Gabriele Boccaccini is a researcher in the
Department of Oriental Studies at the
University of Turin, concentrating on
Judaism and Christian origins.

MIDDLE JUDAISM

MIDDLE JUDAISM

Jewish Thought, 300 B.C.E. to 200 C.E.

GABRIELE BOCCACCINI

With a Foreword by
James H. Charlesworth

FORTRESS PRESS   MINNEAPOLIS

MIDDLE JUDAISM
Jewish Thought, 300 B.C.E. to 200 C.E.

Interior design by Publishers' WorkGroup
Cover design by Publishers' WorkGroup

Library of Congress Cataloging-in-Publication Data

Boccaccini, Gabriele, 1958-
   Middle Judaism : Jewish thought, 300 B.C.E.–200 C.E. / Gabriele Boccaccini.
      p.   cm.
   Includes bibliographical references.
   ISBN 0-8006-2493-9 (alk. paper) :
   1. Judaism—History—Post-exilic period, 586 B.C.–210 A.D.
I. Title.
BM176.B5   1991
296'.09'014—dc20   91-19199
                                                             CIP

The paper used in this publication meets the minimum requirements of American National Standard for Information Sciences—Permanence of Paper for Printed Library Materials, ANSI Z329.48–1984.   ∞™

Manufactured in the U.S.A.   AF 1-2493

95   94   93   92   91   1   2   3   4   5   6   7   8   9   10

To my wife, Aloma,
with love, esteem, and gratefulness

CONTENTS

PART II
A CROSS-SECTION:
THE SECOND CENTURY B.C.E.

PART III
SOME PREPARATORY SKETCHES

FOREWORD

Refreshing Developments
in Italian Research
James H. Charlesworth

A strange thing happened in 1919. After the unprecedented hostilities of the First World War, British scientists were so intent on proving the theories of a German physicist that they committed numerous errors. A British expedition to West Africa proved Einstein's prediction of light deflection, but did so by assuming the result desired.[1] One fact demonstrated by this phenomenon is that the desire to prove a point is stronger than pride or emotion. Scientists, like theologians and all human beings, inadvertently are led in their research by what they hope to find. Precisely this bias, and a host of unexamined presuppositions, have led scholars to miscast the Judaism of Jesus' day. Jewish and Christian scholars, claiming to use objective methodologies but often unintentionally defending a cherished perspective, have portrayed a Judaism that did not exist. One of the purposes of the present book is to argue against such errors and distortions.

Let me attempt to facilitate an understanding and appreciation of what Gabriele Boccaccini is attempting to do in this book. A glimpse of the revolutionary developments within Italian scholarship helps clarify Boccaccini's background and development. Some major insights he stresses are so significant that they deserve singling out. An honest critique of his work may help focus the areas for significant dialogue.

The place of biblical research in Italian universities. Rome was occupied by the army of the Italian state on September 20, 1870. One of the results of this occupation was the separation of church from state. Italian biblical

1. S. W. Hawking, *A Brief History of Time from the Big Bang to Black Holes* (New York and London: Bantam Books, 1988), 32.

research and scholarship were directly affected by the separation. A law of January 26, 1873, demanded the closing of state theological faculties. The church, in its own institutions, was permitted to teach the full range of biblical and theological subjects according to its confessional point of view. At that time the Catholic church did not accept the idea that the Bible may be studied on the basis of strictly scientific principles.

Universities were not permitted to develop institutes (that is, departments) of biblical studies. If related subjects were offered and taught they were sequestered in separate institutes in the universities and usually placed in faculties of letters. Occasionally, institutes of classical studies offered courses in Jewish studies. Institutes of Semitic (or oriental) studies taught courses in Hebrew and Aramaic. Institutes of the history of Christianity presented courses in the history of early Christianity. The approach in these state-supported universities was and remains historical and nonconfessional.

The church reserved the right to teach biblical studies and theology. Only candidates for the ministry were admitted to these courses. The approach to the Bible was typically canonical and confessional.

Between the two world wars the study of early Judaism and Christian origins was constricted. Under Fascism, Jewish studies were contested, and the racial laws of 1938 even prevented Jewish scholars from teaching in universities. Studying Judaism was almost considered a politically suspicious interest. One had to learn Semitic languages under someone like Giorgio Levi della Vida, or social history of the Jews in the Hellenistic age under Arnaldo Momigliano, both of whom were Jews. In those dark years, New Testament philology was fostered by Giorgio Pasquali. Yet, after the Second World War there were no chairs or positions devoted to the Dead Sea Scrolls, the "Apocrypha" (that is, the Pseudepigrapha), early Judaism, or the history of Judaism (including the Maccabean era, so important for Christian theology and culture—including the opera). Such subjects were incidentally taught by scholars whose chairs or positions were in general areas, such as Semitics or the history of Christianity. Moreover, the study of Judaism was almost always considered because of its importance to the study of "Jesus' time" and the origins of Christianity.

Today the great tradition in the field of Semitic languages and philology continues in Italy through scholars such as Pelio Fronzaroli, Sabatino Moscati, and Fabrizio Pennacchietti.[2] However, a change has definitely occurred. Church history departments are now developing programs in the

---

2. In the broader field of oriental studies Giovanni Pettlinato and Luigi Cagni should also be mentioned.

study of Christian origins, under the guidance of New Testament experts such as Franco Bolgiani, Mario Pesce, and Manlio Simonetti. Departments of oriental studies are presently offering courses in Scripture and Judaism taught by renowned experts such as Bruno Chiesa, Giovanni Garbini, Luigi Moraldi, Paolo Sacchi, Jan Alberto Soggin, and Angelo Vivian. Departments of classical studies are offering courses in Judaism and Christian origins under the leadership of scholars such as Eugenio Corsini, Emilio Gabba, and Fausto Parente.

In 1979 the Associazione Italiana per lo Studio del Giudaismo (AISG) was founded. Its purpose is to foster the study of Judaism and Christian origins and to bring together professors who are interested in the study of Judaism. The first president was Paolo Sacchi, who retired from this position in 1989.[3] He was succeeded by Fausto Parente. In 1979, *Henoch* was launched, a journal of Judaic studies that often publishes scholarly research on early Judaism and Christian origins.

Roman Catholic universities—of which the Gregoriana is the most famous—are presently expanding their programs in biblical studies. Courses are no longer offered only to students who are dedicated to the ministry of the church, and women are now admitted. Italian biblical scholars trained in critical methodology have published pioneering research; these include many experts, among them Rinaldo Fabris, Giuseppe Ghiberti, Romano Penna, Gian Luigi Prato, Gianfranco Ravasi, Giuseppe Segalla, Ugo Vanni, and the Archbishop of Milan, Cardinal Carlo Maria Martini.[4] The journal *Rivista Biblica* has been revised to represent the clarified critical and nonconfessional approach to biblical and related subjects. The new trend in Italian Catholic scholarship is noticeable in the Associazione Biblica Italiana (ABI).

The fruit of these labors has been significant. Only a few important and recent volumes can be mentioned here. One of the best collections of the Dead Sea Scrolls, with succinct and insightful introductions, was edited by L. Moraldi and is titled *I manoscritti di Qumrân* (Classici delle religioni; Turin: Unione Tipografico–Editrice Torinese, 1971; 2d ed., 1987). A major international collection of the Old Testament Pseudepigrapha was edited by P. Sacchi (with P. Bettiolo, G. Boccaccini, M. Enrietti, F. Franco, L. Fusella, M. Lana, A. Loprieno, P. Marrassini, F. Pennacchietti, and L. Rosso Ubigli), and titled *Apocrifi dell'Antico Testamento* (2 vols., Classici delle religioni; Turin: Unione Tipografico–Editrice Torinese, 1981, 1989).

3. I wish to express appreciations to Professor Sacchi for his kindness to me during my time in Turin and for helping me improve this foreword.
4. See Carlo Maria Martini's Italian and English contribution to *Jews and Christians: Exploring the Past, Present, and Future*, ed. J. H. Charlesworth (New York: Crossroad, 1990), 19–34.

Critical texts and translations have appeared. The *Exagôgê of Ezekiel*, for example, was edited and translated by Pierpaolo Fornaro in *La voce fuori scena* (Turin: Giappichelli, 1982).

Research has been directed in a singularly significant way to the *Ascension of Isaiah*. The Bologna Research Group of Centro Interdipartimentale di Studi sull'Ebraismo e sul Cristianesimo antico (CISEC) has been focusing its attention on the *Ascension of Isaiah*. Two articles on the *Ascension of Isaiah* appeared in 1980 in the first fascicle of the journal *Cristianesimo nella storia*. Nine critical articles on this pseudepigraphon were edited by Mauro Pesce in *Isaia, il diletto e la chiesa* (Testi e ricerche di scienze religiose 20; Brescia: Paideia Editrice, 1983). According to Pesce, in a letter of December 26, 1990, Enrico Norelli will publish a new critical edition and commentary of the *Ascension of Isaiah* within the next two years.[5]

Particularly of interest to Italian scholars, therefore, is the Jewish apocalyptic literature. (See G. Boccaccini, "Jewish Apocalyptic Tradition: The Contribution of Italian Scholarship," in *Mysteries and Revelations: Apocalyptic Studies since the Uppsala Colloquiom*, ed. J. J. Collins and J.H. Charlesworth [JSPS; Sheffield: Academic Press, in press].) A major study of the historical development of Jewish apocalypticism, with special attention to *1 Enoch*, was published recently by Sacchi under the title *L'apocalittica giudaica e la sua storia* (Brescia: Paideia Editrice, 1990). A major study of the theological development of the Jewish concept of resurrection was published by Cesare Marcheselli-Casale in his *Risorgeremo, ma come? Risurrezione dei corpi, degli spiriti o dell'uomo?* (Associazione Biblica Italiana, Supplementi alla Rivista Biblica 18; Bologna: Edizioni Dehoniane, 1988).

Christian origins are studied in light of the vast increase in our sources of early Judaism. Claudio Gianotto examined the figure of Melchizedek in early Judaism, earliest Christianity (especially *Hebrews*), and Gnosticism in his *Melchisedek e la sua tipologia* (Associazione Biblica Italiana, Supplementi alla Rivista Biblica 12; Brescia: Paideia Editrice, 1984). Internationally significant works are frequently translated into Italian;[6] for example, J. H. Charlesworth's *Gli pseudepigrafi dell'Antico Testamento e il Nuovo Testamento* (Brescia: Paideia Editrice, 1990) was edited and translated by Gabriele Boccaccini.[7] Critical studies on Jesus and other aspects of New Testament

---

5. See Enrico Norelli, "L'Ascensione di Isaia: Analisi e commento" (diss., Université de Genève, 1990).

6. Translated into Italian are works by scholars such as C. K. Barrett, C. H. Dodd, F. Hahn, M. Hengel, E. Käsemann, K. Koch, and C.F.D. Moule.

7. J. H. Charlesworth's *Jesus within Judaism* is now being translated into Italian.

research are appearing in numerous periodicals, including *Rassegna di teo-logia*[8] and *Annali di storia dell'esegesi.*[9]

Boccaccini's Work. Boccaccini's work is an indication of the impressive developments in Italian biblical scholarship. Five aspects of his book are especially appealing. First, he recognizes that the range of early Judaism encompasses the period from the third century B.C.E. to the second C.E. That means that what was called "intertestamental" now antedates the latest book in the Old Testament (or Tanach), *Daniel*, by about one hundred years.

Second, he illustrates that past attempts to reconstruct the thought and history of pre-Mishnaic Judaism were distorted by theological interests. The New Testament books were read first and then the Jewish documents were read in light of them. This methodology misrepresents the Jewishness of the New Testament writings and casts other works as significant only insofar as they are background issues that can, perhaps without proper reflection, be used to prove the superiority of Christianity. The Judaism of the Pharisees and Sadducees must not be branded as legalistic. Jewish prayer was not bound up in the fetters of a rigid legalism. There is a vast chasm between Schürer and the "new Schürer."

Third, he struggles to present a comprehensive study of early Judaism. The Dead Sea Scrolls are not to be sealed apart hermetically from other forms of Judaism. Their authors were living in the desert and they did withdraw from Jerusalem and the Temple; but they were significantly involved with—and inform us of—many other forms of Judaism.

Fourth, he endeavors to present a synthesis of what the various Judaisms were like in and around the first century C.E. Although the documents he examines are highly selective, they are not misrepresentative of much that was vibrantly alive within the various types of Judaism.

Fifth, he rightly stresses that Christianity arose deep within Judaism. In several books, especially *Jesus within Judaism*, I have attempted to argue that we must take more seriously our scholarly conclusion that Jesus was thoroughly Jewish and that he was a devout Jew who worshiped and revered the Temple. His earliest followers were almost all Jews who continued to worship in the Temple and follow almost all Jewish customs and regulations (including the Sabbath, circumcision, the lunar calendar, and devotion to the Scriptures).

8. See, e.g., Vittorio Fusco, "Gesù e la Legge," *Rassegna di teologia* 30 (1989): 528–38.

9. For example, Edmondo Lupieri demonstrates the necessity of studying the *Revelation of John* in light of the Jewish apocalypses, esp. *1 Enoch*; cf. his "Esegesi e simbologie apocalittiche," *Annali di storia dell'esegesi* 7 (1990): 379–96.

However, is it necessarily anachronistic to seek to discern whether a document antedating the Mishnah (200 C.E.) is "Jewish" or "Christian"? Such examinations seem necessary, but we certainly must not proceed as if Christianity were antithetical to or clearly distinct from Judaism.[10]

As much as I appreciate Boccaccini's book I must be candid and express some reservations with two ideas in it. First, the term "early Judaism" does not imply that nothing preceded it. The nomenclature I prefer is that early Judaism should be clearly defined to include everything Jewish from c. 350 B.C.E. to 200 C.E. After that time we have the period of Mishnaic (or rabbinic) Judaism. Before early Judaism there are the periods of postexilic Judaism, exilic Judaism, and the history of Israel. Early Judaism—for me at least—is not a concept that excludes Christianity. Early Judaism encompasses some aspects of earliest Christianity. The New Testament must now be studied within the history of Judaism as well as within the history of the church; obviously, Boccaccini would agree with this claim.

Second, I am reticent in concluding that Christianity is one of the Judaisms of modern times. Obviously Christianity is originally and essentially Jewish. But does not Christianity *emerge* as something different from Judaism? It is not inappropriate to continue to categorize Christianity as a form of Judaism when attempts are made by Christians to convert Jews? Christianity can be labeled "Jewish," but does that mean it is a form of Judaism? Is Christianity no longer to be categorized within Judaism when it proclaims that Jesus is the Messiah, the only one raised from the dead by God, and indeed identical in substance with God? How can Christianity be categorized as a form of Judaism when the law is seen by Paul (at least intermittently) not so much as God's will (the Jewish view) but as an incentive to sin, when the day for the Sabbath is changed, when the Jewish dietary and related rules for purification are rejected, and when the ritual of circumcision and the rite of passage (Bar and Bat Mitzvah) are abandoned? Do not many statements in Paul and the *Gospel of John* indicate that, while Christianity is conceptually Jewish, a movement has begun that distinguishes and separates Christianity from Judaism? If Christianity today is a sister of Judaism, is she not also distinct and different from her sister? Are not the differences today between Christianity and Judaism obvious and indeed essentially attractive?

10. This issue is complex and is clearly placarded by an examination of modern research on the *Testaments of the Twelve Patriarchs*. This foreword is not the place to delve into the perplexities involved.

In summation, this prolegomenous study by a young scholar stimulates significant questions and contains numerous salubrious improvements in the study of Judaism and the origins of Christianity. It also calls for a rejection of the confessional biases that have distorted Judaism. The approach is challenging and fresh.

ACKNOWLEDGMENTS

In conducting research one is never alone but always in debt—for encouragement, advice, an idea, and moral support received. And on one's way one is sometimes lucky enough to meet masters in whom one recognizes both examples and guides. For me, such have been Francesco Adorno of the University of Florence and Paolo Sacchi of the University of Turin. They not only taught me how to be a scholar, but also provided me with living examples of integrity and honesty. I am also grateful to Jacob Neusner of the University of South Florida and James H. Charlesworth of Princeton Theological Seminary. They introduced me to and guided me through American scholarship, patiently sharing their experience and wisdom. Without the teaching, trust, and friendship of these masters, my research would not have been possible.

I have recently worked at the Department of Oriental Studies of the University of Turin. In 1989 and again in 1990 I was in the United States as a visiting scholar at Princeton Theological Seminary. These two prestigious institutions not only offered me their libraries and facilities but also made available to me the support of their professors, the efficiency of their administrations, and the sympathy of their students.

During my stays in the United States I had the opportunity to discuss the present volume—or parts of it—with some of the most distinguished specialists on Judaism and Christian origins. John J. Collins of the University of Notre Dame and Alan F. Segal of Barnard College graciously agreed to review the whole manuscript and gave me good counsel, encouraging my research. I also had significant and helpful meetings with John Barclay of the University of Glasgow, Shaye J. D. Cohen of the Jewish Theological Seminary, Robert A. Kraft of the University of Pennsylvania, Joel Marcus of

Princeton Theological Seminary, and Doron Mendels of the Hebrew University of Jerusalem. Their response provoked new insights and improvements. This does not mean that they share my thesis, nor do I want to suggest that they are responsible for any error I may have made in the present work.

In particular, thanks go to my friends Thomas Kirk and Michael Thomas Davis. The former, a teacher at a language school in Florence, worked with me on the English translation of some parts of the present book, which were originally written in Italian. The latter, a Ph.D. candidate at Princeton Theological Seminary, helped me to refine the language and style of the whole manuscript and checked the technical terminology. Both of them have done their work with great sympathy and competence.

Although I have inserted some material originally written in Italian and taken up ideas already expressed in Italian in several articles of mine, this book is not a translation from an Italian original. It has been planned and written in English for English-speaking readers. I hope to draw attention not only to my personal research but also to the work of Italian scholarship, which recently has achieved significant results in the field of biblical studies. I am especially grateful, therefore, to Fortress Press for publishing the present volume and to Publishers' WorkGroup for their professional and competent help in polishing the presentation.

Gabriele Boccaccini

ABBREVIATIONS

MODERN TEXTS

AAT   P. Sacchi, ed., *Apocrifi dell'Antico Testamento*, 2 vols.,
          Classici delle religioni (Turin, 1981–89)
AB   The Anchor Bible
AOT   H.F.D. Sparks, ed., *The Apocryphal Old Testament* (Oxford,
          1984)
ApAT   A. Díez Macho, ed., *Los apócrifos del Antiguo Testamento*, 5
          vols. (Madrid, 1982–88)
APAT   E. Kautzsch, ed., *Die Apokryphen und Pseudepigraphen des
          Alten Testaments*, 2 vols. (Tübingen, 1900)
APOT   R. H. Charles, ed., *The Apocrypha and Pseudepigrapha of
          the Old Testament in English*, 2 vols. (Oxford, 1913;
          reprint, 1968)
ASB   P. Riessler, *Altjüdisches Schrifttum ausserhalb der Bible*
          (Heidelberg, 1928; reprint, 1966)
BÉI   A. Dupont-Sommer and M. Philonenko, eds., *La Bible
          Ecrits Intertestamentaires* (Paris, 1987)
Bib   *Biblica*
BZAW   Beihefte zur Zeitschrift für die alttestamentliche
          Wissenschaft
CBC   The Cambridge Bible Commentary
DACL   F. Cabrol and H. Leclercq, eds., *Dictionnaire d'Archéologie
          Chrétienne et de Liturgie*, 15 vols. (Paris, 1907–53)
EB   *Estudios Biblicos*
EBib   Etudes bibliques

EncJud	C. Roth, et al., eds., *Encyclopedia Judaica*, 16 vols. (New York, 1971–72)
HNT	Handbuch zum Neuen Testament
HNTC	Harper's New Testament Commentaries
HTKNT	Herdes Theologischer Kommentar zum Neuen Testament
HTR	*Harvard Theological Review*
HUCA	*Hebrew Union College Annual*
ICC	The International Critical Commentary
JBL	*Journal of Biblical Literature*
JQR	*Jewish Quarterly Review*
JSHRZ	W. G. Kümmel and H. Lichtenberger, eds., *Jüdische Schriften aus hellenistisch-römischer Zeit* (Gütersloh, 1973–)
JSJ	*Journal for the Study of Judaism*
JTS	*Journal of Theological Studies*
NICNT	The New International Commentary on the New Testament
NIGNTC	The New International Greek New Testament Commentary
NTS	*New Testament Studies*
OTP	J. H. Charlesworth, ed., *The Old Testament Pseudepigrapha*, 2 vols. (London, 1983–85)
RHR	*Revue de l'histoire des religions*
RivB	*Rivista Biblica*
RQ	*Revue de Qumran*
RSLR	*Rivista di Storia e Letteratura Religiosa*
RT	*Revue Thomiste*
SC	Sources Chrétiennes
SPB	Studia Post-Biblica
SVTP	*Studia in Veteris Testamenti Pseudepigrapha*
TED	Translations of Early Documents
THAT	E. Jenni and C. Westermann, eds., *Theologische Handwörterbuch zum Alten Testament*, 2 vols. (Munich and Zurich, 1971–75)
TNTC	Tyndale New Testament Commentaries
TS	Texts and Studies
TT	Texts and Translations
TU	Texte und Untersuchungen
TWNT	G. Kittel, ed., *Theologisches Wörterbuch zum Neuen Testament*, 9 vols. (Stuttgart, 1933–76). Translated under

	the title *Theological Dictionary of the New Testament*, ed. G. W. Bromiley and G. Friedrich, 10 vols. (Grand Rapids, 1964–76)
VD	*Verbum Domini*
WBC	World Biblical Commentary
WHJP	The World History of the Jewish People
WMANT	Wissenschaftliche Monographien zum Alten und Neuen Testament
WUNT	Wissenschaftliche Untersuchungen zum Neuen Testament

ANCIENT LITERATURE

1 Cor	*1 Corinthians*
Dan	*Daniel*
Deut	*Deuteronomy*
Eph	*Ephesians*
Exod	*Exodus*
Ezek	*Ezekiel*
Gal	*Galatians*
Gen	*Genesis*
Hist	Tacitus, *Historiae*
Jer	*Jeremias*
Jos Asen	*Joseph and Aseneth*
Josephus	
Ant	*Antiquitates Iudaicae*
Ap	*Contra Apionem*
Bellum	*Bellum Iudaicum*
Josh	*Joshua*
Let Aris	Pseudo-Aristeas, *Letter of Aristeas*
Lev	*Leviticus*
Lib Ant Bib	Pseudo-Philo, *Liber Antiquitatum Biblicarum*
m.	Mishnah
1 Macc	*1 Maccabees*
Mal	*Malachi*
Matt	*Matthew*
Mem	Aristotle, *De Memoria et Reminiscentia*
Neh	*Nehemiah*
Num	*Numbers*

Philo of Alexandria

Aet Mund	*De Aeternitate Mundi*
Agric	*De Agricultura*
Apologia	*Apologia pro Iudaeis*
Cherub	*De Cherubim*
Congr	*De Congressu Eruditionis Gratia*
Dec	*De Decalogo*
Det	*Quod Deterius Potiori Insidiari Solet*
Deus Imm	*Quod Deus sit Immutabilis*
Her	*Quis Rerum Divinarum Heres sit*
Jos	*De Josepho*
Leg Alleg	*Legum Allegoriae*
Leg Gai	*Legatio ad Gaium*
Migr Abr	*De Migratione Abrahami*
Mut	*De Mutatione Nominum*
Op Mund	*De Opificio Mundi*
Plant	*De Plantatione*
Post	*De Posteritate Caini*
Praem Poen	*De Praemiis et Poenis*
Quaest Gen	*Questiones in Genesin*
Sac	*De Sacrificiis Abelis et Caini*
Sobr	*De Sobrietate*
Somn	*De Somniis*
Spec Leg	*De Specialibus Legibus*
Virt	*De Virtutibus*
Vit Cont	*De Vita Contemplativa*
Vit Mos	*De Vita Mosis*

Ps	*Psalms*
Qoh	*Qohelet (Ecclesiastes)*

Qumram

1QH	*Hymn Scroll*
1QM	*War Scroll*
IQS	*Rule of the Community*
1Q34[bis]	*Prayer for the Day of Atonement*
11QJN ar	*New Jerusalem*

Rev	*Revelation (Apocalypse) of John*
Rom	*Romans*
Sib Or	*Sibylline Oracles*
Sir	*Sirach (Ecclesiasticus)*
t.	*Tosefta*

T Abr	*Testament of Abraham*
Testaments of the Twelve Patriarchs	
T Ash	*Testament of Asher*
T Benj	*Testament of Benjamin*
T Iss	*Testament of Issachar*
T Jos	*Testament of Joseph*
T Naph	*Testament of Naphtali*
T Reub	*Testament of Reuben*
tg.	Targum
Jo	*Pseudo-Jonathan*
Ne	*Neofiti*
On	*Onkelos*
P	*Fragment-Targum* (MS Paris, Bibliotèque Nationale Hébr. 110, folios 1–16)
V	*Fragment-Targum* (MS Vatican Ebr. 440, folios 198–227)

INTRODUCTION

WRITING A HISTORY OF JEWISH THOUGHT

Reasons and Challenges

Few centuries and few cultural experiences have claimed such a persistent and profound interest as the Judaism of the third century B.C.E. through the second century C.E. It is the common matrix within and from which two great religions took their form, Christianity and Rabbinism. It is also the bridge where the East met the West, laying the foundations of our civilization. Exactly because of its enduring significance it not only belongs to scholars but also impassions and emotionally involves many people today from many different walks of life. Such people see in those centuries an important root, if not *the* root, of their own identity. These centuries are distant, yet they are close to our concerns. They are confusing, even contradictory centuries, which are evoked, celebrated, and discussed but are still largely unknown.

This volume is the result of research conducted between 1983 and 1990. As a prolegomenon, it is not an organic reconstruction of the history of Jewish thought of the period (too many and too relevant are the omissions!). Neither is it a simple collection of miscellaneous studies. Rather, it is a voyage through the thought of some of the protagonists, and through some of the themes that were under discussion at the time. It is a brief voyage taken in long stages, a careful selection aimed at restoring a comprehensive vision of the period from the sect-type (if not sectarian) approach that has impressed upon it a posteriori schemes and misleading hierarchies. I hope to lead the reader to see both the unity and the pluralism of Judaism in these centuries, of this cultural and religious universe in which figures such as Ben Sira and Pseudo-Aristeas, Philo of Alexandria and Jesus of Nazareth, Paul of Tarsus and Flavius Josephus act *on the same plane*, their very different personalities united by the common questions that provoked their various responses.

This book is arranged in three distinct parts, which reflect three different emphases of my research. In the first part ("Methodological Lines," chaps. 1–2), which deals with hermeneutic issues, I describe what I consider to be a better approach to this period than other current options. The confessional biases and artificial divisions that have shaped our understanding for centuries have not yet disappeared. We still face confessionally divided sources as well as a confessionally divided scholarship. The search for a more comprehensive approach and a less biased methodology (chap. 1) is presented, along with a critical review of the whole history of research from Flavius Josephus to the present time (chap. 2).

The second part ("A Cross Section: The Second Century B.C.E.," chaps. 3–5) shows the application of my methodology. A sample of how a history of middle Jewish thought should actually be written is given, limited to a well-defined period (the second century B.C.E.) and to a selected number of documents (*Sirach, Daniel, Book of Dream Visions, Letter of Aristeas*). The result is not a linear history of a "normative" Judaism in evolution (troubled only by some deviations), a description of an early Jewish theology from which early Christianity emerged, or a muddled plot of different opinions. Rather, it is a diachronic history of different ideological systems in competition. Each of them responds to the same questions and with the same bricks builds its own unique system, which is founded upon a particular emphasis, that is, on a self-characterizing generative idea. Each system interacts and competes with the others as a whole, while the search for parallels between documents would simply reveal some common bricks. Hence, the phase of comprehensive identification of the different Judaisms comes methodologically before any comparison.

The third part ("Some Preparatory Sketches," chaps. 6–10) presents the research in its making. It probes a largely virgin field, focusing on some protagonists (Philo, James, Paul, and Josephus) and some emerging issues (memory, universalism, origin of evil, and others). The choice of these topics reflects my own sensibility and interest more than a fixed plan. It is not by chance, however, that authors traditionally considered less Jewish (or not Jewish at all), as well as some of the most Christianized themes, have been chosen here. It is incredible how new and provocative an approach from within Judaism still appears when applied to these topics. To build a comprehensive approach, we must abandon our obsolete criteria of classification, which confine Philo to Greek philosophy, Josephus to Hellenistic historiography, and early Christianity and early Judaism to separate files.

The translations from Hebrew, Aramaic, Greek, and Latin are mine; as for the versions extant in other ancient languages, I refer to the most recent translations. The quotations from ancient documents are usually given in full. As much as possible, I try to let texts speak for themselves and contextualize their own statements. In the notes, I quote the editions, modern translations, and commentaries of the documents examined, as well as the main studies about the issues under discussion. In chapter 2 the reader will find an annotated catalog of the most up-to-date general introductions to this period. I also recommend these works for the essential bibliography.

My approach and interests are historical and philosophical. In order to achieve a comprehensive understanding of Jewish thought, I have borrowed methodologies commonly used in the study of the history of secular philosophy. Applying such methodologies to biblical research may still appear so unusual as to be considered a nonconformist, even provocative intrusion. This is not my intention. I fully recognize the value, importance, and dignity of theology and philology. Theologians and biblical scholars have contributed significantly to our historical knowledge, and obviously any research that has no solid philological foundations is flawed. However, the idea of the scholar of Judaism and Christian origins as a theologian involved in the necessities and questions of a living faith or, otherwise, a philologist restricted to the problems of textual criticism or of language is the fruit of a historically determined—and unfortunately not yet entirely overcome—confessional prejudice (see chap. 1). Our understanding of Judaism and Christian origins has been seriously hindered by the insufficiency of historical and philosophical investigation. We know too little because we have analyzed too few of the internal developments of Jewish thought, the complex ideological links that bind—and diversify—the various Judaisms, both among themselves and in the wider context of ancient thought. I hope to have made a contribution in this area, even if it be a modest one. My wish is that the historian of thought can take an acknowledged place next to both the theologian and the philologist in complementary yet different roles. The goal is to elaborate a history of middle Jewish thought within an ideal history of ancient philosophy that fully embraces the Jewish foundations of Western civilization along with its Greek roots.

PART I

METHODOLOGICAL LINES

1

MIDDLE JUDAISM

Judaism between the Third Century B.C.E. and the Second Century C.E. as a Historiographical Unit

1. THE OBSTACLE OF CONFESSIONAL BIAS

Anyone critically approaching the phase of Judaism that falls between the third century B.C.E. and the second century C.E. faces not only the ordinary difficulties of any reconstructive work but also an impressive array of prejudices, assumptions, clichés, passions, and emotions that have accumulated through the centuries and now form an unfathomable tangle. This period represents a crucial point for the two living faiths we are used to calling "Judaism" and "Christianity." The fundamental roles played by these two religions in our culture (particularly by Christianity, given its demographic and political predominance) have assured the handing down of both the riches of their traditions and their prejudicial paradigms. Historical research, which was born of these religions, could not help but be deeply shaped by their attitudes, even in terms of language.

For example, the term "Judaism" (French *judaïsme*; German *Judentum*; Italian *giudaismo*; Spanish *judaísmo*) in a general sense refers to the monotheistic religion of the people of Israel from its mythical beginnings with Abraham and Moses up to the present. At the same time, in a particular sense it refers to the still vital "normative" system erected by the Rabbis from the second through the tenth centuries C.E. The modern languages, reflecting the common opinion, therefore denote with the same term both the set of all the many Judaisms by which the Jewish religion has been formed over the centuries *and* one definite (ideologically homogeneous) system, namely Rabbinism, the Judaism of the dual Torah.[1]

---

1. See, e.g., the concise definition of Judaism given in one of the most widely used dictionaries of the Bible: "The religion of the Jewish people from the Sinai theophany through the

This ambivalence of meaning reveals a tendency immediately to identify the two referents: rabbinic Judaism and Judaism *tout court*. Here we are dealing with a model that is all the more deeply rooted because it has not been an object of interconfessional debate; instead, it has been the balancing point of a difficult coexistence. From different points of departure and with different aims, Jews and Christians for centuries have tacitly agreed on the idea of Judaism as an unchanging, unchanged (and perhaps unchangeable) system—the idea that since Moses's time there has been only one Judaism, that is, rabbinic Judaism.

For oppressed Jews, the model served to emphasize their enduring fidelity to an ancient and unaltered tradition and polemically to sanction the complete otherness of Christianity (as well as any other "deviation") compared to the one Judaism. Stating the *ab origine* presence of a normative model had a reassuring function for the identity of Jews. This view of Judaism, in which religion and citizenship as well as piety and obedience to the law were identified, immediately transformed any ideological deviation into a radical otherness. Anything in the past—any problem or internal contradiction in history—automatically became "non-Jewish." The most important contradiction, the birth of Christianity from within Judaism, could be removed at the very moment it appeared.

Paradoxically, in the opinion of triumphant Christians the same model served to point out the newness and uniqueness of Jesus of Nazareth, whose message was seen as grafted onto a "late" religion at the end of its role as a "precursor." Judaism, replaced and rendered useless by the advent of Christianity, thus became no more than a pathetic and sclerotic relic without vitality or dignity, proper to an incredulous and even "deicidal" people[2] who remained attached to old and outdated beliefs. Although the New Testament and some later apologetical works (such as Epiphanius's *Panarion*) reminded Christians of the plurality of ancient Judaism, the "Jewish heresies" aroused no interest. In such a decisive conflict between the two main protagonists,

---

present day. Up to and including modern times, Judaism professes the belief in the one, asexual, eternal, creator God, righteous and compassionate judge, king, and parent, who entered into a permanent historical relationship with 'the children of Israel' that would culminate in eschatological redemption. The written and oral Torah perpetually obligated the people to a detailed code of ethical and ritual behavior" (*Harper's Bible Dictionary*, ed. P. J. Achtemeier [San Francisco, 1985], 513).

2. The so-called Jewish "deicide" is, in the words of D. Flusser, "one of the most monstrous inventions in the history of religions" (*Judaism and the Origins of Christianity* [Jerusalem, 1988], xxv). Already in Origen (*In Matthaeum* 27:25) we find the idea that Jesus' blood is not only on those who lived then, but also on all the following generations of the Jews, until the end of the world.

Christians and Rabbis, each so well defined in its respective role, there was certainly no need of walk-ons—in fact, they were quickly forgotten. The humiliated survival of the loser was more than enough to testify to the Christian triumph.[3]

2. CONFESSIONALLY DIVIDED SOURCES

The assumption of such a paradigm, shared by both Jews and Christians, has produced deep and—in many respects—negative consequences. The primary sources have come down to us grouped into distinct corpora following a tripartite division that reflects this paradigm.

First, we have the common inheritance of ancient canonical writings, which Jews call "Tanach" and Christians "Old Testament." Substantially, these two canons or selective collections of ancient Jewish documents are identical, even though they have been handed down in different languages (by Jews in Hebrew and Aramaic; by Christians in Greek, Latin, Syriac, and others) and interpreted differently.

Second, each of the two groups has its own exclusive normative corpus (the Jews' "oral law" and the Christians' "New Testament"), which is handed down with equal care and is held as the indispensable hermeneutical key to the more ancient canonical tradition. These corpora also are the fruit of a selection that gathered and separated documents considered more authoritative from other contemporary documents, which were not rejected but were judged less important and relegated to secondary collections (such as the Christian "Apostolic Fathers" or the Jewish "*Tosefta*").

Finally, we find the formless corpus of the rejected documents, which modern scholars since Fabricius are accustomed to calling "pseudepigrapha." Substantially unrecognized and ignored by Jews and Christians, these documents are considered by both groups to be "apocryphal" and therefore insig-

---

3. Documenting the tenacious presence of such a prejudicial paradigm would be a fascinating research topic. The self-consciousness, relations, "external" debates, and "internal" convictions of Jews and Christians have been based upon it for centuries. Here it is enough to point out its ancient origins. In the middle of the second century C.E., the Christian Justin spoke of an Israel "replaced": "Law placed against law has abrogated that which is before it, and a covenant which comes after in like manner has put an end to the previous one; and an eternal and final law—namely, Christ—has been given to us, and the covenant is trustworthy. . . . We are the true Israel" (Justin Martyr, *Dialogue with Trypho* 11.1–5). Almost contemporaneously, the mishnaic treatise *Aboth* lays the foundations for a rabbinic "normativeness" operating since Moses' times, transforming one group's tradition into the original and necessary complement (the "oral law") of the "written law" through the creation of an uninterrupted and faithful chain of transmission: "Moses received the [oral and written] law from Sinai and committed it to Joshua, and Joshua to the elders, and the elders to the prophets; and the prophets to the men of the great synagogue. . . ."(*m. Aboth* 1:1).

nificant for religious faith and even superfluous as testimony of ancient debates. Their preservation has been due to fortuitous circumstances and sporadic attempts toward normalization that, from time to time, led to the inclusion of some of them in canons that later fell from use. Therefore, these documents sometimes reach us as fragments or only in many different ancient languages. From this indistinct mass of rejected writings, two authors have succeeded in being transmitted since ancient times as autonomous corpora. One is Philo of Alexandria, because he was reinterpreted as a precursor of patristic philosophy. The other is Flavius Josephus, whose historical work lent itself to being reread from different points of view: by Jews as a manifesto of Jewish liberty; by Christians as testimony to the curse cast on an incredulous people. With the discovery of the Dead Sea Scrolls in the 1950s yet another corpus has emerged, which even includes a document until that time considered a classic example of the Old Testament Pseudepigrapha, the so-called *Cairo Damascus Document*.[4]

Thus, today we are faced with a series of corpora that are the fruit of a long and complex process of gathering and selecting from an even greater amount of material. Although a certain degree of randomness has been involved, this process has been based substantially on a continual rereading and reinterpretation of the past according to purely confessional criteria. Hence, originally extraneous documents have been grouped together as units. For example, the Old Testament Pseudepigrapha are a mere miscellany without any ideological homogeneity, in which the *Letter of Aristeas* has been linked with *Jubilees*, and *2 Baruch* with *4 Maccabees*. In contrast, consciously related documents have at times been separated and placed in different corpora. (For example, the "apocryphal" *1 Enoch* is referred to as Scripture in the "canonical" *Letter of Jude*.) Furthermore, through the course of history each corpus has accumulated a number of internal subdivisions that in many cases propose further inappropriate divisions within an already improperly divided body of material, as in the traditional sectioning of the Old or New Testaments, but also in certain modern partitionings of the Pseudepigrapha.[5]

4. The *Cairo Damascus Document* was included in *APOT* 2 (1913): 785–834; and in *ASB* (1928), 920–41. The document is no longer found in the collections of Old Testament Pseudepigrapha published after the 1950s.

5. The most typical case is that of the so-called apocalyptic documents, in which the grouping together of a literary genre in modern times tends to turn into an unverified ideological affinity (see chap. 4). In many respects the destiny of the testaments in the Pseudepigrapha is analogous—they are also perennially suspended between literary genre and ideology.

3. CONFESSIONALLY DIVIDED SCHOLARSHIP

Such a fragmentation is in itself an unpleasant obstacle for the modern scholar who is forced to do the complex and difficult work of reconstructing the ideological and chronological links among documents that history has shuffled and confused. The consequences, however, have been even deeper for scholars. The corpora have given life to a divided body of knowledge that still marks modern scholarship. Confessionally divided sources caused a confessionally divided scholarship.

Universities—the ancient *universitates studiorum*, expressions of Christians' genius (and prejudice)—created two distinct and self-sufficient figures: the "biblical scholar" (the Old or New Testament theologian), whose competence was limited to the Christian canon, every relation with Judaism and its language and culture being considered superfluous and useless; and the "Hebraist," who was eminently a philologist whose interests similarly were devoted to the canonical documents, to "biblical philology," with only occasional extravagances being allowed. A silence fell on the rabbinic literature and the Pseudepigrapha, the former being relegated to the talmudic academies, the latter to the sporadic curiosity of the erudite. Being excluded from the Christian canon also meant being condemned to insignificance, even from the cultural point of view.[6] As for Philo and Josephus, they lived a long exile in the faculties of philosophy and history, respectively, their Jewishness reduced to a mere accident.

Such a division made the corpus a document that belonged to the first hermeneutic criterion for determining the nature of the source itself. Each corpus was considered and studied as a homogeneous and self-sufficient unit, which needed not only distinct research instruments (its own lexicon, concordance, bibliography, and journal) but also an ideological synthesis, namely, its own theology (if not a theology of each of its internal subdivi-

6. Referring to the rabbinic literature, M. Pesce, in a lecture at the University of Bologna (March 17, 1988) during the nine-hundredth anniversary of that oldest *universitas studiorum* in the world, said: "If we turn for a moment to the past, we ascertain with stupor that the great wealth of ancient rabbinical writings that unwind over seven centuries, . . . all the vast literature containing the most varied sectors of the culture, from right to religion, from literature to ethics to folklore, has been totally ignored by our University. And there is not even a trace of a Jewish presence. This absence is not only a gap to be filled, but more importantly it is also a great loss for our tradition, and not only the university tradition, which has amputated one of its principal components, one of the matrices from which it sprang, but one that continued to live in our culture at that time" ("Presentazione del Candidato Jacob Neusner," in *Laurea Honoris Causa a John W. Burrow e Jacob Neusner*, ed. Università di Bologna [Bologna, 1988], 37).

sions). Thus, a confessional criterion for collecting sources became the principal criterion for understanding their contents.

By superimposing the corpora over the documents, ideological and chronological differences were annulled with the utmost carelessness, while related texts were separated and "external" references censured. This phenomenon, which first affected the canonical collections, created a mental habitus and a hermeneutic model that tended to reproduce itself in the study of the other corpora.

A century of historical method, the progressive secularization of Western culture, and the new ecumenical climate in the relationship between Jews and Christians in the wake of the Second Vatican Council have nuanced and complicated the problem but have not modified this perspective at its roots. To a large extent, each corpus still lives its own separate, self-sufficient existence, with its own specialists, journals, bibliographies, and audience. The fact that a document belongs to a corpus largely determines its success, the number and frequency of its editions, its presence in certain series or in the programs of universities and seminaries, and the quantity of its commentaries—in short, its success in public opinion as well as in scholarship.

Today there is no longer an overt ostracism of what is "non-Christian" or "noncanonical." Albeit with difficulty, even the Apocrypha and Pseudepigrapha are reemerging from the centuries-old oblivion to which confessional bias had relegated them.[7] The problem, however, is not simply one of balancing the specific weight of each corpus by giving an introduction, lexicon, and even theological analysis to the previously deprived collections. Nor is it one of drawing together disciplines, so that the specialist of one corpus also becomes the specialist of another and, listing the numerous and significant parallels that unite these corpora, then triumphantly proclaims how the knowledge of one helps to understand the other. The hunt for parallels (a sort of "parallelomania"),[8] usually involving the New Testament and another, more or less contemporary Jewish corpus (be it rabbinic literature, the Dead Sea Scrolls, or the Pseudepigrapha), is an exercise that has delighted genera-

---

7. On the tormented history of research on the Old Testament Pseudepigrapha, see J. H. Charlesworth, *The Old Testament Pseudepigrapha and the New Testament* (Cambridge, 1985), 6–17; and/G.W.E. Nickelsburg and R. A. Kraft, "The Modern Study of Early Judaism," in *Early Judaism and Its Modern Interpreters*, ed. R. A. Kraft and G.W.E. Nickelsburg (Philadelphia, 1986), 1–30.

8. S. Sandmel defines "parallelomania" as "that extravagance among scholars which first overdoes the supposed similarity in passages and then proceeds to describe source and derivation as if implying literary connection flowing in an inevitable or predetermined direction" ("Parallelomania," *JBL* 81 [1962]: 1–13).

tions of scholars and does not yet seem to have gone out of fashion.[9] To be fruitful or even better, to be plausible, however, a comparison should be made between commensurable units, such as two ideological systems taken as wholes, and not between single elements of incommensurable units, such as the traditional corpora.[10]

4. A COMPREHENSIVE APPROACH

We now arrive at the root of the problem: the existence of the corpora. They make sense in relation to epochs and ideologies that formed, delimited, and reinterpreted them. They are absolutely misleading, however, in their prejudicial interposition between the sources (their authors, their age, and their ideological horizons) and the modern interpreter. The task of the historian of thought is to describe an age in its complexity and in the contradiction of its expressions, using *all* the material available, canceling and verifying every traditional division without confessional presupposition. The historian of thought is also to reconstruct as much as possible the chronological and ideological links among the sources. In short, the focus of attention should be shifted from the corpora to the age in which the constituent writings were composed, thus freeing the documents from the cage of their respective corpora and placing them on the same level. In so doing, the interpreter should not be afraid of or surprised at finding forgotten connections or unexpected distances, new hierarchies or unsettling marginalities, supporting roles elevated to protagonists and protagonists reduced to supporting roles.

In the past decade, Judaic studies—in particular those carried out by Jacob Neusner on rabbinic literature, James H. Charlesworth on the Pseudepigrapha, and Paolo Sacchi on apocalyptic tradition[11]—have taught us some important truths about Judaism and, specifically, the Judaism of the period in question here. We are now much more conscious that Judaism is to be seen not as an ideologically homogeneous unit but, in today's world as well

---

9. The best expressions of this methodological approach, whose origins go back to the seventeenth century (see chap. 2), remain the well-known H. L. Strack and P. Billerbeck, *Kommentar zum Neuen Testament aus Talmud und Midrash*, 4 vols. (Munich, 1922–28); and *TWNT*.

10. See the acute methodological observations of E. P. Sanders in *Paul and Palestinian Judaism* (London, 1977), 12–18. The methodology elaborated by J. Neusner also tends toward a global approach; see his *Systematic Analysis of Judaism* (Englewood Cliffs, N.J., 1988).

11. See J. Neusner, *Judaism: The Evidence of the Mishnah* (Chicago and London, 1981); Charlesworth, *Old Testament Pseudepigrapha and the New Testament*; and P. Sacchi, *L'apocalittica giudaica e la sua storia* (Brescia, 1990).

as in the past, as a set of different ideological systems in competition with one another. We have also learned that both Christianity and Rabbinism knew their formative periods and became normative systems only from the second century C.E. on. Prior to that they were only two of the many Judaisms of their time, two instruments of an ancient orchestra, which the canonical myopia prevented us from identifying and enjoying.

Such conclusions mark the end of a prejudicial and conditioning paradigm of the relationship between Judaism and Christianity and are the premise to the passage from a purely quantitative balancing of the attention given to the various corpora to overcoming them completely. Such conclusions also lead us toward a more correct understanding and a more comprehensive approach to the Judaism of that time. The fundamental characteristic of this phase of Judaism, in fact, is its fragmentary nature. A plurality of groups, movements, and traditions of thought coexisted in a dialectic relationship, which was sometimes polemic but never disengaged. This complex and pluralistic period, however, has a clear, distinct, and unitary personality. The multiple and divergent answers offered by the different groups come from the same urgent questions. It is this multifaceted whole (and not a unitary system) that constitutes the common matrix within and from which both Christianity and Rabbinism emerged. The blood-tie between the latter and the former is not a parent–child relationship. Both of these groups mark a fresh development from the common tradition; taking up an effective image from Alan F. Segal, we could more properly say that, like Rebecca's children, they are fraternal twins born of the same womb.[12] Christianity and Rabbinism are the two most successful Judaisms of modern times.

---

12. A. F. Segal writes: "The time of Jesus marks the beginning of not one but two great religions of the West, Judaism and Christianity. . . . Judaism and Christianity were born at the same time and nurtured in the same environment. Like Jacob and Esau, the twin sons of Isaac and Rebecca, the two religions fought in the womb. . . . They are indeed fraternal twins emerging from the nation-state of the second commonwealth Israel" (*Rebecca's Children: Judaism and Christianity in the Roman World* [Cambridge, 1986], 1, 179). The concept and imagery are not new; Segal has developed the intuition of a few enlightened precursors of the Jewish–Christian dialogue. In a 1929 lecture delivered at a conference of the Society of Jews and Christians held at the City Temple, London, F. C. Burkitt stated: "If you ask me what I think of the religion of Jews, I should begin by replying that it is not the Old-Jewish religion itself, but one of its two daughters, the other being Christianity. If you go on to ask me what became of the Old-Jewish religion, I should reply that it died in 70 C.E. of a violent death. . . . The Rabbinical religion, the religion of Johanan B. Zakkai and his followers, is not exactly a continuation of the Old-Judaism, but rather is a new development" ("What Christians Think of Jews," *Hibbert Journal* 28 [1929–30]: 261–72; repr. "Christian Views of Judaism," in *In Spirit and in Truth: Aspects of Judaism and Christianity*, ed. G. A. Yates [London, 1934], 311–31). In 1960, J. W. Parkes presented the first organic historical foundation to this intuition: "The period from Zerubbabel to the first century of the common era was not a period of decline. It was a

5. IS CHRISTIANITY (STILL)
A JUDAISM?

Speaking of Christianity as one of the Judaisms of modern times may be shocking. In the first half of this century, the question as to whether Christianity was Jewish or Hellenistic was still being asked.[13] Scholars now agree on the Jewishness of Jesus and his Palestinian movement.[14] Most scholars also consider the first generation of Christians and its messianic claims on Jesus to be Jewish, the idea and necessity of a divine mediator being a Jewish (apocalyptic or Essene) idea.[15] Some scholars prefer the term "Christian Judaism" to the more frequently used "Judeo-Christianity," thus emphasizing that this phenomenon (still) belongs to Judaism.[16] Significantly, the problem has shifted from the original background of Christianity to the time and modalities of its emancipation from (or its betrayal of) Judaism. Fur-

---

period of such abounding vitality that . . . gave legitimate birth both to the Judaism which survived the destruction of state and Temple, and the Christianity which made Jewish monotheism a world religion. Both are truly rooted in it; and the effort of these two 'disparate twins' each to prove the illegitimacy of the other, is the tragic consequence of the separation between them" (*The Foundations of Judaism and Christianity* [Chicago, 1960], xiii). After Segal, A. Paul speaks of "fraternal twins [Fr. *faux jumeaux*] born together on the ruins of the Second Temple . . . having as their mother something double-faced [Fr. *une chose ambiguë*], whose life extends for centuries and that cannot be called Judaism, but rather 'proto-Judaism' or 'proto-Christianity' according to the side observed" (*Le judaïsme ancient et la Bible* [Paris, 1987], 282). Flusser likes the image of sisterhood, limited to the relationship between "early Christianity and the Judaism contemporary with it": "Both [of them] possess a more or less common broader *Weltanschauung*—a mutual background. Or in other words: Judaism and Christianity are not mother and daughter, but they are in reality sisters, because the mother of both is ancient Judaism" (*Judaism and the Origins of Christianity*, xv–xvi). H. G. Perelmuter eventually settles the question by speaking of "siblings": "Both Rabbinic Judaism and Christianity received their basic form at the same time, each placing a different reading of the messianic force at work within Judaism and the Jewish people. Thus they can be viewed as siblings" (*Siblings: Rabbinic Judaism and Early Christianity at Their Beginnings* [New York, 1989], 2). The debate about the degree of consanguinity between Rabbinism and Christianity is stimulating and reveals different hermeneutic approaches. Drawn out, however, it becomes idle. A scientific classification cannot be founded on an imagery.

13. See H. Odeber, "Ist das Christentum hellenistisch oder jüdisch?" *Zeitschrift für systematische Theologie* 17 (1940): 569–86.

14. Flusser writes, "Without a doubt, Jesus and his message belong within the framework of the Judaism of his time: it is an inseparable part of it" (*Judaism and the Origins of Christianity*, xv).

15. "The second stratum of early Christianity embodied in the so-called *kerygma* of the Christian hellenistic communities was indebted to Essenism. . . . The greatest part of the motifs in Paul, John and other New Testament epistles which previously were assumed to have been derived from Greek or Gnostic thought, now have been shown to have originated in Essene circles" (ibid., xviii, xx). According to A. F. Segal, "Most scholars assume that once Paul had converted, his writings became irrelevant to Judaism. This is simply not so: Paul wrote to a brand-new Christian community that was still largely Jewish, giving us the only witness to a world of everyday Hellenistic Judaism now vanished" (*Paul the Convert: The Apostolate and Apostasy of Saul the Pharisee* [New Haven and London, 1990], xiii).

16. See P. Sigal, *Judaism*, ed. L. Sigal (Grand Rapids, 1988).

thermore, those scholars, such as Segal, A. Paul, D. Flusser, and H. G. Perelmuter,[17] who have pointed out the fraternal relationship between Christianity and Rabbinism, suggest that, although one brother has remained in the parents' house, the other has gone away. The question therefore has become, When and how did Christianity *cease to be* a Judaism? When and how did this former Jewish movement *part from* Judaism?

The question seems legitimate and the answer obvious: this happened when Christians forsook the practice of the law and Christianity became mostly a gentile movement.[18] But the idea of "the" Judaism as a religion linked to a defined people, absolutely free from any foreign cultural influence, and rooted in the legal obedience of the law came to us from Rabbinism—it is merely the rabbinic interpretation of Judaism. Espousing the arguments of one of the parties certainly is not the correct way to try a suit about a contested heritage. Christianity and Rabbinism each had much to gain by disinheriting the other and by cutting off as soon as possible an unpleasant relationship. But a reciprocal excommunication cannot cancel the truth of their common origin, nor has it the authority to sanction before the tribunal of history the idea that a Judaism is no longer a Judaism.

The root of the problem lies in the question, Is it possible that the

---

17. Perelmuter writes, "The short-range messianic movement *out of Judaism* became Christianity. The long-range messianic movement became Rabbinic Judaism" (*Siblings*, 17). Flusser even takes up the parent–child pattern when speaking about the relationship between Christianity and modern Judaism: "Christianity is in the peculiar position of being a religion which, because of its Jewish roots, is obliged to be occupied with Judaism, while a Jew can fully live his Jewish religious life without wrestling with the problems of Christianity. . . . Christianity inherited from her mother [the common Jewish values] she developed in her own manner" (*Judaism and the Origins of Christianity*, 617–18).

18. According to Sigal, "The main body of Christianity *ceased to be* Jewish, not because of Paul's theology or his alternative halakah, but because the church became predominantly gentile, and because the rabbis at Yabneh ca. 90–100 C.E. read even Christian Jews out of Judaism for political reason" (*Judaism*, 80). S.J.D. Cohen writes: "Early Christianity *ceased to be* a Jewish sect when it ceased to observe Jewish practices. It abolished circumcision and became a religious movement overwhelmingly gentile in composition and character. This process was accompanied by the elevation of Jesus to a position far higher and more significant than that occupied by any intermediary figure in Judaism. Its practices no longer those of the Jews, its theology no longer that of the Jews, and its composition no longer Jewish, the Christianity of the early second century C.E. was no longer a Jewish phenomenon but a separate religion" (*From the Maccabees to the Mishnah* [Philadelphia, 1987], 168). According to H. Maccoby: "Christianity developed as a separate religion only when it adopted the doctrine that Jesus was a divine being, and that salvation depended on identification with his sacrificial death, rather than in adherence to the Jewish or Noachian covenants. . . . There can be no doubt . . . that it was through this important change of doctrine that Christianity *ceased to be* part of the scene of first-century Judaism" (*Judaism in the First Century* [London, 1989], 37). It is striking to note that these three authors, in spite of their different approaches to the period, repeat the same word (which I have italicized in quotations) to express the same idea: Christianity was Jewish but "ceased to be" such.

monotheistic faith created by ancient Jews developed *also* into a multinational religion, open to other cultural experiences, in which obedience to the law would not be thought of in legal terms? At the beginning of the Common Era some varieties of Hellenistic and apocalyptic Judaism were already close to what Christianity would later become. Their existence proves that this path was open—it would remain such even in Rabbinism, as the emergence of Reform Judaism in modern times shows. The ancient people of Israel created an extremely dynamic religion, whose enormous potentialities could and can generate divergent systems of thought. Among the many possible Judaisms, Christianity is one of those which has been realized in history. It did happen at the beginning of the Common Era that a particular multinational Judaism called Christianity—which through its faith in Jesus as the Messiah gave a different meaning to obeying the law—became highly successful among Gentiles, that the gentile members very soon composed the overwhelming majority in this community, and that the strong (and reciprocal) debate against other Jewish groups gradually turned, first into bitter hostility against all the other Jews (that is, against all non-Christian Jews), and then against the Jews *tout court* (including the Christian Jews) in a sort of *damnatio memoriae* of their own roots. However, neither a different way of understanding the law nor a claimed otherness nor the emergence of anti-Jewish attitudes does away with the Jewishness of Christianity.

Certainly, Christianity is unique, precisely as unique as Rabbinism.[19] In both cases, uniqueness consists of a peculiar mixture of traditional elements and fresh developments, that is, in the creation of a system capable of giving new sense to the same unrejected heritage. Certainly, Christianity and Rabbinism are distinct and deeply different from one another. From the historical point of view, however, both of them are coherent developments of ancient Judaism; both are in analogous lines of continuity and discontinuity with ancient Judaism. The debate over which of them is the more authentic development (that is, the true Israel) belongs to confessional polemics.[20]

---

19. The idea that Christianity has a *special degree of uniqueness*, such as to display objective superiority, is the last refuge of Christian apologists. See A. J. Tambasco, *In the Days of Jesus: The Jewish Background and Unique Teaching of Jesus* (New York, 1983); and E. Ferguson, *Backgrounds of Early Christianity* (Grand Rapids, 1987).

20. J. Neusner writes: "While the world at large treats Judaism as 'the religion of the Old Testament,' the fact is otherwise. Judaism inherits and makes the Hebrew Scriptures its own, just as does Christianity. But just as Christianity rereads the entire heritage of ancient Israel in light of the 'resurrection of Jesus Christ,' so Judaism understands the Hebrew Scriptures as only one part, the written one, of 'the one whole Torah of Moses, our rabbi.' Ancient Israel no more testified to the oral Torah, now written down in the *Mishnah* and later rabbinic writings, than it did to Jesus as the Christ. In both cases, religious circles within Israel of later antiquity reread

Similarly, the frenzy with which both Christians and Jews argue that Christianity is no longer a Judaism must be recognized as a consequence of confessional bias. For a historian of religion, Rabbinism and Christianity are simply different Judaisms.

6. THE GENUS JUDAISM AND ITS SPECIES

The meaning and use of the term "Judaism" in the scientific study of religion calls for reconsideration. From centuries of confessional polemics we have inherited the image of Judaism as an unchangeable religion, replaced by Christians and maintained by Jews (Figure 1). Modern scholars portray instead a developing and pluralistic religion, which at the beginning of the Common Era exploded into several different groups, producing from within both a new stage of its evolution (Rabbinism) and a different religion (Christianity). This view of Judaism (Figure 2), however, depends too strongly on Rabbinism. All the developments of the ancient religion of Israel that diverge from the line culminating in Rabbinism are simply cut off. What I argue above about the Jewishness of Christianity is valid also for Samaritans,[21] Falashas,[22] and Karaites.[23]

---

the entire past in light of their own conscience and convictions" (*Judaism and Scripture: The Evidence of Leviticus Rabbah* [Chicago and London, 1986], xi). According to Segal: "Both Judaism and Christianity consider themselves to be the heirs to the promises given to Abraham and Isaac. . . . As brothers often do, they picked different, even opposing ways to preserve their family's heritage. . . . It is difficult to judge which religion is the older and which is the younger. . . . Both now claim to be Jacob, the younger child who received the birthright. Rabbinic Judaism maintains that it has preserved the traditions of Israel, Jacob's new name after he wrestled with God. Christianity maintains that it is the new Israel, preserving the intentions of Israel's prophets. Because of the two religions' overwhelming similarities and in spite of their great areas of difference, both statements are true" (*Rebecca's Children*, 179).

21. On the Samaritans, see J. A. Montgomery, *The Samaritans, the Earliest Jewish Sect: Their History, Theology and Literature* (Philadelphia, 1907; repr. 1968); M. Gaster, *The Samaritans: Their History, Doctrines and Literature* (London, 1925; repr. Munich, 1980); idem, *Samaritan Oral Law and Ancient Traditions*, vol. 1, *Samaritan Eschatology* (London, 1932); J. MacDonald, *The Theology of Samaritans* (London, 1964); J. Purvis, *The Samaritan Pentateuch and the Origin of the Samaritan Sect* (Cambridge, Mass., 1968); J. Bowman, *The Samaritan Problem: Studies in the Relationships of Samaritanism, Judaism, and Early Christianity* (Pittsburg, 1975); R. J. Coggins, *Samaritans and Jews: The Origins of Samaritanism Reconsidered* (Oxford and Atlanta, 1975); J. Bowman, *Samaritans: Documents Relating to Their History, Religion, and Life* (Pittsburgh, 1977); R. Pummer, *The Samaritans* (Leiden, 1987); and N. Schur, *History of the Samaritans* (Frankfurt am Main, Bern, New York, and Paris, 1989).

22. On the Falashas, see W. Leslau, *Falasha Anthology* (New Haven, 1951); and M. Wurmbrand, "Falashas," *EncJud* 6:1143–54.

23. On Karaism, see J. Fürst, *Geschichte des Karäerthums*, 3 vols. (Leipzig, 1862–69); W. H. Rule, *History of the Karaite Jews* (London, 1870); Z. Cahn, *The Rise of the Karaite Sect: A New Light on the Halakah and Origin of the Karaites* (New York, 1937); L. Nemoy, ed., *Karaite Anthology* (New Haven, 1952; 3d ed., 1962); A. Paul, *Écrits de Qumran et sectes juives aux premiers*

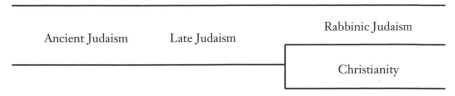

Figure 1. The polemical approach. Judaism is the religion of the Old Testament, revealed to Abraham and Moses. At the "fulness of time" it was replaced by the Christian revelation, although maintained by most of the Jewish people. Judaism in the age of Christ is a decadent religion (late Judaism), which makes sense only as the connection between the Old and New Testaments (intertestamental Judaism). Rabbinism is the conservative (and even degenerative) attempt at the codification of an ancient, unchanged religion.

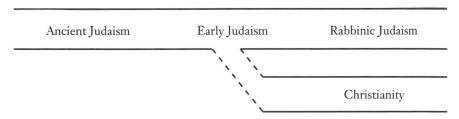

Figure 2. The present approach. Judaism is a developing and pluralistic religion that, at the beginning of the Common Era, split into several different groups. This creative age (early Judaism) produced both a new stage of the inner evolution of Judaism (Rabbinism) and a different religion (Christianity).

In the study of religion, more precise criteria of classification should be adopted. "Judaism" properly denotes the *genus*, that is, the whole family of monotheistic systems that sprang forth from the same Middle Eastern roots as a multibranched tree (Figure 3). To denote the many *species* of which the genus Judaism is composed—that is, the many branches of this luxuriant tree—we should use only more specific terms, such as Samaritan Judaism (or Samaritanism), rabbinic Judaism (or Rabbinism), and Christian Judaism (or Christianity).

siècles de l'Islam: Recherches sur l'origine de Qaraïsme (Paris, 1969); P. Birnbaum, ed., *Karaite Studies* (New York, 1971); S. Szyszman, *Le Karaïsme* (Lausanne, 1980); and E. Trevisan Semi, *Gli ebrei caraiti tra etnia e religione* (Roma, 1984).

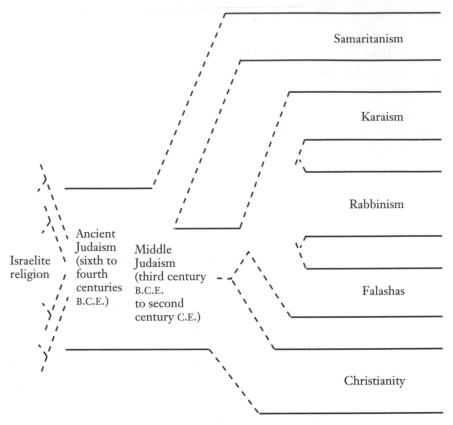

Figure 3. The genus Judaism and its main branches. "Judaism" denotes the whole family of monotheistic systems that sprang forth from the same Middle Eastern roots. More specific terms—such as Samaritanism, Rabbinism, or Christianity— denote the main branches of which Judaism is composed.

"Middle Judaism" is the creative phase of Judaism between the third century B.C.E. and the second century C.E. It encompasses several different species of Judaisms: Pharisaism, early Christianity, Essenism, apocalyptic, and others.

Greater care is required of us when we speak of the first century of the Common Era. At that time, the Jewish family was still roughly united (we should not forget, however, the already separated branch of Samaritans). Both early Christianity and early Rabbinism shared the same branch with many other Judaisms. Nevertheless, we are used to discussing whether a certain document (for instance, a pseudepigraphon) is Christian *or* Jewish. While dealing with a real and important problem—the ideological identification of this document—we scarcely realize that we are incorrectly using the term "Jewish" as a synonym for "non-Christian." More properly, we should discuss whether this document is Christian or belongs to *another* Jewish group. Because early Christianity, like Pharisaism or Essenism, was a first-century Judaism, and even later Christianity is a *species* of Judaism, all the Christian documents are obviously Jewish. Nobody, whether scholar or student, would ever ask if a certain document is Pharisaic or Jewish, Essene or Jewish—rather, if this document is Pharisaic or apocalyptic, Essene or Sadducean. Why should we not do the same when speaking of Christianity (even of early Christianity) in relation with the other Judaisms? Once again the confessional bias reemerges, even in our "neutral" academical discussions.

7. IN SEARCH OF A NAME

Many obstacles still need to be overcome in developing the notion of a "global" specialist in the Judaism of this period, an approach whose interests would not be limited by canons, corpora, or any other artificial division or conditioned by confessional presuppositions. One of the most striking signs of this enduring difficulty is the lack of a universally shared term that adequately covers this phase in the history of Judaism. The confessional names inherited by ancient tradition are rapidly (and fortunately) falling into disuse. The out-of-date Christian image of Judaism as the religion that through its late phase ("late Judaism") or functionally intermediate phase ("intertestamental Judaism") constituted the background and environment of the Christian newness ("Judaism in the time of Jesus") has by now become unsupportable.[24] More recent definitions, such as "Judaism in the Hellenistic and Roman period" and "Judaism of the Second Temple," have had no greater luck. Although more neutral from a confessional point of view, these definitions are chronologically imprecise because they encompass a much longer period of time. The age of the Second Temple actually began three centuries before the terminus post quem of the third century B.C.E.; the

---

24. Noting the rapidity with which the old confessional terms are disappearing should not mean undervaluing the difficulty and work involved in bringing this process about. Such a process requires not only abandoning consolidated conventions and habits, but also searching for correct alternatives. I continued to use the term "giudaismo tardo(-antico)" ("Late Judaism," or, better, "Judaism of late antiquity") until very recently out of respect for the Italian academic tradition and for lack of a better term. I used it, however, in a strictly chronological sense, coherently applying the definition of "movimento tardo-giudaico" ("late Jewish movement") also to early Christianity.

Hellenistic and Roman period extends well beyond the terminus ante quem of the second century C.E.

Recently the term "early Judaism" has been taking root among English-speaking scholars. (What once was "late" is now labeled "early"!) The term is fashioned after "early Christianity" and effectively indicates that this period not only was the cradle of Christianity but also of rabbinic Judaism—a very creative, lively, and not at all "late" period.[25] But in spite of its merits, not even this definition is satisfactory.

First, there is a chronological problem analogous to that of the expression "Judaism of the Second Temple." The intent was to replace the confessionally charged adjective "late" with its opposite, "early," a term charged with positive connotations. But in so doing it has been forgotten that the period was also defined "late" for chronological reasons, in relation to the preceding period(s) of Judaism.[26] Either "early Judaism" leaves out the preceding period (but what could come before "early"!) or it includes it, and we are back to the drawing board, unless we want to propose an improbable "late early Judaism."[27]

Second, the claimed analogy with the term "early Christianity" tends to make "early Judaism" an ideological term, that is, the name of a defined species. The nomenclature suggests that between "early Judaism" and (rabbinic) Judaism there is the same ideological continuity as between "early Christianity" and Christianity. However, not all the Jewish movements active between the third century B.C.E. and the second century C.E. can be defined as "early Judaisms," that is, they cannot be placed in a direct line of continuity with rabbinic Judaism. For example, it is difficult to reconcile the

---

25. Charlesworth writes: "Early Judaism—certainly not 'Late Judaism' or 'Spätjudentum'—should be the term used to refer to the phenomena in Judaism dating from around the end of the third century B.C.E. until the end of the second century C.E. As 'Early Christianity' signifies the origins of Christianity so 'Early Judaism' denotes the beginnings of synagogal (modern) Judaism" (*Old Testament Pseudepigrapha and the New Testament*, 59). The first scholar who used the term "early Judaism" to denote this period of Judaism was F. G. Grant ("Early Judaism," in *The Beginnings of Our Religion*, ed. F. James, et al. [New York, 1934], 79–90). However, only in the past two decades has the term become popular among scholars and students (see chap. 2). Credit goes first to J. Maier and J. Schreiner, eds., *Literatur und Religion des Frühjudentums* (Würzburg, 1973).

26. Until the first half of this century, scholars used the term "early Judaism" to denote the earliest phase of Judaism, that is, the period immediately following the Babylonian exile. See, e.g., L. E. Browne, *Early Judaism* (Cambridge, 1929).

27. Nickelsburg and Kraft also point out that "'early Judaism' is not a particularly precise term, especially with reference to its beginning point" and that they are using it "somewhat by default for its simplicity and relative comprehensiveness" ("Modern Study of Early Judaism," 2). Cohen shares the same reservations: "While 'early Judaism' lacks the anti-Jewish overtones of 'late Judaism,' it is chronologically vague, and therefore other, more precise expressions are preferable" (*From the Maccabees to the Mishnah*, 19–20).

term with Essenism or the apocalyptic tradition. It would seem more correct, therefore, to limit this appellation to Pharisaism, or at least only to those groups for which it is possible to demonstrate a direct link of ideological continuity with Rabbinism, as some scholars do, speaking of "early rabbinic Judaism(s)."[28] Only in this way can the analogy with "early Christianity" be properly maintained. Moreover, denoting this period in relation to rabbinic Judaism as its early phase, we run the risk of symmetrically reproducing the same confessional paradigm we wanted to overcome. "Early Judaism," in fact, is to Rabbinism precisely what "intertestamental Judaism" is to Christianity. But neither Rabbinism nor Christianity can presume to preempt this period, which is the early matrix of both as well as the environment of many other Judaisms.

There is one final, truly decisive objection common to all of the definitions proposed so far. Trying to find a more neutral language is completely in vain if the same confessional schemes are reproduced. However all-inclusive the proposed terms claim to be, they never include early Christianity; that is to say, they include all the Judaisms then active except early Christianity. The absence of the early Christian movement, even in the most recent introductions to "early Judaism," is disturbing.[29] It is like a well-contrived drama. The curtain rises and unveils a marvelous scene, crowded with walk-ons (Jews and Gentiles, men and women, priests and soldiers, rich and poor). The main characters (Pharisees, Sadducees, Essenes) introduce themselves, one after the other. The protagonist, however, keeps the audience waiting!

It is equally disturbing to see scholars discussing the relationship between "early Christianity" and "early Judaism." This is yet another comparison of incommensurable units. How can we pretend to compare a part (a species of Judaism) such as early Christianity to a whole (a set of many Judaisms—a set that should include early Christianity)? No one has ever dreamed of comparing Essenism or Pharisaism, for example, to "early Judaism"—it would immediately appear absurd. Separating early Christianity from the other Jewish groups is an unconscious consequence of confessional bias. How lasting is the Ptolemaic idea that everything revolves around and exists in relation to early Christianity! Once again a confessional notion imposes itself on history in the perception that Christianity is an extraneous seed miraculously planted on the ground destined for, not one of the many fruits

28. See, e.g., A.R.C. Leaney, *The Jewish and Christian World (200 B.C. to A.D. 200)* (Cambridge, 1984); and H. Maccoby, *Early Rabbinic Writings* (Cambridge, 1988).
29. For a discussion of the most recent introductions to "early Judaism" see chap. 2.

brought forth by the same ground. The fact that the original ground of Christianity is now claimed to have been "fertile" (intellectually creative) and not "sterile" (intellectually and morally decadent) does not change the terms of the problem. The internal dialectic of the Judaism of that age will continue to be deprived of an important element until we recognize that historically Christianity is only one of the many Judaisms then active— nothing more and nothing else—and is as unique as each of its contemporary fellows. If it is correct to emphasize the creative contribution of one or another Jewish movement to our knowledge of the period in general, and to Christian origins in particular, the rule of reciprocity should never be neglected: early Christianity can tell us much about other Jewish groups and about first-century Judaism in general.[30]

Because the confessional bias so strongly perdures in our subconscious (if no longer in our consciousness), it is not mere chance that the term "early Judaism" is also born maimed. Once again terminological inadequacy is the agent of hermeneutic difficulty.

8. A NEW NAME FOR A NEW APPROACH

We need a comprehensive term that encompasses chronologically all of the contemporary Judaisms (the so-called early Judaisms as well as early Christianity) without any ideological implication. I propose to denote Judaism(s and Christianities) between the third century B.C.E. and the second century C.E. by the term "middle Judaism" (German *Mitteljudentum*; French *moyen judaïsme*; Italian *medio giudaismo*; Spanish *medio judaísmo*). This period is the bridge between "ancient Judaism" of the sixth through the third centuries B.C.E. and the distinct and separate existence, from the second century C.E., of the two main Judaisms of modern times: Christianity and Rabbinism.

No ideological value should be attributed to this term, only a chronological value. "Middle Judaism" is intended to refer only to a definite chrono-

---

30. M. E. Stone writes: "Christian sources form a valuable body of evidence about Judaism in the first century" (*Scriptures, Sects, and Visions: A Profile of Judaism from Ezra to the Jewish Revolts* [Philadelphia, 1980], 115). According to J. Neusner, "Formative Christianity demands to be studied in the context of formative Judaism and formative Judaism in the context of formative Christianity" (*Judaism in the Beginning of Christianity* [London, 1984], 10). Flusser writes: "Very often not only the synoptic gospels but also the whole New Testament contains witnesses of Jewish thought and life from a period anterior to most of the rabbinic texts. So the evidence from New Testament research is also very fruitful for Jewish studies" (*Judaism and the Origins of Christianity*, xii). According to Segal: "The New Testament gives us evidence of Jewish thought and practice in the first century. . . . A commentary to the Mishnah should be written, using the New Testament as marginalia that demonstrates antiquity" (*Paul the Convert*, xv).

logical period and not to an organic and homogeneous system of thought, much less a theology or a spiritual category. To refer to the plurality of ideological movements active in the period (including early Christianity) we must use the plural and speak of "middle Judaisms" or "middle Jewish" movements.[31] The object of a history of middle Jewish thought, therefore, is not the identification and synchronic study of a Judaism (a particular ideological system) but the identification and diachronic study of many Judaisms (many ideological systems), active and in competition in that historically limited period.

Some may object that the use of one name or another is a secondary question and that, in the end, the definition of a period is simply a convention. This is true; however, I have denounced a name in order to denounce a method, and in proposing a new definition I am rather proposing the hermeneutic approach that I hold to be more correct. Perhaps this period is not well enough known,[32] or perhaps the lingering confessional bias is still too strong for us to write a history of middle Jewish thought. Perhaps, given the current state of research, it is still premature to try to recuperate, in a synthetic perspective, both the unity of the period (which consists in common pressing questions) and its plurality (which consists in different legitimate answers). After the great anti-Roman revolts of the first and second centuries C.E., most of the middle Judaisms fell into oblivion. The only two survivors became more and more estranged and hostile, traumatically separating themselves from one another. Each of them rewrote the (common) history after its own likeness and proclaimed itself the only legitimate heir. Christianity and Rabbinism matured into the two different living and beloved religions we know. For a historian, however, what ensued neither cancels nor distorts what came before, and reconstructing a world of forgotten links provides a fascinating goal.

31. On the use of the plural in the ideological definition of middle Judaism, see J. Neusner, W. S. Green, and E. S. Frerichs, eds., *Judaisms and Their Messiahs at the Turn of the Christian Era* (Cambridge, 1987).

32. Many middle Jewish documents are neglected and need more detailed study; others are still awaiting publication (e.g., portions of the Dead Sea Scrolls).

2

TOWARD A BIBLIOGRAPHY
OF MIDDLE JUDAISM

An Annotated Survey from
Josephus to 1990

1. FROM MANY BIBLIOGRAPHIES TO AN
INCLUSIVE BIBLIOGRAPHY

The history of research in middle Judaism is for the most part the history
of the Christian attitude toward Jews and Rabbinic Judaism. In our Christian-
influenced civilization, contributions made by Jewish historiography have
been significant but not highly influential, at least until the previous century.
The emancipation of historical research from confessional interests and presuppositions is a thoroughly contemporary phenomenon; as I noted in chapter 1, many paradigms of the past are still alive.

Chronologically, the history of research can tentatively be divided into
four periods.

From the First to the Sixteenth Century

The twin birth of Christianity and Rabbinism from within Judaism turns
into a harsh confrontation between "Israel" and the "new Israel." The
emphasis is on the ancient Jewish Scriptures (now labeled by Christians
"Old Testament"), whose later developments are only occasionally visited by
Christian apologists (Eusebius, Epiphanius) and Jewish historians (*Seder
'Olam*, Joseph ben Goryon, Jerahmeel ben Solomon, Abraham ibn Daud).
According to the Christian view of history (Augustine, Otto of Freising),
postbiblical Judaism is important only as the path that prepared humankind
for the Christian revelation. Flavius Josephus becomes the witness par excellence of the "end" of Judaism. His works give the standard patterns, slavishly
repeated in the Christian world chronicles (Sextus Julius Africanus, Hippolytus of Rome, Eusebius, Jerome). Christians and Rabbis share the same

theological indifference to postbiblical Judaism; it is not by chance that the only original and nonconformist portraits of middle Judaism are given in this period by the pagan Tacitus (second century) and the Karaite Ya 'qub al-Qirqisani (tenth century).

The Christian rediscovery (since the thirteenth century, with Raimundus Martini's *Pugio fidei adversus Mauros et Judaeos*) of Jewish postbiblical literature does not change the situation. Christian scholars study these documents for apologetic material to use in their missionary activity among the Jews. In their opinion, the rabbinic tradition and the Old Testament simply prove the Christian truth.

When the formation of national states and the success of the Reformation mark the end of the religious, political, and cultural unity of the medieval world, the distinction between secular and sacred history emerges. As a result of the crisis in the world chronicle genre, the new literary genres of Jewish history (J. Kusthuert, P. Eber) and church history (Matthias Flacius) appear. Jewish historiography takes advantage of a period of greater tolerance (Abraham ben Samuel Zacuto, Samuel Usque).

From the Seventeenth Century to the End of the Nineteenth Century

A new attitude in scholarship emerges when Christians begin to use the Jewish postbiblical literature and history in the interpretation of the Old and New Testaments (C. Cartwright, J. Lightfoot). Introductions to and commentaries on the Christian Scriptures give room to the middle Jewish and rabbinic sources (J. G. Pritius, A. Calmet, J. J. Wettstein, T. H. Horne). The world chronicle is definitively replaced by the *historia sacra* (A. Noël, F. L. von Stolberg), which encompasses the increasingly autonomous genres of biblical history (L. Howell, T. Stackhouse) and church history. These genres in turn split into related subgenres: Old Testament history or history of Israel (S. Cradock, J. F. Buddeus), New Testament history (N. Lardner), the history of early Christianity (L. Echard, J. Le Clerc), and the life of Jesus (K.H.G. Venturini, E. D. de Pressensé). A new historiographical unit appears as the "connection" between the Old and the New Testament, that is, the age "from Malachi to Jesus" (S. Cradock, L. Howell, H. Prideaux). The publication of the first great collections of the Old Testament Apocrypha and Pseudepigrapha (J. A. Fabricius, J.-P. Migne) gives a more defined literary identity to this period.

The emancipation of the Jews from their age-old segregation draws attention to the modern history of the Jewish people (J. Basnage, J. Allen, H. H. Milman), and, beginning in the nineteenth century, causes the emergence of Jewish scholarship (I. M. Jost, L. Herzfeld, H. Graetz), which is generally engaged in presenting this period as a part of a greater—and not yet concluded—whole. The interests of Christian scholars, on the other hand, progressively concentrate upon the history of New Testament times. The period is presented as the late (before Christ) phase of (ancient) Judaism (H. Ewald), the age of Jesus Christ (W. Wotton, J. Langen, A. Hausrath), and the environment of early Christianity (A. F. Gfrörer, J.J.I. von Döllinger).

The work of E. Schürer is the synthesis of these converging research efforts. It is also the evidence of how much the approach of scholarship was shaped by bias at the time: Christianity continues to be seen as the radical replacement of (a decadent) Judaism.

From Schürer to the New Schürer

A century of research shows the climax and then the crisis of such a degenerative idea of the history of Judaism. Interest in the age of Jesus Christ strengthens: new collections of ancient documents (E. Kautzsch, R. H. Charles, P. Riessler) and new syntheses (W. Fairweather, J. Jeremias, G. F. Moore, J. Bonsirven) are published, but stronger polemical approaches also emerge. The characterization of Judaism as a "late," legalistic, and decadent religion (F. W. Weber, W. Bousset) comes with the emergence of harshly anti-Jewish attitudes in the European culture. The Second World War and the Holocaust shake even the most insulated consciences. The exciting archeological discovery of the Dead Sea Scrolls opens large, new horizons. A new and less polemical attitude emerges (R. H. Pfeiffer, M. Simon), even though this ancient period remains above all the "intertestamental" phase of Judaism, which constitutes the background and environment of Christian newness. Pharisaism is commonly seen as the "normative" Judaism. A sectarian approach still prevails. More and more scholars, however, stress the pluralism (Morton Smith) and dynamism (J. Maier) of these centuries, and even their meaning as the common foundations of Christianity and Rabbinism (J. W. Parkes). A revision of Schürer's work is necessary.

Recent Decades

Scholars face confessional biases with a greater awareness (E. P. Sanders). Different scientific methodologies, rather than individual religious backgrounds, now define the differences among specialists. The liveliness of this ancient period—now commonly labelled "early Judaism"—is emphasized (M. E. Stone, G.W.E. Nickelsburg, J. H. Charlesworth), as well as its bonds with early Christianity, which is acknowledged—at least in its first stage—to be a Jewish movement (P. Sacchi, C. Rowland, S.J.D. Cohen,

D. Flusser). Further collections of ancient documents expand the knowledge of the period (W. G. Kümmel, Sacchi, Charlesworth, A. Díez Macho, A. Dupont-Sommer). Specialized introductions (S. Safrai and M. Stern, Stone, R. A. Kraft and Nickelsburg) and bibliographies (G. Delling, S. F. Noll, N. E. Anderson) are published. The supposed "normativeness" of Pharisaic Judaism is questioned, and the plural form (Judaisms) begins to be used to describe the plurality of ideological movements (J. Neusner). The study of the New Testament appears inseparable from the study of its Jewish setting (M. McNamara, Charlesworth, Flusser, G. Strecker and J. Maier). Both Christianity and Rabbinism are seen as fresh developments of ancient Judaism (S. Sandmel, Neusner, A. F. Segal, H. G. Perelmuter).

This brief outline of the history of research in middle Judaism shows how complex the assembly of an inclusive bibliography is. Historically, middle Judaism has been studied within different frameworks and under different labels. The scheme shown in Figure 4 may help in understanding this complex evolution.

The complexity of the history of research in middle Judaism is even more evident when one moves from a chronological survey to a classification *per genera*. The peculiar position of middle Judaism between ancient Judaism and both Rabbinism and Christianity places it at the confluence of different fields of research, each with its own tools and its own introduction and bibliography. Interpreters face different—often noncommunicating— approaches and different emphases on history, literature, or religion, as indicated in Figure 5.

In the following four sections, the most significant studies on middle Judaism, from Flavius Josephus to 1990, are listed. I have attempted to offer an interdisciplinary—not exhaustive—bibliography of this period by encompassing works from different fields and thereby including different approaches. I therefore include general introductions to Jewish history, literature, and religion (A). The list also includes introductions to ancient Judaism (B) and modern (rabbinic) Judaism (C), which deal with the "early" Jewish history, literature, and religion. The introductions to "early" Judaism (D) are included, apart from their Jewish or Christian point of view, based on their emphasis on history, literature, or religion. According to the same criteria, the introductions to early Christianity (E) and Christianity (F) that deal with this period are also considered. Most of these actually ignore Judaism; however, some works contain significant insights that should not be lost. We must be inclusive; middle Judaism is the subject of many approaches, interests, and bibliographies.

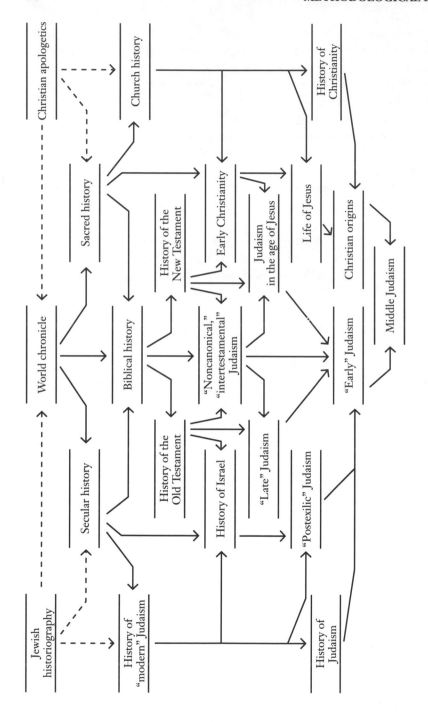

Figure 4. Historical evolution of literary genres in the study of middle Judaism.

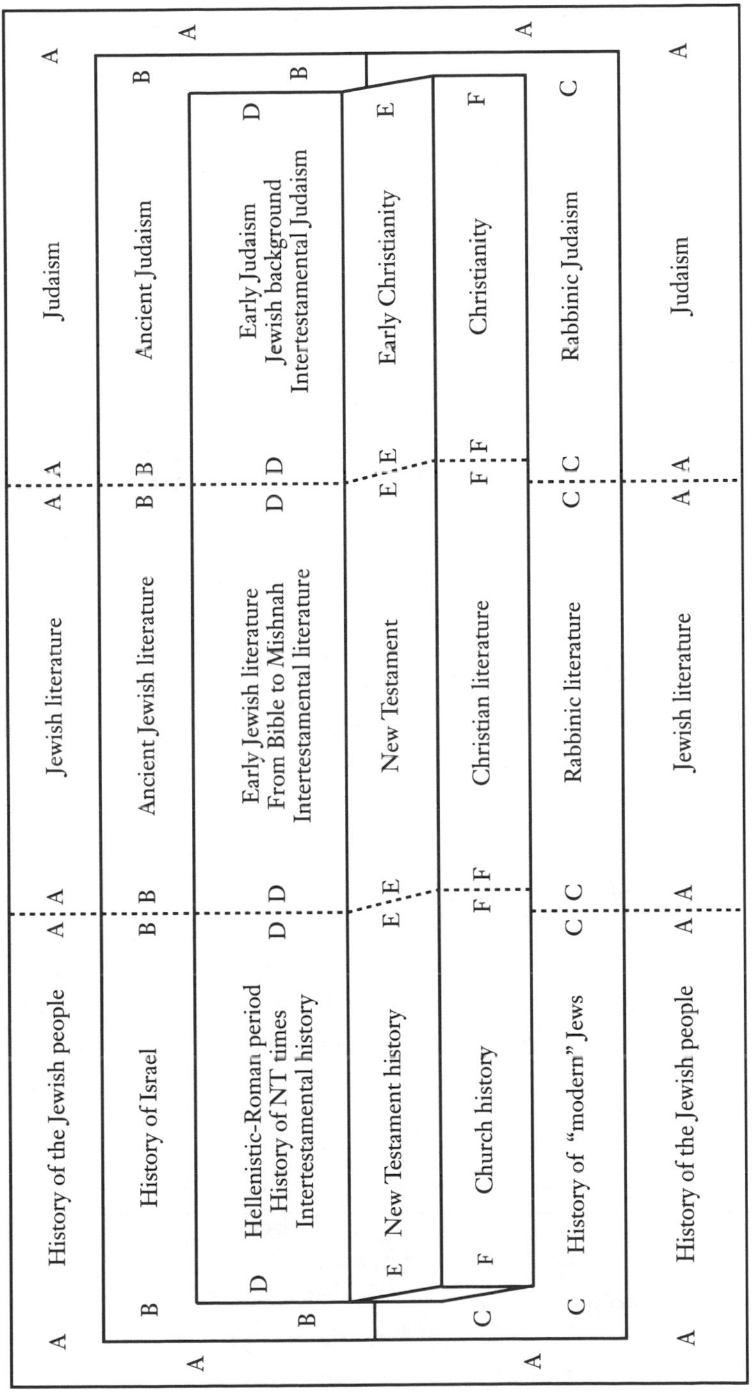

Figure 5. Literary genres dealing with middle Judaism, according to different emphases.

The works are listed chronologically. The brief annotations are not to be taken as exhaustive reviews; they are intended to point out particular contributions and challenges to the understanding of middle Judaism.

2. JEWISH HISTORY, WORLD HISTORY, AND SALVATION HISTORY

First Century

Josephus, Flavius. *Bellum Iudaicum*. 7 books. Circa 78.
   The standard pattern (and main source) of all the following histories of middle Judaism.

Josephus, Flavius. *Antiquitates Iudaicae*. 20 books. Circa 94.
   By harmonizing and integrating the biblical account, Josephus creates the standard history of Israel, from creation to the end of the Jewish War.

Second Century

Tacitus, Publius Cornelius. *Historiae*. 20 books. Circa 110.
   Historiae 5.2–13 gives a brief—yet comprehensive—survey of the history of Jewish people, as seen by a member of the Roman aristocracy and by a historian who mistrusts the Old Testament as a historical source. As such, his work was not to have a following in the Christian world.

Seder 'Olam (Rabbah). Late second century.
   An outline of biblical and postbiblical history, from creation to Bar Kokhba.

Third Century

Julius Africanus, Sextus. *Chronica*. 5 books. 221.
   The pagan world history turns into the Christian world history, which goes from creation through biblical and Roman history to the author's times. For centuries, Christians would know the postbiblical history of the Jews only through and within this framework.

Hippolytus of Rome. *Chronica*. 234.

Fourth Century

Eusebius of Caesarea. *Chronica*. Circa 303; second edition, 325.

Eusebius of Caesarea. *Praeparatio Evangelica*. Circa 315.
   An *ante litteram* history of Christian "backgrounds."

Epiphanius of Salamis. *Panarion*. 375–78.
   In his account of the main heresies, Epiphanius includes Samaritanism (and its four sects: Essenes, Sebuaens, Gorothenes, and Dositheans) and

Judaism (and its seven sects: Sadducees, Scribes, Pharisees, Hemerobaptists, Nazaraeans, Ossaeans, and Herodians).

Jerome. *Chronica*. 380.
A free Latin recasting of the *Chronicle* of Eusebius. With Jerome and Eusebius the middle Jewish history finds its standard pattern, which would be the basis of all the later world chronicles.

Fifth Century

Augustine. *De Civitate Dei*. 22 books. 413–27.
Augustine's conception of history (and his sixfold division) would exercise an enormous influence on all later Western historiography down to the seventeenth century. Book 18 gives a brief account of postbiblical Jewish history.

Tenth Century

Ya 'qub Al-Qirqisani. *Kitab al-anwar*. Circa 927.
Written in Arabic by a Karaite leader, this work gives an original and significant survey of the main Jewish sects (including Christianity) from the biblical age to the times of the author.

Joseph ben Goryon. *Book of Josippon*. Circa 953.
A popular history of the Jewish people within the context of world history, from its origin to the Jewish War. Written by a Jew, probably living in southern Italy, it was considered for centuries a work of Flavius Josephus.

Twelfth Century

Otto of Freising. *Historia de duabus civitatibus*. 8 books. 1143–46; second edition, 1157.
In its original threefold division of history (*ante legem*; *sub lege*; *sub gratia*), it is the most noteworthy attempt at a philosophical interpretation of world history in the Middle Ages. It runs selectively from creation to 1146.

Jerahmeel ben Solomon. *Megillah Jerahmeel*. Circa 1150.
A Jewish world chronicle.

Ibn Daud of Toledo, Abraham ben David Halevi. *Divre malke Yiśrael be-bayit šheni*. Circa 1160.
Ibn Daud's history of the kings of Israel during middle Judaism, in addition to his famous *Sefer ha-Kabbalah*.

Thirteenth Century

Martini, Raimundus. *Pugio fidei adversus Mauros et Judaeos.* 3 books. Circa
1270–80.

> Apologetic motifs shape the beginning of Christian interest in postbiblical
> Judaism (and not just in the history of postbiblical Jews). The attempt to
> convert Jews is carried out by showing that not only the Hebrew Bible
> but even the subsequent rabbinic tradition proves Christian truth. Mar-
> tini's monumental work was for centuries to be the main source of Chris-
> tian knowledge of postbiblical Judaism in its religious aspects.

Fourteenth Century

Salvaticis, Porchetus de. *Victoria adversus impios Hebraeos, in qua tum ex sacris
libris tum ex dictis Talmud ac Caballistarum et aliorum omnium quos Hebraei
recipiunt monstratur veritas catholicae fidei.* 1303.

> An abridged edition of Martini's work, with some original additions.

Sixteenth Century

Zacuto, Abraham ben Samuel. *Sefer ha-Yuḥasin.* 1504.

> A compendium of Jewish political and literary history from creation to
> 1500 C.E.

Kusthuert, J. *Historia Hebreorum ex elegantissimis Marcij Antonij Coccij Sabellicij
Enneadibus excerpa.* Basel, 1515.

> The first modern history of Israel, from the creation to the destruction of
> Jerusalem, was born of a popular Renaissance world chronicle.

Galatinus, Petrus. *De arcanis catholicae veritatis, contra obstinatissimam Iudaeorum nostrae tempestatis perfidiam: ex Talmud, aliisque hebraicis libris nuper
excerptum et quadriplici linguarum eleganter congestum.* Ortona, 1518.

> An enormous (and very successful) plagiarism of Martini's *Pugio.* The
> numerous material additions (chiefly cabalistic) are often inaccurate.

Eber, Paul. *Contexta populi Iudaici historia a reditu ex Babylonico exilio, usqu'ad
ultimum excidium Hierosolymae.* Wittenberg, 1548; second edition, 1560.

> A new historiographical unit emerges: from the Babylonian exile to the
> fall of Jerusalem.

Usque, Samuel. *Consolaçam ás Tribulaçoens de Israel.* Ferrara, 1553.

> This interesting work, written by a Jew in Portuguese, is an account of
> the persecutions borne by the Jewish people in their long history. The
> second part deals with the Second Temple period. It takes the form of a
> dialogue between a suffering shepherd and his comforters, following what
> was then a popular literary convention.

Flacius Illyricus, Matthias. *Ecclesiastica Historia.* 13 vols. Basel, 1559–74; second edition (3 vols.), 1623–24; third edition (*Centuriae Madgeburgenses*), Nuremburg, 1757.

This church history marks the beginning of Protestant historiography. Each century was assigned a volume divided into sixteen basic titles and subjects, among which we find "*De rebus Judaicis*" and "*De religionibus extra Ecclesiam.*" The first volume in particular deals extensively with first-century Judaism.

3. THE EMERGENCE OF JUDAISM IN THE TIME OF JESUS

1649

Cartwright, C. *Mellificium Hebraicum, seu Observationes diversimodae ex Hebraeorum, praesertim antiquiorum, monumentis desumptae, unde plurima cum Veteris tum Novi Testamenti loca vel explicantur vel illustrantur.* 5 vols. London, 1649.

The first organic attempt at applying Jewish postbiblical literature (especially the midrashim) not only to prove but also to illustrate passages of the Christian Scriptures (the Old Testament, including the Apocrypha, and the New Testament).

1658

Lightfoot, J. *Horae Hebraicae et Talmudicae.* 6 vols. Cambridge, 1658–74. Reprint, rev. R. Gandell (4 vols.), Oxford, 1859.

The application of the middle Jewish and rabbinic sources to illustrate the Scriptures turns into a commentary on the New Testament. The work is incomplete: only the parts on the Gospels and *1 Corinthians* were published by the author; *Acts* and some notes to *Romans* were edited posthumously by R. Kidder. Unlike Cartwright, Lightfoot chiefly uses the halakhic literature.

1676

Noël, A. [A. Natalis]. *Historia ecclesiastica Veteris Novique Testamenti: ab orbe condito ad annum post Christum natum millesimum sexcentesimum.* 8 vols. Paris, 1676.

World history is replaced by *historia sacra*, which encompasses the history of the "Jewish church" until the foundation of the Christian church in Jesus and its further modern developments.

1683

Cradock, S. *The History of the Old Testament Methodized: to which is annexed a short History of the Jewish Affairs, from the end of the Old Testament to the birth of our Saviour.* London, 1683; second edition, 1695.

Within *historia sacra*, the "History of Israel" is the content of the Old Testament but also its necessary "appendix," which connects the old covenant with the new covenant and the history of the Old Testament with the history of the New Testament. Confessional reasons, more than historical evidence, make the first century C.E. the fundamental watershed in the history of Israel.

1702

Echard, L. *A General Ecclesiastical History from the Nativity of our Blessed Saviour to the First Establishment of Christianity by Human Laws under the Emperor Constantine the Great. With so much of the Jewish and Roman History as is necessary and convenient to illustrate the Work.* London, 1702; seventh edition, 1729.

1704

Pritius, J. G. *Introductio in lectionem Novi Testamenti: in qua, Quae ad rem criticam, historiam chronologiam et geographiam pertinent, breviter et perspicue exponuntur.* Leipzig, 1704; fourth edition, 1764.

Chapters 32–37 deal extensively with Judaism in the age of Jesus and with its "summa corruptio."

1706

Basnage, J. *Histoire des Juifs depuis Jésus-Christ jusqu'à present.* Paris, 1706; second edition (ed. L. Ellis du Pin), La Haye, 1716. Translated by T. Taylor, under the title *The History of the Jews, from Jesus Christ to the present time.* London, 1708.

The first history of modern Jews since the first century C.E.

1713

Fabricius, J. A. *Codex pseudepigraphis Veteris Testamenti.* 2 vols. Hamburg and Leipzig, 1713–23; second edition, Hamburg, 1722–41.

The first great collection of the Old Testament Pseudepigrapha.

1715

Buddeus, J. F. *Historia ecclesiastica Veteris Testamenti ab orbe condito usque ad Christum natum, variis observationibus illustrata.* 2 vols. Magdeburg, 1715–18; fourth edition, 1744–52.

1716

Howell, L. *A Compleat History of the Holy Bible, in which are inserted the Occurrences that happened during the space of about four hundred years, from the days of the Prophet Malachi to the Birth of our Blessed Saviour.* 3 vols. London, 1716. Reprint, rev. G. Burder (2 vols.), London, 1807–8.

Le Clerc, J. "De statu Iudaeorum, ad religionem quod attinet." In *Historia ecclesiastica duorum primorum a Christo nato saeculorum: e veteribus monumentis deprompta*, 3–47. Amsterdam, 1716.

Prideaux, H. *The Old and New Testament Connected in the History of the Jews, and Neighbouring Nations; from the Declension of the Kingdoms of Israel and Judah to the Time of Christ.* 2 vols. London, 1716–18; fourteenth edition, Edinburgh, 1779. First American edition, Charlestown, Mass., 1815–16.
An erudite English ecclesiastic, retired from his ministry because of a serious infirmity, turns a neglected "appendix" into an autonomous historiographical unit. He creates a new literary genre, that of "intertestamental" history ("for it may serve as an epilogue to the Old Testament in the same manner as . . . a prologue to the New;" from the Preface, 1715). Reprinted dozens of times up to the second half of the nineteenth century and translated into French, Italian, and German, Prideaux's work would dominate scholarship for more than a century. His invention would survive even longer.

1718

Wotton, W. *Miscellaneous Discourses relating to the Traditions and Usages of the Scribes and Pharisees in our Saviour Jesus Christ's time.* 2 vols. London, 1718.
The first portrait—albeit rough—of Judaism "in the time of Jesus." The *Mishnah* is the main source.

1720

Calmet, A. *Dissertations, qui peuvent servir de Prolégomènes de l'Ecriture Sainte, revues, corrigées, considérablement augmentées et mises dans un ordre méthodique.* 3 vols. Paris, 1720.
The first volume contains the dissertations relating to the history, discipline, customs, and opinions of the Jews.

1727

Lardner, N. *The credibility of the Gospel History; or, The Facts occasionally mentioned in the New Testament, confirmed by Passages of Ancient Authors who were contemporary with our Saviour or his Apostles, or lived near their Time.* 2 vols. London, 1727–55.

The first volume is actually a history of Judaism in the age of Jesus.

1733

Schoettgen, C. *Horae Hebraicae et Tamudicae in Universum Novum Testamentum, quibus Horae Jo. Lightfooti in libris historicis supplentur, epistolae et apocalypsis eodem modo illustrantur.* Dresden, 1733.

The author wishes to complete Lightfoot's work (1658). Schoettgen's reading is more extensive, including the *Zohar* and several cabalistic works.

Stackhouse, T. *A New History of the Holy Bible, from the Beginning of the World to the Establishment of Christianity.* 2 vols. London, 1733. Reprint, rev. G. Gleig (3 vols.), London, 1817. Reprint, rev. D. Dewar, Glasgow and London, 1836.

1736

Meuschen, J. G., ed. *Novum Testamentum ex Talmude et Antiquitatibus Hebraeorum illustratum.* Leipzig, 1736.

Psalmanazar, G. *Israel.* In *An Universal History, from the Earliest Account of Time to the Present.* 60 vols. London, 1736–44; second edition, 1779–84.

1737

Mosheim, J. L. *Institutiones historiae ecclesiasticae antiquae et recentioris.* 4 vols. Helmstedt, 1737; second edition, 1764.

1742

Holberg, L. *Jødiske historie.* Copenhagen, 1742. Translated into German by A. Detharding, under the title *Jüdische Geschichte.* Flensburg, 1747.

1744

Ugolino, B., ed. *Thesaurus Antiquitatum Sacrarum.* 34 vols. Venice, 1744–69.

A monumental collection of translations, treatises, and works on Jewish antiquities "*ad illustrationem utriusque Testamenti.*"

1751

Wettstein, J. J. *Novum Testamentum Graecum, editiones receptae cum lectionibus variantibus codicum mss., editionum aliarum, versionum et patrum nec non commentario pleniore ex scriptoribus veteribus Hebraeis, Graecis et Latinis historiam et vim verborum illustrante opera et studio.* 2 vols. Amsterdam, 1751–52.

1766

Baumgarten, S. J. "Von den Juden." In *Geschichte der Religionspartein*, ed. J. Salomo, 257–366. Halle, 1766. Reprint, Hildesheim, 1966.

1776

Hess, J. J. *Geschichte der Israeliten vor den Zeiten Jesu.* 12 vols. Zürich, 1776–88.

1777

Venema, H. *Institutiones historiae ecclesiae Veteris et Novi Testamenti.* 7 vols. Leiden, 1777–83.

1789

Remond, J. *Versuch einer Geschichte der Ausbreitung des Judenthums von Cyrus bis auf den gänzlichen Untergang des jüdischen Staats.* Leipzig, 1789.

1792

Robinson, R. "A General View of Judea at the Birth of Jesus." In *Ecclesiastical Researches*, ed. G. Dyer, 20–32. Cambridge, 1792.

1800

Venturini, K.H.G. "Jehovah und sein Volk." In *Natürliche Geschichte des grossen Propheten von Nasareth.* 1:2–111. Bethlehem, 1800; second edition, 1806.

1806

Stolberg, F. L. von. *Geschichte der Religion Jesu Christi.* 15 vols. Hamburg, 1806–18.

1808

Beer, P. *Geschichte der Juden, von der Rückkehr aus der babylonischen Gefangenschaft bis zur Zerstörung des zweiten Temples.* Vienna, 1808.

1816

Allen, J. *Modern Judaism: or, a Brief Account of the Opinions, Traditions, Rites, and Ceremonies of the Jews in Modern Times.* London, 1816; second edition, 1820.

By "modern Jews" the author means those who lived during and subsequent to the time of Jesus.

1818

Horne, T. H. *An Introduction to the Critical Study and Knowledge of the Holy Scripture*. Vol. 3, *Summary of Biblical Geography and Antiquities*. London, 1818; thirteenth edition, 1872.

1820

Jost, I. M. *Geschichte der Israeliten seit der Zeit der Maccabaer bis auf unsere Tage*. 9 vols. Berlin, 1820–28. Translated under the title *History of the Jews from the Maccabees to the Present Day*. New York, 1848.

Jost's work, an expression of the rationalistic standpoint of a Reform Jew, represents the beginning of modern Jewish historiography. It is the first Jewish history written by a Jew that deals with the life of the Jewish people from antiquity to the modern age. The author touches on the origins of Christianity with a certain degree of sympathy, while giving a low opinion of Pharisaism.

1825

Neander, A. *Allgemeine Geschichte der christlichen Religion und Kirche*. 4 vols. Hamburg, 1825–31; second edition, 1841–47. Translated by J. Torrey, under the title *General History of the Christian Religion and Church*. 8 vols. Edinburgh, 1847–52.

1827

Marsh, J. *An Epitome of General Ecclesiastical History from the Earliest Period to the Present Time with an Appendix Giving a Condensed History of the Jews from the Destruction of Jerusalem to the Present Day*. New York, 1827.

1828

Jahn, J. *The History of the Hebrew Commonwealth from the Earliest Times to the Destruction of Jerusalem, with an Appendix Containing the Continuation of the History of the Jews to the Reign of Adrian Translated from Basnage*, ed. and trans. C. E. Stowe, from the German. Andover, 1828.

1829

Milman, H. H. *The History of the Jews: From the Earliest Period to the Present Time*. 2 vols. London, 1829–30; second edition, 1892.

The first modern history of the Jews from the earliest period to the author's time.

1833

Capefigue, M. [J.B.H. Raymond]. *Histoire philosophique des Juifs depuis la décadence de la race des Machabées jusqu'à la fin du VIe siècle*. Paris, 1833.

1834

Boon, C. "De Judaeis Jesu Christi aequalibus." Chap. 4 in *Specimen Historico-Theologicum, quo continetur Historia conditionis Judaeorum religiosae et moralis, inde ab exsilio Babylonico usque ad tempora Jesu Christi immutatae*. Groningen, 1834.

1838

Gfrörer, A. F. *Geschichte des Urchristenthums*. Vol. 1, *Das Jahrhundert des Heiles*. Stuttgart, 1838.

The first valuable attempt at a systematic presentation of the "Jewish background" of the New Testament. The author uses all the sources then available, including the Pseudepigrapha.

1839

Korn, S. *Rabbinische Quellen und Parallelen zu neutestamentlichen Schriftstellen*. Leipzig, 1839.

1842

Rohrbacher, R. F. *Histoire universelle de l'église catholique*. 29 vols. Nancy and Paris, 1842–49. Reprint, rev. L. Gautier (3 vols.), Montrejeau, 1903.

1843

Ewald, H. *Geschichte des Volkes Israel bis Christus*. 3 vols. Göttingen, 1843–45; second edition (*Geschichte des Volkes Israel*; 7 vols. and supplements; vol. 5, *Geschichte Christus' und seiner Zeit*), 1851–59; third edition, 1864–68. Translated under the title *History of Israel*. 8 vols. London, 1867–86.

Planned as a history of Israel "up to Christ," the work goes on, beginning with the second edition, to connect the history of Christ and early Christianity with the history of the Jews.

1844

Davidson, D. L. *Connection of Sacred and Profane History: Being a Review of the Principal Events in the World, as They Bear upon the State of Religion, from the Close of the Old Testament History, till the Establishment of Christianity*. 3 vols. New York, 1844.

1847

Herzfeld, L. *Geschichte des Volkes Jisrael von der Zerstörung des ersten Tempels bis zur Einsetzung des Makkabaers Shimon zum hohen Priester und Fürsten*. 3 vols. Brunswick, 1847–57; second edition, 1863.

Salvador, J. *Histoire de la domination Romaine en Judée et de la ruine de Jérusalem*. 3 vols. Brussels, 1847.

1852

Henrion, M.R.A. *Histoire ecclésiastique dupuis la création jusqu'au Pontificat de Pie IX*. 27 vols. Paris, 1852–83.

Lutterbeck, J.A.B. *Die neutestamentlichen Lehrbegriffe, oder Untersuchungen über das Zeitalter der Religionswende, die Vorstufen des Christenthums und die erste Gestaltung desselben. Ein Handbuch für älteste Dogmengeschichte und systematische Exegese des neuen Testamentes*. Vol. 1, *Die vorchristliche Entwicklung*. Mainz, 1852.

Reuss, E.W.E. *Histoire de la theologie chrétienne au siècle apostolique*. 2 vols. Strasbourg, 1852; second edition, 1860; third edition, 1864. Translated by A. Harwood, under the title *History of Christian Theology in the Apostolic Age*. 2 vols. London, 1872–74.

1853

Graetz, H. *Geschichte der Juden von den ältesten Zeiten bis auf die Gegenwart*. 11 vols. Leipzig, 1853–76. Translated and abridged, under the title *History of the Jews*. 6 vols. Philadelphia, 1891–98.
    This response of Orthodox Judaism to Jost's *Geschichte* was translated into Hebrew, English, French, Russian, Hungarian, and Yiddish. Graetz indulges in sharp condemnations of movements within Judaism that he dislikes, such as later Christianity, German nationalist trends, Kabbalah, Hasidim, and the Reform movement.

1854

Hale, W. H. *The History of the Jews: From the Time of Alexander the Great to the Destruction of Jerusalem by Titus, A.M. 3595, B.C. 409 to A.D. 70*. Fourth edition, London, 1854.

1855

Raphall, M. J. *Post-Biblical History of the Jews, from the Close of the Old Testament, about the Year 420 B.C.E., till the Destruction of the Second Temple in the Year 70 B.C.* Philadelphia, 1855.

1856

Migne, J.-P. *Dictionnaire des apocryphes, ou collection de tout les livres apocryphes relatifs à l'ancient et au nouveau testament*. 2 vols. Paris, 1856–58.

1857

Döllinger, J.J.I. von. *Heidenthum und Judenthum: Vorhalle zur Geschichte des Christenthums.* Regensburg, 1857. Reprint, Frankfurt, 1965. Translated by N. Darnell, under the title *The Gentile and the Jew in the courts of the Temple of Christ: An Introduction to the History of Christianity.* 2 vols. London, 1862.

Geiger, A. *Urschrift und Übersetzungen der Bibel in ihrer Abhängigkeit von der innern Entwicklung des Judenthums.* Breslau, 1857; second edition, 1928.

Noack, L. *Der Ursprung des Christentums: Seine vorbereitenden Grundlegungen und sein Eintritt in die Welt.* 2 vols. Leipzig, 1857.

1858

Pressensé, E. D. de. "Judaïsme." In *Histoire des trois premiers siècles de l'église chrétienne.* 1.191–238. Paris, 1858. Translated by L. Corkran, under the title *The Religions before Christ, being an Introduction to the History of the First Three Centuries of the Church.* Edinburgh, 1862.

1860

Nicolas, M. *Des doctrines religieuses des Juifs pendant les deux siècles antérieurs à l'ère chrétienne.* Paris, 1860.

1862

Bost, J.-A. *L'époque des Maccabées: Histoire du people juif depuis le retour de l'exil jusqu'à la destruction de Jérusalem.* Paris, 1862.

Darras, J. E. *Histoire général de l'eglise depuis la création jusqu'à nos jorns.* 44 vols. Paris, 1862–1907.

Schneckenburger, M. "Das Judenthum der neutestamentlichen Zeit." In *Vorlesungen über neutestamentliche Zeitgeschichte,* 77–255. Frankfurt am Main, 1862.

1865

Geiger, A. *Das Judenthum und seine Geschichte.* 3 vols. Breslau, 1865–71. Translated by C. Newburgh, under the title *Judaism and Its History.* New York, 1911.

1866

Langen, J. *Das Judenthum in Palästina zur Zeit Christi: Ein Beitrag zur Offenbarungs- und Religions-Geschichte als Einleitung in die Theologie des Neuen Testaments.* Freiburg, 1866.

Like Gfrörer, Langen gives a systematic description of the Jewish theology in the time of Jesus but, unlike him, he does not use the rabbinic writings as sources.

Pressensé, E. D. de. "Le Judaïsme de la décadence." Chap. 3 in *Jésus-Christ, son temps, sa vie, son oeuvre*. Paris, 1866.

1867

Derenbourg, J. "Histoire de la Palestine depuis Cyrius jusqu'à Adrien." In *Essai sur l'histoire et la géographie de la Palestine, d'après les Thalmuds et les autres sources rabbiniques*. Paris, 1867.

Holtzmann, H. J. *Geschichte des Volkes Israel und der Entstehung des Christenthums*. Vol. 2, *Judenthum und Christenthum in Zeitalter der apocryphischen und neutestamentlichen Literatur*. Leipzig, 1867.

Keim, T. *Geschichte Jesu von Nazara in ihrer Verkettung mit dem Gesamtleben seines Volkes*. 3 vols. Zurich, 1867–72; second edition, 1875. Translated by A. Ransom and E. M. Geldart, under the title *The History of Jesus of Nazara, Freely Investigated in Its Connection with the National Life of Israel, and Related in Detail*. 6 vols. London, 1873–83.

Looman, T. M. *Geschiedenis der Israëliten, van de babylonische ballingschap tot op de komst van der Heere Jezus Christus, met een aanhangsel inhoudende de geschiedenis der Israëliten van den dood van Herodes I, tot op de verwoesting van Jeruzalem*. Amsterdam, 1867.

de Witt, H. E. *Histoire du people juif depuis son retour de la captivité a Babylonie jusqu'à la ruine de Jérusalem*. Paris, 1867.

1868

Delitzsch, F. J. *Handwerkerlen zur Zeit Jesu: Ein Beitrag zur neutestamentliche Zeitgeschichte*. Erlangen, 1868; third edition (*Jüdisches Handwerterleben zur Zeit Jesu*), 1879.

Hausrath, A. *Neutestamentliche Zeitgeschichte*. 3 vols. Heidelberg, 1868–74; second edition (4 vols.), 1873–77. Translated by L. Huxley, under the title *A History of the New Testament Times*. 2 vols. London, 1878.

1869

Hengstenberg, E. W. *Geschichte des Reiches Gottes unter dem Alten Bunde*. 2 vols. Berlin, 1869–71.

Hitzig, F. *Geschichte des Volkes Israel von Anbeginn bis zur Eroberung Masada's im Jahre 72 nach Christus*. 2 vols. Leipzig, 1869.

1874

de Saulcy, L.F.J. Caignart. *Sept siècles de l'histoire judaïque depuis la prise de Jérusalem par Nabuchodonosor jusqu'à la prise de Bettir par le Romains.* Paris, 1874.

Schürer, E. *Lehrbuch der neutestamentlichen Zeitgeschichte.* Leipzig, 1874; second edition (*Geschichte des jüdischen Volkes im Zeitalter Jesu Christi*; 3 vols.), 1886–90; third edition, 1898–1901; third-fourth edition, 1901–9; fourth edition, 1911. Translated by J. MacPherson, under the title *A History of the Jewish People in the Time of Jesus Christ.* 5 vols. New York and Edinburgh, 1885–90.

> Planned as an introduction to the New Testament, this work would gain renown as the most authoritative history of Judaism in the time of Jesus. For its erudition and completeness, it is a masterpiece of modern research. Unfortunately, Schürer's attitude toward Judaism is strongly polemical. Borrowing paradigms from Protestant apologetics, he condemns Judaism as a legalistic and formalistic religion. Modern scholarship would be shaped for almost a century by this polemical view.

4. FROM SCHÜRER TO THE NEW SCHÜRER: FROM "LATE JUDAISM" TO "EARLY JUDAISM"

1876

Edersheim, A. *Sketches of Jewish Social Life in the Days of Christ.* London and Boston, 1876.

Stanley, A. P. *The History of the Jewish Church.* Vol. 3, *From the Captivity to the Christian Era.* New York, 1876; second edition, 1879.

Stapfer, E. L. *Les idées religieuses en Palestine à l'époque de Jésus-Christ.* Paris, 1876; second edition, 1878; third edition (*La Palestine au temps de Jésus-Christ d'après le Noveau Testament, l'historien Flavius Josèphe et les Talmuds*), 1885. Translated by A. H. Holmden, under the title *Palestine in Time of Christ.* London, 1886.

1877

Frothingham, O. B. *The Cradle of the Christ: A Study in Primitive Christianity.* New York, 1877.

> A nonconformist attempt "to indicate the place of the N.T. in the literature of the Hebrew people, . . . as a natural product of the Hebrew genius, its contents attesting the creative power of the Jewish mind."

Oort, H. *De laatste Eeuwen van Israëls Volksbestaan.* 2 vols. Leiden, 1877–78; second edition, 1915.

1878

Havet, E. *Le christianisme et ses origines.* Vol. 3, *Le judaïsme.* Paris, 1878.

1879

Ledrain, E. *Histoire d'Israël.* 2 vols. Paris, 1879–82.

1880

Weber, F. W. *System der altsynagogalen palästinischen Theologie aus Targum, Midrash und Talmud dargestellt,* ed. F. J. Delitzsch and G. Schnedermann. Leipzig, 1880; second edition, 1886; third edition, 1897.

Once again, the motive and method of the work are apologetic; the author sets out to prove the superiority of Christianity over Judaism. For Weber, legalism is the sum and substance of the Jewish religion, which transformed God into the inaccessible Lord of Torah.

Wise, I. M. *History of the Hebrews' Second Commonwealth with Special Reference to Its Literature, Culture, and the Origin of Rabbinism and Christianity.* Cincinnati, 1880.

1881

Mears, J. W. *From Exile to Overthrow: A History of the Jews from Babylonian Captivity to the Destruction of the Second Temple.* Philadelphia, 1881.

Reuss, E.W.E. "Die Zeit der Schriftgelehrten." In *Die Geschichte der heilige Schriften: Alten Testaments.* 2 vols. Brunswick, 1881; second edition, 1890.

1883

Edersheim, A. *The Life and Times of Jesus the Messiah.* 2 vols. New York, 1884; second edition, 1886; third edition, 1903; fourth edition, 1943.

1884

Bacher, W. *Die Agada der Tannaïten.* 2 vols. Strasbourg, 1884–90.

Carpenter, J. E. *Life in Palestina When Jesus Lived: A Short Handbook to the First Three Gospels.* London, 1884; second edition, 1893; third edition, 1915; fourth edition, 1926; fifth edition, 1935.

Seidel, M. *Zur Zeit Jesu: Darstellung aus der neutestamentlichen Zeitgeschichte.* Second edition, Leipzig, 1884. Translated under the title *In the Time of Jesus: Historical Pictures.* New York, 1885.

Seinecke, L. *Geschichte des Volkes Israel.* Vol. 2, *Vom Exil bis zur Zerstörung Jerusalems durch die Römer.* Göttingen, 1884.

1885

Craig-Houston, J. D. *Anno Domini; or, A Glimpse at the World into Which Messias Was Born.* London, 1885.

Redford, R. A. *Four Centuries of Silence; or, From Malachi to Christ.* London, 1885.

1886

Cook, K. *The Fathers of Jesus: A Study of the Lineage of the Christian Doctrine and Traditions.* 2 vols. London, 1886.

Cox, H. *The First Century of Christianity,* 15–59. London, 1886.

Karpeles, G. *Geschichte der jüdischen Literatur.* 2 vols. Berlin, 1886; second edition, 1909; third edition (3 vols.), 1920–21.

Kayser, A. "Die Zeit der Zersetzung des Mosaismus unter answärtegen Einflüssen bis zur Zerstörung des zweiten Temples." In *Die Theologie des Alten Testaments in ihrer geschichtlichen Entwicklung dargestellt.* Strasbourg, 1886; second edition (*August Kayser's Theologie des Alten Testaments,* ed. K. Marti), 1894; third edition (*Geschichte der Israelitischen Religion,* ed. K. Marti), 1897; fourth edition, 1903; fifth edition, 1907.

1887

Renan, E. *Histoire du peuple Israël.* 5 vols. Paris, 1887–93. Translated under the title *History of the People of Israel.* 5 vols. London and Boston, 1888–96.

1888

Holtzmann, O. "Das Ende des jüdischen Staatswesens und die Entstehung des Christenthums." In *Geschichte des Volkes Israel,* ed. B. Stade, 2:271–674. Berlin, 1888.

1889

Sack, I. *Die altjüdische Religion im Uebergange vom Bibelthume zum Talmudismus.* Berlin, 1889.

1890

Morrison, W. D. *The Jews under Roman Rule.* London, 1890.

Toy, C. H. *Judaism and Christianity: A Sketch of the Progress of Thought from Old Testament to New Testament.* Boston, 1890.

1891

Bettany, G. T. "Judaism after the Prophets." In *The World's Religions: A Comprehensive Popular Account of all the Principal Religions of Civilised and Uncivilised Peoples*, 649–669. New York, 1891.

1893

Brann, M. *Geschichte der Juden und ihrer Literatur*. 2 vols. Breslau, 1893–95; second edition, 1896–99; third edition, 1910–13.

Moss, R. W. *From Malachi to Matthew: Outlines of the History of Judea 440 to 4 B.C.* London, 1893; second edition, 1899.

1894

Friedländer, M. *Zur Entstehungsgeschichte des Christenthums: Ein Excurs von der Septuaginta zum Evangelium*. Vienna, 1894.

Pfleiderer, O. "The Preparation of Christianity in Judaism." Chap. 2 in *Philosophy and Development of Religion*, vol. 2. New York, 1894. Reprint, 1979.

Wellhausen, J. *Israelitische und jüdische Geschichte*. Berlin, 1894. Reprint, 1958.

1895

Fairweather, W. *From the Exile to the Advent*. Edinburgh, 1895; second edition, 1901.

Holtzmann, O. *Neutestamentliche Zeitgeschichte*. Freiburg and Leipzig, 1895; second edition, Tübingen, 1906.

1896

Kent, C. F. *A History of Israel*. 2 vols. London and New York, 1896–97; second edition (*A History of the Jewish People during the Babylonian, Persian, and Greek Periods*), 1899.

1897

Friedländer, M. *Das Judenthum in der vorchristlichen griechischen Welt: Ein Beitrag zur Entstehungsgeschichte des Christentums*. Vienna, 1897.

Muirhead, L. A. *The Times of Christ*. Edinburgh, 1897; second edition, 1905.

Reville, A. *Jésus de Nazareth: Etudes critiques sur le antecedents de l'histoire evangelique et la vie de Jésus*. Paris, 1897; second edition, 1906.

Valeton, J.J.P. "Die Israeliten." In *Lehrbuch der Religionsgeschichte*, ed. P.D.C. de la Saussaye, 1:242–325. Second edition, Freiburg and Leipzig, 1897.

1898

Cheyne, T. K. *Jewish Religious Life after the Exile.* New York and London, 1898; second edition, 1901; third edition, 1915.

Farrar, F. W. *The Herods.* London, 1898.

Streane, A. W. *The Age of the Maccabees: With a Special Reference to the Religious Literature of the Period.* London, 1898.

1899

Latimer, E. W. *Judea from Cyrus to Titus, 537 B.C.–70 A.D.* Chicago, 1899.

Mathews, S. *A History of New Testament Times in Palestine, 175 B.C. to 70 A.D.* London, 1899; second edition, 1910; third edition, 1943.

1900

Baldensperger, W. *Das spätere Judenthum als Vorstufe des Christenthums.* Giessen, 1900.

Beurlier, E. *Le mond juif aux temps de Jésus-Christ et des apôtres.* Paris, 1900.

Kautzsch, E. *Die Apocryphen und Pseudepigraphen des Alten Testaments.* 2 vols. Tübingen, 1900.

Newman, A. H. "Preparation for Christianity in Jewish Life and Thought." In *A Manual of Church History,* 1:34–64. Philadelphia, 1900.

Riggs, J. S. *A History of the Jewish People during the Maccabean and Roman Periods (including New Testament Times).* New York, 1900.

1901

Schlatter, A. von. *Israel's Geschichte von Alexander dem Grossen bis Hadrian.* Stuttgart, 1901; second edition, 1906; third edition, 1925.

1903

Bousset, W. *Die Religion des Judentums im neutestamentlichen Zeitalter.* Berlin, 1903; second edition, 1906; third edition (*Die Religion des Judentums im späthellenistischen Zeitalter,* ed. H. Gressmann), Tübingen, 1926.
   Bousset radicalizes the ideas of Schürer and Weber, coining the term "Spätjudentum" (late Judaism). The fundamental contrast between Jesus and Judaism is in the idea of God and in the feeling toward God.

Perles, F. *Bousset's Religion des Judenthums im neutestamentlichen Zeitalter: Kritisch Untersucht.* Berlin, 1903.

1904

Bevan, E. R. *Jerusalem under the High-Priest: Five Lectures on the Period between Nehemiah and the New Testament*. London, 1904.

Rae, G. M. *Connection between Old and New Testaments*. London, 1904.

Smith, W. W. *From the Exile to the Advent: The Preparation of the World for Christ: The History of the Apocryphal Age*. Milwaukee, 1904.

Stade, B., et al. "Israel." In *The Historians' History of the World*, ed. H. S. Williams, 2:1–238. New York and London, 1905.

1905

Friedländer, M. *Die religiösen Bewegungen innerhalb des Judentums im Zeitalter Jesu*. Berlin, 1905.

Grant, C. M. *Between the Testaments: A study of the Four Hundred Years Separating the Old and New Testament*, New York and Chicago, n.d. (c. 1905).

Hollmann, G. W. *Welche Religion hatten die Juden als Jesus auftrat?* Halle, 1905; Tübingen, 1906; second edition, Tübingen, 1910. Translated under the title *The Jewish Religion in the Time of Jesus*. Boston, 1909.

Skinner, J. *Historical Connection between the Old and New Testament*. Edinburgh, 1905.

Turnes, M. J. "Religious Beliefs in the Time of Christ." In *Inaugural Lectures Delivered by Members of the Faculty of Theology during Its First Session, 1904–05*, ed. A. S. Peake. Manchester, 1905.

1906

Dujardin, E. *La source de fleure chrétién: Historique critique du judaïsme ancien et du christianisme primitif*. Paris, 1906. Translated by J. McCabe, under the title *The Source of the Christian Tradition: A Critical History of Ancient Judaism*. London and Chicago, 1911.

1907

Abrahams, I. *Judaism*. London, 1907; second edition, 1910.

Gregg, D. *Between the Testaments; or, Interbiblical History*. New York and London, 1907.

Oesterley, W.O.E. *The Religion and Worship of the Synagogue: An Introduction to the Study of Judaism from the New Testament Period*. New York, 1907.

Staerk, W. *Neutestamentliche Zeitgeschichte*. 2 vols. Leipzig, 1907; second edition, Berlin, 1912.

1908

Dummelow, J. R., ed. "The History, Literature, and Religious Developments of the Jews in the Period between the Testaments." In *A Commentary on the Holy Bible*, xlviii–lxxiii. New York, 1906; second edition, 1936; third edition, 1961.

Fairweather, W. *The Background of the Gospel; or, Judaism in the Period between the Old and the New Testament.* Edinburgh, 1908; third edition, 1920. Reprint, 1952.

> The response of English scholarship to Schürer and Bousset. Fairweather is able to coin a new, autonomous, and successful definition ("background"), but he depends strongly on his German models when he portrays (late) Judaism as a legalistic and nationalistic religion.

Kautsky, K. "Das Judentum." In *Der Ursprung des Christentums: Eine historische Untersuchung*, 184–337. Stuttgart, 1908.

1909

Bertholet, A. *Das religionsgeschichtliche Problem des Spätjudentums.* Tübingen, 1909.

Carus, P. "The Origin of Judaism and Its Significance for Christianity." In *The Pleroma: An Essay on the Origin of Christianity*, 83–122. Chicago, 1909.

Dufourcq, A. *L'avenir du christianisme.* Vol. 2, *L'époque syncrétiste: histoire de la fondation de l'église, depuis le temps d'Alexandre jusqu'au temps des Sévèrs.* Paris, 1909; second edition, 1924.

1910

Felten, J. *Neutestamentliche Zeitgeschichte; oder, Judentum und Heidentum zur Zeit Christi und der Apostel.* 2 vols. Regensburg, 1910; second and third editions, 1925.

Schwalm, M. B. *La vie privée du peuple juif à l'époque de Jésus-Christ.* Paris, 1910.

1911

Bertholet, A. *Die jüdische Religion von der Zeit Esras bis zum Zeitalter Christi.* Tübingen, 1911.

Kent, C. F. *The Historical Bible.* Vol. 4, *The Makers and Teachers of Judaism from the Fall of Jerusalem to the Death of Herod the Great.* New York, 1911.

1913

Alford, B. H. *Jewish History and Literature under the Maccabees and Herod.* London, 1913.

Bouillon, L. *L'église apostolique et les juifs philosophes jusqu'à Philon*. 2 vols. Orthez, 1913–14.

Charles, R. H. *The Apocrypha and Pseudepigrapha of the Old Testament in English*. 2 vols. Oxford, 1913.

1914

Case, S. J. "The Early Christians' Jewish Connections." Chap. 4 in *The Evolution of Early Christianity: A Genetic Study of First-Century Christianity in Relation to Its Religious Environment*. Chicago, 1914.

Charles, R. H. *Religious Developments between the Old and the New Testament*. New York and London, 1914.

> Christianity is the heir of the prophetic and apocalyptic line, which in Judaism was choked back by the emergence of the legalistic line of Pharisaism.

Juster, J. *Les Juifs dans l'Empire romain, leur condition juridique, économique et sociale*. 2 vols. Paris, 1914.

1915

Prideaux, S.P.T. *The Cradle of Christianity; or, Some Account of the Times of Christ*. New York, 1915.

1916

Barnes, W. E., ed. *A Companion to Biblical Studies*. Cambridge, 1916.

> See the articles by H. E. Ryle, H.C.O. Lanchaster, V. H. Stanton, and H. M. Gwatkin.

1919

Knopf, R. "Neutestamentliche Zeitgeschichte." In *Einführung in das Neue Testament: Bibelkunde des Neuen Testaments, Geschichte und Religion des Urchristentums*, 166–225. Giessen, 1919; second edition, 1923; third edition, 1929; fourth edition, 1933.

1920

Foakes-Jackson, F. J., K. Lake, and C. G. Montefiore. "The Jewish World." In *The Beginnings of Christianity*, ed. F. J. Foakes-Jackson and K. Lake, 1:1–168. London, 1920.

1921

Bernfeld, S. *Die jüdische Literatur: Bibel, Apocryphen und jüdisch-hellenistisches Schrifttum*. Berlin, 1921.

Meyer, E. *Ursprung und Anfänge des Christentums.* Vol. 2, *Die Entwicklung des Judentums und Jesus von Nazareth.* Stuttgart and Berlin, 1921. Reprint, Darmstadt, 1962.

1922

Braley, E. R. *A Neglected Era: From the Old Testament to the New.* New York, 1922.

Büchler, A. *Types of Jewish-Palestinian Piety from 70 B.C.E. to 70 C.E.: The Ancient Pious Men.* London, 1922.

Fillion, L. C. *Vie de N.S. Jésus-Christ: exposé historique, critique et apologetique.* 3 vols. Paris, 1922. Translated under the title *The Life of Christ: A Historical, Critical, and Apologetic Exposition.* 3 vols. St. Louis and London, 1928–29.

Hölscher, G. *Geschichte der israelitischen und jüdischen Religion.* Giessen, 1922.

Strack, H. L., and P. Billerbeck. *Kommentar zum Neuen Testament aus Talmud und Midrasch.* 4 vols. Munich 1922–28; seventh edition, 1978.

Wade, G. W. *New Testament History.* London, 1922.

1923

Jeremias, J. *Jerusalem zur Zeit Jesu.* 2 vols. Leipzig, 1923–37; third edition, 1962. Translated by F. H. Cave and C. H. Cave, under the title *Jerusalem in the Time of Jesus.* Philadelphia, 1969.

Montefiore, C. G. *The Old Testament and After.* London, 1923.

Sell, E. *After Malachi.* Madras, 1923.

Walker, T. *The Teaching of Jesus and the Jewish Teaching of His Age.* London, 1923.

1924

Union of Jewish Literary Societas, ed. *Judaism and the Beginnings of Christianity: A Course of Lectures Delivered in 1923 at Jew's College, London.* London, 1924.

See articles by A. Cohen, F. C. Burkitt, E. N. Adler, R. T. Herford, and H.St.J. Thackeray.

Blunt, A.W.F. *Israel before Christ: An Account of Social and Religious Development in the Old Testament.* London, 1924.

1925

Dubnow, S. *Weltgeschichte des jüdischen Volkes,* German trans. from the Russian. 10 vols. Berlin, 1925–26. Translated by M. Spiegel, under the title *History of the Jews.* 5 vols. South Brunswick, 1967–73.

Klausner, J. *Jesus of Nazareth: His Life, Times, and Teachings*, trans. H. Danby from the Hebrew. New York, 1925.

Lightley, J. W. *Jewish Sects and Parties in the Time of Christ.* London, 1925.

1926

Annett, E. A. *The Hidden Centuries: Malachi to Matthew.* London, 1926.

Browne, L. E. *From Babylon to Bethlehem: The Story of the Jews for the Last Five Centuries before Christ.* Cambridge, 1926. Reprint, 1951.

Fiebig, P.W.J. *Die Umwelt des Neuen Testament: Religionsgeschichte und geschichtliche Texte, in deutscher Übersetzung und mit Anmerkungen versehen, zum Verständnis des Neuen Testaments.* Göttingen, 1926.

Gibson, G. M. *History of New Testament Times.* Nashville, 1926.

Keith, K. E. *The Social Life of a Jew in the Time of Christ.* Liverpool, 1926. Reprint, London, 1950.

Kreglinger, R. "La religion d'Israël pendant et depuis l'exil." In *La Religion d'Israël.* Second edition, 248–359. Brussels, 1926.

1927

Bevan, E. R. "Hellenistic Judaism." In *The Legacy of Israel*, ed. E. R. Bevan and C. Singer, 29–67. Oxford, 1927.

Bergmann, J. "Das Judentum in der hellenistisch-römischen Zeit." In *Entwicklungsstufen der jüdischen Religion*, ed. I. Elbongen. Giessen, 1927.

Moore, G. F. *Judaism in the First Centuries of the Christian Era: The Age of the Tannaim.* 3 vols. Cambridge, Mass., 1927–30. Reprint, 1971.
  Moore portrays Rabbinism as the "normative" Judaism in the first century. His anachronistic view (much more than his sympathetic attitude) was to have a deep influence on subsequent research.

1928

Dana, H. E. *The New Testament World: A Brief Sketch of the History and Conditions Which Composed the Background of the New Testament.* Second edition, Nashville, 1928; third edition, 1937.

Gore, C., ed. *A New Commentary on Holy Scripture.* London, 1928.
  See articles by V. M. Benecke and W.O.E. Oesterley.

Herford, R. T. *Judaism in the New Testament Period.* London, 1928.

Riessler, P. *Altjüdisches Schrifttum ausserhalb der Bibel.* Heidelberg, 1928. Reprint, 1966.

1929

Booth, H. K. *The Bridge between the Testaments: A Survey of the Life and Literature of the Period of the Connections.* New York and London, 1929.

Charue, A. "Le milieu juif." In *L'incrédulité des Juifs dans le Noveau Testament: Etude historique, exégétique et théologique,* 1–66. Gembloux, 1929.

Eiselen, F. C. ed. *The Abingdon Bible Commentary.* New York, 1929.
    See the articles by T. H. Robinson, L. E. Fuller, and G. H. Box.

Hunkin, J. W. *From the Fall of Nineveh to Titus.* London, 1929.

1930

Cook, S. A., F. E. Adcock, and M. P. Charlesworth, eds. *The Cambridge Ancient History,* vols. 8–10. Cambridge, 1930–34.
    See the articles by E. R. Bevan and A. Momigliano.

Hempel, J. *Die althebräische Literatur und ihr hellenistisch-jüdisches Nachleben.* Wildpark-Potsdam, 1930. Reprint, Berlin, 1968.

Waxman, M. *A History of Jewish Literature from the Close of the Bible to Our Own Days.* 4 vols. New York, 1930–41; second edition (6 vols.), 1960.

1931

Bindley, T. H. *Religious Thought in Palestine in the Time of Christ.* London, 1931.

Boulenger, A. "Le mond juif." In *Histoire générale de l'église,* 1:49–80. Lyon and Paris, 1931.

Glover, T. R. *The World of the New Testament.* Cambridge and New York, 1931.

Lagrange, M.-J. *Le judaïsme avant Jésus-Christ.* Paris, 1931.

Marshall, F. H. *The Religious Backgrounds of Early Christianity.* St. Louis, 1931.

1932

Box, G. H. *Judaism in the Greek Period, from the Rise of Alexander the Great to the Intervention of Rome (333–63 B.C.).* Oxford, 1932.

Holzmeister, U. *Historia aetatis Novi Testamenti.* Rome, 1932; second edition, 1938. Translated into Italian and revised by C. Zedda, under the title *Storia dei tempi del Nuovo Testamento.* Rome, 1950.

Kittel, G. *Die Religionsgeschichte und das Urchristentum.* Gütersloh, 1932.

Levison, N. *The Jewish Background of Christianity: A Manual of the Political, Religious, Social and Literary Life of the Jews from 586 B.C. to A.D. 1.* Edinburgh, 1932.

Oesterley, W.O.E. *A History of Israel.* Vol. 2, *From the Fall of Jerusalem, 586 B.C., to the Bar-Kokhba Revolt, A.D. 135.* Oxford, 1932.

Ricciotti, G. *Storia d'Israele.* Vol. 2, *Dall'esilio al 135 dopo Cristo.* Turin, 1932; second edition, 1934. Translated by C. Della Penta and R. T. Murphy, under the title *The History of Israel.* Milwaukee, 1955.

1933

Kittel, G., ed. *Theologisches Wörterbuch zum Neuen Testament.* 9 vols. Stuttgart, 1933–76. Translated under the title *Theological Dictionary of the New Testament*, ed. G. W. Bromiley and G. Friedrich. 10 vols. Grand Rapids, 1964–76.

Sell, E. *The Return From Exile.* Madras, 1933.

1934

Bonsirven, J. *Le judaïsme palestinien au temps de Jésus-Christ: Sa théologie.* 2 vols. Paris, 1934–35; abridged edition, 1950. Translated by W. Wolf, under the title *Palestinian Judaism in the Time of Jesus Christ.* New York, 1964.

The author tries to give a systematic presentation of Judaism "in the age of Christ" according to the criteria of (Catholic) dogmatics. Judaism is seen as a homogeneous whole.

Grant, F. C. "Early Judaism." In *The Beginnings of Our Religion*, ed. F. James, et al., 79–90. New York, 1934.

Grant is the first scholar to use the term "early Judaism" in place of "late Judaism."

Lebreton, J. "Le monde juif." In *Histoire de l'église*, ed. A. Fliche and V. Martin, 1:26–62. Paris, 1934. Translated under the title *The History of the Primitive Church*, Vol. 1. Oxford, 1942.

Schneider, C. *Einführung in die neutestamentliche Zeitgeschichte.* Leipzig, 1934.

1935

Guignebert, C. *Des prophetes à Jésus: Le monde juif vers le temps de Jésus.* Paris, 1935; second edition, 1950. Translated under the title *The Jewish World in the Time of Jesus.* London, 1939; second edition, New York, 1953.

James, E. O. "The Jewish Background." In *In the Fulness of Time: A Course of Public Lectures in the University of Leeds on the Historical Background of Christianity*, 44–64. London and New York, 1935.

Welch, A. C. *Post-exilic Judaism*. Edinburgh and London, 1935.

Woolf, B. L. *The Background and Beginnings of the Gospel Story*. London, 1935.

1936

MacGregor, G.H.C., and A. C. Purdy. *Jew and Greek: Tutors unto Christ: The Jewish and Hellenistic Background of the New Testament*. London, 1936.

Scott, W. "Jewish History." In *A History of the Early Christian Church*, 15–78. Nashville, 1936.

Stamm, R. T. "The Historical Relationships of Christianity: A Study of Man's Quest for Salvation." In *New Testament Commentary*, ed. H. C. Alleman, 25–82. Philadelphia, 1936; second edition, 1944.

1937

Baron, S. W. *A Social and Religious History of the Jews*. 3 vols. New York, 1937; second edition (17 vols.), 1952–83.

Oesterley, W.O.E. *The Age of Transition*. Vol. 1, *Judaism and Christianity*. London, 1937.

Preisker, H. *Neutestamentliche Zeitgeschichte*. Berlin, 1937; second edition, 1965.

1938

Cassuto, U. *Storia della letteratura ebraica postbiblica*. Florence, 1938.

Enslin, M. S. "The Background." In *Christian Beginnings*, 1:1–143. New York and London, 1938. Reprint, 1956.

Jones, A.H.M. *The Herods of Judaea*. Oxford, 1938; second edition, 1967.

1939

Lods, A. "La recontre du judaïsme et de la civilization gréco-romaine." In *La religion d'Israël*, 210–45. Paris, 1939.

Manson, T. W., ed. *A Companion to the Bible*. New York, 1939.
    See articles by W.O.E. Oesterley, T. H. Robinson, and M. Black.

McNeill, J. T., ed. *Environmental Factors in Christian History*. Chicago, 1939.

1940

Albright, W. F. *From the Stone Age to Christianity: Monotheism and the Historical Process*. Baltimore, 1940; second edition, 1946. Reprint, Garden City, 1957.

Foerster, W. *Neutestamentliche Zeitgeschichte*, Vol. 1. Hamburg, 1940; second edition, 1955. Translated by G. E. Harris, under the title *Palestinian Judaism in the New Testament Times*. Edinburgh, 1964. American edition (*From the Exile to Christ: An Historical Introduction to Palestinian Judaism*), Philadelphia, 1964.

1941

Nilsson, M. P. *The Historical Hellenistic Background of the New Testament*. Cambridge, Mass., 1941.

Oesterley, W.O.E. *The Jews and Judaism during the Greek Period: The Background of Christianity*. London and New York, 1941.

1943

Eissfeldt, O. *Einleitung in das Alte Testament*. Tübingen, 1943; second edition, 1956; third edition, 1964. Translated by P. R. Ackroyd, under the title *The Old Testament: An Introduction*. Oxford and New York, 1965.

This introduction to the Old Testament is still one of the most complete with respect to the Old Testament Apocrypha and Pseudepigrapha.

1944

Oldaker, W. H. *The Background of the Life of Jesus*. London, 1944; second edition, 1956.

1945

Browne, L., ed. "The Post-Biblical Period." In *The Wisdom of the Jewish People*, 91–156. New York, 1945. Reprint, 1987.

1946

Bultmann, R. *Urchristentum im Rahmen der antiken Religionen*. Zurich, 1946; second edition, 1956; third edition, 1963. Translated by R. H. Fuller, under the title *Primitive Christianity in Its Contemporary Setting*. New York, 1956.

1948

Davis, W. H., and E. A. McDowell. *A Source Book of Interbiblical History*. Nashville, 1948.

1949

Finkelstein, L., ed. *The Jews: Their History, Culture and Religion.* New York, 1949; second edition, 1955; third edition, 1960; fourth edition (3 vols.), 1971–72.

See articles by E. J. Bickerman, J. Goldin, and R. Marcus.

Pfeiffer, R. H. *A History of New Testament Times with an Introduction to the Apocrypha.* New York, 1949.

Snaith, N. H. *The Jews from Cyrus to Herod.* New York, 1949; second edition, 1956.

1950

Filson, F. V. *The New Testament against Its Environment: The Gospel of Christ, the Risen Lord.* London, 1950; second edition (*A New Testament History: The Story of The Emerging Church*), Philadelphia and London, 1965.

Klausner, J. *History of the Second Temple* (Hebrew). Jerusalem, 1950. Reprint, 1968.

Lods, A. *Histoire de la littérature hébraïque et juive depuis les origines jusqu'à la ruine de l'état juif (135 après J.-C.).* Paris, 1950.

Noth, M. *Geschichte Israels.* Göttingen, 1950; second edition, 1954. Translated by S. Godman, under the title *The History of Israel.* London and New York, 1958.

1951

Allen, I. "The World to Which Christ Came." In *The Early Church and the New Testament*, 1–68. London, 1951.

Waszink, J. H., ed. *Het oudste Christendom en de antieke Cultuur.* 2 vols. Haarlem, 1951.

1952

Abel, P. M. *Histoire de la Palestine depuis la conquête d'Alexandre jusqu'à l'invasion arabe.* 2 vols. Paris, 1952.

1953

Bouquet, A. C. *Everyday Life in New Testament Times.* New York, 1953.

Tenney, M. C. "The World of the New Testament." In *The New Testament: An Historical and Analytic Survey*, 1–121. Grand Rapids, 1953; second edition, 1961; third edition (ed. W. M. Dunnett), 1985.

1954

Baron, S. W., and J. L. Blau, eds. *Judaism: Post-Biblical and Talmudic Period*. New York, 1954.

Goppelt, L. *Christentum und Judentum im ersten und zweiten Jahrhundert*. Gütersloh, 1954.

1955

Bonsirven, J. *Textes rabbiniques des deux premiers siècles chrétiens*. Rome, 1955.

Schubert, K. *Die Religion des nachbiblischen Judentums*. Vienna and Freiburg, 1955.

1956

Barrett, C. K. *The New Testament Background: Selected Documents*. London, 1956; second edition, San Francisco, 1987.

Davis, M., ed. *Israel: Its Role in Civilization*. New York, 1956.
   See articles by H. L. Ginsberg, M. Smith, and S. W. Baron. Smith attacks the myth of "normative Judaism," showing the great diversity of shades of Judaism that coexisted in first-century Palestine.

Marcus, R. "The Hellenistic Age." In *Great Ages and Ideas of the Jewish People*, ed. L. W. Schwartz, 93–139. New York, 1956.

1957

Gift, J. *Life and Customs in Jesus' Time*. Cincinnati, 1957.

Johnson, S. E. *Jesus in His Homeland*. New York, 1957.

Kee, H. C. *Understanding the New Testament*. Englewood Cliffs, N.J., 1957; second edition, 1965; third edition, 1973; fourth edition, 1985.

Stauffer, E. *Jerusalem und Rom im Zeitalter Jesu Christi*. Bern, 1957.

1958

Eller, M. F. *The Beginnings of the Christian Religion: A Guide to the History and Literature of Judaism and Christianity*. New York, 1958.

Perowne, S. *The Later Herods: The Political Background of the New Testament*. London, 1958; second edition, 1965.

Philippides, L. I. *Historia tês epochês tês kainês diathêkês* (Greek). Athens, 1958.

1959

Alfaric, P. *Origines sociales du christianisme*. Paris, 1959.

Bright, J. *A History of Israel*. Philadelphia, 1959; second edition, 1972; third edition, 1981.

Pfeiffer, C. F. *Between the Testaments*. Grand Rapids, 1959; second edition, 1975.

Rossano, P. "L'ambiente di Gesù." In *Introduzione alla Bibbia*, ed. L. Moraldi, Vol. 4. Turin, 1959.

Tcherikover, V. *Hellenistic Civilization and the Jews*. Translated by S. Applebaum from the Hebrew. Philadelphia, 1959.

Tricot, A. "Jewish World and Literature." In *Introduction à la Bible*, ed. A. Robert. Vol. 2, *Noveau Testament*. Tournai, 1959. Translated by P. W. Skehan, et al., under the title *Introduction to the New Testament*, 30–139. New York, 1965.

1960

Grant, F. C. *Ancient Judaism and the New Testament*. Edinburgh, 1960.

Henry, C.F.H., ed. *The Biblical Expositor*. 3 vols. Philadelphia and New York, 1960; second edition, 1973.
    See articles by D. H. Wallace and J. R. Mantey.

Kee, H. C., and F. W. Young. *The Living World of the New Testament*. London, 1960.

Parkes, J. W. *The Foundations of Judaism and Christianity*. Chicago, 1960.
    Parkes's work is a landmark in the new approach that sees Second Temple Judaism as "the common foundation" of both Rabbinism and Christianity.

Russell, D. S. *Between the Testaments*. Philadelphia, 1960.

Simon, M. *Les sectes juives au temps de Jésus*. Paris, 1960. Translated by J. H. Farley, under the title *Jewish Sects in the Time of Jesus*. Philadelphia, 1967.

Toombs, L. E. *The Threshold of Christianity: Between the Testaments*. Philadelphia, 1960.
    The author speaks of "rabbinic Judaism and modern Christianity as the two legitimate successors of the Old Testament tradition."

1961

Démann, P. *Judaism*. Translated by P. J. Hepburne-Scott from the French. New York, 1961.

Hertzberg, A., ed. *Judaism*. New York, 1961.

Price, J. L. "Reconstructing the Setting of Early Christianity." In *Interpreting the New Testament*, 31–84. New York, 1961; second edition, 1971.

Purinton, C. E. *Christianity and Its Judaic Heritage: An Introduction with Selected Sources*. New York, 1961.

1962

Black, M. "The Development of Judaism in the Greek and Roman Periods (c. 196 B.C.–A.D. 135)." In *Peake's Commentary on the Bible*, ed. M. Black and H. H. Rowley, 693–98. London, 1962.

Blaiklock, E.M. *The Century of the New Testament*. London, 1962.

Davies, W. D. *Christian Origins and Judaism*. Philadelphia, 1962.

Nötscher, F. *Vom Alten zum Neuen Testament*. Bonn, 1962.

Zeitlin, S. *The Rise and Fall of the Judean State: A Political and Religious History of the Second Commonwealth*. 3 vols. Philadelphia, 1962–78.

1963

Bruce, F. F. *Israel and the Nations: From the Exodus to the Fall of the Second Temple Period*. London and Grand Rapids, 1963; second edition, Exeter, 1975.

1964

Noack, B. "Det Nye Testamentes Baggrund." In *Det Nye Testamente og de Første kristne Årtier*, 39–95. Copenhagen, 1964; second edition, 1966.

Schedl, C. *Geschichte des Alten Testaments*. Vol. 5, *Die Fulle der Zeiten*. Innsbruck, 1964. Translated under the title *History of the Old Testament*, Vol. 5. Staten Island, N.Y., 1973.

Tamisier, P. *Les deux derniers siècles de l'Ancient Testament*. Paris, 1964.

1965

Boys, M. *Life in the Time of Jesus*. London, 1965.

Howie, C. G. *The Creative Era between the Testaments*. Richmond, Va., 1965.

Lace, O. J. "The Historical Background of New Testament Times." In *Understanding the New Testament*, ed. O. J. Lace, 11–63. Cambridge, 1965.

Leipoldt, J., and W. Grundmann. *Umwelt des Urchristentums*. 3 vols. Berlin, 1965–67; fifth edition, 1979.

Metzger, B. M. "The Background of the New Testament." In *The New Testament: Its Background, Growth and Content*, 17–70. Nashville, 1965.

Nichol, F. D., ed. *The Seventh-Day Adventist Bible Commentary*, 5:17–102. Washington, 1965.

Reicke, B. *Neutestamentliche Zeitgeschichte: Die biblische Welt 500 v.–100 n. Chr.* Berlin, 1965. Translated by D. Green, under the title *The New Testament Era: The World of the Bible from 500 B.C. to A.D. 100*. Philadelphia, 1968.

1966

Glatzer, N. N. *Anfänge des Judentums: Eine Einführung*. Gütersloh, 1966.

Newman, B. M. "The Old Wine." In *The Meaning of the New Testament*, 1–60. Nashville, 1966.

Schultz, H. J., ed. *Die Zeit Jesu*. Stuttgart, 1966. Translated by B. Watchorn, under the title *Jesus in His Time*. London and Philadelphia, 1971.

1967

Bronkhorst, A. J. *Von Alexander bis Bar Kochba: 400 Jahre Fremdherschaft in Israel*. Wuppertal, 1967.

Bronner, L. *Sects and Separatism during the Second Jewish Commonwealth*. New York, 1967.

Malherbe, A. J., ed. *The World of the New Testament*. Austin, 1967.

Russell, D. S. *The Jews from Alexander to Herod*. London, 1967; second edition, 1970.

1968

Anderson, H. "The Intertestamental Period." In *The Bible and History*, ed. W. Barclay, 153–244. Nashville, 1968.

Brown, R. E., J. A. Fitzmyer, and R. E. Murphy, eds. *The Jerome Biblical Commentary*. Englewood Cliffs, N.J., 1968.
    See articles by C. Stuhlmueller, R. E. Brown, G. Wright, R. E. Murphy, and J. A. Fitzmyer.

Cazelles, H. *Naissance de l'église: Secte juive rejetée?* Paris, 1968.

Gaubert, H. *L'attente du Messie*. Paris, 1968.

Simon, M., and A. Benoit, *Le judaïsme et le christianisme antique d'Antiochus Epiphane à Costantin*. Paris, 1968; second edition, 1985.

1969

Bauer, J. B. *Die Zeit Jesu: Herrscher, Sekten und Parteien*. Stuttgart, 1969.

Bleeker, C. J., and G. Widengren. *Historia religionum: Handbook for the History of Religions*. 2 vols. Leiden, 1969–71.
    See articles by G. Widengren and R.J.Z. Werblowsky.

Bruce, F. F. *New Testament History*. London, 1969; New York, 1972.

Hengel, M. *Judaism und Hellenismus*. Tübingen, 1969; second edition, 1973. Translated by J. Bowden, under the title *Judaism and Hellenism*. 2 vols. Philadelphia, 1974.

McKenzie, J. "The Jewish World in the New Testament Times." In *A New Catholic Commentary on Holy Scripture*, ed. R. C. Fuller, 766–83. London, 1969.

Menzies, W. W. *Understanding the Times of Christ*. Springfield, Mo., 1969.

Michel, O., ed. *Studies on the Jewish Background of the New Testament*. Assen, 1969.

Toynbee, A. J., ed. *The Crucible of Christianity: Judaism, Hellenism, and the Historical Background to the Christian Faith*. New York, 1969.

1970

Bosler, E. *Als die Zeit etfüllet ward: Zeitgeschichte des Neuen Testaments*. Metzinger and Württ, 1970.

Cohon, B. D. *Men at the Crossroads between Jerusalem and Rome, Synagogue and Church: The Lives, Times, and Doctrines of the Founders of Talmudic Judaism and New Testament Christianity*. South Brunswick, N.J., 1970.
    An interesting approach to middle Judaism as the period of "the beginnings of Rabbinic Judaism and New Testament."

Guthrie, D., and J. A. Motyer, eds. *The New Bible Commentary Revised*. Grand Rapids, 1970.
    See articles by G. R. Beasley-Murray and F. F. Bruce.

Michelini Tocci, F. *La letteratura ebraica*. Florence, 1970.

Qwarnström, R. "Nytestamentlig tidhistoria." In *En bok om Nya Testamentet*, ed. B. Gerhardsson, 137–254. Lund, 1970.

Schubert, K. *Die jüdischen Religionsparteien in neutestamentlicher Zeit*. Stuttgart, 1970.

1971

Allegro, J. M. *The Chosen People: A Study of Jewish History from the Time of the Exile until the Revolt of Bar Kocheba, Sixth Century B.C. to Second Century A.D.* London, 1971.

Baumbach, G. *Jesus von Nazareth in Lichte der jüdischen Gruppenbildung.* Berlin, 1971.

Bowden, D. J. *The World of the New Testament.* Oxford, 1971.

Castellani, G., ed. *Storia delle religioni,* Vol. 3. Turin, 1971.
See articles by A. Penna and J. Maier.

Layman, C.M., ed. *The Interpreter's One-Volume Commentary on the Bible.* Nashville and New York, 1971.
See articles by J. C. Greenfield and L. Mowry.

Lohse, E. *Umwelt des Neuen Testament.* Göttingen, 1971; second edition, 1974; third edition, 1977; fifth edition, 1980. Translated by J. E. Steely, under the title *The New Testament Environment.* Nashville, 1976.

Rost, L. *Einleitung in die alttestamentlichen Apokryphen und Pseudepigraphen.* Heidelberg, 1971. Translated by D. E. Green, under the title *Judaism outside the Hebrew Canon: An Introduction to the Documents.* Nashville, 1976.

1972

Caquot, A. "Le judaïsme depuis la captivité de Babylone jusqu'à la révolte de Bar-Kokheba." In *Histoire des religions: Encyclopédie de la Pléiade,* ed. H.-C. Puech, 2:114–84. Paris, 1972.

Connick, C. M. "Background of the Christian Community." In *The New Testament: An Introduction to Its History and Thought,* 1–76. Encino, Calif., and Belmont, Calif., 1972; second edition, 1978.

Maier, J. *Geschichte der jüdischen Religion: Von der Zeit Alexander der Grossen bis zur Aufklärung mit einem Ausblick auf das 19./20 Jahrhundert.* Berlin and New York, 1972.

Salomonsen, B. "Das Spätjudentum." In *Handbuch des Religionsgeschichte,* ed. J. P. Asmussen and J. Laessøe, 149–90. Göttingen, 1972.

Schalit, A. *The Hellenistic Age: Political History of Jewish Palestine from 332 B.C.E. to 67 B.C.E.* WHJP 6. Jerusalem and New Brunswick, N.J., 1972.

Temporini, H., and W. Haase, eds. *Aufstieg und Niedergang der römischen Welt.* Berlin, 1972–.
This is a monumental collection of essays on the history, literature, and religion of the Roman age. Many volumes refer to middle Judaism.

1973

Kee, H. C. *The Origins of Christianity: Sources and Documents.* Englewood Cliffs, N.J., 1973.

Kümmel, W. G., and H. Lichtenberger, eds. *Jüdische Schriften aus hellenistisch-römischer Zeit*. Gütersloh, 1973–.

Maier, J., and J. Schreiner, eds. *Literatur und Religion des Frühjudentums*. Würzburg, 1973.

First in German and later in English, the term *Frühjudentum* (early Judaism) replaces the confessionally charged *Spätjudentum* (late Judaism).

Saltrand, G.A.E. *The Time Was Right*. Nashville, 1973.

Schürer, E. *The History of the Jewish People in the Age of Jesus Christ*, a new English version rev. and ed. G. Vermes, F. Millar, M. Black, and M. Goodman. 3 vols. Edinburgh, 1973–87.

Besides a traditional formulation that sees the "Judaism in the age of Jesus Christ" in relation to early Christianity and that recognizes its pluralistic character "despite the predominance of Pharisaism," the work represents an indispensable tool for the quantity and quality of information it offers on the history, literature, political and religious institutions, and ideological trends of the period. The revision of Schürer's masterpiece marks the beginning and follows the developments of a new (more positive and historically correct) approach to middle Judaism.

Wells, G. A. *The Origins of Christianity: From the Pagan and Jewish Backgrounds*. London, 1973.

5. "EARLY JUDAISM(S)" AND "EARLY CHRISTIANITY"

1974

Boertien, M. *Het joodse leerhuis: Van 200 voor tot 200 na Christus*. Kampen, 1974.

Jendorff, B. *Jesus und seine Zeit*. Aschaffenburg, 1974.

Safrai, S., and M. Stern, eds. *The Jewish People in the First Century: Historical Geography, Political History, Social, Cultural and Religious Life and Institutions*. 2 vols. Philadelphia, 1974–76.

Unnik, W. C. van, ed. *La littérature juive entre Tenach et Mishna*. Leiden, 1974.

1975

Avi-Yonah, M., and Z. Baras. *The Herodian Period*. WHJP 7. Jerusalem, 1975.

Conzelmann, H., and A. Lindermann. "Neutestamentliche Zeitgeschichte—Die Umwelt des Urchristentums." Part 2 in *Arbeitsbuch zum Neuen Testament*. Tübingen, 1975; third edition, 1977; eighth edition, 1985. Translated under the title *Interpreting the New Testament: An Introduction to the Principles and Methods of New Testament Exegesis*. Peabody, Mass., 1988.

Delling, G. *Bibliographie zur jüdisch-hellenistischen und intertestamentarischen Literatur: 1900–1970*. Berlin, 1975.

Martin, R. P. "The Jewish Background." In *New Testament Foundations: A Guide for the Christian Student*, 1:53–116. Grand Rapids, 1975.

McCullough, W. S. *The History and Literature of the Palestinian Jews from Cyrus to Herod, 550 B.C. to 4 B.C.*. Toronto and Buffalo, 1975.

Surburg, R. F. *Introduction to the Intertestamental Period*. St. Louis, 1975.

1976

Ben-Sasson, H. H., ed. *A History of the Jewish People*, trans. from the Hebrew. Philadelphia, 1976.
See articles by M. Stern and S. Safrai.

Ellison, H. L. *From Babylon to Bethlehem: The Jewish People from the Exile to the Messiah*. Exeter, 1976; second edition (*From Babylon to Bethlehem: The People of God Between the Testaments*), Grand Rapids, 1984.

Gowan, D. E. *Bridge between the Testaments: A Reappraisal of Judaism from the Exile to the Birth of Christianity*. Pittsburgh, 1976; second edition, 1979; third edition, 1985.

Johnson, P. "The Rise and Rescue of the Jesus Sect." In *A History of Christianity*, 1–63. New York, 1976.

Sacchi, P. *Storia del mondo giudaico*. Turin, 1976.
This work attempts to trace a synthetic framework of the "principal themes over which Hebrew and Jewish thought had toiled before the rise of Christianity." Of methodological note is the use of canonical documents (including those of early Christianity) and noncanonical documents on the same level.

Weingreen, J. *From Bible to Mishnah: The Continuity of Tradition*. Manchester and New York, 1976.

Whitelocke, L. T. *The Development of Jewish Religious Thought in the Intertestamental period*. Kampen, 1976.

1977

Avi-Yonah, M., and Z. Baras. *Society and Religion in the Second Temple Period*. WHJP 8. Jerusalem, 1977.

Dommershausen, W. *Die Umwelt Jesu: Politik und Kultur in neutestamentlicher Zeit*. Freiburg, Basel, and Vienna, 1977.

Moeller, H. R. *The Legacy of Zion: Intertestamental Texts related to the New Testament*. Grand Rapids, 1977.

Sanders, E. P. *Paul and Palestinian Judaism: A Comparison of Patterns of Religion*. Philadelphia, 1977.

In many ways Sanders's conclusions are debatable. Above all, the idea that Palestinian Judaism can be brought back to a unitary pattern of religion (defined as "covenantal nomism") impoverishes and reduces the period's pluralism to a homogeneity from which only the "heresy" of Paul emerges. This work is noteworthy, however, for some of its lucid methodological observations: Sanders challenges the validity of a comparative analysis of the various Judaisms of the period when based on the search for parallels.

Hayes, J. H., and J. M. Miller, eds. *Israelite and Judean History*. Philadelphia, 1977.

See articles by P. Schäfer, A.R.C. Leaney, and J. Neusner.

Stemberger, G. *Geschichte der jüdischen Literatur: Ein Einführung*. Munich, 1977.

This introduction to Jewish literature deals with the New Testament "als jüdische Schrift."

1978

Sandmel, S. *Judaism and Christian Beginnings*. New York, 1978.

This book surveys the "common roots of synagogue Judaism and Christianity."

1979

Gaebelein, F. E., ed. *The Expositor's Bible Commentary*, Vol. 1. Grand Rapids, 1979.

See articles by B. M. Metzger, H. W. Hoehner, and W. S. LaSor.

Villaneuva, M. "Palestina en tiempos de Jesús." In *Iniciacion a la lectura del Nuevo Testamento*, ed. S. Garcia, et al., 17–42. Bilbao, 1979.

Howley, G.C.D., F. F. Bruce, and H. L. Ellison, eds. *The New Layman's Bible Commentary in One Volume*. Grand Rapids, 1979.

See articles by J. M. Houston and H. L. Ellison.

Kippenberg, H. G., and G. A. Wewers. *Textbuch zur neutestamentlichen Zeit-geschichte*. Göttingen, 1979.

1980

Freyne, S. *The World of the New Testament*. Wilmington, Del., 1980.

Köster, H. "Geschichte, Kultur und Religion des Hellenistischen Zeitaltus." In *Einführung in das Neue Testament im Rahmen der Religionsgeschichte und Kulturgeschichte der hellenistischen und römischen Zeit*, 1–293. Berlin and New York, 1980. Translated under the title *Introduction to the New Testament*. 2 vols. Philadelphia, 1982.

Seltzer, R. M. "From the Hellenistic Period to Late Antiquity." Part 2 in *Jewish People, Jewish Thought: The Jewish Experience in History*. New York and London, 1980.

Sigal, P. *The Foundation of Judaism from Biblical Origins to the Sixth Century A.D.* Pittsburgh, 1980.

Stone, M. E. *Scriptures, Sects, and Visions: A Profile of Judaism from Ezra to the Jewish Revolts*. Philadelphia, 1980.

1981

Conzelmann, H. *Heiden-Juden-Christen: Auseinandersetzungen in der Literatur der hellenistisch-römischen Zeit*. Tübingen, 1981. Translated under the title *Gentiles-Jews-Christians*. Minneapolis, 1991.

Musaph-Andriesse, R. C. *From Torah to Kabbalah: A Basic Introduction to the Writings of Judaism*, trans. J. Bowden from the Dutch. New York, 1981.

Nickelsburg, G.W.E. *Jewish Literature between the Bible and the Mishnah: A Historical and Literary Introduction*. London, 1981.
    The first attempt to offer an organic "introduction to the Jewish litera-ture of the so-called intertestamental period," redistributing the materials according to exclusively chronological criteria. A Christian text, the *Gos-pel of Matthew*, is included, but only because it is considered "the most Jewish of the Gospels." The book sometimes fails in its methodological premises (part of the material is presented along other than chronological lines—following ideological or geographical criteria) and has some important omissions (Flavius Josephus, Philo of Alexandria, the Sep-tuagint, and others).

Sacchi, P., ed. *Apocrifi dell'Antico Testamento*. 2 vols. Turin, 1981–89.
    In the introduction to the first volume, Sacchi gives an interesting outline of the history of middle Jewish thought.

Schiffman, L. H. "Jewish Sectarism in Second Temple Times." In *Great Schisms in Jewish History*, ed. R. Jospe and S. M. Wagner, 1–46. New York, 1981.

Yamauchi, E. M. *Harper's World of the New Testament*. San Francisco, 1981.

1982

Díez Macho, A., ed. *Los apócrifos del Antiguo Testamento*. 5 vols. Madrid, 1982–88.

1983

Ayers, R. H. *Judaism and Christianity: Origins, Developments, and Recent Trends*. Lanham, Md., 1983.

Charlesworth, J. H., ed. *The Old Testament Pseudepigrapha*. 2 vols. Garden City, N.Y., 1983–85.
    This is the most complete collection of Old Testament Pseudepigrapha, the fruit of the work of an international team.

Collins, J. J. *Between Athens and Jerusalem: Jewish Identity in the Hellenistic Diaspora*. New York, 1983.

McNamara, M. *Intertestamental Literature*. Wilmington, Del., 1983.
———*Palestinian Judaism and the New Testament*, Wilmington, Del., 1983.
    The Targumic sources are extensively used by this competent author.

Nickelsburg, G.W.E., and M. E. Stone. *Faith and Piety: Text and Documents*. Philadelphia, 1983.

Tambasco, A. J. *In the Days of Jesus: The Jewish Background and Unique Teaching of Jesus*. New York, 1983.

1984

Davies, W. D., and L. Finkelstein, eds. *The Cambridge History of Judaism*. Cambridge and New York, 1984–.

Leaney, A.R.C. *The Jewish and Christian World 200 B.C. to A.D. 200*. Cambridge, 1984.

Neusner, J. *Judaism at the Beginning of Christianity*. Philadelphia, 1984.
    Neusner's studies have individuated the testimony of a "formative Judaism" in rabbinic literature and, with it, the inconsistency of a normative model projected backward to the period before the second century C.E. The history of middle Judaism is coherently read as the history of two

Judaisms in formation: "Formative Christianity demands to be studied in the context of formative Judaism and formative Judaism in the context of formative Christianity."

Otzen, B. *Den antike Jødedom: Politisk undvikling og religiose stromninger fra Aleksander den Store til Kejser Hadrian*. Copenhagen, 1984.

Penna, R. *L'ambiente storico-culturale delle origini cristiane: Una documentazione ragionata*. Bologna, 1984; second edition, 1986.

Soggin, J. A. *Storia d'Israele*. Brescia, 1984. Translated by J. Bowden, under the title *A History of Ancient Israel*. Philadelphia, 1985.

Sparks, H.F.D., ed. *The Apocryphal Old Testament*. Oxford, 1984.

Stone, M. E., ed. *Jewish Writings of the Second Temple Period: Apocrypha, Pseudepigrapha, Qumran Sectarian Writings, Philo, Josephus*. Assen and Philadelphia, 1984.
　　The collective work of a group of specialists, this volume is part of a series (Compendia Rerum Iudaicarum ad Novum Testamentum) for the study of early Christianity. For the most part documents are presented according to their literary genre (apocalyptic texts, testaments, wisdom literature, and so on) and in part according to ideologically homogeneous corpora (Philo, Josephus, Dead Sea Scrolls). The choice of material is quite wide, although selective: on the one hand, it includes only "material that was not transmitted by Jewish (rabbinical) tradition"; on the other hand, it excludes the writings in the New Testament. Two Christian texts (the *Magnificat* and the *Benedictus*) are included because they are considered "pre-Christian" hymns.

Tyson, J. B. "The Jewish Context." In *The New Testament and Early Christianity*, 66–105. New York and London, 1984.

1985

Caquot, A., ed. *La littérature intertestamentaire: Colloque de Strasbourg (17–19 Octobre 1983)*. Paris, 1985.

Charlesworth, J. H. *The Old Testament Pseudepigrapha and the New Testament: Prolegomena for the Study of Christian Origins*. Cambridge, 1985.
　　In this work Charlesworth underlines the decisive importance that modern research on the Old Testament Pseudepigrapha has for the knowledge of New Testament documents and, more generally, for a better understanding of the period. Far from being the evidence of "heretical" movements or the testimony of a degenerate phase of Judaism, the

Pseudepigrapha are the primary sources for the reconstruction of the history of thought of middle Judaism.

Harrington, D. J. "The World of the New Testament." In *The New Testament: A Bibliography*, 193–232. Wilmington, Del., 1985.

Jagersma, H. *Geschiednis van Isräel van Alexander de Grote tot Bar Kochba.* Kampen, 1985. Translated by J. Bowden, under the title *A History of Israel from Alexander the Great to Bar Kochba.* Philadelphia, 1986.

Noll, S. F. *The Intertestamental Period: A Study Guide.* Madison, Wisc., 1985.
  The first study guide completely devoted to the "intertestamental" period.

Rowland, C. *Christian Origins: From Messianic Movement to Christian Religion.* Minneapolis and London, 1985.
  Early Christianity is presented as a Jewish messianic movement.

Saulnier, C. (with C. Perrot). *De la conquête d'Alexandre à la destruction du temple (331 a.c.–135 a.d.).* Paris, 1985.

1986

Anderson, N. E. *Tools for Bibliographical and Backgrounds Research on the New Testament.* South Hamilton, Mass., 1986; second edition, 1987.

Fondazione, S. Carlo, ed. *L'ebraismo.* Modena, 1986.
  See articles by M. Pesce and P. Sacchi.

Hooker, M. D. *Continuity and Discontinuity: Early Christianity in Its Jewish Setting.* London, 1986.

Kraft, R. A., and G.W.E. Nickelsburg, eds. *Early Judaism and Its Modern Interpreters.* Philadelphia, 1986.
  The goal of this collaboration by a group of specialists is to sharpen the most recent developments in the research of "early" Judaism, meaning "the phenomena collectively designated 'Judaism' in the period bounded approximately by Alexander the Great (330 B.C.E.) on the one hand and the Roman Emperor Hadrian (138 C.E.) on the other." Structurally, however, it is yet another work on "intertestamental" Judaism. The book, in fact, is the central volume of a triptych that covers and heteronomously defines its contents as "a miscellany of what remains from Jewish sources not covered in the other two volumes—chronologically, from roughly the close of volume 1 (Hebrew Bible, Old Testament) to roughly the close of volume 3 (New Testament)."

Russell, D. S. *From Early Judaism to Early Church.* Philadelphia, 1986.

Segal, A. F. *Rebecca's Children: Judaism and Christianity in the Roman World.* Cambridge, Mass., 1986.

Christianity and Rabbinism are seen as "fraternal twins," the results of a twofold reform within ancient Judaism.

1987

Charlier, J.-P. *Jésus au milieu de son people.* Paris, 1987.

Cohen, S.J.D. *From the Maccabees to the Mishnah.* Philadelphia, 1987.

Judaism at the turn of the Common Era is a set of different movements (including early Christianity). Rabbinism emerges as the "winning" group, while Christianity—abandoning the law—ceases to be a Judaism and becomes a new religion.

Dupont-Sommer, A., and M. Philonenko, eds. *La Bible: Écrits intertestamentaires.* Paris, 1987.

Ferguson, E. "Judaism." In *Backgrounds of Early Christianity*, 315–463. Grand Rapids, 1987.

Neusner, J., W. S. Green, and E. S. Frerichs, eds. *Judaisms and Their Messiahs at the Turn of the Christian Era.* Cambridge, 1987.

This collective work is exemplary of how research on a theme in middle Judaism should be conducted. The newness of the critical approach, lucidly theorized by Neusner in the preface and concretely followed up in the contributions of the illustrious specialists represented here (among them Charlesworth, Stone, and Nickelsburg), is mirrored in the simple and brilliant use of the plural "Messiahs" and "Judaisms." Hence, both the period and the theme are dealt with in their globality and integrity without giving in to a historical synthesis, while safeguarding the dynamic pluralism of the various components (among them and on an equal basis, early Christianity).

Paul, A. *Le judaisme ancien et la Bible.* Paris, 1987.

By "ancient Judaism" the author refers to the Judaism from the fifth century B.C.E. to the tenth century C.E.

1988

Flusser, D. *Judaism and the Origins of Christianity.* Jerusalem, 1988.

This work is a collection of essays on first-century Judaism (including early Christianity).

Nisworger, R. L. "Judaism in the Christian Era." In *New Testament History*, 53–78. Grand Rapids, 1988.

1989

Maccoby, H. *Judaism in the First Century*. London, 1989.

Perelmuter, H. G. *Siblings: Rabbinic Judaism and Early Christianity at Their Beginnings*. New York, 1989.

Prato, G. L., ed. *Israele alla ricerca di identità tra il III sec. a.C. e il I sec. d.C.* Ricerche storico-bibliche 1. Brescia, 1989.

Strecker, G., and J. Maier. *Neues Testament—Antikes Judentum*. Stuttgart, 1989.

> This work houses in the same volume (but does not amalgamate) two literary genres: the introduction to "early" Judaism and the introduction to the New Testament.

1990

Brown, R. E., J. A. Fitzmyer, and R. E. Murphy, eds. *The New Jerome Biblical Commentary*. Englewood Cliffs, N.J., 1990.

> See articles by J. J. Collins, R. E. Brown, P. Perkins, A. Saldarini, G. Wright, R. E. Murphy, and J. A. Fitzmyer.

Riches, J. *The World of Jesus: First-Century Judaism in Crisis*. Cambridge, 1990.

Stemberger, G., ed. *Die Juden: Ein historische Lesebuch*. Munich, 1990.

> This is an anthology of modern scholarly treatments of Jewish history: see articles by A. Momigliano, P. Schafer, M. Stern, S. Safrai, and G. Stemberger.

PART II

A CROSS-SECTION:
THE SECOND CENTURY B.C.E.

3
BEN SIRA, QOHELET, AND APOCALYPTIC

A Turning Point in the History of Jewish Thought

It cannot be said that Ben Sira is a fortunate author.[1] The position of his work in the Old Testament—an "apocryphon" belonging to the marginal and often neglected subgroup of the wisdom literature—certainly has not helped familiarize him to biblical scholars. In addition, a number of very complex textual problems surround the *Book of Sirach*. The rediscovery of a large part of the original Hebrew text, instead of helping to resolve these difficulties, has complicated them. Clear traces of successive Essene redactions are present, introducing substantial conceptual modifications not present in the original.[2]

1. On the *Book of Sirach* (*Ecclesiasticus*), see O. F. Fritzsche, *Die Weisheit Jesus Sirach's* (Leipzig, 1859 [German trans.]); I. Lévi, *L'Ecclésiastique ou la Sagesse de Jésus fils de Sira*, 2 vols. (Paris, 1898–1901 [Hebrew text and French trans.]); V. Ryssel, *APAT* 1 (1900): 230–475 (German trans.); I. Lévi, *The Hebrew Text of the Book of Ecclesiasticus*, (Leiden, 1904; 2d ed., 1951; 3d ed., 1969 [Hebrew text]); R. Smend, *Die Weisheit des Jesus Sirach*, 2 vols. (Berlin, 1906 [Hebrew text and German trans.]); G. H. Box and W.O.E. Oesterley, *APOT* 1 (1913): 268–517 (English trans.); N. Peters, *Das Buch Jesus Sirach oder Ecclesiasticus* (Münster, 1913 [German trans.]); A. Eberharter, *Das Buch Jesus Sirach* (Bonn, 1925 [German trans.]); A. Rahlfs, *Septuaginta* (Stuttgart, 1935 [Greek text]); M. H. Segal, *Sefer Ben-Sira ha-šalem* (Jerusalem, 1953; 2d ed., 1958 [Hebrew text]); H. Duesberg and P. Auvray, *Le livre de l'Ecclésiastique* (Paris, 1953; 2d ed., 1958 [French trans.]); O. Schilling, *Das Buch Jesus Sirach* (Freiburg, 1956 [German trans.]); J. Ziegler, *Sapientia Jesu filii Sirach* (Göttingen, 1965 [Greek text]); H. Duesberg and I. Fransen, *Ecclesiastico*, La Sacra Bibbia (Turin, 1966 [Italian trans.]); A. A. Di Lella, *The Hebrew Text of Sirach* (The Hague, 1964); L. Alonso Shökel, *Proverbios y Ecclesiastico* (Madrid, 1968 [Spanish trans.]); F. Vattioni, *Ecclesiastico* (Naples, 1968 [Hebrew, Greek, Latin, and Syriac texts]); Akademyah la-lashon ha-Ivrit, ed., *The Book of Ben Sira: Text, Concordance and an Analysis of the Vocabulary* (Jerusalem, 1973 [Hebrew text]); J. G. Snaith, *Ecclesiasticus*, CBC (Cambridge, 1974 [English trans.]); G. Sauer, *JSHRZ* 3.5 (1978 [German trans.]); A. Minissale, *Siracide (Ecclesiastico)* (Rome, 1980 [Italian trans.]); and P. W. Skehan and A. Di Lella, *The Wisdom of Ben Sira*, AB 39 (Garden City, 1987 [English trans.]).
2. On the history of the Hebrew recensions of *Sirach*, see A. Di Lella, *The Hebrew Text of Sirach: A Text-Critical and Historical Study* (The Hague, 1966); and H. P. Ruger, *Text und Textform im hebräischen Sirach: Untersuchungen zur Textgeschichte und Textkritik der hebräischen*

Even so, it is an extremely significant document in which we find contemporary anxieties emerging from within Judaism and from its contact with Hellenistic culture. What would come to be the basic themes of middle Judaism are already present: the great questions about the mechanisms of knowledge, the value of the law, the origin of evil and the freedom of human will, the relationship between God's mercy and justice, and salvation.

Ben Sira composed his work at the beginning of the second century B.C.E., a particularly critical moment in the history of Jewish thought. The characteristic tension of ancient Jewish thought—a tension never completely resolved between the ideas of the covenant and promise, in other words, between an idea of salvation that rests on human forces and one that rests on the hope of God's intervention—was by that time definitely in crisis.[3] Contemporaneously with that corpus of writings destined to become "canonical," another post-exilic tradition of thought was being formed. Later it would be considered "apocryphal"; at this time, however, it was alive, working, and authoritative. This other tradition took the form of an alternative pentateuch, that of Enoch (1 Enoch). Today we call this other tradition "apocalyptic."[4]

By the beginning of the second century B.C.E. two volumes (surviving today) of this "pentateuch" had already been composed: the *Book of the Watchers* and the *Book of Astronomy* (*1 Enoch* 6–36; 72–82).[5] The distin-

---

Sirachfragmente aus der Kairoer Geniza, BZAW 112 (Berlin, 1970). On the relationships between the Hebrew text and the Greek version, see B. G. Wright, *No Small Difference: Sirach's Relationship to Its Hebrew Parent Text* (Atlanta, 1989). On the Syriac version in relation to the Hebrew text and the Greek version, see M. D. Nelson, *The Syriac Version of Ben Sira Compared to the Greek and Hebrew Materials* (Atlanta, 1988). Given the lack of a work that clarifies comprehensively the document's history in relation to its recensions and versions, as a rule I will hold to the Greek version (ed. Rahlfs). I will discuss the ideologically significant variations in the Hebrew text or in the other ancient versions, when they aid in better understanding the document.

3. On the "theology of the covenant" and the "theology of the promise" as interpretative categories of ancient Jewish thought, see P. Sacchi, *Storia del mondo giudaico* (Turin, 1976).

4. On the nature and essence of the apocalyptic tradition, see the more detailed discussion in chap. 4.

5. On the *Book of the Watchers* and the *Book of Astronomy*, see R. Laurence, *The Book of Enoch the Prophet* (Oxford, 1821 [English trans.]); idem, *Libri Enoch Versio Aethiopica* (Oxford, 1838 [Ethiopic text]); A Dillmann, *Liber Henoch Aethiopice* (Leipzig, 1851 [Ethiopic text]); idem, *Das Buch Henoch übersetzt und erklärt* (Leipzig, 1853 [German trans.]); R. H. Charles, *The Book of Enoch* (Oxford, 1893 [English trans.]); G. Beer, *APAT* 2 (1900): 217–310 (German trans.); J. Flemming and L. Radermacher, *Das Buch Henoch* (Leipzig, 1901 [German trans.]); J. Flemming, *Das Buch Henoch* (Leipzig, 1902 [Ethiopic text]); F. Martin, *Le livre d'Hénoch* (Paris, 1906 [French trans.]); R. H. Charles, *The Ethiopic Version of the Book of Enoch* (Oxford, 1906 [Ethiopic text with the fragmentary Greek and Latin versions]); F. Feiers and E. De Giovanni, "Il libro di Enoc," *Rivista delle riviste* 6 (1908): 297–319, 377–84, 412–19 (Italian trans.); H. B. Swete, *The Old Testament in Greek according to the Septuaginta* (Cambridge, 1909) 3:789–808 (Greek

guishing element that places these books at the origin of the apocalyptic tradition is precisely the idea that the cause of evil does not stem so much from freedom of will, that is, choice, but from humankind's own nature.

The *Book of the Watchers* speaks of an "angelic sin" that corrupted creation, turning human nature, originally good, toward an inclination to do evil and thus causing the spread of iniquity: "And the whole earth has been corrupted by Azaz'el's teaching of his [own] actions; and write upon him all sin" (*1 Enoch* 10:8).

In the *Book of Astronomy* sinfulness comes to coincide with humankind's status as a creature: "No one of the flesh can be just before the Lord; for they are merely his own creation" (*1 Enoch* 81:5). The context seems to assign *ab aeterno* to all their own individual destinies, to the extent that Enoch can read them in the "tablets of heaven."

> So I looked at the tablet[s] of heaven, read all the writing [on them], and came to understand everything. I read that book and all the deeds of humanity and all the children of the flesh upon the earth for all the generations of the world. (*1 Enoch* 81:2)

In both the *Book of the Watchers* and the *Book of Astronomy*, individual responsibility is gravely compromised. Salvation is entrusted to an extraordinary intervention by God and the idea of the covenant is emptied of all substance.

The wisdom tradition dialectically had to confront this interlocutor, bearer of its own autonomous and complete system of thought. The confrontation—traces of which are already present in both *Job* and *Qohelet*[6]—becomes all the more pressing as the very possibility of a theology of the covenant appears compromised. This concept had already been subjected from within to a progressive process of crumbling, made more evident by the influence of Greek rationalism. Experience contradicts the affirmation of the complete freedom of human will and the notion of the existence of

---

text); R. H. Charles, *APOT* 2 (1913): 163–281 (English trans.); P. Riessler, *ASB* (1928), 355–451, 1291–97 (German trans.); C. Bonner, *The Last Chapters of Enoch in Greek* (London, 1937); M. Black, *Apocalypsis Henochi Graece* (Leiden, 1970 [Greek text]); J. T. Milik, *The Books of Enoch: Aramaic Fragments of Qumran, Cave 4* (Oxford, 1976 [Aramaic fragments]); M. A. Knibb (with E. Ullendorf), *The Ethiopic Book of Enoch: A New Edition in the Light of the Aramaic Dead Sea Fragments*, 2 vols. (Oxford, 1978 [Ethiopic text, Aramaic fragments, and English trans.]); L. Fusella and P. Sacchi, *AAT* 1 (1981): 413–667 (Italian trans.); E. Isaac, *OTP* 1 (1983): 5–89 (English trans.); F. Corriente and A. Piñero, *ApAT* 4 (1984): 11–143 (Spanish trans.); M. A. Knibb, *AOT* (1986), 169–319 (English trans.); M. Black (with J. C. VanderKam), *The Book of Enoch or I Enoch: A New English Edition with Commentary and Textual Notes*, SVTP 7 (Leiden, 1985); and A. Caquot, *BÉI* (1987), 463–625 (French trans.).
   6. See P. Sacchi, "Giobbe e il Patto (Gb. 9, 32–33)," *Henoch* 4 (1982): 175–83; and L. Rosso Ubigli, "Qohelet di fronte all' apocalittica," *Henoch* 5 (1983): 209–34.

individual retribution in a present life regulated through obedience to the
covenant. Too many exceptions exist to a rigidly and, by then, simplistically
structured system of retribution.

The personal experience of Job,[7] that righteous man who protested before
God his right to happiness and well-being, is already emblematic in itself.
However, if the wisdom writing that bears Job's name still allows God an
appeal and a happy ending to the protagonist's doubts, with *Qohelet* the crisis
is already complete and the conceptual impossibility of a theology of the
covenant clearly affirmed. Qohelet's analysis is lucid,[8] almost merciless. The
just suffer while the unjust triumph too many times for us to believe in any
rule that guarantees vindication for the just (cf. *Qoh* 8:14). Too many times a
righteous life is not even accompanied by the comfort of an everlasting
memory (cf. *Qoh* 8:10). Meanwhile, the inherent difficulties in humankind's
efforts to be just appear more and more insuperable. "There is not a righteous man on earth who does good and never sins" (*Qoh* 7:20).

If the covenant is the rule against which the just and unjust are measured,
then the only conclusion left is that an equivalent end awaits both, which
amounts to an affirmation of the vanity of the traditional ideas on salvation:

> Since one fate comes to all,
> to the righteous and the wicked,
> to the good [and the evil],
> to the clean and the unclean,
> to he who sacrifices and he who does not sacrifice.
> As is the good man, so is the sinner;
> [as] is he who swears, so is he who shuns swearing.
>   (*Qoh* 9:2)[9]

The restorative work of Ben Sira has to be understood within this context. Ben Sira is intent on reaffirming the centrality of the covenant and the
retributive principle, overcoming the aporias and doubts of Job and Qohelet.
At the same time he directly confronts the suggestions of the apocalyptic
movement. The calm and asystematic style of this wisdom book should not
lead us to lose sight of the terms of a bitter debate, addressing such precise
referents and such urgent questioning. Let us retrace this unique itinerary of
thought as it develops around two great themes: the problem of knowledge,

---

7. On the *Book of Job*, see K. Elliger and W. Rudolph, eds., *Biblia Hebraica Stuttgatensia*
(Stuttgart, 1967–77 [Hebrew text]).

8. On the *Book of Qohelet* (*Ecclesiastes*), see esp. D. Buzy, *L'Ecclésiaste*, La Sainte Bible (Paris,
1946); R.B.Y. Scott, *Ecclesiastes*, AB (Garden City, 1965); L. di Fonzo, *Ecclesiaste*, La Sacra
Bibbia (Turin, 1967); Elliger and Rudolph, eds., *Biblia Hebraica Stuttgatensia* (Hebrew text);
P. Sacchi, *Qohelet* (Rome, 1981); and M. Diethelm, *Qohelet* (Darmstadt, 1988).

9. The parallelism of the Hebrew text is restored on the basis of the Greek version.

which Ben Sira confronts within the relationship between wisdom and law; and the theme of salvation, which for him poses disturbing questions on the origin of evil as well as the freedom of human will.

I. The Problem of Knowledge: Wisdom and Law

1. WISDOM AND LAW: AN IDENTITY?

It is a common notion that wisdom and law are identified for the first time in the history of Jewish thought in the *Book of Sirach*. Some have complained that scholars have not sufficiently sounded the nature, motives, and consequences of such an identification; however, this equivalence is beyond debate because it seems to emerge explicitly from the text. This is the prevalent approach to the problem of the relationship between wisdom and law in *Sirach*, as summarized in a recent book by E. J. Schnabel, the most complete study dedicated to the subject to date.[10] Schnabel reviews earlier contributions made by scholars and offers a broad and detailed analysis with the intention of giving depth to what he defines as "Ben Sira's significant and portentous identification of law and wisdom."[11]

That wisdom and law are closely linked in *Sirach* is beyond doubt. More open to discussion, however, is whether such a relationship should be expressed in terms of an "identification." This model of relationship, when applied to Ben Sira, risks being misleading insofar as it is unable to express the complex relationship that he establishes between wisdom and law. Besides, flattening this complex relationship as Schnabel does—taking it to be a constant in Jewish thought "from Ben Sira to Paul"—fails to account for the profound and significant differences on this point among the various components of middle Jewish thought.

It is therefore necessary to get to the root of the problem, submitting the passages in which Ben Sira seems to identify wisdom and law to another perspective and being careful not to isolate these passages unnaturally from the whole of his reflection and from the particular historical phase of Jewish thought in which Ben Sira was forging his own ideological identity.

---

10. See E. J. Schnabel's *Law and Wisdom from Ben Sira to Paul* (Tübingen, 1985). The book contains a rich bibliography on the topic.

11. Ibid., 89. Similar expressions are also found on p. 9.

2. WISDOM AS A GIFT FROM GOD

Faced with a view of humankind in *Job* (and even more so in *Qohelet*) that seems to want to impose reason as the judge of God's actions, Ben Sira draws attention first of all to the ambiguity of reality. Human judgment is often revealed to be fallacious.

> A man can find profit in misfortune
> and loss in good fortune.
> There are gifts that produce gain
> and gifts that must be paid back double.
> There is fortune that does not bring glory,
> while from humiliation a man can lift up his head.
> A man may buy much for little,
> but in the end pay seven times over.
>
> (*Sir* 20:9-12)

For Ben Sira it is not so much a difficulty as an epistemological impossibility. Humans are incapable of penetrating the underlying sense of things and can only recognize their own limits and hold themselves back in the face of mysteries. "For wonderful are the works of the Lord, yet remain hidden [Gr. *krypta*] from men His works" (*Sir* 11:4b; cf. 18:1-7; 43:27-33).

This results in a peculiar conception of "wisdom" (Heb. *ḥkmh*; Gr. *sophia*). In *Qohelet* wisdom is a human faculty, the cognitive tool used to investigate reality. It is in this faculty that rational analysis is founded. *Qohelet* says, "I applied my soul to seek and to search out by wisdom all that is done under heaven" (1:13). For Ben Sira, however, wisdom, as a deep and universal knowledge of things, is not of humankind but of God. Only God can properly be defined as "wise" (omniscient). Humankind can acquire wisdom, but only as a gift from God.

The importance of such affirmations is emphasized by their placement at the incipit of the book in an effective synthetic formulation:

> All wisdom [is] from the Lord
> and with Him it is forever.
> The sand of the seas, the drops of rain,
> the days of time, who can count them?
> The height of the heaven, the breadth of the earth,
> [the depth of the] abyss,[12] who can explore them?
> Wisdom was created before all things,
> the understanding intelligence is from eternity.

---

12. Although lacking the possibility of a comparison with the Hebrew text, the Latin version ("the depth of the abyss") seems in this case preferable to the Greek ("the abyss and wisdom"), which improperly breaks the parallelism with the preceding verse.

To whom has wisdom's root been revealed?
Who knows her designs?
There is but one, wise and truly awe-inspiring,
seated upon His throne.
The Lord Himself created [wisdom],
has seen her and measured her;
He has poured her forth upon all His works,
upon every living thing according to His gift,
he has lavished her upon those who love Him [Gr. *tois agapôsin auton*].
(*Sir* 1:1-10)

The theme is taken up again in similar terms in the broader passage (*Sir* 42:15—43:33), in which it is affirmed that not even

to God's holy ones has it been conceded
to tell all of His wonders. . . .
He examines the abyss and the heart,
and penetrates all their secrets.
Because the Highest knows all of science
and observes the signs of the time,
announcing the things of the past and those that are to come
and unveiling the traces of hidden things [Gr. *apokrypha*].
(*Sir* 42:17-19)

The passage continues glorifying God for the wonders of creation, those that humankind can contemplate, and concludes:

There are many hidden things [Gr. *apokrypha*] greater than these;
only a few of His works have we seen.
Indeed the Lord created everything,
and to those who are pious He has given wisdom.
(*Sir* 43:32-33)

3. THE FEAR OF GOD, OBEDIENCE TO THE LAW, AND THE GIFT OF WISDOM

Ben Sira seems to be obliged to align himself with the apocalyptic idea of knowledge as illumination granted to an "elect,"[13] such as Enoch in the *Book of the Watchers* and the *Book of Astronomy*, "whose eyes were opened by God" (*1 Enoch* 1:2). Wisdom is the revelation Enoch received and then passed to future generations through his own son, Methuselah.

---

13. On knowledge as "illumination," see P. Sacchi, "La conoscenza presso gli ebrei da Amos all' essenismo," in *Israele alla ricerca di identità tra il III sec. a.C. e il I sec. d.C.*, ed. G. L. Prato (Brescia, 1988), 98–119; and idem, *Storia*, 156–61.

Now, Methuselah, my son, I shall recount all these things to you and write
them down for you. I have revealed to you and given you the book concerning
all these things. Preserve, my son, the book from your father's hands in order
that you may pass it to the generations of the world. I have given wisdom to
you, to your children, and to those who shall become your children in order
that they may pass it [in turn] to their own children and to the generations that
are discerning. (*1 Enoch* 82:1-2)

However, it becomes clear that Ben Sira is far from this apocalyptic
conception when he states the determining conditions for the gift of wisdom. In the passages previously cited, he speaks of "those who are pious"
(*Sir* 43:33) and "those who love [God]" (1:10) as the recipients of the gift of
wisdom. If to these qualities we add "the fear of God," we have the three
expressions, so equivalent as to be interchangeable, with which Ben Sira
designates the correct relationship between humankind and its Lord. Being
pious, loving God, and fearing God represent one thing: obeying the law.
On this point the text is univocal, even polemically so.

Those who fear the Lord disobey not His words,
those who love Him keep His ways.
Those who fear the Lord seek to please Him,
those who love Him observe His law.
(*Sir* 2:15-16)

Just as observing the law defines the righteous person (cf. 23:27; 37:12),
injustice consists in transgression.

Whose offspring can be in honor? Those of men.
Which offspring are in honor? Those who fear the Lord.
Whose offspring can be in disgrace? Those of men.
Which offspring are in disgrace? Those who transgress the commandments.
(*Sir* 10:19; cf. 41:8)

Observance of the law comes to be affirmed as the propaedeutically indispensable condition by which people become worthy of receiving wisdom.
With this, the recipient of such a gift is immediately placed on a very different level than that of the apocalyptic "seer." "If you desire wisdom, keep the
commandments, and the Lord will bestow her upon you" (*Sir* 1:26; cf. 6:37;
15:1). And in this sense the fear of God is coherently exalted as "the beginning . . . the fullness . . . the crown . . . the root of wisdom" (*Sir* 1:14-20).

4. INTELLIGENCE, OBEDIENCE TO THE LAW,
AND THE GIFT OF WISDOM

Ben Sira does not deny that human intelligence (Gr. *synesis*) and the
knowledge (Gr. *epistêmê*) people are able to acquire with it are involved in

the search for wisdom: "He who has intelligence [Gr. *pas synetos*] knows wisdom" (*Sir* 18:28a). Neither does he seem to have the intention of downgrading the importance and usefulness of experience.

> He who has traveled knows many things,
> and he who has much experience speaks with intelligence [Gr. *synesis*].
> He who has no experience knows little,
> whereas he who travels becomes very capable.
> I have seen many things in my travels,
> my intelligence [Gr. *synesis*] is greater than my words.
> I have often faced the danger of death
> and because of my experience have remained safe.
>
> (*Sir* 34:9-12; cf. 39:4)

For Ben Sira, however, for intelligence to be authentic it must be intimately linked with obedience to the law. An intelligence that claims to be self-sufficient is transformed into foolishness, or rather, into impiety. The fool is identified with the sinner and the intelligent person with the righteous person, even to the point of putting people on their guard against the use of intelligence.

> Don't look for things that are too difficult,
> and don't investigate things that are too obscure;
> What is commanded to you, attend to;
> for you have no need of the hidden things [Gr. *krypta*].
> With what is superfluous to your works, meddle not;
> for what is beyond man's intelligence [Gr. *synesis*] was shown to you.
> Presumption, in fact, has misled many,
> an evil illusion seduced their thoughts.
>
> (*Sir* 3:21-24)

As soon as it appears as a guilty contrast, intelligence loses all value; it becomes an obstacle to be removed, a useless presumption: "Fearing [God] with little intelligence is better than excelling at sense and then offending the law" (*Sir* 19:24).

Only in becoming complementary to the "law of life and knowledge" (*Sir* 45:5; cf. 17:11) does human knowledge obtain a certain degree of legitimate autonomy. A very significant example of this is presented by the way Ben Sira reconciles—without contrasting, but also without separating from one another—the effectiveness of the art of medicine with the conception that identifies health as God's compensation to the righteous and, therefore, the law as the first authentic "medicine." The Lord

> has given knowledge [Gr. *epistêmê*] to men,
> to be glorified in His wonders;

through which [the doctor][14] cures and overcomes suffering
and the druggist prepares his potion . . .
Son, in your sickness don't scorn [this],
but pray to the Lord and He will heal you.
Renounce the error and correct [the works of] your own hands,
cleanse your heart of every sin . . .
Then make room for the doctor, the Lord created him too;
lest he leave, for you need him.
There are times when healing is in his hands;
[the doctors] too pray to the Lord
so that He allows them to comfort and heal their patients.

(*Sir* 38:6-7, 9-10, 12-14)

Beyond these rigidly drawn limits, for which the law is the criterion, there is no wisdom, only a foolish and impious presumption of wisdom.

All wisdom is fear of God,
and in all wisdom there is the practice of the law.
The knowledge of evil [Gr. *ponêrias epistêmê*] is not wisdom
and there is no sense [Gr. *phronêsis*] in the counsel of sinners.

(*Sir* 19:20-22)

The completeness (even in an epistemological sense) of the law and of wisdom (and of their link) excludes all other forms of knowledge. Ben Sira says of dreams:

Empty and false are the hopes of the foolish [Gr. *asynetos*],
dreams give wings to the senseless [Gr. *aphrôn*].
Like a man who catches at shadows or chases the wind,
is the one who believes in dreams. . . .
Divinations, omens and dreams are vain;
like the raving heart of a woman in labor.
Unless it be a vision specially sent by the Most High,
fix not your heart on it;
for dreams have led many astray,
and those who believed in them have perished.
The law will be fulfilled without lies
and wisdom is perfect in a faithful mouth.

(*Sir* 34:1-2, 5-8)

On this point Ben Sira allows no exceptions. Wisdom is specifically and uniquely the fruit of a synergy between human beings and God in which human beings must manifest their fear toward God and, at the same time, apply their own intelligence to the obedience of the law.

---

14. That the subject of the stich is "doctor" is explicit in the Hebrew text. The Greek omits the subject.

Happy is the man who takes care for wisdom
and reflects with his intelligence [Gr. *synesis*].
He who ponders her ways in his heart,
understands even her hidden things [Gr. *apokrypha*].
Pursue her like a scout
and lie in wait at her entry way.
He who peeps through her windows
and listens at her doors,
who encamps near her house
and fastens his tent pegs within her walls;
this man pitches his tent beside her
and lives in the lodging of goods,
gets his children under her cover
and lodges in her branches,
takes shelter with her from the heat
and dwells in her glory.
    He who fears the Lord will do this,
he who keeps the law will acquire [wisdom].
    Motherlike she will meet him,
like a virgin bride she will receive him,
nourish him with the bread of intelligence
and give him the water of wisdom.
She will exalt him above his fellows,
in the assembly she will make him eloquent.
Joy and gladness he will find,
an everlasting name inherit.
The fool [Gr. *asynetos*] will not attain her,
the sinner will not behold her.
Far from pride is she,
not to be spoken of by liars.
    Unseemly is praise on a sinner's lips,
for it is not accorded to him by God.
Praise speaks where wisdom is,
and it is the Lord who leads it.

(Sir 14:20—15:10)

This is a remarkable text, for both its synthetic effectiveness and its poetic force. The passage is literally the result of a contemporary and simultaneous movement of human beings toward God (14:20-27) and of God toward human beings (15:2-8). The respective points of departure are in the person who seeks wisdom (14:20) and in God, who offers wisdom to the righteous as "mother" and "virgin bride" (15:2). This symmetrical movement converges in the affirmation of 15:1 ("He who fears the Lord will do this, he who keeps the law will acquire [wisdom]"), the central verse in both its content and its location in the text. In this verse Ben Sira expresses the decisive moment of synthesis of fear of God, human intelligence, practice of the law, and the gift of wisdom. The "praise" (15:9-10), which comes from God, is the just coronation of a wisdom thus acquired.

5. WISDOM AND LAW:
AN ASYMMETRICAL RELATIONSHIP

For Ben Sira, the law not only is the *conditio sine qua non* by which the "righteous" and "intelligent" person can attain the gift of wisdom but it is itself a manifestation of wisdom.

In the speech in which personified wisdom "sings her own praises . . . before her own people . . . and in the assembly of the Most High" (*Sir* 24:1-2), she reaffirms her origin in and dependence on God and states that she has pitched her tent in Jacob, put down roots there, and produced abundant fruit.

> From the mouth of the Most High I came forth,
> and mistlike covered the earth.
> In the highest heavens did I dwell,
> my throne on a pillar of cloud. . . .
> Over waves of the sea, over all the land,
> over every people and nation I held sway.
> Nevertheless I sought a resting place,
> someone in whose inheritance I could abide.
>   Then the Creator of all gave me His command . . .
> and said: "In Jacob make your dwelling,
> in Israel your inheritance." . . .
> I have struck root among a glorious people,
> in the portion of the Lord, His inheritance.
> Like a cedar of Lebanon I am raised aloft,
> like a cypress on Mount Hermon . . .
> I bud forth delights like the vine,
> my blossoms become fruit of glory and richness.
> Come to me, all you that yearn for me,
> and be filled with my fruits. . . .
> He who eats of me will hunger still,
> he who drinks of me will thirst for more.
> He who obeys me will not be put to shame,
> he who serves me will never sin.
>   (*Sir* 24:3-4, 6-8, 12-13, 17-19, 21-22)

The author's comment immediately follows wisdom's speech.

> All this is the book of the Most High's covenant,
> the law which Moses imposed upon us,
> the inheritance for the assemblies of Jacob.
>   (*Sir* 24:23)

More than any other, it is this passage that has rashly led to the notion of an identification of wisdom and law in *Sirach*. However, saying that the law is the historical manifestation in Israel of a pretemporal wisdom[15] is far from an affirmation of identity. It is more the indication of a relationship conceived in strongly asymmetrical terms. It is possible that the influence of later conceptions of the pretemporality of the law[16] has conditioned the commentators on the reading of this passage, but in *Sirach* the terms of the question are unequivocally different.

Wisdom is "eternal" (Gr. *eis ton aiôna, heôs aiônos*; *Sir* 1:1b; 24:9b), but it is also before history, "before all things" (1:4a), "before the times" (Gr. *pro tou aiônos*; 24:9a). The fact that it has historically become immanent in the law is not the reason for the loss of its pretemporal condition and transcendence that places it second, as a created thing, only to its atemporal Creator. God "has ordered the wonders of His wisdom; He only exists before the times and forever" (42:21).

The covenant is also "eternal," but its eternal nature belongs to history—to the relations between humankind and its Creator—as the foundation necessary for a partnership based on the retributory principle. The law comes after the creation of humankind.

> The Lord from the earth created man . . .
> good and evil He showed them. . . .
> An everlasting covenant He has made with them,
> His decrees He has revealed to them. . . .
> He said to them: "Avoid all evil";
> each of them He gave precepts about his fellow men.
>   (*Sir* 17:1a, 7b, 12, 14)

The law has neither autonomy nor function beyond the limits of the relationship between human beings and God. It exists to be observed; to be observed it had to be made accessible. The law is an already-given gift, the application of which depends on the free will of the individual (cf. *Sir* 15:11-20).

Wisdom, on the other hand, has a degree of autonomy in relation to God, as God's eternal possession, and to all of creation, which is its manifestation. Its enduring condition as gift is owed to its autonomy with respect to the relationship between human beings and God. It remains a gift—that is, a

15. Here I prefer to speak of pretemporality and not atemporality because wisdom too has its beginning in God's act of creation, even though it exists "before time" and "before history." God alone is properly atemporal.

16. The pretemporality of the law is a concept common to the rabbinic tradition. See E. E. Urbach, *The Sages: Their Concepts and Beliefs* (Jerusalem, 1975).

superfluous good—sought after but not granted to all, indeed denied to the majority.

6. COSMIC ORDER, WISDOM, AND LAW

It is Ben Sira's firm conviction that humankind lives in an ordered universe. Such an order is the manifestation of wisdom and the effect of God's creative command. The universe is ruled by certain, immutable, and above all uncorrupted laws.

This is the sense of the passage that in a glance embraces all the "wonders" of creation (*Sir* 42:15—43:33):

> Now will I recall God's works;
> what I have seen, I will describe;
> At God's words were His works brought into being. . . .
> He has ordered the wonders of His wisdom. . . .
> All these things live and last forever
> in every need, and all obey Him. . . .
> The sun, resplendent at its rising, proclaims
> to be a wonderful work of the Most High. . . .
> The moon, too, always respects her times,
> governing the seasons as their lasting sign. . . .
> The beauty of the heavens [is] the glory of the stars,
> shining order in the heights of God;
> to the command of the Holy One they keep according to His decree,
> never relax in their vigils. . . .
> In obedience to His will blow the southern wind,
> the northern storm and the whirlwind. . . .
> However much we add, we say little;
> let the last word be, He is all . . .
> He is greater than all His works.
>   (*Sir* 42:15, 21a, 23; 43:2, 6, 9-10, 16b, 17b, 27, 28b)

The insistence on the immutability and obedience of creation, underscored here with particular emphasis in reference to the stars ("to the command of the Holy One they keep according to His decree [Gr. *krima*]"; *Sir* 43:10), is anything but random. In fact, according to the apocalyptic tradition, immediately after the creation (the fourth day) the stars (that is, the angels who guide them) chose to refuse the role and place assigned to them by God. This original sin overturned the order of the universe and was the beginning and cause of every sin. In the *Book of the Watchers*, in his otherworldly voyage Enoch comes upon "a desolate and terrible place" where he sees "seven stars [which] were like great, burning mountains." The angel accompanying him (Uriel) explains:

> This place is the [ultimate] end of heaven and earth: it is the prison house for the stars and the powers of heaven. And the stars which roll over upon the fire, they are ones which have transgressed the commandments of God from the beginning of their rising because they did not come in their [allotted] time. (*1 Enoch* 18:14-15; cf. 21:3-6)

The idea is taken up again in the *Book of Astronomy*. Describing "the rules concerning all the stars of heaven" (*1 Enoch* 79:1)—that is, the original order of the universe—the author of this apocalyptic document is aware that this order does not exist any more, that it has been dramatically corrupted.

> In those days, the angel Uriel responded and said to me: "Behold, I have shown you everything, Enoch, and I have revealed everything to you [so that] you might see this sun, this moon, and those that guide the stars of heaven as well as those who interchange their activities and their seasons and rotate their processions. In the days of the sinners the years shall be cut short. Their seed[s] shall lag behind in their lands and in their fertile fields, and all the activities upon the earth shall be altered. . . . The rain will be withheld. . . . The moon shall alter its order, and will not be seen according to its [normal] cycles. . . . The [sun][17] shall shine [more brightly], exceeding the normal degree of light. Many of the chiefs of the stars shall make errors in respect to the orders given to them; they shall change their courses and functions and not appear during the seasons which have been prescribed for them. (*1 Enoch* 80:1-6)

The presence of such conceptions makes Ben Sira careful to emphasize the uncorrupted nature of the universe. In accordance with the *Book of Genesis*, he admits the appearance of only one variation since the moment of creation: death, as a consequence of (Adam and) Eve's sin: "In woman was sin's beginning, and because of her we all die" (*Sir* 25:24). In Ben Sira's thought, however, this notion remains a given, hardly touched upon and to a large extent demythologized so as to be inert. The transgression of the first progenitors, the fruit of a foreseen freedom, was certainly grave, but was limited and circumscribed in its effects. The entire order of the universe was in no way subverted. Rather, by the will of God a new rule (death) was included within creation and from that moment became one of God's decrees, an "eternal covenant" (Gr. *diathêkê ap'aiônos*; *Sir* 14:17) for all creatures.

> Fear not death's decree [Gr. *krima*];
> remember it embraces those before you and those after.

---

17. The text is corrected according to Charles (*APOT* 2:245), who suggests that the Ethiopic simply read *šmym* ("sky"), instead of *šmš* ("sun").

[Death] is God's decree [Gr. *krima*] for all flesh,
why then should you reject the will of the Most High?
(*Sir* 41:3-4a; cf. 14:17-18; 38:22)

Having reaffirmed the general rule through the only apparent exception,
Ben Sira must now clarify the compatibility of the necessary and immutable
order of the universe with the law. This had been the problem in *Qohelet*,
according to which the moral order also follows the necessary and immutable rhythms of the universe, discovered in the "law of the times."

For everything there is a season,
and a time for every matter under heaven:
a time to be born, and a time to die;
a time to plant, and a time to pluck up;
a time to kill, and a time to heal;
a time to break down, and a time to build up;
a time to weep, a time to laugh;
a time to mourn, and a time to dance;
a time to cast away, and a time to gather together;
a time to embrace, and a time to refrain from embracing;
a time to seek, and a time to lose;
a time to keep, and a time to cast away;
a time to rend, and a time to sow;
a time to keep silence, and a time to speak;
a time to love, and a time to hate;
a time for war, and a time for peace.
What does man gain from all his work?

(*Qoh* 3:1-9)

The final question reveals *Qohelet*'s basis theme. Humankind does not know
the succession of times for any individual, nor can it grasp the meaning of
this law that governs even the moral order ("whether it is love or hate man
does not know"; *Qoh* 9:1b). The author of *Qohelet* does not doubt that
everything that happens is in conformity with the will of God ("I know that
whatever God does endures for ever; nothing can be added to it, nor nothing taken from it"; *Qoh* 3:14), but the author realizes from experience that,
in applying the "law of the times" to the righteous and the unjust alike, there
is no room for retributory justice ("one fate comes to all . . ."; *Qoh* 9:2).

For Ben Sira, on the other hand, there is no contradiction between the
cosmic order, the law of necessities for all creatures, and a moral order that
through the law relies on human freedom. It is in fact the cosmic order that
offers the certain and necessary rules within which human obedience to the
law is made possible. Life and death, intelligence and feeling, the capacity to
distinguish good and evil and to "see" God in the greatness of God's works

all are the necessary premises to a covenantal relationship between God and humankind.

Step by step, *Sir* 16:24—17:24 follows the unfolding of the divine order: from the immutable cosmos to the mutable creature whose freedom and responsibility are brought into action within the equally certain and defined limits represented by the law and the application of retributory justice.

> At the first God created IIis works,
> and, as He made them, set their bounds. . . .
> Each of them will not squeeze its neighbor,
> nor will they ever disobey His word. . . .
> The Lord from the earth created man,
> and makes him return to earth again. . . .
> Will,[18] tongue, eyes,
> ears and heart gave He to them for reasoning.
> With the knowledge of intelligence He filled them;
> good and evil He showed them.
> He posed His eye in their hearts,
> for showing them the greatness of His works. . . .
> He gave them knowledge,
> a law of life as their inheritance.
> An everlasting covenant He has made with them,
> His decrees He has revealed to them. . . .
> He said to them: "Avoid all evil,"
> each of them He gave precepts about his fellow men.
> Their ways are even known to Him,
> they cannot be hidden from His eyes. . . .
> Finally He will rise up and repay them,
> and requite each of them as they deserve.
>   (*Sir* 16:26, 28; 17:1, 6-8, 11-12, 14-15, 23)

In the great diptych that makes up the final part of *Sirach*, a panegyric on the history of Israel (*Sirach* 44–49) follows the description of the cosmic order in *Sir* 42:15—43:33. It is a story of faithfulness rewarded and unfaithfulness punished, a story marked by the succession of alliances and culminating in the gift of the Mosaic law. The Lord

---

18. G. L. Prato (*Il problema della teodicea in Ben Sira* [Rome, 1975], 276–77) and other scholars hold that the insertion of the Greek term *diaboulion* ("free will") in *Sir* 17:6a is due to an error in the Greek translation where the (missing) Hebrew text would have placed a verb (*wbr*'; "and [God] created"), as suggested by the Siriac version. This objection, which is not unanimously accepted (see J. Hadot, *Penchant mauvais at volonté libre dans la Sagesse de Ben Sira* [Brussels, 1970], 106–7), does not change the sense of the verse. As a whole—and even Prato agrees—the verse is intended to show how humankind has been given by God all the instruments necessary to "reason," that is, to distinguish good from evil.

permitted [Moses] to hear His voice,
and led him into the dark cloud
and, face to face, gave him the commandments [Gr. *entolai*],
the law of life and knowledge [Gr. *nomos zôês kai epistêmês*],
that he might teach the covenant [Gr. *diathêkê*] to Jacob,
[the Lord's] decrees [Gr. *krimata*] to Israel.

(*Sir* 45:5)

In a cosmos ordered by certain rules, the law is the certain rule that governs the relationship between God and humankind in history, marking the limits of human freedom such that the mutability of the creature has its assigned place in the harmony of all things. The error of identifying wisdom with the law is once again confirmed. The law, which is the manifestation of wisdom in history, in the cosmic context is but one of the rules that God in God's wisdom has established to govern creation.

7. THE LAW AS WISDOM'S EDUCATION

That the relationship between wisdom and law in *Sirach* is an asymmetrical relationship is even more apparent from the text itself than from critical reflection. The law is not identified with wisdom but with the "education" (Gr. *paideia*) of wisdom.

Indeed, for Ben Sira there is a real pedagogy of wisdom, expression of the mercy God lavishes on all flesh, "reproving, admonishing, teaching, as a shepherd He guides His flock" (*Sir* 18:13; cf. 18:8-14).

Wisdom [Gr. *sophia*] instructs her children
and takes care for those who seek her. . . .
If one trusts her, he will possess her. . . .
At first she perversely walks with him;
fear and dread she brings upon him
and tries him with her education [Gr. *en paideia autês*];
until she might trust his soul,
with her precepts she puts him to the proof.
Then she makes him come back to the straight path and makes him happy
and reveals her hidden things [Gr. *krypta*] to him.

(*Sir* 4:11, 16-18)

This education (Gr. *paideia*), which those who seek wisdom must undergo as a true pedagogical course, is nothing more than observance of the law. This is explicitly stated in *Sir* 6:18-37 and is particularly clear in the two parallel sentences (vv. 18 and 37) that open and close the passage.

Son, from your youth embrace education [Gr. *paideia*],
thus will you find wisdom [Gr. *sophia*] with graying hair.

As though plowing and sowing, draw close to her,
then await her bountiful crops;
for in cultivating her you will labor but little,
and soon you will eat of her fruits. . . .
Put your feet into her fetters,
your neck under her yoke.
Stoop your shoulders and carry her,
be not irked at her bonds.
With your soul draw close to her,
with all your strength keep her ways.
Search her out, seek her, and she will make herself found;
Then when you have her, do not let her go.
At the end you will find rest in her,
and she will become your joy.
Her fetters will be for you a strong shelter,
her bonds, a robe of glory. . . .
Reflect on the precepts [Gr. *prostagmata*] of the Lord,
let His commandments [Gr. *entolai*] be your constant meditation;
then He will make your heart sound,
and the wisdom you desire He will grant.

(*Sir* 6:18-19, 24-29, 37)

The equivalence of *paideia* and law is confirmed by the interchangeable relationships they have, within the same synergetic dynamic, on the one hand with the fear of God and human intelligence, and on the other hand with the gift of wisdom.

He who fears the Lord accepts education [Gr. *paideia*],
he who seeks Him obtains His request.
He who studies the law masters it,
but the hypocrite finds it a trap. . . .
The thoughtful man does not neglect reflection,
the foreigner and the proud man do not feel fear. . . .
He who trusts in the law keeps the commandments [Gr. *entolai*],
he who trusts in the Lord shall not be disappointed. . . .
The wise man [Gr. *anêr sophos*] does not hate the law,
he who simulates it is like a boat in a storm.
The intelligent man [Gr. *anthrôpos synetos*] trusts in the law,
and the law is dependable for him as the response of the Urim.

(*Sir* 32:14–15, 18, 24; 33:2-3)

The same elements are present also in *Sir* 21:11-28, in which Ben Sira insists on the moral contrast between the intelligent person and the fool.

He who keeps the law controls his thoughts,
perfection of fear toward the Lord is wisdom.
He can never be taught who is not shrewd,
but one form of shrewdness is thoroughly bitter. . . .

Like fetters on the legs is education [Gr. *paideia*] to a fool [Gr. *anoêtos*],
like a manacle on his right hand. . . .
Like a chain of gold is education [Gr. *paideia*] to an intelligent man
  [Gr. *phronimos*],
like a bracelet on his right hand.

(Sir 21:11–12, 19, 21)

8. THE LAW AS WISDOM'S BLESSING

On more than one occasion Ben Sira reminds us that the gift of wisdom, humankind's most sought-after goal, is not an end in itself. Wisdom is not given to be hidden.

Hidden wisdom and unseen treasure
—of what value is either?
Better the man who hides his folly
than the one who hides his wisdom.
        (Sir 20:30-31 = 41:14-15)

The blessings linked with the gift of wisdom not only concern the one who receives it (to whom the greatest good, the everlasting name, is promised) but are to be spread to all people through the words of the "wise." From "learning" (Gr. *paideia*) the law becomes "teaching" (Gr. *didaskalia*).

When a man is wise in his own soul,
the true fruits of his intelligence are seen also in his mouth.
The wise man educates his own people,
the fruits of his intelligence are true.
The wise man will be blessed . . .
and his name will live forever.

(Sir 37:22-24a, 26b)

Having delineated on the one hand the pedagogical-spiritual course that leads people to wisdom, and on the other the diffusive effects of the gift of wisdom, Ben Sira identifies the ideal model of the wise person in the figure of the scribe (cf. *Sir* 39:1-11). In seeking wisdom, the scribe consecrates all of his intelligence and experience, his fear of God, and his ability to obey the law (vv. 1-5). His striving for perfection synergetically meets the will of God and eventually gains the gift of wisdom with its countless blessings both for himself and for the people benefiting from his teaching (vv. 7-11). The scribe

  devotes his soul
to the study of the law of the Most High.
He explores the wisdom of the men of old
and occupies himself with the prophecies. . . .

He travels among the peoples of foreign lands
to experience what is good and evil among men. . . .
He makes supplications before the Most High
and opens his lips in prayer,
asks pardon for his sins.
Then, if it pleases the Lord Almighty,
he will be filled with the spirit of intelligence:
he will pour forth the words of His wisdom
and in prayer give thanks to the Lord.
He will give advice and knowledge,
and meditate upon the hidden things which have been revealed to him;
he will show the education of his teaching [Gr. *paideia didaskalias autou*],
and glory in the law of the Lord's covenant.
Many will praise his intelligence [Gr. *synesis*];
his fame can never be effaced;
unfading will be his memory,
through all generations his name will live.
Peoples will speak of his wisdom,
and the assembly [of Israel] sing his praises.

(Sir 39:1, 4b, 5b-10)

This is also—Ben Sira claims—his personal experience. Through prayer
and practice of the law he became a disciple of wisdom. It is to this training
that he owes his quality as a master and the authority of his teaching.

When I was young, before I traveled,
I sought wisdom openly in prayer.
Before the Temple I begged for her,
and to the end I will seek her. . . .
I have devoted my soul to her,
and I have been scrupulous in keeping the law. . . .
The Lord has granted me a tongue as a reward,
and with it I will sing His praises.
Come to me, you who need education [Gr. *apaideutoi*],
and take your place in my school [Gr. *oikos paideias*; Heb. *byt mdršy*]. . . .
I opened my mouth and I said:
"Gain, at no cost, [wisdom] for yourselves.
Submit yourselves to [her] yoke,
let your souls bear [her] education [Gr. *paideia*].
It is so easy to find her!"

(Sir 51:13-14, 19a, 22-23, 25-26)

The circle closes; the law is the learned education (Gr. *paideia*) that enabled
Ben Sira to be a master and now is the subject of his teaching. That which
benefited him now benefits others through him. The law

overflows, like the Phison, with wisdom [Gr. *sophia*],
like the Tigris in the days of the new fruits.

cal systems, such as the Pauline doctrine of "Adam's sin"[21] or the rabbinic idea of *yeṣer haraʿ* ("the evil inclination").[22] However, even at the beginning of this century F. R. Tennant drew attention to the limits of such a statement of the problem in relation to Paul.[23] In more recent years J. Hadot has pointed out that the term *yeṣer* does not at all have the same technical value, strongly ideologized, in *Sirach* that it would later acquire in rabbinic thought, where it is used in a coherent system that sees "two opposing inclinations" struggling within human beings.[24]

Far from being the precursor of later theories, Ben Sira offers a significant testimony within the context of the problems emerging in his era. At the beginning of the second century B.C.E., in the conscience of a Jew—even a Jew proposing to restore a theology of the covenant—evil is no longer conceivable as simply an act deriving from free transgression of the law. It is something much more complex and even more terrible; it is an evil presence that makes its force and destructive power known before and beyond any and all transgressions.

Taking up the image found in *Genesis* 4:7, *Sirach* often compares sin to a beast of prey lying in ambush: "As a lion lies in ambush [Gr. *enedreueô*] for prey, so does sin [Gr. *hamartia*] for evildoers" (*Sir* 27:10; cf. 6:2; 21:2; 28:23).

The force of evil is all the more terrible inasmuch as it is not external to human beings; rather, it is fomented and unleashed from inside like a weed: "For the distress of the proud man there is no cure; the plant of evil has taken root in him" (*Sir* 3:28).

Ben Sira discovers a radical ambivalence in human beings; their senses, even their entire self, seems to be capable of either good or evil.[25] The tongue is perhaps the most immediate sign of this: "If you blow upon a spark, it quickens into flame, if you spit on it, it dies out; yet both you do with your mouth!" (*Sir* 28:12).

---

21. See I. Lévi, *Le péché originel dans les anciennes sources juives* (Paris, 1907); N. P. Williams, *The Ideas of the Fall and Original Sin* (London, 1927); A. M. Dubarle, "Le péché originel dans les livres sapientiaux," *RT* 56 (1956): 597–619; and L. Ligier, *Péché d'Adam et péché du mond* (Paris, 1960).

22. See F. C. Porter, *The Yeser Hara: A Study in the Doctrine of Sin* (New York, 1901); G. H. Box and W.O.E. Oesterley, "The Wisdom of Ben Sira," *APOT* 1 (1913): 268–517; W. Eichrodt, *Theologie des Altes Testaments* (Göttingen, 1964), 273, 287; M. Hengel, *Judentum und Hellenismus*, 2d ed. (Tübingen, 1973), 254ff.; and G. H. Cohen Stuart, *The Struggle in Man between Good and Evil: An Inquiry into the Origin of the Rabbinic Concept of Yeser Hara* (Kampen, 1984).

23. Tennant, *Teaching of Ecclesiasticus and Wisdom*; cf. Hadot, *Penchant mauvais*, 105; and Prato, *Il problema della teodicea*, 377–78.

24. Hadot, *Penchant mauvais*; cf. Prato, *Il problemo della teodicea*, 238–42.

25. Some interesting ideas on this topic can be found in Hadot, *Penchant mauvais*, 177–92.

Humankind's being, every person's being, in essence has two faces, show-ing itself at times good and at times bad, at times the source of good and at times that of evil. In *Sirach* this is a fact of experience, disturbing and dra-matic but so obvious that there is no need to explain it. It is precisely in this ambivalence that the cause of evil is to be searched out; when humankind's being, practically in a doubling process, reveals its evil face, the person who experiences this is pushed toward sin and ruin.

This happens with the "sinner with a double tongue." The Greek expres-sion *ho hamartôlos ho diglôssos* corresponds perfectly with the original Hebrew: *'yš r' b'l štym* ("evil man, master of two [tongues]").

> Honor and dishonor through talking!
> A man's tongue is his downfall.
> Be not called a slanderer [Gr. *psithyros*; Heb. *b'l štym*];
> and lie not in ambush [Gr. *mê enedreue*; Heb. *'l trgl r'*] with your tongue;
> for shame is for the thief
> and blame for the double-tongued [Gr. *diglôssos*; Heb. *b'l štym*].
> Go not wrong in the small and great things
> and from friend become not enemy;
> as a bad name draws upon itself shame and blame,
> so [does] the sinner with a double tongue [Gr. *ho hamartôlos ho diglôssos*;
>   Heb. *'yš r' b'l štym*].
>
> (*Sir* 5:13-15)

The condemnation of an evil tongue is not new to the wisdom tradition,[26] but here the emphasis is no longer simply on the devastating effects the tongue can have on one's neighbor. The "friend become enemy" is above all one's *own* tongue, whose destructive power of evil is manifested in a more insidious way: "Through his lips is the sinner [Gr. *hamartôlos*] ensnared; the railer and the proud man fall thereby" (*Sir* 23:8; cf. 20:18).

Once again, in an ample passage dedicated to the "sinner with a double tongue," *Sirach* speaks of the damages brought about (a) against the slan-dered, (b) against those who listen, but most of all (c) against oneself. According to an expression that would later become common in rabbinic literature,[27] a bad tongue is "a tongue with threefold power" (Gr. *glôssa tritê*, literally "the third tongue").

> Cursed be the slanderer and the double-tongued [Gr. *psithyros kai diglôssos*],
> for they have destroyed many who lived in peace.

---

26. See J. Behm, "*glôssa*," *TWNT*; and Hadot, *Penchant mauvais*, 183.
27. "The bad tongue [Aram. *lšwn br'*] . . . [is called] the third tongue [Aram. *lšwn tlt'*] . . . because it kills three people: he who speaks, he who is spoken to, he who is spoken of" (*Babylonian Talmud, Arakhin* 15b).

[a] The third tongue has subverted many,
and made them refugees among the people;
it has destroyed walled cities,
and overthrown powerful dynasties.
The third tongue has made virtuous women repudiated
and robbed them of [the fruit of] their toil
    [b] Whoever heeds it has no rest,
nor can he dwell in peace.
A blow from a whip raises a welt,
but a blow from the tongue smashes bones.
Many have fallen by the edge of the sword,
but not so many as by the tongue.
    [c] Happy is he who is sheltered from it,
and has not endured its wrath;
who has not borne its yoke
nor been fettered with its chains.
For its yoke is a yoke of iron
and its chains are chains of bronze.
Dire is the death it inflicts,
besides which even Hades is a gain.

(Sir 28:13-21)

The passage ends with an invocation for people to defend themselves from
their *own* tongues, a source of ruin and a foe lying in ambush.

As you hedge round your vineyard with thorns,
and seal up your silver and gold,
so balance and weigh your words
and set barred doors over your mouth.
Take care not to slip by your tongue
and fall victim to it which is lying in ambush [Gr. *enedreuô*].

(Sir 28:24-26)

Other senses too, taking part in the same ambivalence, can show an evil
face. *Sirach* speaks of a "bad eye" in analogous terms: "Remember that a bad
eye is evil; what was created worse than the eye?" (*Sir* 31:13; cf. 14:8-10;
26:11; 27:22). The same is true of the heart and soul (Gr. *kardia, psychê*; Heb.
lb, npš), which represent the core of one's being. A "bad heart" pushes one to
sin and calls down God's punishment:

A hard heart [Gr. *kardia sklêra*; Heb. *lb kbd*]
will fare badly in the end,
and he who loves danger will perish in it.
A hard heart will be burdened with sorrow,
and the sinner will heap sin upon sin.

(Sir 3:26-27; cf. 1:28; 2:12-13; 16:10;
22:18; 36:20)

A "bad soul" also leads its possessor to ruin:

> Abandon not yourself in the power of your soul [Gr. *psychê*],
> lest, like a bull, your soul [Gr. *psychê*] knock you down.
> Your leaves it will eat and you will lose your fruits,
> and you will be left a dry tree.
> A bad soul [Gr. *psychê ponêra*; Heb. *npš 'zh*] destroys his owner
> and makes him the laughing-stock of his enemies.
>
>   (*Sir* 6:2-4; cf. 23:6, 17)

The uncontrolled emergence of shameful thoughts and passions is one of the most obvious signs of ambivalence, seen in its negative aspect. In fact, from a bad heart and soul come "jealousy" [Gr. *zêlos*; Heb. *qn'h*; cf. 30:24], "passion" (Gr. *epithymia*; Heb. *t'wh*; cf. 5:2; 23:5), "rage" (Gr. *thymos*; Heb. *'p*; cf. 1:22; 28:19; 30:24), "pride" (Gr. *hyperêphania*; Heb. *g'wh*; cf. 10:6-18), "anxiety (of possession)" (Gr. *merimna*; Heb. *d'gh*; cf. 30:24—31:2); in short, any sort of sentiment hateful to God.

> Odious before God and man is pride. . . .
> Why are dust and ashes proud? . . .
> The beginning of man's pride is his fleeing God,
> his heart [Gr. *kardia*] has left his Maker.
>
>   (*Sir* 10:7a, 9a, 12)

Ben Sira's exhortation puts human beings on their guard against blindly following their own selves, because a dangerous enemy could be hidden there.

> Go not after your passions [Gr. *epithymiai*],
> but keep your desires in check.
> If you let your soul [Gr. *psychê*] satisfy passion [Gr. *epithymia*],
> it makes you the laughingstock of your enemies.
>
>   (*Sir* 18:30-31)

Beyond the textual difficulties,[28] the statement of *Sir* 37:3 also appears clearer in this context. In this passage the complaint about a friend's betrayal gives voice to the daily experience of an even more radical betrayal.

> Every friend says: "I love you";
> but there are friends who are friends in name only.
> Is it not a sorrow unto death
> when your companion and friend becomes your enemy?
> Alas, bad decision [Gr. *ponêron enthymêma*]!
> Where did you come from, to blanket the earth with deceit?
>
>   (*Sir* 37:1-3; cf. 6:5-17)

---

28. On the textual problems of *Sir* 37:3, see Prato, *Il problema della teodicea*, 239–40.

The text might imply the Hebrew expression *yeṣer haraʿ* but the ideological context is quite different from the rabbinic one. In *Sirach* an "evil inclination" as a part of human beings, with its opposite counterpart, "good inclination," (the *yeṣer ṭob*), does not exist. This idea already represents an attempt to explain rationally the condition of ambivalence, common to all human beings, which is described but not explained by Ben Sira. The exclamation of *Sir* 37:3 is the stuporous exclamation of a human being who discovers his or her own self, who should be his bosom friend, transformed into his worst enemy.

Human ambivalence does not imply that human nature is ontologically bad; evil is simply a possibility innate in the human self. People possess tongues, hearts, and minds that may reveal themselves to be bad; however, they may also show themselves to be good and faithful when they bare the benign face of their ambivalence.

> The heart [Gr. *kardia*] of a man changes his countenance,
> either for good or for evil.
> The sign of a good heart [Gr. *kardia en agathois*; Heb. *lb ṭwb*]
> is a cheerful countenance. . . .
> Happy the man whose mouth brings him no grief.
> > (*Sir* 13:25-26a; 141a; cf. 37:17-18)

A good heart (soul) is a faithful friend whom one can trust completely:

> Heed your own heart's counsel,
> for nothing is more trustworthy than it.
> A man's soul can tell him his situation
> better than seven watchmen in a lofty tower.
> > (*Sir* 37:13-14; cf. 3:29; 22:16-17; 36:19)

It is certainly necessary to be prudent and, in the various circumstances of life, not to lose control of one's own soul (cf. 37:27-31). Ben Sira exhorts, however, not to be "ashamed" without reason, to value one's own self for what it is worth, to repress it if it is bad and to follow it if it is good.

> Mind your situation and guard yourself from evil,
> and be not ashamed of your soul [Gr. *psychê*].
> There is a shame that leads to sin,
> and a shame that causes honor and respect.
> Extol not your soul,
> but be not ashamed of it to your own downfall.
> > (*Sir* 4:20-22; cf. 10:28-29)

2. HUMAN FREEDOM AND THE
OMNIPOTENCE OF GOD

Once again it seems that Ben Sira must take up a position near the apocalyptic tradition with the conviction that evil is based on human nature or, at any rate, is fed by it. His position appears radically different, however, when he denies iniquity as an ontological given. The debate on this point is bitter, confirming that similar ideas were widespread among his contemporaries.

First of all, Ben Sira excludes the idea that the ambivalence of human nature should be attributed to an agent external to human beings themselves. Such an idea is even "impious": "When an impious man curses the satan [Gr. *satanas*], he really curses his own soul [Gr. *psychê*]" (*Sir* 21:27). The figure of "the satan," the angelic being depicted in the *Book of the Watchers* as guilty of the corruption of the world and therefore responsible for evil (cf. *1 Enoch* 10:8), is thus radically demythologized. That which the impious man calls "the satan" is in truth an internal human reality, deprived of any autonomous existence.

Although the evidence of the Hebrew text unfortunately is missing,[29] such an idea appears in line with the thought of Ben Sira, who scrupulously avoids any speculation on angels and demons. Even the reference to the "ancient giants," within a tally of examples of God's retributory justice (cf. *Sir* 16:6-14), does not seem random when it is borne in mind that these are the protagonists of the biblical episode (cf. *Gen* 6:1-4) at the center of the reflection on the origin of evil in the *Book of the Watchers*. With the same demythologizing scheme used by the final redactor of *Genesis*, the episode is inserted in a context that removes all uniqueness from both the sin and the punishment of the "ancient giants." It is but one of many incidents in human history; the regular sequence of transgression and punishment confirms the validity of the covenant.

> Against the assembly of the sinners fire was enkindled,
> upon a godless people [God's] wrath flamed out.
> [The Lord] forgave not the ancient giants,
> who rebelled in their might.

---

29. Hadot (*Penchant mauvais*, 95–96) holds that in this case Ben Sira is referring to the figure of the "personal adversary," a figure characteristic of wisdom literature. In his opinion this is a gloss added to the Greek version. However, his reasons for upholding this thesis are not valid because they are based on an inaccurate dating of *1 Enoch*, which he places at the beginning of the second century B.C.E. We now know that the conception of an angelic being responsible for evil is anterior to the period in which Ben Sira was active.

He spared not the neighbors of Lot
whom He detested for their pride;
nor did He spare the doomed people
who were uprooted because of their sins;
nor the six hundred thousand foot soldiers
who perished for the hardness of their hearts.
                                              (*Sir* 16:6-10)

Ben Sira shows greater affinity with the *Book of Astronomy*. In some contexts, sin can appear to be a consequence of humankind's status as a flesh-and-blood creature. There is, in fact, an unbridgeable distance between the creature and its Maker, a distance that Ben Sira turns into an equation: mortality is to immortality as sin is to righteousness.

There cannot be everything in man,
for not immortal is any son of man.
Is anything brighter than the sun? Yet it can be eclipsed.
The flesh and body have evil thoughts.
[The Lord] watches over the host of highest heaven,
while all men are dust and ashes.
The Eternal created all things,
the Lord alone is righteous.
                                              (*Sir* 17:30—18:2)

But that which is a bitter consideration in *Genesis* (cf. 8:21) and an onto-logical reality in the *Book of Astronomy* (cf. *1 Enoch* 81:5) is in *Sirach* only the condition of those who *intentionally* distance themselves from God. The misery or the greatness of human beings' status as creatures depends on their will and on faithful obedience to the law.

Whose offspring can be in honor? Those of men.
Which offspring are in honor? Those who fear the Lord.
Whose offspring can be in disgrace? Those of men.
Which offspring are in disgrace? Those who transgress the commandments.
                                              (*Sir* 10:19)

Now we have arrived at the central problem: the freedom of human will. Although Ben Sira locates the cause of the evil done by human beings in the ambivalence of their selves, this does not at all compromise human ability to choose. Free will is also an integral part of human nature as creatures. This original, constitutional condition has not been changed; it maintains its completely unaltered validity.

Any deterministic solution, such as the one already touched upon with the image of the "heavenly tables" in the *Book of Astronomy* (cf. *1 Enoch* 81:2), is resolutely denied.

Say not: "It was the Lord's fault if I sinned,"
for what He hates He does not do.
Say not: "It was He who set me astray,"
for He has no need of sinful man.
The Lord hates every abomination,
even those who fear Him do not love [abomination].
In the beginning He created man
and made him subject to his own will [Gr. *diaboulion*; Heb. *yṣr*].[30]
If you choose you can keep the commandments;
being faithful depends on your good will.
He set fire and water before you;
to whichever you choose you shall stand your hand.
Before man are life and death,
whichever one he chooses shall be given to him.
Immense is the wisdom of the Lord;
He is mighty in power, and all-seeing.
His eyes [are] upon those who fear Him,
He knows man's every deed.
No man does He command to be impious,
to none does He allow to sin.

(*Sir* 15:11-20)

This is the first time in the history of Jewish thought that we find the theme of free will conceptually developed, even though it constitutes one of the postulates of any theology of the covenant.[31] It is significant, and also natural, that this should happen after the first appearance of an explicit denial of human responsibility for evil, even though this too is the expression of a long tradition of thought.[32] The theme of the freedom of human will has been brought from the periphery to the core of Jewish thought.

30. The Hebrew in v. 14b contains a significant addition: "In the beginning [God] created man—and placed him in power to his abductor [Heb. *ḥwtpw*]—and made him subject to his own will [Heb. *yṣrw*]." This is a clear interpolation that breaks the rhythm of the verse and whose intent is through parallelism to give a negative value to the term *yeṣer* where it has a neutral value. Conceptually, the gloss is related to the dualistic anthropology of Qumran. See Hadot, *Penchant mauvais*, 94; Maier, *Mensch und freier Wille*, 88; and Prato, *Il problema della teodicea*, 221, 242.

31. The idea of the covenant implies the presupposition that humankind is capable of obeying its stipulations, as is clearly expressed by the author of *Deuteronomy*: "For this commandment which I command you this day is not too hard for you, neither is it far off. It is not in heaven, that you should say, 'Who will go up for us to heaven, and bring it to us, that we may hear it and do it?' Neither is it beyond the sea, that you should say, 'Who will go over the sea for us, and bring it to us, that we may hear it and do it?' But the word is very near you; it is in your mouth and in your heart, so that you can do it" (*Deut* 30:11-14).

32. A certain pessimism as to humankind's ability to do good is implicit in any theology of the promise, a pessimism particularly evident in some passages of the so-called Yahwist, who has God say dejectedly after the flood that "the *yeṣer* [will] of man's heart is evil from his youth" (*Gen* 8:21; cf. 6:5).

But if human beings are free and their choices are not preordained, how can the ambivalence of their nature, the evil force that seems to spring from their own selves, be explained? How can this be reconciled with God's omnipotence?

For Ben Sira the problem has a wider context than the human one and rather belongs to the cosmological plane. The ambivalent structure of human beings simply repeats the equally ambivalent structure of the entire cosmos, in which good and evil, life and death coexist.

> As good is facing evil
> and life is facing death,
> so the righteous is facing the sinner.
> See now all the works of the Most High,
> they come in pairs, the one is facing the other.
> <div align="center">(<i>Sir</i> 33:14-15; cf. 42:24)</div>

These words sound like the prelude to a dualistic solution. The following statement is not sufficient to contradict this impression: "Good and evil, life and death, poverty and riches, are from the Lord" (*Sir* 11:14). Although deprived of an autonomous reality in relation to God, evil can still vindicate its equal dignity in relation to good. Ben Sira denies, however, any ontological depth to this duality. It exists only in the eyes of human beings; it is apparent, fictitious.

> The works of the Lord are all of them very good,
> in its own time every order of His shall be fulfilled.
> No cause then to say: "What is this? What is its purpose?"
> for everything will be used in its own time. . . .
> No cause then to say: "What is this? What is its purpose?"
> for everything was created to an end. . . .
> As good things were created for the good from the beginning,
> so for the sinner bad things. . . .
> So from the first I have been persuaded,
> I reflected and wrote it down:
> The works of the Lord are all of them good;
> every need when it comes He fills.
> No cause then to say: "This is worse than that,"
> for each will show its goodness in its own time.
> <div align="center">(<i>Sir</i> 39:16, 21, 25, 32–34)</div>

As G. L. Prato has demonstrated in a rich and thorough monograph, Ben Sira's theodicy is based upon a *coincidentia oppositorum* that assumes and annuls opposites in the inscrutable unity of divine will.[33] Evil, which for humankind

---

33. See Prato, *Il problema della teodicea.*

is a concrete and tangible reality, in relation to God immediately loses all consistency; everything is good because it obeys God's project and evil exists only as the other side of good.[34]

3. DOMINATING ONE'S OWN AMBIVALENCE

Resolved on the metaphysical plane, the problem of evil is still dramatic on the anthropological plane. The call of freedom and its consequent individual responsibility make the human condition all the more burdensome, oppressed by the ambivalence of human nature itself. The ideal would be to attain a "simplicity," an inner unity that would annul the evil face that is always lying in wait.[35]

> Winnow not in every wind,
> and walk not in every path;
> so [does] the sinner with a double-tongue.
> Be consistent in your intelligence [Gr. *synesis*],
> and one be your word.
>   (*Sir* 5:9-10; cf. 2:2-3)

In entreaty, human beings question themselves about their chances for salvation and turn to God for help.

> Who will set a guard over my mouth,
> and upon my lips an effective seal,
> that I may fail through it,
> that my tongue may not destroy me?
> Lord, Father and Master of my life,
> abandon me not into their power,
> let me not fall by them!
> Who will apply the lash to my thoughts,
> to my heart the education of wisdom [Gr. *paideia sophias*]? . . .
> Lord, Father and God of my life,
> abandon me not into eyes' excitement,
> remove me from passion [Gr. *epithymia*].
> Let not the lustful cravings of the flesh master me,
> surrender me not to a shameless soul [Gr. *psychê*].
>   (*Sir* 22:27—23:2a, 4–6; cf. 51:1-12)

---

34. The origins of this conception can be traced to the influence of Egyptian cosmology, in which evil has the same fictitious consistence. In any case, we are faced with elements extrapolated and isolated from their original context and inserted into a problematic made typically Jewish. See D. Hellholm, ed., *Apocalypticism in the Mediterranean World and the Ancient Near East* (Tübingen, 1983); A. Loprieno, "Il pensiero egizio e l'apocalittica giudaica," *Henoch* 3 (1981): 289–320; and idem, "Il modello egizio nei testi della letteratura intertestamentaria," *RivB* 34 (1986): 205–32.

35. See Hadot, *Penchant mauvais*, 177–92.

The first response is given in negative terms; people must avoid every occasion that could lead their own selves to go astray and to become bad. We find repeated exhortations to flee the company of sinners, not to fall into the same ruin (cf. *Sir* 8:10; 11:29—13:18). This does not simply mean avoiding dangerous company and bad examples; the risk is even more insidious—that of being contaminated. As *Qohelet* already tells us (cf. *Qoh* 9:2), in the mentality of the day sin and uncleanness are seen as equivalent terms; the sinner is unclean to such a degree that contact should be avoided.[36]

> Waste not your words with the stupid man,
> be not the companion of the foolish man;
> beware of him lest you have trouble
> and contaminate yourself not [Gr. *molynô*] in contact with him.
> Turn away from him and you will find rest
> and not be wearied by his foolishness.
>
> *(Sir* 22:13)

A contamination contracted in this way seems directly to influence the manifestation of the evil side of human ambivalence. This link is really more intuited than developed by Ben Sira, but it sufficiently explains his insistence when he urges against any kind of relationship with the sinner so that one's own soul may not be corrupted.

> Who pities a snake charmer when he is bitten,
> or anyone who goes near a wild beast?
> So it is with the companion of the sinner,
> who dirties himself with his sins. . . .
> He who touches pitch contaminates [Gr. *molynô*] himself,
> he who associates with the proud man becomes like him.
>
> *(Sir* 12:13–14; 13:1)

There are some occasions that, although not communicating uncleanness, are equally dangerous. The most serious seems to be the company of woman, to whom the power of stirring up wicked desires in men's souls is attributed.

> Give not your soul to [your] woman. . . .
> Give not your soul to harlots. . . .
> With another's woman not be seated . . .
> lest your soul be drawn to her
> and you ruined because of your spirit.
>
> *(Sir* 9:2a, 6a, 9b; cf. 25:13-26;
> 26:5-12; 42:9-14)

---

36. On the conception of impurity in ancient and middle Judaism, see Sacchi, *Storia*, 229–59; and idem, "Omnia munda mundis (Tito 1,15): Il puro e l'impuro nel pensiero ebraico," in *Il pensiero di Paolo nella storia del cristianesimo antico*, ed. Università di Genova (Genoa, 1984), 29–55.

It is certainly significant that Ben Sira gives no weight to the contaminating value of the sexual act, even though he is aware of the link between uncleanness and sin and hence between uncleanness and human ambivalence. There are countless misogynous statements in his work, but the danger represented by women is never linked to the danger of contamination, as it is in the case of the sinner. Again, the care Ben Sira takes to distinguish his positions from those of the apocalyptic tradition seems obvious; the *Book of the Watchers* placed the sexual sin of the angels with the daughters of men at the origin of evil and identified sex as the means of communicating and spreading the corruption of human nature.[37]

Also for this reason, it is not at all plausible to claim that in *Sirach* we find the idea of "Adam's sin" for the first time in the history of Jewish thought, an idea that would be developed only later in the apocalyptic tradition and by Paul. Following the example of *Genesis*, Ben Sira intends simply to recall that it was from the nearness of a woman that sin had its beginning (only in a temporal sense!) and that because of this all people must experience death:[38] "In woman was sin's beginning, and because of her we all die" (*Sir* 25:24). Woman, therefore, was only the first temptation of man; other no less insidious temptations followed. Banquets, for example, with their abundance of food and wine, are another occasion for putting human hearts to a hard test.

> Let not wine-drinking be the proof of your strength,
> for wine has been the ruin of many.
> As the furnace probes the work of the smith,
> so does wine the hearts in a competition among proud men.
> (*Sir* 31:25-26; cf. 31:12—32:13)

Even in wealth lies a mortal threat. Wealth is so easily transformed into a love of possession, covetousness, and pride that a rich person who does not have these passions is celebrated with amazed admiration as one who has overcome a difficult test.

> The lover of gold will not be free from sin,
> he who pursues wealth will be led astray by it.
> Many have been ensnared by gold,
> though destruction lay before their eyes.
> It is a stumbling block to those who are avid for it,
> a snare for every fool.

---

37. See L. Rosso Ubigli, "Alcuni aspetti della concezione della 'porneia' nel tardo-giudaismo," *Henoch* 1 (1979): 201–42.

38. See Tennant, *Teaching of Ecclesiasticus and Wisdom*; Hadot, *Penchant mauvais*; and Prato, *Il problema della teodicea*. For a different opinion, see T. Gallus, " 'A muliere initium peccati et per illam omnes morimur'—*Sir* 25, 24 (33);" *VD* 23 (1943): 272–77.

> Happy the rich man found without fault,
> who turns not aside after gain!
> Who is he? We will praise him,
> for he has done wonders among his people.
> Who has been tested by [gold] and come off safe?
> This will remain his glory.
> Who could have sinned but did not,
> could have done evil, but did not?
> > (*Sir* 31:5-10; cf. 8:2; 26:29—27:3)

Ben Sira is not, however, a rigid moralist; wine was created "for the joy of man" (cf. *Sir* 31:27-28; 32:6); a judicious woman is the greatest happiness (cf. 26:1-4, 13-18; 36:21-27); even wealth is one of God's blessings (cf. 11:21-22) and is good if it is not accompanied by sin (cf. 13:24a). The important thing is to find the right measure in all actions.

> Listen to me, son, and scorn me not;
> later you will find my advice good.
> In whatever you do, be moderate,
> and no sickness will befall you.
> > (*Sir* 31:22)

This measure, this education (Gr. *paideia*; Heb. *mwsr*) by which all actions are regulated, is the law. Those who entrust themselves to it protect themselves from all temptations.

> He who trusts in the law, keeps the commandments,
> he who trusts in the Lord shall not be disappointed.
> No evil can harm the man who fears the Lord;
> through trials, again and again he is safe.
> > (*Sir* 32:24—33:1; cf. 27:3)

Above all, Ben Sira is anxious to emphasize the positive sense in which the law, and only the law, gives human beings the power to dominate the ambivalence of their own nature. He shares with the apocalyptic tradition the idea that the force of evil is so great that it cannot be defeated without God's help. This help, however, in its modality is brought back within the traditional limits of a theology of the covenant; it is subordinated to the commitment to obedience of the law. Between humankind and God a kind of synergy is created in the struggle for salvation. "Trust [the Lord] and He will help you" (*Sir* 2:6a). "Even to the death fight for truth, and the Lord God will battle for you" (4:28).

Because the point of departure of this synergy is constituted by humankind's attitude toward the covenant and is the fruit of its free choice, Ben Sira can reaffirm the centrality of the law as the instrument of salvation.

Obedience to the law, in fact, makes the heart sound (cf. *Sir* 6:37), assures dominion over one's own thoughts (cf. 21:11), and even frees one from the destructive power of the "third tongue" (cf. 28:22). In short, the law is that "whip of thoughts," that "education of wisdom" (Gr. *paideia sophias*; 23:2a) that human beings so ardently implore as the only remedy to the evil manifestation of their own ambivalence.

> Son, from your youth embrace education [Gr. *paideia*],
> thus will you find wisdom [Gr. *sophia*] with graying hair. . . .
> Reflect on the precepts of the Lord,
> let His commandments be your constant meditation;
> then He will make your heart sound,
> and the wisdom you desire He will grant.
>
> (*Sir* 6:18, 37)

Hence Ben Sira attributes extraordinary importance to the learning of such an education (Gr. *paideia*; cf. *Sir* 6:32-36) and to the teaching function of the "wise man" (cf. 39:1-11). The words with which he takes leave of the reader are an appeal (perhaps to some degree a commercial) to come to his school willing to buy a richness "with much money" that is incomparably greater—salvation, which is "rest" and "reward," the supreme goal of all people.

> Come to me, you who need education,
> and take your place in my school! . . .
> Gain [wisdom], at no cost, for yourselves.
> Submit yourself to [her] yoke,
> let your souls bear [her] education [Gr. *paideia*];
> it is so easy to find her!
> See for yourselves! I labored but a little for her sake,
> and found great rest.
> Buy education [Gr. *paideia*] even with much money,
> you will win gold through it! . . .
> Do your work in due season,
> and in His own time [the Lord] will give you your reward.
>
> (*Sir* 51:23, 25b-28, 30)

On the other hand, those who transgress against the precepts and thus refuse the education of wisdom find themselves exposed, defenseless, and hopeless before the forces of evil: "If [the man] goes astray, [wisdom] will abandon him and deliver him into the hands of his ruin" (*Sir* 4:19; cf. 28:23). The decision to flee from evil or to fall victim to it is once again entrusted totally to human responsibility: "Do no evil, and evil will not overtake you; avoid wickedness and it will turn aside from you" (7:1-2).

4. THE FOUNDATION OF DIVINE RETRIBUTION: BETWEEN MERCY AND WRATH

The reaffirmation of human responsibility makes the principle of individual retribution plausible again. Its validity was so much discussed at that time that Ben Sira feels the need to affirm it more than once. Based on the covenant, God's justice punishes the impious and recompenses the righteous.

> The sinner will not escape with [his] plunder,
> and the righteous man's perseverance [Gr. *hypomonê*] will be not disappointed.
> [The Lord] will hold every righteous deed [Gr. *eleêmosynê*] in account,
> each will receive according to his own deeds.
> (*Sir* 16:13-14; cf. 2:8-10; 16:6-23; 35:10-23)

This insistence can well be linked to the internal criticisms of a theology of the covenant by *Job* and *Qohelet*, criticisms Ben Sira refutes with historical examples and personal experience. He has a much more insidious adversary before him, however, who is elaborating a different hypothesis of salvation that is entirely independent of the covenant, based instead on God's mercy. For Ben Sira this is another foolish impiety.

> Of [God's] forgiveness be not overconfident,
> adding sin upon sin;
> and say not: "Great is His mercy [Gr. *oiktirmos*],
> my many sins He will forgive."
> For mercy [Gr. *eleos*] and wrath [Gr. *orgê*] alike are with Him;
> upon the wicked will alight His anger.
> (*Sir* 5:5-6)

The question of the relationship between God's mercy and God's justice is thus posed very clearly. This question will be central to middle Judaism.[39] Perhaps the clearest formulation of the problem is found in *2 Baruch*, in which the apocalyptic author openly contests to God what seems to him an absurd behavior in the face of the misery of God's creatures.

> Hear your servant,
> and regard my appeal.
> For we are born in a short time,
> and in a short time we return. . . .
> Be, therefore, not angry at man because he is nothing;
> and do not take count of our works;

---

39. See G. Schrenk, "*dikaiosynê*," *TWNT* (esp. par. 4, "The Relationship between God's Punitive Justice and His Mercy"); and G. Boccaccini, "Il dibattito sul valore salvifico della Torah nel I sec.," in *Il dono della Torah*, ed. I. Gargano (Camaldoli, 1985), 112–20, and below, pp. 169–71, 217–20.

for what are we?
For behold, by your gift we come into the world,
and we do not go of our own will.
For we did not say to our parents: "Beget us,"
nor have we sent to the realm of death saying: "Receive us."
What therefore is our strength that we can bear Your wrath,
or what are we that can endure Your judgment?
Protect us in Your grace,
and in Your mercy help us.

(*2 Baruch* 48:11-18)

Second Baruch is a late apocalyptic document from the end of the first century C.E.[40] However, the tendency to separate distinctly God's mercy from God's justice is implicit in the apocalyptic tradition from its origins. From a viewpoint that accentuates the force of evil and at the same time limits human responsibility, God's punitive justice must have seemed a tragic joke and God's mercy the only hope for salvation.

At the beginning of the second century B.C.E. Ben Sira already tells us that the traditional balance has been broken; his is a difficult work of reconstitution. Certainly, he states, the God of Israel is "a merciful God, who forgives sins and saves in time of trouble" (*Sir* 2:11); God "sees and knows" the misery of humankind and therefore "multiplies His forgiveness" (18:12). This aspect of God, however, does not cancel the reality of judgment and the covenant, nor does it prevail over God's justice, which remains the measure of God's mercy.

Mercy [Gr. *eleos*] and wrath [Gr. *orgê*] are with [the Lord],
mighty when He forgives and when he alights His wrath.
Great as His mercy is His justice,
He will judge men, each according to his deeds.

(*Sir* 16:11-12)

---

40. On *2 Baruch*, see A. M. Ceriani, *Monumenta sacra et profana*, Vol 1.2 (Milan, 1866), 73–98 (Latin trans.), Vol. 5.2 (Milan, 1871), 113–80 (Syriac text); R. H. Charles, *The Apocalypse of Baruch* (London, 1896); V. Ryssel, *APAT* 2 (1900): 402–46 (German trans.); B.P. Grenfell and A. S. Hunt, *The Oxyrhynchus Papyri* (London, 1903 [Greek fragments]); M. Kmosko, "Liber Apocalypseos Baruch Filii Neriae," in *Patrologia Syriaca*, ed. R. Graffin, Vol. 1.2 (Paris, 1907), 1056–1305; R. H. Charles, *APOT* 2 (1913): 470–526 (English trans.); Riessler, *ASB* (1928), 55–113 [German trans.]; P.-M. Bogaert, *L'Apocalypse syriaque de Baruch*, 2 vols., SC 144–45 (Paris, 1969 [French trans.]); S. Dedering, "Apocalypse of Baruch," in *The Old Testament in Syriac*, ed. The Peshitta Institute of the University of Leiden, Vol. 4.3 (Leiden, 1973), 1–50 (Syriac text); A.F.J. Klijn, *JSHRZ* 5.2 (1976): 101–91 (German trans.); idem, *OTP* 1 (1983): 615–52 (English trans.); R. H. Charles (rev. L.H. Brockington), *AOT* (1984), 835–95 (English trans.); F. Leemhuis, A.F.J. Klijn, and G.J.H. van Gelder, *The Arabic Text of the Apocalypse of Baruch* (Leiden, 1986); J. Riaud, *BÉI* (1987), 1471–1557 (French trans.); and P. Bettiolo, *AAT* 2 (1989): 147–233 (Italian trans.).

5. FROM A NEW CONCEPTION
OF THE RIGHTEOUS TO A
NEW CONCEPTION OF JUDGMENT

The postulates of a theology of the covenant—namely, the freedom of human will and the retributory principle—having thus been reaffirmed, it becomes necessary to redefine the corollaries by solving the problems that *Job* and *Qohelet* have brought to light within the system.

Ben Sira speaks of the righteous and the wicked as two distinct groups of people (cf. *Sir* 13:17) and proclaims the blessedness of those who have no reason to reproach themselves (cf. 14:1-2). The force of evil, however, makes the existence of a righteous person without sin implausible, as already had been stated in *Qohelet* (cf. *Qoh* 7:20). This is true even independently of the individual's will: "A man can slip and not mean it; who has not sinned with his tongue?" (*Sir* 19:16). For human beings, sinning is practically inevitable; in collective experience it is even natural, almost physiological, like old age and death.

> Shame not a repentant sinner;
> remember, we are all guilty.
> Insult no man when he is old,
> for some of us, too, will grow old.
> Rejoice not when a man dies;
> remember, we are all to die.
>
> (*Sir* 8:5-7)

The problem of forgiveness and the atonement of sin becomes central. In the traditional framework of the "return to God" through repentance (cf. *Sir* 17:24-26; 18:21), prayer (cf. 21:1; 28:2), and sacrifice (cf. 7:31; 35:4-6), Ben Sira emphasizes in particular the expiatory value of observing the law. "Water quenches a flaming fire, and righteousness [Gr. *eleêmosynê*; Heb. *ṣdqh*] atones for sins" (3:30; cf. 3:3; 35:3). This is not a new given; even Ezekiel had affirmed that "if a wicked man turns away from all his sins which he has committed . . . and does what is lawful and right . . . none of the transgressions which he has committed shall be remembered against him; for the righteousness [Heb. *ṣdqh*] which he has done he shall live" (*Ezek* 18:21-22). In reality the similarity is only apparent. Ben Sira gives a completely different meaning to this idea, which he clarifies when speaking of the expiatory value of duties toward parents. The importance of this theme for the question of salvation is solemnly emphasized by the incipit of the discourse.

> Children, listen to me, your father;
> do so that you may be saved. . . .

He who honors his father atones for his sin;
he stores up riches who reveres his mother. . . .
For righteousness [Gr. *eleêmosynê*; Heb. *ṣdqh*] to a father will not be forgotten,
it will be counted in place of your sins;
in time of tribulation [it will be remembered in your favor],[41]
like warmth does upon frost, so your sins will be melted.

(*Sir* 3:1, 4-5, 14-15)

This passage represents a radical shift in the conception of the retributory principle from that expressed by Ezekiel, for whom merits could not be accumulated: "If the righteous man turns from the path of righteousness to do evil . . . none of his good deeds shall be remembered . . . he shall die" (*Ezek* 18:24). Ezekiel sees being righteous and being wicked as two distinct phases in the life of an individual; one is either righteous or wicked; the righteous can become wicked and the wicked can become righteous (cf. *Ezek* 18:1-32; 33:10-20). For Ben Sira the situation is obviously more nuanced because human beings are always and in every moment of their lives subject to sin. The relationship between good and bad deeds becomes the problem, and its resolution requires a reconceptualization of the retributory principle. For Ezekiel, the good deeds done before sinning shall be forgotten simply because they were done before. For Ben Sira, good and bad deeds shall not be forgotten because they are done together. The idea that a person's merits can somehow compensate for inevitable transgressions in the eyes of God is stated here for the first time in the history of Jewish thought.

This is a decisive step in the direction of the idea that God's judgment is carried out with measure and with mercy, just as it would be understood later in the Pharisaic-rabbinic tradition.[42] It is also significant that the premises for a new judgmental modality are stated independently of the conception of retribution after life by the necessity of redefining the "righteous." The experience of sin that inevitably marks a person's whole life does

41. An expression typical of biblical language is used in *Sir* 3:15a: God "remembers" sins in order to punish them and good works in order to pay them back (see W. Schottroff, "*zkr*," *THAT*). In the translation I have preferred to follow the Hebrew text, which expresses God's saving memory in humankind's favor through the passive form of the verb *zakar* ("to remember") followed by the *dativus commodi* (Heb. *tzkr lk*: "in your favor"), thus respecting the parallelism with the preceding verse: "Righteousness to a father will not be forgotten . . . it will be remembered in your favor." Faced with the difficulty of a literal translation, the translator of the Greek version chose to use the reflexive form: "[God] will remind Himself of you" (*Gr. anamnêsthêsetai sou*). The transformation of the *dativus commodi* in object genitive makes the phrase less effective, obscuring the real object of God's memory. The object is not generically the devoted son, but the works of justice he has done toward the father, works that in God's memory stand beside sins committed.

42. See P. Sacchi, "Retribuzione e giudizio fra ebraismo e cristianesimo," *RSLR* 9 (1973): 407-20; and below, pp. 217-20.

not compromise the possibility of being "righteous"; the "righteous" person is the person whose inevitable transgressions are compensated for by a multitude of good deeds.

6. THE JOY OF THE WICKED AND THE SUFFERING OF THE RIGHTEOUS

Job and *Qohelet* had also underlined the suffering of the righteous and the joy of the wicked as insupportable contradictions. Ben Sira does not deny the evidence but searches instead for a reason.

God's patience can easily explain the delay in punishing sinners and silence those who doubt the validity of the retributory principle: "Say not: 'I have sinned, yet what has befallen me?' for the Lord is patient" (*Sir* 5:4). God, in fact, is provident and merciful before the misery of creatures and continually renews the offer of salvation, delaying the moment of punishment and giving more and more opportunities for repentance to all.

> What is man? What is his utility?
> The good, the evil in him, what are these?
> The sum of a man's days
> is great if he reaches a hundred years.
> Like a drop of sea water, like a grain of sand,
> so are these few years among the days of eternity.
> That is why the Lord is patient with men
> and showers upon them His mercy.
> He sees and knows that their lot is grievous,
> and so He multiplies His forgiveness.
> Man may be merciful to his fellow man,
> but the Lord's mercy reaches all flesh.
> Reproving, admonishing, teaching,
> as a shepherd He guides His flock,
> merciful to those who accept His education [Gr. *paideia*],
> who are diligent in His decrees [Gr. *krimata*].
>   (*Sir* 18:8-14)

Even the suffering of the righteous must be understood within the terms of this divine pedagogy; just as God corrects and admonishes the sinners, God also tests the righteous to reinforce and confirm their righteousness.

> Wisdom instructs her children
> and takes care for those who seek her. . . .
> If one trusts her, he will possess her. . . .
> At first she perversely walks with him;
> fear and dread she brings upon him
> and tries him with her education [Gr. *en paideia autês*],

until she might trust his soul [Gr. *psychê*],
with her precepts she puts him to the proof [Gr. *peirazô*].
Then she makes him come back to the straight path
and makes him happy
and reveals her hidden things to him.

(Sir 4:1, 16-18)

The best possible response of the righteous to the test of suffering is, therefore, patience and perseverance in obeying the covenant. This perseverance is affirmed in Sir 2:1-14 as the principal virtue.

Son, when you come to serve the Lord,
prepare your soul [Gr. *psychê*] for trial [Gr. *eis peirasmon*]. . . .
Accept whatever befalls you,
in crushing misfortune be patient [Gr. *makrothymeô*],
for in fire gold is tested,
and worthy men in the crucible of humiliation. . . .
Woe to you who have lost perseverance [Gr. *hypomonê*]!
What will you do when the Lord visits you?

(Sir 2:1, 4-5, 14)

7. DEATH AND BEYOND DEATH

Ben Sira points out that before judging the life of anyone it is necessary to await the day of that person's death; it is only in death and its modalities that God's judgment is revealed in full.

For it is easy with the Lord on the day of death
to repay man according to his deeds.
A moment's affliction brings forgetfulness of past delights;
when a man dies, his life is revealed.
Call no man happy before his death,
for [by how he ends,] a man is truly known.[43]

(Sir 11:26-28; cf. 9:11-12)

For Ben Sira, death is a natural prospect that no one can avoid, fixed by God's relentless decree.

All flesh grows old, like a garment;
the covenant has been forever [Gr. *ap'aiônos*]: All must die.
As with the leaves that grow on a vigorous tree:
one falls off and another sprouts;

---

43. I have corrected v. 28b on the basis of the Hebrew text because the Greek ("for a man is truly known in his sons") makes no sense in the context of the passage.

so with the generations of flesh and blood:
one dies and another is born.
>   (*Sir* 14:17-18; cf. 38:22; 41:3-4a)

After death there is only *šeol*, the common destiny of all and the eternal
resting place of the dead. According to the traditional description, it is a
dark and sad place, far from God where there is no joy (cf. *Sir* 14:16;
17:27).[44] Any hypothesis of an afterlife, such as that already expressed within
Judaism through the doctrines of the immortality of the soul (cf. *Book of the
Watchers*) and resurrection (cf. *Apocalypsis of Isaiah*), is peremptorily refused;
from death "there is no return."

>   Son, shed tears for one who is dead . . .
>   then compose yourself after your grief. . . .
>   Turn not your heart to grief again,
>   turn it away, recall rather the end.
>   Forget not: there is no return;
>   you will not help the dead, but will do yourself harm. . . .
>   With the departed dead, let memory fade;
>   rally your courage, once the breath of life [Gr. *pneuma*] has left.
>   (*Sir* 38:16a, 17b, 20-21, 23)

It is thus understandable that every human being should view death with
anguish and dismay (cf. *Sir* 40:1-2). However, because of the link posed by
Ben Sira with the problem of retribution, death acquires a very different
importance for the righteous and for the wicked.[45]

For the sinner, death is a haunting, threatening presence that can intervene at any time and in any way to cancel an apparent happiness.

>   A man may become rich through privations and savings,
>   and this is his allotted reward:
>   when he says: "I have found rest,
>   now I will feast on my possessions,"
>   he does not know how long it will be,
>   till he dies and leaves them to others.
>   (*Sir* 11:18-19; cf. 40:3-10)

The prospect of being forgotten that condemns both the sinner and the
sinner's memory in death only accentuates the dramatic and resolute character that this inevitable appointment has for the impious.

>   Woe to you, O impious men,
>   who forsake the law of the Most High.

---

44. See E. Jacob, *Théologie de l'Ancient Testament*, 2d ed. (Neuchâtel, 1968), 243 (*Theology of
the Old Testament* [New York, 1958]).
45. On the ambivalent value of death in *Sirach*, see Prato, *Il problema della teodicea*, 332–63.

When you are born, you are born for curse;
when you die, you inherit curse.
Whatever is of earth returns to earth,
so too the impious from curse to destruction.
Men's mourning concerns their own bodies,
but the bad name of sinners will be annihilated.

(Sir 41:8-11; cf. 10:17; 16:4; 23:25-26)

The *memento mori*—the recurring reminder, You must die!—becomes one of the most characteristic elements in Ben Sira's parenesis, placing him at the beginning of a long and successful tradition of thought: "In whatever you do, remember your end, and you will never sin" (Sir 7:36; cf. 14:12; 18:24; 28:6).

The righteous person, on the other hand, can approach death with serenity and even with the hope of God's blessing: "He who fears the Lord will have a happy end, on the day of his death he will be blessed" (Sir 1:13). But death, even the *bona mors*, is not the last word for the righteous; a prospect of everlasting memory is opened up for them beyond death.

Happy is the man who takes care for wisdom. . . .
She will exalt him above his fellows;
in the assembly she will make him eloquent.
Joy and gladness he will find,
an everlasting name inherit.

(Sir 14:20a; 15:5-6; cf. 39:9-11)

In this way, Ben Sira goes decidedly beyond the limit of death in his discussion of retribution while remaining anchored to a system that excludes any hypothesis of life to come. The theme of the conservation of one's name as a reward for the righteous, corresponding to that of the *damnatio memoriae* for the wicked, is certainly not new to the Jewish tradition,[46] but here it receives singular emphasis. It is obvious that the boundaries of individual existence, so uncertain and fleeting, were by then felt to be too narrow for divine retribution to fulfill. The conservation of one's name is thus affirmed as the truest and most authentic reward for the righteous, better than any riches or even a long and happy life.

Have a care for your name, for it will endure for you
better than a thousand great precious treasures.
The days of a happy life are limited,
but a good name will endure forever.

(Sir 41:12-13)

46. See below, p. 231 n. 11.

Among the objections put forward by *Qohelet* in the name of experience, this is the only one for which Ben Sira denies all evidence, reproposing *sic et simpliciter* the traditional assumption. It is not true, he claims, that the righteous and the wicked share a common destiny in oblivion (cf. *Qoh* 2:16); on the contrary, the memory of the righteous lives in the people of Israel and continues to live from generation to generation.

The only significant correction that Ben Sira brings to the theme concerns the mechanisms of transmitting this memory. The traditional way— that it is entrusted to the sons (cf. *Sir* 30:4; 40:19)—is not always confirmed by experience; their birth and above all their righteousness are not at all guaranteed. Even the righteous cannot trust this traditional route.

> Desire not a brood of worthless children,
> or rejoice in wicked offspring.
> Many though they be, exult not in them
> if they have not the fear of the Lord.
> Count not on their [length of] life,
> have no hope in their number.
> For one can be better than a thousand;
> rather die childless than have wicked children!
> (*Sir* 16:1-3)

To overcome this obstacle, Ben Sira imposes an immediate link between the life of the individual and that of Israel; the memory of the righteous person is given a more concrete guarantee, anchored to collective memory.

> Limited are the days of one man's life,
> but the days of Israel are without number.
> The wise man will be honored among his people
> and his name will live forever.
> (*Sir* 37:25-26)

Ben Sira's insistence upon specifying and emphasizing the apparently marginal theme of the conservation of the name of the righteous reveals its importance in the economy of his thought, that is, in the difficult balance he is trying to reestablish between God's retributory justice and the objections raised by human experience. For Ben Sira the theme occupies the same delicate role that will later be held by the ideas of judgment after death and retribution in both the rabbinic and Christian traditions. The aporias of existence are solved by removing reward and punishment from experience's critical eye. Bringing this theme under discussion would prejudice the entire system, while the hope of future fulfillment, which escapes the immediate perception of the individual, validates the entire system. It is for this reason that Ben Sira's work is drawn to a close with a poem (*Sirach* 44–49) that even more than praising the "biblical heroes" praises the collective memory of Israel.

In the prologue to the poem (*Sir* 44:1-15), the selective capability of this memory is exalted. Not all of the many illustrious people celebrated in history and glorified by their contemporaries are conserved in memory.

> Rulers in their kingdoms,
> men of renown for their might,
> or counselors in their intelligence,
> or announcers in prophecy.
> Heads of peoples in their counsels,
> and in the intelligence of their decrees;
> wise words [were] in their education.
> Composers of melodious psalms,
> or discourses on lyric themes.
> Stalwart men, solidly established
> and at peace in their own estates.
> All they were glorious in their time,
> each illustrious in his day.
> Some of them have left behind a name
> that is still remembered to their praise;
> but of others there is no memory,
> they vanished as though they had never lived,
> they are as though they had never been,
> they and their children after them.
>
> (*Sir* 44:3-9)

The debate with *Qohelet* is once again direct; if there is unmerited glory, such as that even the wicked may know among their contemporaries (cf. *Qoh* 8:9-14), it does not bear time's examination. Only righteousness guarantees the conservation of the righteous' name forever; the conclusive evidence is given by the "biblical heroes," whose memory is still green in Israel and whose praises Ben Sira sings so proudly. These heroes

> were godly men,
> whose good deeds have not been forgotten;
> With their offspring there is
> a good heritage, their descendants.
> Their offspring are faithful to the covenants,
> the children thanks to their fathers.
> Their offspring will endure forever,
> and their glory will not be canceled.
> Their bodies were buried in peace,
> and their name will live from generation to generation.
> Peoples will tell their wisdom,
> and the assembly [of Israel] sing their praises.
>
> (*Sir* 44:10-15)

All the expressions of good wishes contained in this section are to be interpreted in this metaphorical yet extremely concrete sense and not as possible evidences of the idea of the resurrection of the righteous, as some scholars have claimed,[47] as the following passage about the judges of Israel demonstrates:

> The judges, too, each one of them,
> whose hearts were not deceived,
> who did not abandon the Lord:
> may their memory be as blessing,
> their bones bloom from their resting place again,
> and their names endure
> in the decendants of such glorious men!
> *(Sir* 46:11-12; cf. 49:10)

It is true that the step from a metaphorical conception of the resurrection, such as the conservation of the name, to a true conception of survival after death is short in the wisdom tradition (cf. *Wisdom of Solomon*). However, such an interpretation does not seem justified in Ben Sira, neither from the general economy of his thought nor from the particular context, in which the accent is clearly placed on the endurance of the name. Even the literary structure points to the fact that the protagonist of the "praise of the fathers" is the collective memory of Israel. After concluding the celebratory list of the principal biblical characters, from Adam to Nehemiah, with a brief summary *(Sir* 49:14-16), Ben Sira follows with the praises of a contemporary: "Simon the High Priest, son of Oniah" (see 50:1-21). This is not a random addition. True to its past, the memory of Israel knows no interruptions and its endurance becomes proof of the blessing promised to the righteous and a seal of the rediscovered validity of the principles of a theology of the covenant.

8. AT THE ORIGINS OF A LONG DEBATE

Ben Sira has the great merit of having reorganized a coherent theology of the covenant and of having done so at a particularly delicate moment, without fear of facing the suggestions of the apocalyptic tradition. Many of the solutions he proposed were destined to have a long life, others a more ephemeral one. The book's fortunes are paradoxical. Born with precise polemical intentions, it would prove most successful among the adversaries it was meant to fight (as demonstrated by the Essene redaction and its

---

47. See F. Saracino, "Resurrezione in Ben Sira?" *Henoch* 4 (1982): 185–203.

acquisition by Christianity), while it would be viewed with increasing suspicion by its closest heirs, who would not even think it worthy of being included in the rabbinic canon.

Ben Sira's theodicy lent itself easily to a dualistic reading. In the end, few interpolations were sufficient to deny the freedom of choice he had defended so strenuously because human nature did not appear already determined as good or bad for each individual.[48]

But even in its original formulation the idea that the whole of human being was subject to a radical ambivalence must have seemed to the rabbis to limit the individual's freedom too much. The rabbis preferred to circumscribe human inclinations toward good and evil in two distinct parts of human nature (the *yeṣer haraʿ* and the *yeṣer ṭob*).

I would not meet the aims of this investigation if I measured the value of this document in the light of subsequent ideological systems and not in terms of its specific role in the history of Jewish thought. In this dimension Ben Sira still has many things to say. The classic image of Ben Sira as a representative of the conservative wisdom tradition against advancing Hellenism[49] seems inadequate in expressing the complexity and novelty of his thought. He already fully belongs to middle Judaism, not only for chronological reasons but because the problems and tensions he interprets are the same ones around which the confrontation will develop in the following three centuries. Superimposed on the classic image of Ben Sira, another perhaps no less real image can be seen—that of an author who, in his accomplished attempt at a synthesis, is fully connected to the origins of the debate within Judaism that will impassion and divide generation after generation, leading finally to the great schism between Christians and Pharisees.

---

48. The interpolation of *Sir* 15:14b discussed above, p. 107 n. 30, is emblematic of this.

49. This is the prevalent image that emerges from the introductions. See O. Eissfeldt, *Einleitung in das Alte Testament* (Tübingen, 1943, 3d ed., 1964) (*The Old Testament: An Introduction*, trans. P. R. Ackroyd [Oxford and New York, 1965]); J. A. Soggin, *Introduzione all'Antico Testamento* (Brescia, 1968; 4th ed., 1987) (*Introduction to the Old Testament*, trans. J. Bowden [Louisville, 1989]); G.W.E. Nickelsburg, *Jewish Literature between the Bible and the Mishnah* (London, 1981), 55–65.

4

DANIEL AND
THE DREAM VISIONS

The Genre of Apocalyptic and the
Apocalyptic Tradition

1. APOCALYPSES AND APOCALYPTIC
TRADITION

A comparison between the *Book of Daniel*[1] and the so-called *Book of Dream Visions* (*1 Enoch* 83–90)[2] yields significant results. The documents are very nearly contemporary, both being dated to the first years of the Maccabean

1. On the *Book of Daniel*, see K. F. Friedrich, *Biblischer Commentar über den Propheten Daniel* (Leipzig, 1869) (*The Book of the Prophet Daniel*, trans. M. G. Easton [Edinburgh, 1872]); A. A. Bevan, *A Short Commentary on the Book of Daniel* (Cambridge, 1892); S. R. Driver, *The Book of Daniel* (Cambridge, 1900); K. Marti, *Das Buch Daniel* (Tübingen, 1901); W. Baumgartner, *Das Buch Daniel* (Giessen, 1926); J. A. Montgomery, *A Critical and Exegetical Commentary on the Book of Daniel* (Edinburgh, 1927; 3d ed., 1959); J. Goettsberger, *Das Buch Daniel* (Bonn, 1928); R. H. Charles, *A Critical and Exegetical Commentary on the Book of Daniel* (Oxford, 1929); A. Rahlfs, ed., *Septuaginta* (Stuttgart, 1935 [Greek versions: Septuagint and Theodotion]); J. Linder, *Commentarius in Librum Daniel* (Paris, 1939); G. Rinaldi, *Daniele* (Turin, 1947; 2d ed., 1962); C. Lattey, *The Book of Daniel* (Dublin, 1948); F. Nötscher, *Daniel* (Würzburg, 1948); J. Steinmann, *Daniel* (Paris, 1950); A. Bentzen, *Daniel* (Tübingen, 1952); J. Ziegler, *Susanna, Daniel, Bel et Draco* (Göttingen, 1954 [Greek version]); R. Augé, *Daniel* (Montserrat, 1954); H. Schneider, *Das Buch Daniel* (Freiburg, 1954); P. J. de Manasce, *Daniel* (Paris, 1954; 2d ed., 1958); E. W. Heaton, *The Book of Daniel* (London, 1956); J. Steinmann, *Daniel: Texte français, introduction et commentaires* (Bruges, 1961); R. E. Brown, *The Book of Daniel* (New York, 1962); O. Plöger, *Das Buch Daniel* (Gütersloh, 1965); N. W. Porteous, *Daniel* (Philadelphia, 1965; 2d ed., 1979); K. Elliger and W. Rudolph, eds., *Biblia Hebraica Stuttgartensia* (Stuttgart, 1967–77 [Hebrew-Aramaic text]); M. Delcor, *Le livre de Daniel* (Paris, 1971); J. Alonzo Díaz, *Daniel* (Madrid, 1971); L. Wood, *Commentary on Daniel* (Grand Rapids, 1973); G. Bernini, *Daniele* (Rome, 1975); R. Hammer, *The Book of Daniel* (Cambridge, 1976); A. Lacocque, *Le livre de Daniel* (Neuchâtel, 1976) (*The Book of Daniel*, trans. D. Pellauer [Atlanta, 1979]); L. Alonso Schökel, M. I. Gonzales, and J. Mateos, *Daniel* (Madrid, 1976); J. J. Collins, *The Apocalyptic Vision of the Book of Daniel* (Missoula, Mont., 1977); L. F. Hartmann and A. A. Di Lella, *The Book of Daniel* (Garden City, 1978); A. Lacocque, *Daniel et son temps: Recherches sur le mouvement apocalyptique juif au IIe siècle avant Jésus-Christ* (Geneva, 1983) (*Daniel in His Time* [Columbia, S.C., 1988]); W. S. Towner, *Daniel* (Atlanta, 1984); and J. J. Collins, *Daniel: With an Introduction to Apocalyptic Literature* (Grand Rapids, 1984).

2. On the *Book of Dream Visions*, see the works cited above, pp. 78–79 n. 5.

revolt (ca. 164 B.C.E.). They are written in related styles, to a large extent share the same conceptual framework, and substantially answer the same questions. A comparative analysis is thus doubly valuable. First, it brings to light the problems then emerging in Jewish thought, not least of all the resistance to or shattering of the system painfully constructed only a few years earlier by Ben Sira,[3] in the face of the deep crisis (more internal than external) experienced by Judaism during the period of the Maccabean revolt. Second, by examining the answers given to commonly addressed questions, it allows us to determine whether *Daniel* and the *Dream Visions* belong to the same tradition of thought or take different sides, that is, whether they are complementary or heatedly opposed to one another.

The need for such an analysis may seem paradoxical. Are we not considering two of the best-known "apocalypses"? Is not the *Dream Visions* an integral part of the apocalyptic *1 Enoch*? Is not *Daniel*, if not the prototype of every apocalypse, at least the apocalyptic book par excellence of the Hebrew Bible?[4] The term "apocalyptic" seems to define the two documents, even from an ideological point of view. It gives the impression of a well-defined system and therefore seems to offer clear connotations and precise points of reference for the thoughts of the two documents. But is this really the case, or is this just a misleading set of presuppositions? The very liveliness of today's debate on the definition of "apocalyptic"[5] justifies the need for reassessment.

The designation "apocalyptic" was coined in modern times to categorize intuitively a vaguely defined group of middle Jewish texts, which share the same peculiar genre with *Revelation*—so much so as to be named for its incipit (*Apokalypsis Iêsou Christou . . .*). Lack of critical reflection has allowed these texts to be presented as a homogeneous corpus, which appears only in need of some a posteriori reasoning to legitimize its obvious uniqueness. Meanwhile, detached from any precisely defined contents, the term "apocalyptic" has taken on a life of its own, acquiring many and varied meanings in historical criticism and even in common language. The problem thus

---

3. For the frequent references to the *Book of Sirach* and its ideology, see chap. 3.

4. See O. Eissfeldt, *Einleitung in das Alte Testament* (Tübingen, 1943, 3d ed., 1964) (*The Old Testament: An Introduction*, trans. P. R. Ackroyd [Oxford and New York, 1965]); J. A. Soggin, *Introduzione all'Antico Testamento* (Brescia, 1968; 4th ed., 1987) (*Introduction to the Old Testament*, trans. J. Bowden [Louisville, 1989]); G.W.E. Nickelsburg, *Jewish Literature between the Bible and the Mishnah* (London, 1981).

5. See D. Hellholm, ed., *Apocalypticism in the Mediterranean World and the Near East: Proceedings of the International Colloquium on Apocalypticism (Uppsala, August 12–17, 1979)* (Tübingen, 1983).

becomes one of bringing a name back into a precise hermeneutic framework, a name that today may seem cumbersome but that we cannot do without. What exactly is "apocalyptic"? Is it literary form and nothing else, as the late J. Carmignac claimed? A form that ties together a well-defined complex of ideas, as put forward by J. J. Collins? A tradition of thought consistently expressed by the "apocalypses," as P. Vielhauer and K. Koch have tried to demonstrate with varying results? Or is it even something else?[6]

There is no doubt that *Revelation* indicates the existence of a particular literary form within the literature of middle Judaism. Following convention, we can continue to call this literary genre "apocalyptic," and the documents written in this form "apocalypses." We can also agree with Collins in seeing in this literary genre a linkage of a certain complex of ideas. Analysis of the frequency of the most recurrent themes in the apocalypses shows that the apocalyptic form is the expression of a wide cultural phenomenon spread well beyond the confines of Israel. The apocalypses witness not only a form but a content; they are the vehicles of a definitive world view.[7]

We can therefore legitimately define and delimit on a formal basis a literary corpus within Jewish literature (the "apocalypses") and catalogue the ideas related to this corpus, even the related world view (Collins's "apocalypticism"). However, a fundamental question remains: Is this apocalyptic corpus also the expression of a single tradition of thought or have authors of various traditions of thought used the same literary genre to express their various convictions?

The presence of some recurring themes, even the same themes, is not sufficient to identify a tradition of thought. Not only can an identical form be used by different traditions but identical ideas (even the same world view) can assume a different meaning (a role, a specific weight) in different contexts. This is well stated by E. P. Sanders, who writes: "One may consider the analogy of two buildings. Bricks which are identical in shape, color, and weight could well be used to construct two different buildings which are

---

6. See J. J. Collins, *The Apocalyptic Imagination: An Introduction to the Jewish Matrix of Christianity* (New York, 1984); J. Carmignac, "Qu'este-ce que l'apocalyptique? Son emploi à Qumrân," *RQ* 10 (1979): 3–33; P. Vielhauser, "Apocalypses and Related Subjects," in *New Testament Apocrypha*, ed. E. Hennecke and W. Schneemelcher (Philadelphia, 1965), 2:581–607; K. Koch, *Ratlos vor der Apokalyptik* (Gütersloh, 1970) (*The Rediscovery of Apocalyptic: A Polemical Work on a Neglected Area of Biblical Studies and Its Damaging Effects on Theology and Philosophy*, trans. M. Kohl [London, 1972]); and K. Koch and J. M. Schmidt, *Apokalyptic* (Darmstadt, 1982).

7. See Collins, *Apocalyptic Imagination*.

totally unlike each other."[8] Two documents do not necessarily belong to the same tradition of thought simply because they share the same literary genre and even the same world view. An ideological affinity exists only if the authors have consciously organized and developed their thoughts out of the same generative idea. Therefore, we can and must ask ourselves whether an "apocalyptic" tradition of thought exists and, if it does, what its generative idea might be and what relationship it has with the apocalyptic literary genre.

The possibility of a comparative analysis of the apocalyptic and the various movements of middle Judaism (Essenism, Pharisaism, early Christianity, and so forth) depends on the answers to these questions. To be correct, such an analysis must only be made between commensurable units, that is, between sets defined according to homogeneous criteria. If apocalyptic is only a literary genre (albeit, one with its own definite world view), it can be compared only with the other forms of middle-Jewish literature, such as poetry, testament, halakah, midrash, and hymns, each with its own definite world view. At most we could ask why a certain movement of thought tends to prefer one or another literary genre, that is, one or another world view. But only an apocalyptic tradition defined according to ideological criteria—if such a tradition exists—can be compared to other ideological traditions of middle Judaism. Early Christianity, Pharisaism, and Essenism are not phenomena defined according to literary criteria.

The studies of P. Sacchi on *1 Enoch* opened the way for a coherent solution.[9] His primary reference to the *Pentateuch of Enoch* is not at all arbitrary. *First Enoch* is a collection of five books (six, if we consider the removed *Book of Giants*). Through a consistent system of literary connections, allusions, and quotations, each book consciously refers to the preceding one(s). Their compilation, from the *Book of the Watchers* (and its archetype, the *Book of Noah*) to the *Book of the Similitudes*, covers a vast span of time—from the fifth

---

8. E. P. Sanders, *Paul and Palestinian Judaism* (London, 1977), 13. This quotation from Sanders does not mean that I agree with all aspects of his methodology.

9. See P. Sacchi, "'Il Libro dei Vigilanti e l'apocalittica," *Henoch* 1 (1979): 42–92; idem, "Riflessioni sull'essenza dell'apocalittica: peccato d'origine e libertà dell' uomo," *Henoch* 5 (1983): 31–58; idem, "L'apocalittica del I sec.: Peccato e giudizio," in *Correnti culturali e movimenti religiosi del Giudaismo: Atti del V Congresso dell'AISG (S. Miniato, 12–15 Nov. 1984)*, ed. Associazione Italiana per lo Studio del Giudaismo (Rome, 1987), 59–77; and idem, *L'apocalittica giudaica e la sua storia* (Brescia, 1990). Sacchi's research has been supported by a group of his collaborators, principally L. Rosso Ubigli and myself, and has caused the emergence of an Italian school. See G. Boccaccini, "Jewish Apocalyptic Tradition: The Contribution of Italian Scholarship," in *Mysteries and Revelations: Apocalyptic Studies since the Uppsala Colloquium*, ed. J. J. Collins and J. H. Charlesworth (Sheffield, 1991), 38–58.

or fourth century B.C.E. to the first century C.E. The constant reconstitution of these works into one book testifies in itself to the active and conscious presence of an uninterrupted ideological tradition in the history of Jewish thought. It is certainly a complex and dynamic trend of thought, with its own developments and deepenings, and therefore cannot be fit entirely into a unitary scheme or a univocal definition. But in spite of all the differences, its core can be identified in a peculiar conception of evil, understood as an autonomous reality antecedent even to humanity's ability to choose, the fruit of "a contamination that has spoiled [human] nature . . . and was produced before the beginning of history."[10] This conception of evil is not simply one among many ideas put forth in one of many books belonging to the apocalyptic literary genre: it is the generative idea of a distinct ideological tradition, the cornerstone on which and out of which the whole apocalyptic tradition is built.

We do not know what this tradition was called or what it called itself in ancient times. The fact that a large number of the apocalypses (*2 Baruch* and *4 Ezra*, for example) can be identified with this tradition, not to mention the weight of (ab)use that has given an ideological sense as well to the traditional term, authorizes Sacchi's designation of this current of thought as "apocalyptic." I do not mean that the apocalyptic literary genre and the apocalyptic tradition are coincident nor that this apocalyptic is a sort of subgroup of the apocalyptic literary corpus. The documents belonging to the apocalyptic tradition are neither all nor only apocalypses. The composite and multiform structure of the *Pentateuch of Enoch* shows how the apocalyptic tradition is expressed historically through different literary genres. Conversely, some of the major apocalypses share different (if not opposite) traditions of thought with documents written in other literary genres. The most striking (and most paradoxical) example is *Revelation*, which ideologically is undoubtedly a Christian document, the expression of a Judaism different from yet related to that of *1 Enoch*. How is it possible to think of *Revelation* and the *Book of Similitudes* as belonging to the same ideological movement? For the former the "Son of man" is Jesus of Nazareth (cf. *Rev* 1:12-18); for the latter that eschatological figure is Enoch (cf. *1 Enoch* 71:14).[11]

Describing a literary genre, a world view, and a tradition of thought (three distinct and nonoverlapping categories) by the term "apocalyptic"

---

10. Sacchi, "Riflessioni," 57.

11. On the identification of the "Son of man" with Enoch, as the fruit of a first-century apocalyptic interpolation of the *Book of the Similitudes*, see L. Fusella and P. Sacchi, *AAT*, 1:571–72; and J. H. Charlesworth, *The Old Testament Pseudepigrapha and the New Testament* (Cambridge, 1985), 18.

may appear to be a careless use of terminology. Another label could be chosen, of course. However, the problem is not terminological; it deals with method. Terms may be interchangeable; hermeneutic categories such as literary genre, world view, and tradition of thought are not. The call for a better methodological clarity in the study of apocalyptic remains valid, whatever labels we decide to use in cataloging the different aspects of this complex phenomenon.

The clear distinction between the formal (and form-content) level and the ideological level represents an essential spur to a greater hermeneutic clarity. It points out the danger of an insidious confusion inherent in the common use of the term "apocalyptic" and helps us to avoid the inappropriate comparison of incommensurable sets, such as that of an intuitively defined apocalyptic corpus (which we later find to be apocalyptic only in a formal sense) with "other" movements of middle Judaism.

The association of a document with the apocalyptic ideological tradition, as indicated and defined in the studies of Sacchi, must be weighed critically, not on the basis of its literary form or the complex of ideas it expresses but solely on the basis of a comprehensive examination of its thought. Even the ideological affinity imposed by common opinion among the apocalypses, and therefore between the *Book of Daniel* and the *Book of Dream Visions*, cannot be taken for granted but should be verified only when the ideological traits of each apocalypse have been independently defined.

Today the *Book of Daniel* is part of both the rabbinic and Christian canons; the *Book of Dream Visions*, on the other hand, is a pseudepigraphon that several times was going to be included in the Christian canons and owes its conservation to the Ethiopian church. A comparative investigation will tell us if the diverse destinies of the two books are random or should be read as the clue to an ideological difference perceived by the ancients with an immediateness that is not so obvious to us.

2. THE *BOOK OF DREAM VISIONS* IN THE APOCALYPTIC TRADITION

The *Book of Dream Visions* belongs undoubtedly to the apocalyptic tradition. Above all its conscious placement in the Enochic pentateuch (*1 Enoch*) witnesses to this. The *Book of Dream Visions* is even formally linked to the other documents in the *Book of Enoch*, practically continuing without interruption the first-person narration of the preceding chapters, which belong to the *Book of Astronomy*. The protagonist, Enoch, appears on the scene as a character already known; a few verses (*1 Enoch* 83:1-2) are sufficient to introduce the two visions, or dreams, that constitute the body of the work. The first vision (83:3—84:6) deals specifically with the flood; the second (chaps. 85–90), more ample and characterized by a rich symbology drawn from the animal world, offers a comprehensive framework for the history of humanity, from Adam and Eve to the eschatological reign.

This attention to the historical dimension markedly distinguishes the *Dream Visions* from the preceding tradition. The ahistoric "world of the spirit," where the battle between good and evil is played out in the *Book of the Watchers*, disappears and with it the idea of the immortality of the soul. History ceases to be a pale reflection of the world beyond and regains its concreteness; the future and not the spirit is the site of the eschaton, of judgment and salvation.[12]

Even in this radical shift of perspective, the idea that the angels' sin is the cause of the spread of evil on earth remains the central idea. Evidently, more than any other element (content, form), this is enough to guarantee ideological continuity. Thus, in the first vision Enoch explains the manifestation of God's wrath and with it the sense of history: "The angels of your heavens are now committing sin, and your wrath shall rest upon the flesh of the people until the great day of judgment" (*1 Enoch* 84:4).

This "sin" is historically specified in its various stages in the second vision, in which the author first speaks of the devil's sin ("a star fell down from heaven"; *1 Enoch* 86:1) and later dwells on the sin of the angels with the "daughters of men." We know well this second episode from the *Book of the Watchers*; traces of it are also preserved in the Bible (see *Gen* 6:1-4). In the *Dream Visions*, the sexual union of angels and women is crudely described:

> I kept observing, and behold, I saw all of them extending their sexual organs like horses and commencing to mount upon the heifers, the bovids; and [the latter] all became pregnant and bore elephants, camels, and donkeys. (*1 Enoch* 86:4)

The insistence on the modality of the angelic sin (see also *1 Enoch* 87:3; 90:21) is not without meaning: through the sexual union evil not only penetrated into human nature and contaminated it but it continues to be transmitted from generation to generation.[13] Neither the intervention of the good angels—who reduce the rebels to impotence (see *1 Enoch* 87–88)—nor

---

12. For the development of apocalyptic thought from the *Book of the Watchers* through the *Book of Dream Visions*, see Sacchi, *L'apocalittica giudaica e la sua storia*.

13. On the morally negative value attributed to sexual impurity in middle Judaism, see L. Rosso Ubigli, "Alcuni aspetti della concezione della 'porneia' nel tardo-giudaismo," *Henoch* 1 (1979): 201–45.

the flood (see 89:2-8) can eradicate evil from the earth. Evil descendants are bound to arise, even from the holy survivors. From Noah, "the snow-white cow which became a man" (i.e., like the angels), are born "three cows," but

> one of those three cows was snow-white, similar to that [first] cow [Shem], and one red like blood [Japheth], and one black [Ham]. . . . They began to bear the beasts of the fields and the birds. There arose out of them many [different] species. (*1 Enoch* 89:9-10)

In like manner Abraham,

> the snow-white cow which was born in their midst begat a wild ass [Ishmael], and a snow-white cow with it [Isaac]; and the wild asses multiplied. And that cow which was born from him bore a black wild boar [Esau] and a snow-white sheep [Jacob]; the former then bore many wild boars and the latter bore twelve sheep. (*1 Enoch* 89:11-12)

History thus witnesses a continuous expansion of evil, with no way for human beings to oppose its spread. Even the nature of the "elect" was changed: in the span of time from Adam to Jacob, from "cows" they became "sheep."

The vision continues going over the various episodes of biblical history in great detail: slavery in Egypt, the exodus, the conquest of Palestine, the monarchy, and so on. Without doubt the most striking element of this narration is the absence of any reference to the covenant. The march through the desert is described in detail, including Moses' ascent of Mount Sinai (see *1 Enoch* 89:29-33), but no reference is made to the alliance. In all evidence we find a context radically different from that of a theology of the covenant. In fact, the idea of the covenant presupposes a recognition of human freedom of choice between obedience and transgression. Even if this freedom is not explicitly denied, in the *Dream Visions* it appears gravely compromised; humankind, more than being responsible for evil, is its victim. Above all, in this perspective the idea that human beings can be responsible authors of their own salvation is unthinkable. Only God's intervention can oppose evil. The ideal of the righteous person who fulfills the law is replaced by the figure of the elect who is chosen and justified by God.

After Babylonian exile the situation collapses; God entrusts God's people to "seventy shepherds" (angels), who show themselves to be evil, trespassing upon their assigned tasks in such a way that the entire history of Israel in the post-exilic period unfolds under a demonic influence (see *1 Enoch* 89:59ff.). God's response is limited to watching the dramatic succession of events and assigning the task of checking the work of the "seventy shepherds"—to write down and to relate to God their actions—to one of God's angels (who has the characteristics of Michael, although not mentioned by name). The task, however, excludes any direct intervention:

Do not reveal them [what they should do], neither admonish them, but write down every destruction caused by the shepherds—for each and every one in his appointed time—and elevate all of it to Me. (*1 Enoch* 89:64)

History thus follows its course until the final catharsis when God intervenes and pronounces judgment, eliminating the guilty and offering to the elect of every race and nation the prospect of eternal salvation in a world totally purified of evil ("they had all become gentle and returned to God's house"; *1 Enoch* 90:33). God's wrath can thus be laid down (90:34) and the Messiah, "a snow-white cow . . . with huge horns" (90:37), prototype of a new humanity, is called to rule the eschatological reign. The circle closes; the elect return from "sheep" to being "cows."

I went on seeing until all their kindred were transformed, and became snow-white cows; and the first among them [the Messiah] became something [new], and that something was a great beast with huge black horns on its head. The Lord of the sheep rejoiced over them and over all the cows. (*1 Enoch* 90:38)

3. THE IDEOLOGICAL UNITY AND COMPOSITIVE SCHEME OF THE *BOOK OF DANIEL*

A definition of *Daniel* from an ideological standpoint appears quite problematic. We have before us a complex document that presents a unique structure, a composite both in language (part Hebrew and part Aramaic) and in literary genre (apocalyptic visions alternate with edifying stories, prayers, and so forth). Furthermore, it is commonly accepted that some sections have their own "prehistory," that is, they are the fruit of a tradition that brings a vast wealth of material together around the name of Daniel, more than is collected in the *Book of Daniel* (see the so-called apocryphal additions to the Greek version).

This explains the uncertainty with which commentators approach the scheme of composition of the book. This problem is not without consequences from the ideological viewpoint because it implicates the existence or the lack of a unitary project of composition. The traditional distinction, reaffirmed in the most recent introductions, between *Daniel* A (stories of the Diaspora; *Daniel* 1–6) and *Daniel* B (apocalyptic visions; *Daniel* 7–12) makes sense on a formal level, and perhaps also on a chronological level, but does not at all resolve the problem of their having been placed together. Instead, it tends to exclude any reciprocal relationship aside from the reference to the same protagonist, so that even the ideology of the book risks being resolved (or better, dissolved) in the ideologies of the two separate parts.

Yet there is something that makes *Daniel* a profoundly unitary work and shows that its presentation as a collection of passages written in different periods with different ideological intentions is inadequate.[14] More than the presence of a few recurring themes, the juxtaposition of the parts to form a whole appears too coherent to be due to chance. There are, in fact, precise thematic connections between chapters 2 and 7 (the succession of the four kingdoms), chapters 3 and 6 (Daniel's experience in the lions' den repeats that of his three friends in the fiery furnace), chapters 4 and 5 (God punishes the kings' pride), and chapters 8 and 10–12 (the characteristics and duration of the fourth kingdom). Therefore, excluding the first chapter, which functions as an introduction, *Daniel* is constituted of two sections (chaps. 2–7 and chaps. 8–12), whose parts are disposed symmetrically around chapters 4–5 and chapter 9.

This hypothesis has unquestionable merits. First, it allows us to establish an identity between the book's scheme of composition and its linguistic structure, making sense of the unresolved problem of its bilingualism. Second, it decisively shifts the accent from the "prehistory" of the single parts to the unity of the composition project, the context that brings the parts together and gives them meaning. The scholars that have held this hypothesis, however, have only been able to exhibit formal evidence in its favor.[15] The hypothesis has thus remained sterile, its hermeneutic potential not well exploited. However, I believe the chiastic structure of the document is perfectly functional for the unitary ideological project carried out by its author.

In my investigation of *Daniel* I will let myself by guided by two reference points. The first, "external" to the document, has already been mentioned—the comparison with the contemporary *Book of Dream Visions*. The other, equally important, is "internal"—the coherence of the scheme of composition. On these bases I believe it is possible to offer a comprehensive presentation of the principal lines of thought in *Daniel* and, therefore, to answer the question of its apocalyptic nature.

4. ENOCH AND DANIEL:
THE KNOWLEDGE OF THE MEDIATOR

A comparison between *Daniel* and the *Dream Visions* can well begin with an analysis of the respective protagonists, Daniel and Enoch, focusing on their personal traits and clarifying the nature of their knowledge.

---

14. A similar critical formulation is found in J. G. Gammie, "The Classification, Stages of Growth and Changing Intentions in the Book of Daniel," *JBL* 95 (1976): 191–204; and Nickelsburg, *Jewish Literature between the Bible and the Mishnah*.

15. See A. Lenglet, "La structure littéraire de Daniel 2–7," *Bib* 53 (1972): 169–90; and Bernini, *Daniele*.

Practically nothing is said of Enoch except that he knew how to write (this concerns his ability to receive and transmit the revelation; cf. *1 Enoch* 83:2) and that he was not yet married (this regards his pure status in a context that, as we have seen, assigns a fundamental role to sexual activity in the spread of evil; cf. *1 Enoch* 83:2; 85:3). In either case, his personal righteousness is not involved. The apocalyptic mediator is not chosen for his merits; the knowledge imparted to him is a gratuitous act of illumination on God's part.

Daniel, on the other hand, is presented as a "wise" man who has received (or won) the gift of divine wisdom in virtue of his faithfulness to the covenant (*Daniel* 1). He is a Jew in the court of Nebuchadnezzar, the king of Babylonia, and, unlike most of his companions, he refuses to "defile himself with the king's food or the wine from his table" (*Dan* 1:8), asking "vegetables to eat and water to drink" (1:12) in order to avoid breaking the dietary laws. To Daniel, and to the three youths who followed his example (Hananiah, Mishael, Azariah), as recompense "God gave . . . learning and skill in all letters *and wisdom* [Heb. *ḥkmh*]; and Daniel had understanding in all visions and dreams" (1:17). In short, Daniel is not made a mediator because he is of the elect, but because he is righteous.

The relationship between obedience to the covenant and knowledge is resolved, therefore, according to the scheme already formulated in the wisdom tradition in the *Book of Sirach*. Knowledge of the "hidden things" must be a gift from God, but such illumination is granted only to the worthy, those who merit it through faithfulness to the covenant ("If you desire wisdom, keep the commandments; and the Lord will bestow her upon you"; *Sir* 1:26; cf. 6:37; 21:11).

Thematically, this is the meaning of the episode placed as the introduction to *Daniel*. It can also be read as an edifying story directed at the Jews of the Diaspora. However, in the ecology of the book it plays a more specific role: to present the figure of Daniel as righteous and to clarify the limits of his knowledge, bringing the apocalyptic illumination back into the sphere of a theology of the covenant. The first chapter provides, in substance, the key to reading the book, the frame of reference for both Daniel's cognitive experiences and the continuous reminders that wisdom is the property and gift of God.

Without doubt, the period in which *Daniel* was written was one thirsty for knowledge, but also one for which knowledge had assumed a complexity unknown to preceding generations. Knowledge had lost any immediateness. In fact, the cognitive process in *Daniel* consists of two sharply distinct phases: God's revelation is not complete if it is not followed by God's gift of its interpretation.

The revelation comes in different modalities: sometimes in a dream (*Dan* 2:1; 4:2; 7:1), sometimes in a vision (8:1; 12:5), once in a miraculous apparition (5:5), in a written word (9:2), and in a prophetic word (10:1). It is not always Daniel who receives the revelation; other people are or have been the repository: Nebuchadnezzar (2:1; 4:2); his son Belteshazzar, along with his dignitaries, wives, and concubines (5:5); and the prophet Jeremiah (9:2).

An element common to each revelation is its incomprehensibility; the revelation remains obscure if God does not also reveal its hidden meaning. The passage from the phase of revelation to that of interpretation is emphasized in the narrative structure by a "space of time" (*Dan* 2:16). In the face of the incomprehensible there is disturbance and fear; even Daniel does not seem able to understand immediately the meaning of the revelation, and his desire for knowledge pushes him to supplication and penitence (cf. *Dan* 2:16-18; 4:16; 7:15-16; 8:15; 9:3; 10:2-3; 12:8).

This "space of time" between revelation and interpretation exalts God's further intervention of illumination, through which the gift of wisdom is given and by which the righteous person is turned into a mediator. Daniel is the unique and absolute protagonist of this second decisive phase, a phase that usually comes through a dream (cf. *Dan* 2:19; 7:17ff.; 8:16ff.) or through a vision (cf. 9:21ff.; 10:1, 5ff.; 12:9ff.). If other people may receive the revelation, join Daniel in supplication to God (cf. 2:17-18), and be present at the moment of the interpretive vision (cf. 10:7), God gives the fullness of knowledge only to Daniel. And it is only through Daniel that the hidden meaning of the revelation is publicly unveiled (cf. 2:24ff.; 4:16ff.; 5:17ff.) or jealously kept, "sealed" in writing, "for the last days" (cf. 7:1, 28; 8:27; 12:4, 9).

As an object of an illumination and instrument of its transmission, Daniel plays a role that is certainly analogous to that of the apocalyptic mediator. Thanks to *Daniel* 1, however, the reader knows that Daniel's election is due to his righteousness. In Daniel's election the reader sees an explicit example of the synergetic relationship that, in its ideological horizon, links humankind to God—as in the terms already delineated by Ben Sira.

This complex cognitive scheme, here synthesized only in its essential outline (revelation → space of time → interpretation), repeats itself constantly in *Daniel*, although with different emphases and developments (cf. *Daniel* 2; 4–5; 7; 8; 9; 10:1—12:4; 12:5-13).

In chapter 2, King Nebuchadnezzar receives a revelation in a dream. He is deeply disturbed (v. 1) and commands the wise men of his court ("the

> I, Daniel, had seen the vision and sought to understand it. . . . And on the Ulai
> I heard a man's voice that cried out and said, "Gabriel, explain the vision to
> this man." (*Dan* 8:15-16)

The affirmation of a new cognitive model necessarily poses the problem for the author of also readapting the past cognitive models—first and foremost the prophetic model, which is at the base of most Scripture—to the new one in which revelation and interpretation are no longer coincident.

The relationship between knowledge and Scripture constitutes the theme of *Daniel* 9. God has spoken to the prophet Jeremiah; the exile will last "seventy years" (v. 2). Daniel is engaged in trying to understand "in the books" the meaning of this prophecy, an attempt that appears to be beyond his ability. He turns to God in prayer and fasts (vv. 2-20) and the angel Gabriel comes to him in a vision ("I have now come to make you understand all"; v. 22). The angel emphasizes that the interpretation is inseparably linked to the "word" of Jeremiah: "Consider the word and understand the vision" (v. 23).

Between knowledge and Scripture there is a deep bond; the wisdom knowledge is not foreign to the Torah, it is its interpretation. The books cannot unveil the hidden meaning, however, which remains a gift from God. Ben Sira resolved the relationship between wisdom and the law in the same way, including rather than identifying the law in wisdom's project, affirming at the same time the Torah and its incompleteness, the superiority of divine illumination and its role as complement to Scripture.

Daniel 10 clarifies the way in which prophetic knowledge must be interpreted. The story is introduced by a characteristic formula of prophetic language: "a word was revealed to Daniel" (v. 1). But the prophetic word is not enough, it requires interpretation. Daniel is aware of this and does penitence "for three weeks" (vv. 2-3), until he receives divine illumination in a vision. The text is forced to follow a tortuous turn of phrases:

> A word was revealed to Daniel. . . . And the word was true. . . . He sought to
> understand the word and had understanding through a vision. (*Dan* 10:1)

In conclusion, even if Daniel, as a righteous man, has different traits from those of the apocalyptic mediator, he is not the wise man who solves enigmas (like Joseph in *Genesis*), the prophet who speaks the word of God (like Jeremiah), or the scribe whom God's gift of wisdom enables to interpret Scripture through his studies (like Ben Sira). The immediateness of their knowledge is replaced by the necessary mediation between divine revelation and its interpretation, which Daniel develops out of the wisdom cognitive model affirmed by Ben Sira at the beginning of the second century B.C.E.

5. THE SENSE OF HISTORY

In *Daniel* we find the same degenerative conception of history that we have seen in the *Dream Visions*, as well as the same anticipation of the eschatological reign; however, these elements do not have the same meaning for the two authors.

The entire course of history is revealed to Enoch, from the creation until the eschatological reign. History is a drama that unfolds with humankind as both protagonist and victim. "All of the men's deeds were shown to me, each in all of their parts" (*1 Enoch* 90:41), states Enoch at the book's conclusion. The explanation of everything that has happened, is happening, and will happen is contained in the *Book of Dream Visions*, which explains the origin of evil, sets the limits of human freedom, and indicates the characteristics of future salvation.

The idea of causality within the unfolding of history corresponds to the apocalyptic idea of a world corrupted by an original sin. For *Dream Visions* this sin effects its degenerative action in the succession of increasingly iniquitous kingdoms up until the cathartic intervention of God.

This concept appears completely extraneous to the author of *Daniel*, who organizes his thought, as well as the literary structure of the book, around two fundamental ideas: first, sovereignty belongs to God, who grants it and revokes it according to God's will and established times (chaps. 2–7); second, the cause of history's degeneration is the breaking of the covenant, which has brought down upon the people the curse contained therein (chaps. 8–12). Because of their chiastic structure, I will begin the analysis of the two sections with their central nuclei (chaps. 4–5; chap. 9).

In *Daniel* 4–5, the affirmation of God's absolute sovereignty ("His dominion is an everlasting dominion, and His kingdom endures from generation to generation"; *Dan* 4:31; cf. 3:33; 4:23) runs parallel to the affirmation of God's supreme control in granting sovereignty to kings, even gentile kings ("the Most High rules over the kingdom of men, and gives it to whom He will"; *Dan* 4:14, 22, 29; cf. 5:21). The power exercised by God is absolute and unquestionable: neither human beings nor angels can oppose it.

> All the inhabitants of the earth are accounted as nothing; and He does according to His will with the host of heaven as well as with those who live on the earth; and there is no one who can stay His hand or say to Him: "What are you doing?" (*Dan* 4:32)

This idea is demonstrated in the individual destinies of King Nebuchadnezzar and his son, Belshazzar. God has granted them sovereignty but is always ready to revoke it whenever they show themselves to be unworthy.

In one case, Nebuchadnezzar is punished for having dared to proclaim himself the origin of his sovereignty.

> The king was walking on the roof of the royal palace of Babylon, and said: "Is not this great Babylon, which I have built by my mighty power as a royal residence and for the glory of my majesty?" (*Dan* 4:26-27)

The consequences are immediate. The king is condemned to madness and is deprived of sovereignty (*Dan* 4:28) for as long as he refuses to recognize that it does not belong to him. God is the absolute protagonist of history; the sovereignty of kings is only a reflection of God's sovereignty.

> The Most High God gave Nebuchadnezzar . . . kingship and greatness and glory and majesty. And because of the greatness that He gave him, all peoples, nations, and languages trembled and feared before him; whom he would he slew, and whom he would he kept alive; whom he would be raised up, and whom he would he put down. But when his heart was lifted up and his spirit was hardened so that he dealt proudly, he was deposed from his kingly throne, and his glory was taken from him. He was driven from among the sons of men, and his mind was made like that of a beast, . . . until he recognized that the Most High God rules over the kingdom of men, and sets over it whom He will. (*Dan* 5:18-21)

As for King Belshazzar, guilty of having profaned the vessels of the Temple by using them at his table (*Dan* 5:2-4, 23a), Daniel accuses him of having committed an act of idolatry, "instead of glorifying God in whose hand is your breath and whose are all your ways" (5:23b). Through the mysterious and terrifying apparition of a hand writing incomprehensible words on the wall, God once again expresses judgment and reconfirms God's power. In this case the withdrawal of sovereignty is irrevocable.

> "God has numbered your kingdom and put an end to it; . . . you have been weighed in the steelyard and been found wanting; . . . your kingdom has been divided and given to the Medes and Persians." . . . That same night Belshazzar the Chaldean king was slain. And Darius the Mede received the kingdom at the age of sixty-two. (*Dan* 5:26—6:1)

God, therefore, possessor of an eternal and absolute power, is the source of the sovereignty of gentile kings who govern by God's will and within the limits set by God's judgment.

It follows that a dual fidelity is required of the Jews because they are subject to a sovereignty exercised by two authorities: God and, through God, the gentile king. The possibility of a conflict of fidelity between that owed to God and that owed to the king is confronted in *Daniel* 3 and 6, the first frame around *Daniel* 4–5.

The same story is told in these two chapters, although with different nuances. Daniel and his companions are presented as faithful subjects, placed in charge of the very administration of the kingdom, honored and esteemed by the gentile king for their services (cf. *Dan* 3:12; 6:2-4). Taking advantage of a royal decree that goes against the Jewish religious obligations, imposing an act of idolatry (3:4-6) or denying certain religious practices (6:8), some "envious men" denounce Daniel (6:5ff.) and his companions (3:8-12). God miraculously intervenes, sparing them from punishment and allowing them to emerge unharmed from the furnace (3:25-28) and from the lions' den (6:23). The "envious men" pay for their deeds with their lives. The fire devours those who threw Shadrach, Meshach, and Abednego (the Babylonian names of Hananiah, Mishael, and Azariah, according to *Dan* 1:7). As for those who denounced Daniel, they and their families end up as food for the lions in place of Daniel (6:25). The king recognizes God's power and the privileges of the Jews, making himself guardian of their diversity. Nebuchadnezzar orders that, under penalty of death and the loss of belongings, no one in his kingdom "speaks anything against the God of Shadrach, Meshach, and Abednego . . . for there is no other god who is able to deliver in this way" (3:29). Darius puts out an edict that "in all [his] royal dominion men tremble and fear before the God of Daniel, for He is the living God enduring for ever; His kingdom shall never be destroyed, and His dominion shall be to the end" (6:26-28). Daniel and his companions are eventually restored to their court responsibilities (3:30; 6:29).

As disconcerting as it seems, even though the order to perform idolatry came from the king, he is not at all blamed for it. The king can be benevolent like Darius, who sees himself "forced" to punish Daniel against his will and "spend the night fasting," begging God for salvation (*Dan* 6:15-19); or he can be malevolent like Nebuchadnezzar, who "was full of fury" when faced with the unexpected rebellion of the three young functionaries (*Dan* 3:19). Only those who maintain that the king's edict should also be valid for the Jews are guilty, those "envious men" who do not consent to the particular status of Israel. Kings pass away; they are good or bad: the pious Jew follows the same course with both. Daniel and his companions show no difficulty in continuing faithfully to serve the gentile king whose orders they have broken with such determination.

This is not a contradiction. The king's power is not so holy that it should not be contradicted, because it originates in and is limited by a "jealous" God; however, *for the same reason* its legitimacy remains unquestionable, even when it is wielded in opposition to the law of God and the Jew, in the name of fidelity to the covenant, is led to disobedience. In the vision of *Daniel*, Jewish particularism contests the idolatrous pretenses of the royal authority, not its essence; sovereignty is from God, is granted by God, and only subsists by God's will.

The outer frame (chaps. 2 and 7) is an announcement that this situation is destined to change, however, because "at the end of time" God will give sovereignty to God's people: "The kingdom and the dominion and the greatness of the kingdoms under the heavens shall be given to the people of the saints of the Most High" (*Dan* 7:27; cf. 2:44; 7:14).

First, however, the "four kingdoms" must pass, represented in two visions by a "great statue" made of various materials (chap. 2) and by "four beasts" (chap. 7). Sovereignty is granted to these four kingdoms, but not forever; only the eschatological kingdom that God will give to God's people will have no successors and will last for eternity, mirroring the characteristics of divine sovereignty. "The God of heaven will set up a kingdom which shall never be destroyed, nor shall its sovereignty be left to another people" (*Dan* 2:44). "[T]his dominion is an everlasting dominion, which shall not pass away, and [t]his kingdom is one which shall not be destroyed" (*Dan* 7:14; cf. 7:18, 27).

The author again insists on God's absolute freedom to grant and revoke sovereignty; even the eschatological kingdom will be exclusively God's work ("without the hand of man"; *Dan* 2:45; cf. 7:9-14, 26-27). Just as *Daniel* derived the idea that all knowledge is a gift of God from the idea that wisdom is from God, from the idea that sovereignty belongs to God it follows that every kingdom is God's gift. In the prayer of benediction that Daniel offers to God in chapter 2, the two themes are closely linked:

> Wisdom and power are His.
> He changes times and seasons;
> He removes kings and sets up kings.
> He gives wisdom to the wise
> and knowledge to those who understand.
> (*Dan* 2:20-21)

The religious conception of the origin of sovereignty that emerges in *Daniel* 2–7 contrasts radically with the secular vision with which Ben Sira confronted the same subject only a few decades earlier (cf. *Sir* 10:4-18). Of course, for Ben Sira too kings are subject to God's judgment.

> Sovereignty over the earth is in the hand of God,
> who raises up on it the man of the hour. . . .
> The throne of the arrogant God overturns
> and establishes the lowly in their stead.
> (*Sir* 10:4, 14)

However, God's interest is turned exclusively to the ethical qualities of the kings (whose pride is reproached; cf. *Sir* 10:7, 12, 13, 18), not to the origin or foundation of their power. The succession of kingdoms is the work of human beings, of their ambitions and strength: "Domination passes from one people to the other because of injustices, violence and riches" (*Sir* 10:8).

This is the element that most clearly distinguishes *Daniel* from *Sirach*, two documents linked by many deep ties. It is not by chance that the same element also characterizes the *Dream Visions* with respect to its own tradition. For *Sirach*, as for the early apocalyptic tradition (*Book of the Watchers* and *Book of Astronomy*), the unfolding of history holds no interest at all. In both traditions the problem of evil, as well as salvation, is played out on the cosmic and anthropological levels, certainly not on the historical level. History is autonomous simply because it has no value. In this respect *Daniel* and the *Dream Visions* signal a change of perspective. Given all evidence, the Maccabean crisis brought the problem of history back to the center of Jewish thought.

The ideas expressed in *Dan* 2–7—that God wields supreme power over the kingdoms of the earth and that nothing happens outside of God's will and working control—are certainly consoling. However, suffering and difficult tests are to be expected. Even Daniel and his companions, as we have seen them, are pushed to heroic acts of resistance and survive thanks only to God's miraculous intervention. The narratives in *Daniel* do not indulge in idyllic descriptions; even the imagery used to describe the four kingdoms is decidedly disturbing, the dream taking on the traits of a nightmare. The vision in chapter 7 communicates even more, something that seems to fracture the very universality of the stated principle of God's unchallenged sovereignty. It is prophesied that an "iniquitous king" will come who "shall speak words against the Most High and afflict the saints of the Most High" (*Dan* 7:25; cf. 7:8). At that time, however brief it may be, God will not intervene.

This element constitutes the bridge between the first and second sections of *Daniel* (chaps. 8–12). What remains to be understood is not so much why God in freedom will grant sovereignty to a gentile king, but why God will permit a power subject to God to "afflict" God's people and even show itself rebellious to God without immediately being punished.

The *Book of Daniel* responds directly to this question in chapter 9. Daniel reflects upon Jeremiah's prophecy regarding the time of exile (cf. *Jer* 25:11-12). In the prayer he offers to God (*Dan* 9:4-19) Daniel lucidly shows that he knows the cause of what is happening. He confesses the transgressions of the people before a "great and terrible God, who keeps covenant and steadfast love with those who love Him and keep His commandments" (9:4). The people have sinned; they did not listen to the appeals of the prophets and brought down a just punishment. "The curse and the oath which are written in the law of Moses, the servant of God, have been poured out upon us, because we have sinned against Him" (9:11).

This explains the history that awaits Israel; God is "righteous" (*Dan* 9:14) and therefore punishes the people who have revealed themselves to be unfaithful. In this way *Daniel* establishes a cause-and-effect link between the idea of the covenant and the apocalyptic theory of the degeneration of history, deliberately placing it within the context of a theology of the covenant. It is not coincidental that Daniel's prayer takes *Neh* 1:5-11 as its model; the self-consciousness of Israel as the people of the covenant was then traditionally linked to Nehemiah and to his "memoirs."

Such an explicit reference to the covenant in a document considered apocalyptic has seemed rather strange to several scholars, who have preferred to speak of it as a later addition.[17] However, without this prayer *Daniel* lacks any internal logic. The vision of history in *Daniel* does not have the same comprehensive character seen in the *Dream Visions*. The entire course of history is not revealed to Daniel, only the events that await Israel in the period immediately following the exile, that is, since the time in which revelation is imagined to have taken place. Nothing is said of the preceding history. In this sense the vision does not set itself up as a tool for a universal and self-sufficient interpretation of reality. The events described do not make sense in themselves; their cause must be found elsewhere.

Daniel answers this call for a meaning in history simply by recalling the givens of a known tradition—the curse pronounced by God on Sinai against those who broke the covenant.[18] What Daniel is seeking in Jeremiah's prophecy is not the cause of the degenerative process of history (he demonstrates that he already knows that) but the consequences the realization of the divine threat has on history and the individual. To pose the question about the duration of the exile means to question the possibility of a redemption of history once the punitive mechanism has been set in motion. It is to question the enduring validity of the covenant on the collective and the individual level in the new situation the people find themselves in—subject to the divine curse.

For Nehemiah a simple return to obedience seems sufficient for God's curse to be replaced by God's blessing:

---

17. E.g., see Eissfeldt, *Eileitung in das Alte Testament.*

18. See *Lev* 26:14-39; *Deut* 28:15-68. According to *Exod* 24:3-8, the foundation for such a curse lies in the modalities in which the covenant was stipulated on Sinai, when Moses contaminated the people with the blood of the covenant. See P. Sacchi, *Storia del mondo giudaico* (Turin, 1976), 16–17.

> We have acted very corruptly against You, and have not kept the commandments, the laws, and the ordinances which You commanded Your servant Moses. Remember the word which You commanded Your servant Moses, saying, "If you are unfaithful, I will scatter you among the peoples; but if you return to Me and keep My commandments and do them, though your dispersed be under the farthest skies, I will gather them thence and bring them to the place which I have chosen, to make My name dwell there." (*Neh* 1:7-9)

For Daniel the mechanism is not so immediate or simple. Israel is faced with a real crisis, not simply a stumbling-block, in its relationship with God. Once unleashed the divine curse can in no way be stopped before it has followed its entire course. Good deeds are useless to divert it; it is necessary to await and implore God in mercy to show *first* forgiveness. The conclusion of the prayer signals the distance of *Daniel* from its model, *Nehemiah*:

> We do not present our supplications before You on the ground of our righteousness, but on the ground of Your great mercy. . . . O Lord, forgive! . . . For Your own sake, O my God, because Your name is called over Your city and Your people. (*Dan* 9:18-19)

The awareness of living under the curse of the covenant and the plea for forgiveness as the only way of salvation creates a dramatic context for Daniel's question concerning duration of the exile and emphasizes its decisive importance. The angel responds to Daniel's doubts and reveals that the seventy years of Jeremiah's prophecy should in reality be understood as seventy weeks of years and that this span of time corresponds to the time necessary to expiate the guilt.

> Seventy weeks of years are decreed
> concerning your people and your holy city,
> to finish the transgression,
> to put an end to sin,
> and to atone for iniquity.
>
> > (*Dan* 9:24)

We are dealing, therefore, with a fairly long, yet chronologically determined historical period in which God's punishment will culminate in the coming of an "iniquitous king":

> And after sixty-two weeks . . .
> the people of the prince who is to come
> shall destroy the city and the sanctuary; . . .
> for half of the week
> he shall cause sacrifice and offering to cease;
> upon the wing [of the sanctuary] there shall be desolating abominations,
> until destruction and the decreed end are poured out on the desolator.
>
> > (*Dan* 9:26-27)

Daniel 8 and 10–12, placed as a frame to chapter 9, further specify the characteristics of this period, describing the various steps with abundant detail. Although the same story is told, it is seen from a different point of view. In chapter 8 the attention is concentrated on the Temple and the continuity of the cult. In chapters 10–12 emphasis is placed upon the covenant and the retributory principle. Later we will see the results of *Daniel*'s reflection on these two traditional pillars of Judaism. In the meantime it is worth noting the presence and great importance given in these chapters to the figure of the "iniquitous king," who in chapter 9 signals the climax of God's punishment. It is undoubtedly the same figure already introduced in chapter 7. His actions against God and God's people are identical ("he shall speak words against the Most High . . . and think to change the times and the law"; *Dan* 7:25; cf. 8:9-12, 23-25; 9:26-27; 11:28-39), as well as the duration of his apparent success ("a time, [two] times, and half a time"; *Dan* 7:25 = 12:7; cf. 9:27)[19] and his end ("he shall be consumed and destroyed"; 7:26; cf. 8:25; 9:27; 11:45).

The emphasis is significant. In the two sections of *Daniel*, two different periodizations are used: history seen phenomenologically by humankind as a succession of kingdoms ("the four kingdoms") and history seen by God as the instrument of God's punishment ("the seventy weeks"). The common figure of the "iniquitous king" allows the two periodizations to be synchronized just as the visual and aural presence of clapsticks allows the image and sound of a film to be synchronized exactly. In this sense chapter 8 plays a particularly important role as a hinge between the two sections of the book. It draws explicitly on chapter 7 ("a vision appeared to me, Daniel, after that which appeared to me at the first"; *Daniel* 8:1) and echoes the same imagery.

This connection explains the apparent contradiction between God's supreme control over the kingdoms and their iniquity. The kings are not "stray bullets," but docile instruments of divine punishment. Even Antioch, whose sacrilegious actions would seem to challenge God, acts "not with his power . . . and, by no human hand, he shall be destroyed" (*Dan* 8:24-25).

---

19. The Aramaic *'dn w'dnyn wplg 'dn* (*Dan* 7:25) corresponds exactly to the Hebrew *mw'd mw'dym wḥṣy* (*Dan* 12:7), as clearly perceived in the most ancient versions (see Septuagint and Theodotion). Scholars agree that this chronological indication ("a time, [two] times, and half a time") corresponds to the "half a week," that is, the "three and a half years" (1260 days) of *Dan* 9:27, interpreting the Hebrew *mw'dym* as a dual and making the Aramaic *'dnyn* a mold of the same. Scholars equally agree that the two chronological indications of *Dan* 8:14 (1150 days) and 12:11-12 (1290–1335 days) refer to the same time, although the former is approximative by defect, the latter by excess in respect to the 1260 days of the previous computation. In this chapter I will demonstrate that these figures actually represent three different "times" that share the same starting point but are clearly and consciously distinct.

However, identifying the time of history ("the four kingdoms") with the time of divine punishment ("the seventy weeks") also means making the end of history coincide with the end of punishment. In both periodizations the "iniquitous king" represents the last link in the chain; after that there is only the eschatological kingdom and God's forgiveness (cf. *Dan* 7:26-27; 12:1-3). Daniel discovers that there is no redemption in history: since the Babylonian exile, history is destined to be the time of God's wrath. After the divine punishment there is no more history; God's forgiveness marks the end of history.

We can speak, then, of historical predeterminism in *Daniel* even though we are dealing with a sui generis predeterminism, limited to a single historical season and not to the entire course of history, the consequence of a misused opportunity (the covenant) on humankind's part and not the result of an *ab aeterno* design on God's part. The problem of human freedom, the crucial problem of all forms of predeterminism, remains within a history that is no longer free. With great lucidity the author of *Daniel* will meet the challenge and deal with individual retribution in chapters 10–12.

6. HUMAN RESPONSIBILITY AND
THE RESPONSIBILITY OF THE ANGELS

In the *Book of Dream Visions*, corruption is brought about in creation because the angels' sin directly influences the very possibility of human resistance to evil. It drastically limits human freedom of choice and responsibility. Humankind is thus more the victim than the doer of evil. The degeneration of history is the collective manifestation of a corruption at work against individuals on the ontological level.

In *Daniel*, on the other hand, history degenerates because God has made it the instrument of punishment of the people of Israel who, fully exercising their freedom, failed to meet the commitments of the covenant. Nothing intervened to modify human ability to choose; human beings were and remain free.

However, if the times of history are now fixed, if every possibility to modify them has been denied, and if salvation depends solely on an act of God's mercy, it is worth asking what sense there is to the notion that human beings continue to enjoy a state of freedom. Breaking the link between freedom and salvation means denying the very presuppositions of a theology of the covenant. Does unleashing the divine curse signal the end of the covenant itself?

Daniel confronts and resolves this problem in the last part of the book (chaps. 10–12). The author brings into operation a clear distinction between the collective and the individual dimensions of guilt and salvation. In condemning history, God has collectively punished the people for a sin committed collectively. Judgment of the individual has not yet been pronounced, and will not be pronounced until the end of time, when everyone living and dead will be called individually to answer for their own actions before the divine tribunal. The collective guilt does not condemn the individual, nor will the individual be saved by God's forgiveness. Individual salvation will not necessarily correspond to collective salvation; the day that history and the people are redeemed will be the day of judgment for the individual. Coherently, at the announcement of God's collective forgiveness ("at that time your people shall be delivered"; *Dan* 12:1a), *Daniel* follows immediately with a proposition that limits the effects of the divine intervention on the individual level ("every one whose name shall be found written in the book"; 12:1b). The various destinies to which each person is brought by the resurrection are then indicated: "And the multitude of those who sleep in the dust of the earth shall awake, some to everlasting life, and some to shame and everlasting contempt" (12:2).

The idea of the resurrection certainly emerges in Jewish thought from the process of progressive subtraction from human verification of God's retributory work, as it appears already carried to its (pen)ultimate consequences by Ben Sira.[20] This is made even more necessary, however, by the ecology of *Daniel*'s thought. In this way our author can restore meaning to individual freedom as well as saving value to the covenant.

The distinction brought about between the collective and individual dimensions of salvation and guilt also allows a different meaning to be given to the suffering that inevitably comes with a history seen as punishment. On a collective level this suffering is the expiation of a collectively committed sin. On the individual level it becomes the context within which human beings are called to demonstrate their faithfulness to the covenant. Those who succumb will be damned; those who persevere will be rewarded.

The idea of suffering as a test is already a part of the heritage of Jewish thought; Ben Sira made it an element of the pedagogical project of wisdom (cf. *Sir* 4:11-18). In *Daniel* suffering returns to being a consequence of guilt. Even though individuals are innocent because they did not personally commit the sin, as part of an unfaithful collective they must suffer the conse-

---

20. Ben Sira pointedly denies any possibility of life after death, but his discourse on retribution already prevents humankind from verifying God's action, because it makes a "good death" and an everlasting memory the true compensation for the righteous (see above, pp. 119–24).

quences of collective guilt. The time of wrath and punishment is, therefore, also the time of expiation and testing. The protests of Job and the skepticism of Qohelet by now belong to a distant past. From contradiction and scandal, the suffering of the righteous has become the norm of existence.

Every space for earthly retribution will progressively be reduced until, with the coming of the "iniquitous king," only "sword and flame, captivity and exile" await the righteous (*Dan* 11:33), as well as death without guilt (cf. 9:26).[21] The only choice will be between apostasy and obedience to the covenant, a heroic obedience carried even to self-sacrifice. The "iniquitous king"

> shall take action against the holy covenant. He shall turn back and give heed to those who forsake the holy covenant. . . . He shall seduce with flattery those who violate the covenant; but the people who know their God shall stand firm and take action. And those among the people who are wise shall make many understand, though they shall fall by sword and flame, by captivity and exile. (*Dan* 11:30, 32-33)

It is significant that in the context of chapters 10–12—and only in this context—*Daniel* returns explicitly and repeatedly to speaking about the "covenant" or the "holy covenant" (Heb. *bryt*; *bryt qwdš*; *Dan* 11:22, 28, 30 [bis], 32). The reference in chapter 9 was to the covenant as the remote and irrevocable source of the curse for the entire community; chapters 10–12 restate its enduring validity as a "measure" of human responsibility. The covenant marks the boundaries of apostasy and obedience. In the concrete choice between the two ways, human beings put their freedom into action and construct their own salvation. At the moment of resurrection the sufferings of the righteous will be redeemed and their perseverance rewarded. "Those who are wise shall shine like the brightness of the firmament; and those who turn many to righteousness, like the stars for ever and ever" (12:3).

Perseverance in the test is affirmed as the principal virtue, decisive for salvation. The book, in fact, finishes with a general invitation to persevere and the promise of resurrection and future recompense for the "righteous" Daniel. In a brief appendix (*Dan* 12:5-13), which concludes both the second section and the entire book, the predetermined duration of history is confirmed. The persecution of the "iniquitous king" will last, as announced in *Dan* 7:25 and 9:27, three and a half years (1260 days), "a time, [two] times,

---

21. The Greek version of Theodotion allows us to complete the Hebrew and to make sense of the otherwise incomprehensible words of Daniel, commenting on the bloody death of a "consecrated" man (probably the high priest Oniah III) under Antioch IV: *kai krima ouk estin en autô* (cf. Heb. *w'yn lw* [*dyn*]).

and half a time" (12:7). The moment that the difference in individual destiny is noted ("Many shall purify themselves, and make themselves white, and be refined; but the wicked shall do wickedly; and none of the wicked shall understand, only those who are wise shall understand"; 12:10), the times are unexpectedly lengthened, passing in rapid succession first to 1290 days, with the addition of one month ("From the time that the continual burnt offering is taken away, and the desolating abomination is set up, there shall be a thousand two hundred and ninety days"; 12:11); then to 1335 days, with the addition of another month and a half—without, however, giving even this term a final character ("Happy is he who waits and comes to the thousand three hundred and thirty-five days!"; *Dan* 12:12). This dissonance of times has not failed to create obstacles for the commentators. Many have held that later additions were inserted with the intention of justifying the late arrival of "the end."[22] However, the detail fits well in the perspective of salvation in *Daniel*. Through this mechanism of a progressive lengthening of time, the centrality of perseverance for the individual is emphasized. The indeterminate extension of the end beyond the limits of history to include the beginning of the new times, evidently up until the time of judgment, reaffirms the independence of the collective and individual dimensions of guilt and salvation.

As for the angels, in *Daniel* and in the *Dream Visions* they are unquestionably presented with common traits. There is a distinction between the angels and human beings but not a complete separation. In the *Dream Visions* the elect, who through God's will accomplish a superhuman action, are made equal to the angels; this is said of Noah ("the snow-white cow which became a man"; *1 Enoch* 89:1, 9) and of Moses ("the sheep which became a man"; *1 Enoch* 89:36). Analogously, in *Daniel* the same expression, "holy one," or "holy ones" (Aram. *qdyš, qdyšyn*; Heb. *qdwš, qdwšym*), designates both angels (*Dan* 4:10, 14, 20; 8:13 [bis]) and the Jews who are faithful to the covenant (7:18, 21, 22 [bis], 25, 27; 8:24). Furthermore, the worship service identifies the priests with a "heavenly host" (8:10).

Once again, we are faced with a common cultural heritage elaborated according to divergent ideological perspectives. Even the formulation of the problem of the angels' freedom and responsibility in relation to evil is reversed in the two documents. In the *Dream Visions* the angels' sin, corrupting human nature, negatively conditions history; in *Daniel* it is the history of the relationship between humanity and God that conditions, so to speak, the

---

22. See, e.g., Eissfeldt, *Eileitung in das Alte Testament*.

angelic world, which follows the unfolding of history as a docile instrument of the divinity (cf. *Dan* 4:31-32: "[God's] dominion is an everlasting dominion. . . . He does according to His will with the host of heaven; . . . and there is no one who can stay His hand or say to Him: What are you doing?"). In *Daniel*, the angels never appear as rebellious against God; they protect Israel, free Daniel and his companions from every mortal danger (*Dan* 3:25, 28; 6:23), and above all they are the messengers of divine knowledge, both in the phase of revelation (4:10; 8:13; 12:5-7) and in the phase of interpretation (7:16, 23; 8:15-19; 9:21-22; 10:5-6, 9-11, 21b; 12:8-9). Strikingly, in the significant context of *Daniel* 4–5 God's absolute sovereignty over creatures is entrusted to one of the "watchers" (4:10-14, 20-24). *Daniel* obviously intends to restore the reputation of those angels, which the apocalyptic tradition (*Book of the Watchers*) had made protagonists of the rebellion against God.

Only on one occasion (chap. 10) does the vision present a conflict among angels. This occurs, once again, in a significant context: in the section of *Daniel* (chaps. 10–12) that indicates most strongly human freedom and responsibility. The conflict pits the guardian angel of Israel against the "prince of the kingdom of Persia" (that is, the guardian angel of Persia; 10:12-14) and then the "prince of the kingdom of Jawan" (the guardian angel of Greece; *Dan* 10:20-21).[23] But here the argument already discussed about the kingdoms is still valid; the battle among the angels only corresponds to the struggle among the kingdoms, which, as we have seen, takes place by the will and under the direct control of God. The battle is entirely fictitious. The active presence of Michael ("the great prince who has charge of your people"; *Dan* 12:1; cf. 10:21a) on the side of the guardian angel of Israel guarantees that the final results will conform to God's plan. Israel never appears to be abandoned to itself. Even for the brief moment that the guardian angel of Israel leaves the field of battle to reveal himself to Daniel, Israel is not alone; Michael takes his place for the necessary time (10:13). When the vision is made explicit, the conflict dissolves as a purely symbolic image, and if the angels are granted an active role, it is in no way in opposition to God.

Here we are obviously quite far from the positions of the *Book of Dream Visions*, in which the angel world has gone out of control, Israel is caught by demonic forces without heavenly protection, and Michael appears relegated

---

23. The angel revealed to Daniel has the function of "protector angel of Israel" (as I have taken him to be here), whose role in the heavenly struggle is exactly analogous to that of the protector angels of Persia and Greece. If Daniel reserves this title for Michael, it is because Michael's decisive role relegates the works of the true "protector angel of Israel" to a secondary position.

to the passive position of onlooker—all until the time established by God for definitive intervention.

7. GOD'S JUDGMENT:
RETRIBUTION OR PURIFICATION?

A different way of understanding the freedom and responsibility of the angels and of humanity necessarily corresponds also to a different conception of the judgment that both *Daniel* and the *Dream Visions* place at the climax of history. This event, with God as its protagonist, is presented in the ritual form of a trial: the seating of the divine court ("the placed throne"; cf. *Dan* 7:9; *1 Enoch* 90:20a); the reading of the charges (opening of the heavenly book; cf. *Dan* 7:10; 12:1b; *1 Enoch* 90:20b); the convocation of the accused and the execution of the sentence (cf. *Dan* 7:11-14, 26-27; 12:1-3; *1 Enoch* 90:21ff.).

Daniel, consistent in its distinction between the collective and individual dimensions of guilt and salvation, speaks of the judgment on two occasions (chaps. 7 and 12).

In chapter 7 the judgment is seen in its collective dimension of salvation; sovereignty has been taken away from the kingdoms and entrusted forever to Israel. In this dimension the judgment signals God's last intervention in history, signifying the manifestation of God's forgiveness and the end of punishment, as is clarified in the second part of *Daniel*. The definitiveness of the divine decision is emphasized: in contrast to the three preceding kingdoms, no "prolongation of life" is granted to the last kingdom after its power has been removed:

> The [fourth] beast was slain, and its body destroyed and given over to be burned with fire. As for the rest of the beasts, their domination was taken away, but their lives were prolonged for a certain time. (*Dan* 7:11-12)[24]

In *Dan* 12:1-3, on the other hand, the judgment is presented in its ambivalent individual dimension: salvation for the righteous and condemnation for the unrighteous. Recompense and punishment give meaning to the individual's attitude in facing history. This well explains the insistence on individual resurrection and on the personal nature of the judgment: each person will be

---

24. The Aramaic expression '*d-zmn w'dn* is extremely vague and is therefore translated with the equally vague "for a certain time." It indicates an imprecise yet historically defined period when "the beasts" (the reigns), although deprived of any power over Israel, continue to exist before disappearing completely from history. No "prolongation of life" will be granted, however, to the "fourth beast" because its end marks the end of history itself.

called to answer for his or her own actions. Significantly, only humankind is involved in this event; the absence of the angels is further proof of their innocence.

As for the retributory criteria of individual judgment, it is clear from the whole of *Daniel* that it is based on the covenant. The resolution to the problem of the relationship between good and bad deeds, however, is not made explicit.[25] The image of the "steelyard" used in *Dan* 5:27 is traditional (cf. *Job* 31:6) and in itself does not imply a weighing of the quantity of actions. Daniel's words to Nebuchadnezzar are more significant: Daniel advises him to "redeem his sins by practicing righteousness, and his iniquities by showing mercy to the oppressed" (*Dan* 4:24). These words echo analogous expressions of Ben Sira (cf. *Sir* 3:3, 14, 30; 35:3), who drew the idea of God's comprehensive evaluation of an individual's actions from the expiatory value of righteous deeds in relation to transgressions. But even if *Daniel* shows awareness of the reform of Ben Sira, the radicality and emphasis of the alternative *Daniel* places between apostasy and obedience cancels a problem that belongs more to the day-to-day nature of living than to the exceptional nature of the last days.

In the *Dream Visions*, judgment has a completely different value. It is more a reestablishment of a corrupted order through an indistinctly operated elimination of both those who are responsible and those who have been involved against their will. Judgment, therefore, is made primarily against the rebellious angels (cf. *1 Enoch* 90:21-25) and, only by association, human beings and their institutions (cf. *1 Enoch* 90:26-28). Hence, we have this order: "the star which had fallen down first" (the devil); "the stars whose sexual organs were like those of the horses" (the fallen angels; the watchers); "the seventy shepherds" (the rebellious angels); "the blinded sheep" (the wicked); and "the old house" (Jerusalem; the Temple).

Regarding humankind, individual judgment is not insisted upon, nor is an accounting of actions. The cause of evil does not lie in human responsibility and freedom. As a result, the theme of the resurrection, central in *Daniel*, is much more nuanced in the *Dream Visions*, to the point that it is not even mentioned explicitly, although the dead—both the wicked ("the blinded sheep"; *1 Enoch* 90:26) and the elect (the white sheep "who had perished"; *1 Enoch* 90:33)—are all manifestly present before God. It is not a retributory judgment that God carries out (only a free act of obedience or transgression

25. See P. Sacchi, "Retribuzione e giudizio fra ebraismo e cristianesimo," *RSLR* 9 (1973): 407–20; G. Boccaccini, "Il dibattito sul valore salvifico della Torah nel I secolo," in *Il dono della Torah*, ed. I. Gargano (Camaldoli, 1985), 112–20; and above, pp. 116–18.

can correspond to retribution) but a work of purification. Through the fire of Gehenna God erases from the earth every trace of the evil originating from the angels' sin.

Having freed judgment from any tie to the covenant, the *Dream Visions* broadens the horizons of salvation and includes even Gentiles among the elect, whereas *Daniel*'s interests lie concentrated on the righteous of Israel.

> All those [white sheep] which had perished and those which have been dispersed, and all the beasts of the field and the birds of the sky were gathered together in that house; and the Lord of the sheep rejoiced with great joy because they had all become gentle and returned to His house. (*1 Enoch* 90:33)

8. FACED WITH THE EVENTS OF HISTORY

The falsely *ante eventum* reading of contemporary historical events offered by *Daniel* and the *Book of Dream Visions* allows us to assess their attitudes toward the principal political subjects of the day: the philo-Hellenists, the Hasmoneas, and the priesthood.

The two documents are united by an equal contempt for those "blinded sheep" and the apostates that have betrayed the people, making themselves accomplices to the "iniquitous king" Antioch IV (cf. *1 Enoch* 90:7, 16; *Dan* 11:30). In this respect, the attitude of *Daniel* and the *Dream Visions* is objectively coincident with that of the Hasmoneas (cf. *1 Macc* 2:15-26), although their commitment to the Maccabean revolt had to be conditioned by the distrust that both felt (though for different reasons) toward the possibility of a human intervention capable of modifying the course of events from within.

The most rigid position is certainly that of *Daniel*. Because of the unleashing of the divine curse, human responsibility toward history has been suspended; opposing it means opposing divine punishment. The only alternative is that of passive resistance, followed and suffered by each individual. The "iniquitous king," as we have seen, "by no human hand, shall be destroyed" (*Dan* 8:25; cf. 2:34). This position, as scholars have unanimously noted, is difficult to reconcile with the activism (the zeal for the law) of the Maccabees, whose political action is, in effect, completely disregarded.[26]

The *Dream Visions*' perspective, on the other hand, is more disposed to

---

26. According to G. von Rad: "Without any doubt, the writer of Daniel sides with those who endure persecution rather than those who take up arms against it, and in so doing he is only being true to his own basic conviction that what must be will be. He is far removed from the Maccabees and their policy of active resistance; their large following is actually suspect in his eyes" (*Old Testament Theology*, trans. D.M.G. Stalker, 2 vols. [New York, 1962–65], 2:315).

allow a space for the elect to act as instruments of God's action. As a result, the figure of Judas Maccabeus ("the sheep on which a great horn had sprouted"; *1 Enoch* 90:9) acquires great importance. His coming appears to be a fundamental step in the process of preparing God's intervention, and his success is a sure sign of election. The angel Michael has finally abandoned his passive role to deploy himself at Judas's side (cf. *1 Enoch* 90:14). Judas Maccabeus is, therefore, an instrument of God's wrath, used by God to rout the impious just before the erection of the thrones and the judgment.

Both *Daniel* and the *Dream Visions*, however, agree on the idea that the eschatological kingdom will be exclusively God's work and that any messianic claim on the part of human beings is to be excluded. This insight is significant; it is more probable that the first Hasmoneas were not entirely insensitive to messianic suggestions.[27] In the *Dream Visions* the messiah appears only after the establishment of the eschatological kingdom and divine judgment—events in which he does not appear to be involved (cf. *1 Enoch* 90:37-38). In *Daniel* there is no individual messiah; the figure of the "Son of man" is more a collective symbol of the people of Israel, to whom God has entrusted sovereignty (cf. *Dan* 7:13-14, 18, 27). In any case, he is present only after judgment and is limited to receiving that which God has prepared as a gift.

The interest in the cult and the centrality of the Temple of Jerusalem links both authors closely to the priesthood.[28] An equally positive judgment of Honias III probably unites them, if the symbolically shaded figure in *1 Enoch* 90:8 and *Dan* 9:26 really represents the high priest assassinated under Antioch IV. However, the judgment these authors express on the religious life of their time remains radically different.

As we have seen, in the *Dream Visions* the entire post-exilic history of Israel unfolds under a demonic influence, and even the Temple is no exception. The Temple, whose Mosaic origins and construction by Solomon are emphatically evoked (cf. *1 Enoch* 89:36, 50), after the Babylonian destruction is also involved in the common ruin. Reconstructed "under the seventy shepherds" it can only be a contaminated temple.

> They again began to build as before; and they raised up that tower which is called the high tower, and they placed a table before [the tower], but all the bread which was upon it was polluted and impure. (*1 Enoch* 89:73)

---

27. It is not difficult, for example, to make out messianic traits in the eulogy of Simon (*1 Macc* 14:4-15), although within the framework of an eschatology fulfilled within the confines of history.

28. A priestly origin of *Daniel* has been suggested by J.C.H. Lebram, "Perspektiven der gegenwärtigen Danielforshung," *JSJ* 5 (1974): 1–33.

The argument is drawn from an episode narrated in *Mal* 1:6ff. In the context of the *Dream Visions*, however, it is raised to the level of a paradigm of the condition in which the entire worship activity of the Temple has fallen. The profaning action of Antioch IV adds nothing to an already compromised situation, and as a result, it is not even mentioned. In the time of judgment the Temple ("the ancient house") will be devoured by the same purifying fire of Gehenna into which the wicked are thrown. In its place a "new house" will be built by God in which all of the elect will be reunited.

> Then I went seeing until that ancient house caught [fire]. . . . I went on seeing until the Lord of the sheep brought about a new house, greater and loftier than the first one. . . . All the sheep were within it. . . . And the Lord of the sheep rejoiced with great joy because they had all become gentle and returned to His house. (*1 Enoch* 90:28-33)

For *Daniel*, who specifically dedicates chapter 8 to this theme, the cult in the Temple of Jerusalem is absolutely legitimate. No religious or political event seems to have tarnished this legitimacy, neither the end of the Zadokite priesthood nor the philo-Hellenistic politics of the high priest Menelaus. The break does not come until the perpetual sacrifice is interrupted and the Temple is profaned by the "desolating abomination" (cf. *Dan* 8:13; 9:27; 11:31; 12:11), that is, when the very raison d'être of the Levite priesthood is challenged.[29] Antioch IV's intervention is presented as a sacrilegious action against God.

> He grew great, even to the host of heaven; and some of the host and of the stars he cast down to the ground, and trampled upon them. He magnified himself, even up to the Prince of the host; and the continual burnt offering was taken away from Him, and [their place was overthrown. The sanctuary was made desert and] sin was posed instead of the continual burnt offering, and the truth was cast down to the ground. He acted thus and was successful. (*Dan* 8:10-12; cf. 11:36-39)[30]

The interruption of the continuity of the cult and the introduction of idolatrous practices in the Temple, therefore, create a qualitatively new situation. History itself is indelibly stained. From the historical-political point of view these events signal the beginning of the "half week" when the "iniquitous king" will appear to triumph over the righteous (cf. *Dan* 9:27), just as

---

29. On the opposition of the Levite and Sadokite priesthoods and on the break represented by the end of the Sadokite priesthood for certain ideological components of middle Judaism, see Sacchi, *Storia*; and G. Garbini, *Storia e ideologia nell'Israele antico* (Brescia, 1986), 208–35 (*History and Ideology in Ancient Israel*, trans. J. Bowden [New York, 1988]).

30. The Masoretic text, at some points corrupted, has been reconstructed based on the Greek version of the Septuagint.

they mark for the individual the beginning of the "time of perseverance" (cf. 12:11-12). Now we see that from the point of view of the cult also these events are the beginning of a time in which the cult in the Temple of Jerusalem is delegitimated.

> For how long is the vision concerning the continual burnt offering [to be taken away], the desolating abomination to be posed instead, the sanctuary and the host to be trampled? . . . For two thousand and three hundred evenings and mornings; then the sanctuary shall be restored to its rightful state. (*Dan* 8:13-14; cf. 8:26)

Here we have another date differing from the three and a half years (1260 days) that mark the duration of the persecution under Antioch IV. In this case, the period is slightly shorter ("two thousand and three hundred evenings and mornings," that is 1150 days). It seems difficult, however, to make it coincide with the preceding period, as generally proposed by scholars.[31] The discrepancy is intentional; the profanation of the Temple is only an episode of the divine punishment, a parenthesis destined to be closed before the end. In restoring the preceding situation God commits an act of justice owed to the Temple and its legitimate cult.

As we have seen, even in judgment of contemporary events *Daniel* and the *Dream Visions* take different positions, for anything but marginal reasons. This is an effect, and yet another proof, of the distance that separates them ideologically and makes them witnesses of two independent currents of thought within middle Judaism.

9. DANIEL AND THE APOCALYPTIC TRADITION

The preceding analysis now permits an answer to our initial question, that is, whether or not the *Book of Daniel* belongs to the apocalyptic tradition of thought. Given the hermeneutic premises, the answer can only be negative.[32] From the formal point of view, *Daniel* contains so-called apocalyptic sections and even shares the same world view with the *Dream Visions*. However, the ideology that this canonical document expresses differs in its essential traits from those principles that distinctly characterize the Enochian tradition in post-exilic Jewish thought. With respect to that tradition—and

31. See above, p. 149 n. 19
32. I expressed such conclusions for the first time some years ago in "E' Daniele un testo apocalittico? Una (ri)definizione del pensiero del Libro di Daniele in rapporto al Libro dei Sogni e all'Apocalittica," *Henoch* 9 (1987): 267–302.

in this sense the comparison with the contemporary *Book of Dream Visions* has been exemplary—*Daniel* offers a different and in no way compatible vision of the meaning of history, God's action, and human responsibility. Because we give the name "apocalyptic" to the movement of thought systematically expressed in the *Book of Enoch*, we can only take note that *Daniel* does not belong to such a movement and contest its traditional definition as an ideologically apocalyptic document.

Daniel can even be considered an anti-apocalyptic document, at least to the same extent as *Sirach* is. For many verses the procedures used are analogous: assuming themes and forms of the apocalyptic tradition while inserting them in an ideological context (such as the whole of *Daniel*) that denies them their original characteristics and draws them into the sphere of a theology of the covenant.

In the light of these critical insights, the image prevalent in the introductions to *Daniel*—that of a book primarily concerned with encouraging the anti-Hellenistic Jews in a period of persecution, practically an anthology of consoling stories—appears reductive. *Daniel* offers something more; it offers a comprehensive vision of history and of individual destiny that is capable of overcoming historical contingency and presenting itself as a model for future generations.

The operation performed by *Daniel* was certainly not a painless one. The centrality of the covenant is reconfirmed only through courageous choices and painful renunciations. Humankind saves its freedom and denies evil any autonomy, yet accepts life in a history condemned to inexorable degeneration ("the four kingdoms"). The idea of the resurrection on the one hand solves a problem that had tormented the generations from *Job* to *Sirach* by removing God's judgment from any possible human determination; on the other hand it painfully distances the hope of seeing merit compensated and guilt punished from the horizons of existence.

The force and necessity of such innovative choices are proven by their long history in Jewish thought (up to Christianity and Rabbinism), and were already proven in the short term in the various ideological traditions of middle Judaism. The document was widespread in Qumran, influenced the apocalyptic tradition (e.g., it caused the development of the figure of the "Son of man" in the *Book of the Similitudes)*, offered several ideas to early Christianity, and was accepted without reserve in the rabbinic canon. This is yet another proof of the richness and suggestiveness of a book that, from its appearance, has imposed its originality of thought as a milestone in the ideological history of middle Judaism.

5

THE *LETTER OF ARISTEAS*

A Dialogical Judaism Facing
Greek *Paideia*

1. A SOMEWHAT SHAMELESS GRANDSON

In the second half of the second century B.C.E., the *Book of Sirach*[1] was translated into Greek by a self-proclaimed "grandson" of the author and thus made available to the debate within the Jewish community of Alexandria.

In the prologue written specifically for the occasion, the translator declares, first of all, Israel's excellence in education (Gr. *paideia*) and wisdom (Gr. *sophia*), which is founded in Scripture transmitted by the Jewish religious tradition.

> Many and important [teachings] have been handed down to us through the law, the prophets, and the later [writings]; and for these [teachings] Israel must be celebrated in education [Gr. *paideia*] and wisdom [Gr. *sophia*]. (*Prologue to Sirach* 1–3)

The translator delineates three categories of people, according to their relationship with the Scripture. Hierarchically ordered, they are: "the readers" (Gr. *hoi anaginôskontes*), "the lovers of learning" (Gr. *hoi philomathountes, hoi philomatheis*), and "those outside" (Gr. *hoi ektos*). The bind that ties each category to its superior is one of discipleship, measured by the distance from the scriptural text and having as its declared aim the following of "a life in conformity to the law."

This principle can be seen in the figure of the "grandfather." He was a "reader" and expert in the Scripture and therefore was qualified to exercise his function as teacher to the "lovers of learning."

---

1. On the *Book of Sirach* and its ideology, see chap. 3.

> My grandfather, Jesus, having devoted himself for a long time to the reading
> [Gr. *anagnôsis*] of the law, the prophets, and the rest of the books of [our]
> ancestors, and having developed a thorough familiarity with them, was moved
> to write something himself about education [Gr. *paideia*] and wisdom [Gr.
> *sophia*], in order that the lovers of learning [Gr. *hoi philomatheis*], by acquainting
> themselves with what he too had written, make even greater progress in living
> in conformity to the law. (*Prologue to Sirach* 7–14)

The teaching example of the "reader" triggers the teaching commitment
of the "lovers of learning," who direct this commitment to their own disciples, "those outside."

> It is necessary that not only the readers become themselves expert, but that the
> lovers of learning are able, in speech and in writing, to help also those outside.
> (*Prologue to Sirach* 4–6)

Motivated by this principle, the "grandson" translated the book

> for the benefit of those living in the diaspora [Gr. *hoi en tê paroikia*] who wish
> to become lovers of learning [Gr. *philomatheô*], in order that they live according
> to the law, conforming their customs [to it]. (*Prologue to Sirach*
> 34–36)

The primacy of reading the text brings with it the primacy, explicitly and
polemically affirmed, of the original Hebrew over any translation, whose
worth is limited to a didactic role.

> You therefore are invited to read [this translation] with good will and attention
> and to be indulgent if, despite our earnest efforts, we could not render the
> strength of certain expressions. These do not have the same force spoken in
> the original Hebrew or translated into another language. [That is true] not
> only of this book but of the law itself, the prophets and the rest of the books,
> which differ not little when they are spoken in the original. (*Prologue to Sirach*
> 15–26)

Stating the absolute incapacity of a translation to replace the original is
not simply a scruple on the part of a particularly conscientious translator,
nor is it a question of purism; it is the necessary corollary of the exclusive
and self-sufficient link posed by Ben Sira between law and wisdom. More
than being a translator, then, the "grandson" is the conscious and coherent
preacher of a precise religious address within the Jewish community of Alexandria. He openly warns his interlocutors that the necessity of his work is
derived from personal contact with the Egyptian situation and from his
judgment formed concerning his experience.

In the thirty-eighth year of the reign of King Euergetes I arrived in Egypt and settled there. As I accounted that a translation[2] would be of not little educational value, I therefore considered it quite necessary to devote also by myself diligence and industry to translate this book. (*Prologue to Sirach* 27–30)

It is impossible not to see the bitterness of the debate in the way he shamelessly presents himself as a master exhorting his coreligionists of the Diaspora (assimilated without compromise to "those outside") of the necessity of a discipleship, "in order that they live [or rather, begin to live] according to the law, conforming their customs [to it]."

2. THE *LETTER OF ARISTEAS*: BETWEEN APOLOGY AND DEBATE

The polemical slant that animates the *Prologue to Sirach* leads us to consider in the Alexandrian Diaspora an active, vital, and truly different tradition of thought. Such a tradition is precisely indicated by the contemporary *Letter of Aristeas*.[3]

Scholars have been more concerned with questioning what the writing

2. The term *aphomoion* is a hapax in the known Greek literature; this, combined with the ambiguity of its meaning, significantly complicates the interpretation of the passage. Generally it is understood as "a copy" of the *Book of Sirach* (or the Bible or a collection of wisdom literature) that the "grandson" claims to have found and about which he gives his value judgment. Others prefer to link the term to the previous mention of "Egypt," in whose regard the grandson noted a "difference" (see V. Ryssel in *APAT* 1 (1900): 268–517; and R.A.F. MacKenzie, *Sirach* [Wilmington, 1983]) or, on the contrary, a "similarity" (see P. Auvray, "Notes sur le prologue de l'Ecclésiastique," in *Mélanges bibliques rédigée en l'honneur d'André Robert*, ed. Institut Catholique de Paris [Paris, 1957], 281–87) between the cultures. Others, finally, lean toward the variant *aphormên* ("opportunity"; see, e.g., L. Alonso Schökel, *Proverbios y Ecclesiastico* [Madrid, 1968]; and J. G. Snaith, *Ecclesiasticus* [Cambridge, 1974]), but this option is simply the *lectio facilior*. None of the proposed solutions seems satisfactory to me. I prefer to hazard a new hypothesis: the "similar yet different thing" is the "translation" the grandson prepares to make, which he holds would be a useful pedagogical tool.

3. On the *Letter of Aristeas*, see P. Wendland, *Aristeae ad Philocratem epistula* (Leipzig, 1900 [Greek text]); idem, *APAT* 2 (1900): 4–31 (German trans.); H. St. J. Thackeray, "The Letter of Aristeas," in *An Introduction to the Old Testament in Greek*, ed. H. B. Swete (Cambridge, 1900), 533–606; idem, "The Letter of Aristeas," *JQR* 15 (1903): 337–91 (English trans.); H. T. Andrews, *APOT* 2 (1913): 83–122 (English trans.); H. St. J. Thackeray, *The Letter of Aristeas*, *TED* 2 (London, 1917 [English trans.]); P. Riessler, *ASB* (1928), 193–233 (German trans.); R. Tramontano, *La Lettera di Aristea a Filocrate* (Naples, 1931 [Greek text and Italian trans.]); H. G. Meecham, *The Oldest Version of the Bible* (London, 1932 [English trans.); idem, *The Letter of Aristeas* (Manchester, 1935 [Thackeray's Greek text with philological annotations]); M. Hadas, *Aristeas to Philocrates* (New York and London, 1951 [Thackeray's Greek text and English trans.]); A. Pelletier, *Lettre d'Aristée à Philocrate*, SC 89 (Paris, 1962 [Greek text and French trans.]); N. Meisner, *JSHRZ* 2.1 (1973): 35–85 (German trans.); C. Kraus Reggiani, *La Lettera di Aristea a Filocrate* (Rome, 1979 [Italian trans.]); N. Fernández Marcos, *ApAT* 2 (1983): 9–63 (Spanish trans.); and R.J.H Shutt, *OTP* 2 (1985): 7–34 (English trans.).

says, or seems to say, about the translation of the Septuagint—in spite of the pseudepigraphic character of the *Letter*, its many legendary traits, and the anachronisms that inevitably distance it from the events narrated. The role of "witness" attributed to Pseudo-Aristeas is, furthermore, the reason behind the affection with which first Hellenistic Judaism and then Christianity passed on the writing as well as its legend. Upon close examination, however, the story of the translation is only the frame for a quite complex, profoundly consistent, and articulated system of thought that still asks to be explored and identified in its entirety.

The *Letter*—which is not a letter so much as a "written account" (Gr. *diêgêsis*; *Let Aris* 1, 8, 322)—presents both polemical and apologetic characteristics. But it is an apology whose object is not very clear, and a polemic whose referents remain unnamed.

An early critical approach was to see this document as a Jewish propaganda pamphlet, motivated solely by the missionary prospect of presenting the superiority of Judaism to a pagan audience. Out of such a prospect, the *Letter* would demonstrate little originality of thought.[4] Time has overturned this judgment, shifting attention more and more decisively (especially after the Second World War) to the specific role played by the writing in the internal life of the Jewish community in Alexandria and to its Jewish interlocutors.[5]

At the same time, the debate over the object of the apology took form. It soon ran into the paradox of a document that propagandizes for a translation composed at least a century earlier. The hypotheses proposed to deal with this difficulty have been varied, and some have been suggestive—for example, that the Septuagint was in reality a revised edition of previous translations, the contemporary *Letter* offering an ancient and therefore authoritative foundation to this revision;[6] or that the defense of the Septuagint had

4. Andrews claims that "the Epistle is not directly interested in theological problems," (*APOT* 2:88). According to Meecham: "The *Letter* is of no great value from the standpoint of religion and ethics. The theological and ethical questions that indirectly emerge are treated in a conventional fashion. . . . It reflects a Judaism fundamentally true to itself but attenuated by contact with Hellenic thought. . . . In brief the author of the *Letter* is not a profound or original thinker" (*Oldest Version of the Bible*, 238–41).

5. An article by V. Tcherikover, "The Ideology of the *Letter of Aristeas*," *HTR* 51 (1958): 59–85 (published in Hebrew in 1945), marks the beginning of this new critical approach. Tcherikover writes, "The *Letter of Aristeas* was not written with the aim of self-defense or propaganda and was addressed not to Greek, but to Jewish readers."

6. This hypothesis is generally attributed to P. E. Kahle (*The Cairo Genizah* [Oxford, 1947; 2d ed., 1959]), but it appears already formulated in its essential terms by B. Motzo ("Aristea," *Atti Accademia di Torino* 50 [1914–15]: 202–25, 547–70).

become necessary by the appearance of a rival translation, which the institution of the Temple of Leontopolis could have produced and supported.[7] Although none of these hypotheses, when carefully weighed, has withstood the burden of proof, the growing concentration of interest on the life and internal tensions of the Jewish community in Alexandria has given new plausibility to Pseudo-Aristeas's defense of an already ancient translation (and the *Prologue to Sirach* has furnished an essential clue). Given the evidence, the authority of the Septuagint in respect to the original was strongly questioned in Alexandria at the end of the second century B.C.E.

With all of this the debate on the object and referents of the *Letter*, although much better focalized in its terms, certainly cannot be considered closed. The most recent studies have tried to bring to light above all the political nature and implications of the *Letter*, given that Pseudo-Aristeas clearly sided with philo-Ptolemaic and loyalist positions. Certainly these positions were hardly adaptable to the renewed national pride of Hasmonaic Israel and perhaps even went against the nascent (and growing) influence of the Pharisee "party."[8] The impression, however, is that the struggle by then clearly present within the Jewish community of Alexandria is linked to a much deeper and more decisive level than the political one. The prejudice that the *Letter* contains little originality of thought and is not directly related to theological problems lies beneath the undervaluation, if not silence, concerning the religious ideology of this document. It is precisely its affinity with the *Book of Sirach* and its prologue that should demonstrate to us that we are faced with an alternative conception of Judaism—a very different way of conceiving the religion of Israel, both in itself and in relation to Hellenistic culture. The *Letter of Aristeas* signals much more than the existence of a philo-Ptolemaic "party"; it is the testimony (extraordinary in its uniqueness) to an evolutionary possibility for Judaism that must have still seemed practicable at the end of the second century B.C.E.—but no later, at least not in the same terms.

---

7. A. Momigliano ("Per la data e la caratteristica della Lettera di Aristea," *Aegyptus* 12 [1932]: 161–72) was the first to see in the *Letter of Aristeas* "a reaffirmation of the Jewish forces in Egypt that remained faithful to Jerusalem against the predominance of the Temple of Leontopolis. . . . It seems natural to me that a version accepted or edited by the priests of Leontopolis circulates in competition with that of the Septuagint" (pp. 170–71). The hypothesis was reconsidered and developed by S. Jellicoe in "The Occasion and Purpose of the *Letter of Aristeas*," *NTS* 12 (1965–66): 144–50.

8. On the *Letter of Aristeas* as a political document, see F. Parente, "La Lettera di Aristea come fonte per la storia del Giudaismo alessandrino durante la prima metà del I sec. a.C.," *Annali della Scuola Normale Superiore di Pisa* 2 (1972): 177–237, 517–67; and D. Mendels, "On 'Kingship' in the 'Temple Scroll' and the Ideological Vorlage of the Seven Banquets in the 'Letter of Aristeas to Philocrates,'" *Aegyptus* 59 (1979): 127–36.

3. THE MONARCH-GOD OF PSEUDO-ARISTEAS

The God depicted by Pseudo-Aristeas exercises sovereignty with a logic that is quite different from that put forth by Ben Sira. In the *Letter*, the ideal model—explicitly evoked—is more the option offered by Hellenistic thought; God is the Supreme Monarch, Creator, Lord, and Benefactor of all of humanity. By placing the proclamation of the existence of the only God in the mouth of the gentile Aristeas, the Jewish author of the *Letter* betrays his own models in a curious play on roles.

> These people [the Jews] worship God the overseer and creator of all, whom all men worship including ourselves, O king, except that we use a different name, Zeus or Dia. In this way the ancient men not improperly[9] intended to say that the one by whom all live and are created is the master and Lord of all. (*Let Aris* 16)

The *Letter* offers an impressive and unobscured vision of the lordship of the only God, who is "pantocrator" (*Let Aris* 185) and omniscient (cf. *Let Aris* 189, 210), "lover of the truth" (*Let Aris* 206) and "lover of justice" (*Let Aris* 209).

> God is one, and His power is shown in everything, every place being filled with His sovereignty, and none of the things on earth which men do secretly are hidden from Him, but rather all the deeds of any man are manifest to Him, as well as that which is to come to pass. (*Let Aris* 132)

God's power is revealed specifically in the providence shown to all God's subject creatures. "God does good to the whole world" (*Let Aris* 210; cf. 281); "He blesses the humankind, giving them health and food and all other gifts in their season" (*Let Aris* 190; cf. 259); "He is the source of blessings to everyone" (*Let Aris* 205).

God looks to the poor with particular benevolence. By definition, God is their protector: "God by His very nature welcomes that which is humbled" (*Let Aris* 257). "He destroys the proud, and exalts the gentle and humble" (*Let Aris* 263).

In short, the qualities attributed to the ideal monarch by Hellenistic political thought are transposed to a universal scale and stripped of every difficulty and imperfection known to human experience, while their willful and even unexpectedly creative character is maintained and emphasized through their attribution to a person-God. This explains why the author saw a treatise on the art of governing as the most adequate form for speaking

---

9. God's name means God's essence through a play of words, untranslatable into English. The same etymology is found in Diodorus of Sicily, *Bibliotheca historica* 1.12:2; 3.61:6.

about God, a treatise that the Jewish translators are said to have presented to King Ptolemy at his dining hall. This is another clever pseudo-epigraphic ploy by the pseudo-epigraphic author. The protagonist of the treatise is not the king, it is God—God's nature and actions. The king is not even the primary interlocutor. Pseudo-Aristeas's audience is his coreligionists of Alexandria, the only ones capable of distilling in its entirety the religious message hidden under the disguise of a political treatise. The section on the banquets (*Let Aris* 187–294) is not the "teaching on kingship" (Gr. *didachê pros to basileuein*) that it claims to be (*Let Aris* 294), but a *summa theologica* in the form of a treatise on political ethics. Read in this way it offers precious information about the religious ideology of the author, information that is perfectly coherent with the whole of the *Letter* and confirms the intimate unity of both the thought and the composition of the writing. A Hellenistic political philosophy inferred from the Stoic conceptions of an impersonal divinity is thus the occasion for a synthesis of Jewish theology at the end of the second century B.C.E.[10] Recast as a "teaching on kingship" and offered to the King's imitativeness,[11] this religious synthesis would produce new philosophical syntheses in an uninterrupted chain of borrowing and reciprocal influences destined for centuries to characterize the encounter of the "philosophical" West with the "religious" East, first through Hellenistic Judaism and later through Christianity.

4. IMPERFECT AND SINNING HUMANKIND

Before the only God, omnipotent and provident King, there is humankind, as a beloved subject, the supremely inferior creature who is therefore liable to good and evil and to the happiness and suffering of living. "All men have been created by God to share the greatest ills as well as the greatest blessings, and it is impossible, being a man, to be without some of both" (*Let Aris* 197a).

Because it is God's will, experiences such as "death, disease, pain, and the like" are part of human existence "despite our will" (*Let Aris* 233), part of the only earthly prospect of life known to the *Letter*. Only death can quit this situation, with the end *tout court* of human existence, so that "reason does not legitimate any pain for those who are dead and released from evils" (*Let Aris* 268a).

---

10. See F. Adorno, *La filosofia antica*, 2 vols. (Milan, 1961–65), 2:70–83.
11. "Providence" (cf. *Let Aris* 190; 205; 210; 281) and "mercy" (cf. *Let Aris* 188; 191–92; 254) are the two divine qualities that the *Letter* invites the king to "imitate."

That which human beings cannot avoid must be confronted with the "goodness of soul" (Gr. *eupsychia*), a quality the author does not entrust to the self-discipline of the wise but invites request in prayer as God's gift. "God gives the goodness of soul; we must pray Him [to receive it]" (*Let Aris* 197b).

Apart from the evils that humankind undergoes, there is the evil that each individual commits. Pseudo-Aristeas knows that human beings not only are imperfect but also sinners. He even offers a natural, almost benevolent explanation of this by recalling humankind's constitutional inclination toward pleasure according to models once again borrowed from Hellenistic culture:

> By nature [Gr. *physikon esti*] all men incline their heart [Gr. *dianoia*] toward something. The majority are likely to incline toward things to eat and drink and pleasure. (*Let Aris* 222–23)

Of course, he does not fail to recall the greater vulnerability and weakness of women—the Jews and the Greeks were in perfect agreement on this.

> The female sex is bold, positively active for something which it desires, easily liable to change its mind because of poor reasoning powers; by nature [Gr. *tê physei*] [woman] has been constituted [Gr. *kataskeuastai*] weak. (*Let Aris* 250)

Every injustice is triggered by this natural inclination, common to all people, although more accentuated in women.

> By nature [Gr. *physikôs*] all men are intemperate and incline to pleasures; hence injustice and the mass of greed result by nature [Gr. *pephyke*]. (*Let Aris* 277)

In contrast to Ben Sira, Pseudo-Aristeas does not dramatize this point. The constant and almost nonchalant repetition that this happens "by nature" is intended to be calming in itself. It excludes the existence of an external principle adverse to the divinity, as well as any corruption in the universal order. It also anticipates an impact with the experience of evil that subjectively would be too traumatic. The claimed conformity with the divine will is even further accentuated when we bear in mind that in our author's religious ideology "by nature" does not so much express a state of objective and impersonal necessity as it does a constituting act of the person-God. Nature (Gr. *physis*) is the result of God's intervention; it is a constitution by God (Gr. *kataskeuê*). The two terms in the *Letter* are interchangeable. "By [divine] constitution [Gr. *tê kataskeuê*) all men are inclined to pleasures" (*Let Aris* 108; cf. 277).

Faced with evil, whose natural origin and inevitability are found in the passions, the first remedy is obviously temperance—the "middle way" or "happy medium" (cf. *Let Aris* 122, 223, 256): "Control of oneself, and not being carried away by one's impulses [is] the highest power" (*Let Aris* 221–22).

At this point we would expect the prescription for a regimen of self-control, the elaboration of an ascetic life style, or, as in the *Book of Sirach*, a call to the law as "medicine." Instead, the *Letter* renews its invitation to prayer, to entrusting oneself to God's merciful providence.

> What is philosophy? To have a well-reasoned assessment of each occurrence . . . , and not to be carried away by impulses but to study carefully the harmful consequences of the passions, and by exercising proper and necessary restraint in carrying out what the occasion demands. But in order to have due care for these things, it is necessary to pray God. (*Let Aris* 256; cf. 252)

5. MERCY AS THE CORE OF THE RELATIONSHIP BETWEEN GOD AND HUMANKIND

In the theological vision of the *Letter*, mercy is in fact God's attribute par excellence, the corollary of God's self-sufficient power and perfection: "God does not want anything and is merciful" (Gr. *epieikês*; *Let Aris* 211).

Mercy is the "constant" (Gr. *dia pantos*; *Let Aris* 188), guiding principle of divine action in relation to humankind in general, to every individual human being, and in every circumstance. This is what grounds the golden rule of love taught to the king as a "teaching of wisdom" (Gr. *sophias didachê*):

> As you do not wish evils to come upon you, but to partake of every blessing, so you will put this into practice with your subjects, including the sinners, and admonish the good and upright even more mercifully [Gr. *epieikesteron*]. For God guides all men in mercy [Gr. *epieikeia*]. (*Let Aris* 207)

That mercy is the only face God presents to humankind, even the sinner, is an absolute truth for Pseudo-Aristeas. It does not matter if the very logic of the retributory principle as a result is diminished, compromised, or even denied: "God does not smite [the sinners] in proportion to their offenses nor by the greatness of His strength, but exercises mercy" (Gr. *epieikeia*; *Let Aris* 192).

The reason for such action lies, first, in God's benevolent compassion for the misery of creatures. God knows well the burden of suffering in life. In proposing the ideal of philanthropy, Pseudo-Aristeas holds God's attitude up as a model.

> The human race increases and reproduces over many years and in painful suffering, so that it is your duty neither to inflict punishments easily nor to

submit men to torments, knowing that the life of mankind is constituted in pain and suffering. If you bear in mind each set of facts, you will be inclined to mercy [Gr. *eleos*], even as God is merciful [Gr. *eleêmôn*]. (*Let Aris* 208)

Second, the *Letter* maintains that there is a real pedagogical value in the principle of love toward enemies, a value for both those who receive it and those who give it. Pseudo-Aristeas is very conscious that this opinion runs against the general current:

It is a man's duty [to be generous] toward those who are amicably disposed to us. That is the general opinion. My belief is that we must [also] show liberal charity to our opponents so that in this manner we may convert them to what is proper and fitting to them. (*Let Aris* 227)

Even the king, "to conserve his kingdom safe and whole until the end," must know how

to imitate the constant mercy [Gr. *to epieikes*] of God. By being long-suffering and by treating the guilty more mercifully [Gr. *epieikesteron*] than they deserve, you will convert them from evil and bring them to repentance. (*Let Aris* 188)

But most of all, God is merciful precisely because God's power is absolute and unquestionable. Applying retributory logic toward humankind would be the equivalent, for Pseudo-Aristeas, of a manifestation of weakness. It would mean that the divine authority to a certain extent can be challenged, that through sin, humankind has the ability to affirm its own autonomy before God. Given that this prospect is precluded by divine absoluteness and omnipotence, the unleashing of God's wrath (even God's "just," retributory wrath) would mark a useless and even reproachable act of cruelty on the part of an incomparably stronger power. In teaching the king to be fair in his judgments and to avoid wrath in the use of his power, Pseudo-Aristeas is once again speaking of God and revealing God's action.

Let [the king] take no action arrogantly or in [his] own strength against the sinners. . . . [The king], in fact, has absolute power, and any recourse to anger [Gr. *thymos*] brings death, which is indeed a useless and painful thing to do if many are deprived of life simply because he is their lord. But since all are subject to him and there is no opposition, why should he be carried away by anger? You must know that God governs the whole cosmos with mercy [Gr. *met'eumeneias*] and without any wrath [Gr. *chôris orgês hapasês*]. (*Let Aris* 191, 253–54)

We are polemically very far from the rigid, almost mathematically deter-mined proportion between God's mercy and justice proposed by Ben Sira. For him God's wrath is one of the necessary foundations of the retributory principle.

> Mercy and wrath [Gr. *orgê*] are with [the Lord],
> mighty when He forgives and when He alights His wrath.
> Great as His mercy is His justice,
> He will judge men, each according to his deeds.
>
> (*Sir* 16:11-12)

Of course, the sinners are lost also for the author of the *Letter*, and the law does not fail to warn them by listing "the manifest damages and the visitations sent by God upon the guilty" (*Let Aris* 131). But for God it is enough to demonstrate almighty power from time to time in order to show the complete impotence of God's enemies and to confound their presumptuousness. Like a king who maintains peace and *parat bellum*, "God by granting a truce and demonstrating His power implants His fear in every heart" (*Let Aris* 194).

One thing is certain: in Pseudo-Aristeas's vision of divine omnipotence (and its unquestionability) there is no room for a God challenged by sin and forced to wrath in order to reaffirm authority over humankind and the cosmos.

6. A THEOLOGY OF GRACE

The emphasis placed on God's omnipotence and mercy pushes Pseudo-Aristeas to develop a true theology of grace.

We discover, first of all, that not only is the goodness of the soul (Gr. *eupsychia*) from God, but the escape from the evils of life and the acquisition of blessings are also the immediate consequences of divine will. "The escape from every evil takes place only through the power of God. . . . God controls all glory, directing it where He wishes" (*Let Aris* 268b–69).

Before the supreme freedom with which "God takes away prosperity [from some] while magnifying others and promoting them to receive glory" (*Let Aris* 244), humankind seems little more than a powerless spectator who, in its aspirations to become an actor, sees its every initiative as null and void from the very beginning. The most emblematic case is that of the kingdom:

> It is God who assigns glory and greatness of wealth to kings, each and every one, and no king is such by himself [Gr. *par'heautou*]. All wish to share this glory, but they cannot—it is a gift from God. (*Let Aris* 224)

Human initiative is excluded even in the case of acceding to the throne by hereditary succession.

> It is God who bestows the glory and greatness of wealth and neither do [the descendants of the king] obtain the power by themselves [Gr. *di'heautous*]. (*Let Aris* 196)

As for the conservation of power, again it is only God who defends the king from his enemies and assures him of the favor of his subjects. "Even being liked by every people is to have received a handsome gift from God—this is the highest good" (*Let Aris* 225; cf. 265).

The most amazing statement we find in the *Letter*, however, is that in addition to an individual's social status and success, moral being and action also depend on God; being happy and being good are both gifts from God. Whenever the value of an ethical principle—even a simple preliminary call to temperance—is put forth, Pseudo-Aristeas repeats that every good deed and every good thought are possible only through God's work; even the very capability of doing good (and not evil) is a gift: "It is a gift of God to do good and not its opposite" (*Let Aris* 231).

From this perspective, the question "Can good be taught?" (*Let Aris* 236) is inevitably answered in the negative. From the point of view of human capacities, it is even a dishearteningly negative answer, which emphasizes human impotence and incapability of doing or even wanting the good. On the other hand, the stress Pseudo-Aristeas places on the greatness of God's mercy makes it a bit of good news. The theological assumption is that the good depends on a constituting act of God: "It is a constitution [Gr. *kataskeuê*] of the soul, caused by the power of God, to accept every good and to reject its opposite" (*Let Aris* 236).

In fact, God is the master of the human "heart" (Gr. *kardia*, *dianoia*),[12] and it is in God's power to force it to the good, modifying God's creature. Aristeas's prayer to God, that his plea in favor of the Jewish prisoners be well accepted by the king, is exemplary of this idea:

> I prayed God with all my soul, that He constitute the heart [Gr. *dianoia*] of the king to the release of all [the prisoners]. For mankind is God's creation and is changed and converted by Him. Therefore with many diverse prayers I besought Him who is the Master of man's heart [Gr. *kardia*], that [the king] be compelled [Gr. *sunanagkazô*] to accomplish my request. (*Let Aris* 17)

If the king consented to his functionary's request, the merit must go to God, who used God's power. Aristeas does not hesitate to recognize this:

> God had fulfilled all my purpose, and compelled [Gr. *synanagkazô*] [the king] to release [the prisoners]. . . . God had bestowed him strength to bring salvation to a large multitude. (*Let Aris* 20–21)

---

12. With the Greek term *dianoia* the *Letter* indicates the intention of the intellect and the will, the thought and the sentiment of humankind, the self in the most intimate and total sense. Metaphorically it is the "mind" or, more fully, the "heart" of humankind (cf. *Let Aris* 17, where *dianoia* is a synonym of *kardia* ["heart"]).

We find the same language in *Let Aris* 237, in reference to "temperance":

It is impossible unless God constitutes [Gr. *kataskeuazô*] the heart [Gr. *dianoia*] toward it.

And again in *Let Aris* 238 regarding "love toward parents":

It is impossible unless God guides the heart [Gr. *dianoia*] toward the noblest things.

As for "love toward neighbors," enemies included,

you must pray God that this be taken in action, for He rules the hearts [Gr. *dianoia*] of all. (*Let Aris* 227)

Therefore, it is not an individual who does good, but God the omnipotent who does good through that individual, (re)molding God's creature.

God is Lord over all and we do not ourselves direct our plans in the finest of actions, but God brings to completion the affairs of all men and guides [them], since He has the power. (*Let Aris* 195)

This is a general rule that allows no exceptions:

The fulfillment of our deeds depends on God. (*Let Aris* 239)

Even the conception of good thoughts is held to be the work of God:

God directs us toward good deliberations on everything. (*Let Aris* 243)

It follows that there is no practice, code, or norm that human beings must (or can) propaedeutically fulfill. God's freedom to give is in no way conditioned by the ethical actions of humankind. For Pseudo-Aristeas there is only one option that comes before every law—the recognition of God's supreme power, which opens humankind to the reception of God's gifts, qualifying human beings to do good.

Realizing that God has given legislators the purpose of saving men's life, is the basis of the obedience of any law. (*Let Aris* 240)

In this consists the right attitude that humanity owes to God's mercy: the "fear of God" (Gr. *phobos tou theou*), which is the absolute "principle" (cf. *Let Aris* 159, 189); and "piety" (Gr. *eusebeia*), which is the "greatest good" (*Let Aris* 2, 229).

The base of piety [is] the realization that God continually directs everything and is omniscient. (*Let Aris* 210)

The centrality of prayer springs from this "realization"; the invocation of God is the primary stance of the righteous person.

> Life prospers when the helmsman knows the goal to which he must make the
> passage. Life is completely steered by invocation of God. (*Let Aris* 251)

The sole rule that orients all of human existence is made clear: it is only the
rule of prayer that makes good behavior and a good will possible and that
opens humankind to the gifts of salvation. It is neither a moral nor a cultic
rule, but a state of being ("the purity of soul") and a "holy conviction," even
a "faith," if that term did not evoke other and different theological perspectives. Human initiative and freedom find new space and value in this conviction. It is truly the greatest glory

> honoring God, and this not with gifts or sacrifices, but with purity of soul [Gr.
> *psychês katharotês*] and the holy conviction [Gr. *dialêpsis hosia*] that everything is
> constituted [Gr. *kataskeuazô*] by God and is directed according to His will. (*Let
> Aris* 234)

At this point I would even dare to define the "righteous" person according to Pseudo-Aristeas. It is not the person who strives hard to do good but
the one who, with purity of soul and serene awareness, directs life toward
the righteous goal: recognizing the beginning and end of everything as being
in God and receiving from God salvation, that is, blessings and the good,
well-being and well-doing.

7. THE MEANING OF THE MOSAIC LAW

What sense is there, then, in the law, particularly in the purity laws that
separate Israel from every other people? It is of this alone that Pseudo-
Aristeas speaks when he offers an allegorical explanation of these norms
through the person of the high priest Eleazar.

Again, the theological concerns of the author—and not incongruous missionary ends—emerge in the foreground. The aspects drawn from the allegory, in their specificity and even in their marginality, make sense only as a
justification for a rereading of Judaism from within. Not one reference is
made to the more striking features of the Mosaic law, such as circumcision
or rest on the Sabbath. The author of the *Letter* intends to redefine the
traditional foundations of Judaism, not to advertise it to the Gentiles. In the
statement, "most people . . . show a certain amount and difficulty of concern
for the parts of the law dealing with meats and drink and beasts considered
to be unclean" (*Let Aris* 128), we must not see the curiosity of Gentiles or
proselytes reflected, but the doubts and questions of the Jewish readers of
the *Letter*. Does claiming that "everything is God's gift" not perhaps risk
sanctioning the notion that the law is useless and obedience to it unneces-

sary? In particular, how can the purity laws be reconciled with the principle that "everything is similarly constituted in regard to natural reasoning, being governed by one supreme power" (*Let Aris* 143; cf. 129)?

The author of the *Letter* does not at all intend to diminish, much less deny, the force of the divine commandment that obliges Israel to observe legal norms. Nor does he want to bring into question the existence of the "clean" and the "unclean," a distinction that remains an active and vital part of the lived religion and even the utopian imagination of the author:[13] the "purity of soul" is a condition for salvation (cf. *Let Aris* 234). In the *Letter*, the law given by God to Israel holds a dual function that legitimates its existence in God's "logic" and its faithful observance on the part of the Jew.

First, the law defends Israel from any possible contamination that could come from the company of unworthy or evil people. This is a constant concern of Pseudo-Aristeas, as well as of Ben Sira (cf. *Sir* 22:13).

> Through bad relationships men become perverted, and are miserable their whole life long; if, however, they mix with wise and prudent companions, they rise above ignorance and achieve progress in life. . . . So, to prevent our being perverted by contact with others or by mixing with bad influences, [our lawgiver] hedged us in on all sides with purity laws connected with meat and drink and touch and hearing and sight. (*Let Aris* 130, 142)

Through the Mosaic revelation Israel was "constituted" pure by God's intervention. Such status of purity consists in the recognition of the only God. Because "all the rest of humankind, except ourselves, believe that there are many gods" (*Let Aris* 134), the separation of Israel as a people from idolatrous peoples (from "all the rest of humankind") makes sense.

> In his wisdom [our] lawgiver, being endowed by God for the knowledge of universal truths, surrounded us with unbroken palisade and iron walls to prevent our mixing with any of the other peoples in any matter, since we have been constituted [Gr. *kathestôtes*] pure in body and soul, preserved from false beliefs, and worshiping the only God omnipotent over all creation. (*Let Aris* 139)

Keeping the Jews whole in their "constituted" purity, the law, through the pedagogy of obedience, keeps them fast in the "holy conviction" of the supremacy of the one God. This is the second function of the law: being the

---

13. The description of Jerusalem offered in *Let Aris* 83–120 is not the recounting of a journey or a guide for pilgrims; it is a utopian portrait of the holy city with the Temple as its center, its raison d'être. The description of the inhabitants is part of this utopian portrait—they "ascend and descend" the long stairways of the city "keeping their distance as much as possible as they walk, in order for those who are in the state of purity to avoid coming into contact with something forbidden" (*Let Aris* 106).

reminder of Israel. Next to "distinction," another fundamental characteristic of the Jews emerges—"memory."

> The cloven hoof, that is the separation of the claws of the hoof, is a sign of setting apart each of our actions for good. . . . The symbolism conveyed by these things compels us to make a distinction in the performance of all our acts, with righteousness as our aim. This moreover explains why we are distinct from all other men. . . . The man with whom the aforesaid manner of disposition is concerned is the man on whom the legislator has also stamped that of memory. For all cloven-footed creatures and ruminants quite clearly express to those who perceive it, the phenomenon of memory. . . . So [Moses] has ordained every time and place for a continual reminder of the supreme God and upholder [of all]. Accordingly in the matter of meats and drinks he commands men to offer first fruits and to consume them there and then straightaway. Furthermore in our clothes he has given us a distinguishing mark as a reminder, and similarly on our gates and doors he has commanded us to set up the "Words," so as to be a reminder of God. He also strictly commands that the sign shall be worn on our hands, clearly indicating that it is our duty to fulfill every activity with justice, having in mind our own condition, and above all the fear of God. He also commands that "on going to bed and rising" men should meditate on the ordinances of God. . . . I have thus demonstrated to you the extraordinary nature of the sound reason behind our distinctive characteristic of memory by expounding the cloven hoof and chewing the cud. . . . In the Scripture all the regulations have been made with righteousness in mind, and no ordinances have been made without purpose or fancifully, but to the intent that through the whole of our lives we may also practice justice to all mankind in our acts, remembering the all-sovereign God. (*Let Aris* 150–68)

In substance, the law is the education (Gr. *paideia*) of Israel. Its role is to defend, educate, and conserve the Jews in the requirements for salvation: the "purity of soul" and the "holy conviction" of the absolute and watchful supremacy of the one God. Obeying the law means following an effective pedagogical path toward morality and salvation, as the high priest Eleazar notes at the end of his discourse: "in the matter of meats, the unclean reptiles, the beasts, the whole underlying rationale is directed toward righteousness and righteous human relationship" (*Let Aris* 169; cf. 144).

8. SALVATION AMONG THE GENTILES

For Pseudo-Aristeas, therefore, the principle of salvation does not consist in being separate in itself nor in obedience to the law in itself. Salvation lies in what separation and obedience mean and produce. The true difference is not between Jew and non-Jew *tout court*, but between those who can justly be defined as "men of God," recognizing the beginning of everything in the only God, and those who, on the contrary, "are concerned with meat and drink and clothes, their whole attitude [to life] being concentrated on these concerns" (*Let Aris* 140b).

This takes nothing away from the superiority of Israel; in fact, it confirms Israel's primacy as the chosen people, because in relation to this condition Israel shines as the *unicum* among peoples, thanks to the effective education (Gr. *paideia*) of the law. The *Letter* does not fail to give voice to national pride:

> Such concerns are of no account among the people of our race, but throughout the whole of their lives their main objective is concerned with the sovereignty of God. (*Let Aris* 141)

However, shifting the stress from obedience to the law to its effects is a premise with enormous consequences. For example, it allows the high priest Eleazar almost carelessly to pronounce a few words (culminating in an astonishing parenthetical statement) that mark a profound change in the attitude toward Gentiles—namely, the admission that the qualification "men of God," properly due to the Jews, can be recognized by non-Jews and even lived by some of them.

> The leading priest among the Egyptians, conducting many close investigations and with practical experience of affairs, gave us the title "men of God" which is not ascribed to others, except a few who worship the true God. (*Let Aris* 140a)

Thus, the *Letter* provides its readers with a list of distinguished gentile "witnesses." The list encompasses not only fictitious characters, such as Aristeas and his brother Philocrates, but also well-known historical personalities (although all of these figures belong to an unverifiable past).[14]

For example, witnesses are the "most renowned priests in renowned Egypt" cited by the high priest. Attention to and a knowledge of the most minute details of Jewish things must be attributed to these men. Aristeas states that he has learned from these priests the information necessary for writing a previous "work on the people of the Jews" (*Let Aris* 6).

The list of witnesses continues with the philosopher Demetrius of Phalerum, presumed to be the librarian at the time of King Ptolemy Philadelphus and to whose authoritative advice the translation of the Hebrew Bible is ascribed (cf. *Let Aris* 9-11). In recognizing the philosophical and divine character of the law, Demetrius recalls the testimony of the historian Hecataeus of Abdera:

---

14. On the personalities of Greek philosophy and literature mentioned in the *Letter*, see Adorno, *La filosofia antica*; R. Cantarella, *La letteratura greca classica* (Florence, 1967); and A. A. Long, *Hellenistic Philosophy: Stoics, Epicureans, Sceptics* (London, 1974).

> Information has reached me that the lawbooks of the Jews are worth translation
> and inclusion in the royal library. . . . Because of their divine nature these
> books are very philosophical and pure. . . . A holy and pure speculation is
> contained in [these books], as Hecataeus of Abdera says. (*Let Aris* 10, 31)

Finally, even King Ptolemy is a "witness." He fills the Temple of Jerusalem with bountiful gifts (cf. *Let Aris* 51–82), calls those translators sent by the
high priest "men of God" (cf. *Let Aris* 179) and before the scrolls of the law

> bows down seven times, and says: "I offer to you my thanks, gentlemen, and to
> him who sent you even more, and most of all to the God whose oracles these
> are." (*Let Aris* 177)

However, Eleazar's parenthetical statement ("except a few who worship
the true God") implies something more than the general recognition that a
non-Jew can fully understand the value of the law and show it respect. It
means admitting that a non-Jew can share the same reality of salvation with
the Jew. In this respect the *Letter* contains some truly scandalous statements:
at least they must have seemed so to Flavius Josephus two centuries later
when he scrupulously avoided repeating them in his long and even slavish
paraphrase (*Ant* 12.11–118).[15] For example, the *Letter* speaks of a gentile
functionary, Aristeas, who without being or even posing as a proselyte prays
to God, is satisfied, and even dares not to perceive anything exceptional:

> For I had great hope, as I presented the case for the saving of men, that God
> would execute the fulfillment of my request, inasmuch as whatsoever men
> think to do in piety in the way of righteousness and attention to good works,
> God the Lord of all directs their acts and intentions. (*Let Aris* 18)

Above all, the *Letter* tells of a gentile king who is not content to be presented
as only a friend and benefactor of the Jews, nor simply to show respect for
their God: he even claims to share the same piety (Gr. *eusebeia*; cf. *Let Aris*
24, 37). Of even greater note, the high priest finds nothing strange in this
pretense; on the contrary, he is happy to inform of this fact the assembly of
the people of Jerusalem (cf. *Let Aris* 42). The translators then seem to
compete in glorifying the king's piety (Gr. *eusebeia*, *Let Aris* 215–216, 255,
261). This is not just laudatory rhetoric or vain hope, much less a moral
appeal; the translators state that the king already fully lives the reality of
salvation. God grants him the kingdom (cf. *Let Aris* 219), preserves his
existence from all evil (cf. *Let Aris* 233), directs his heart toward the most
beautiful things (cf. *Let Aris* 247) so that he desires the good (cf. *Let Aris*

---

15. On Josephus's paraphrase of the *Letter*, see Meecham, *Oldest Version of the Bible*, 333–39;
and A. Pelletier, *Flavius Josèphe adaptateur de la Lettre d'Aristée; une réaction atticisante contre la
koinê* (Paris, 1962).

267, 270, 271), and God realizes this good and brings it to term (cf. *Let Aris* 199, 255, 283, 287). The blessings that he has in abundance and the good he is capable of doing are unquestionable signs of God's favor. If salvation consists of "purity of soul and the holy conviction that everything is constituted by God and is directed according to His will, this is also [the king's] attitude, evidence of which can be seen by all from [his] past and present accomplishments" (*Let Aris* 234).

9. THE GREEK *PAIDEIA* AS AN ITINERARY OF SALVATION

There must therefore be a road to salvation open to the Gentiles too, a road of both "purification" and "awareness." This road is traced out in the prologue of the *Letter of Aristeas*. At the base of all we still find "the love of learning" (Gr. *philomatheia*). But this quality is not tied to the discipleship of the "readers" and therefore subordinated to the "reading" of the law, as in the *Prologue to Sirach*; it is presented by Pseudo-Aristeas as a gift common to every person of culture, the object of a recognized universal value. In praising the "disposition of the soul that loves to learn" that pervades his "brother," Philocrates, Pseudo-Aristeas makes this the fundamental quality of humankind and, by referring to the authority of a poetic text,[16] the very core of the Greek education (Gr. *paideia*):

> This is the supreme quality in man: "learning always something and always increasing," whether from the accounts [of others] or by actual experience. (*Let Aris* 2)

The religious potential of this "disposition of the soul" is even more extraordinary. Through it God "purifies" the human soul and makes it capable of receiving the most beautiful things, so that once the piety (Gr. *eusebeia*) has been established (that is, the "holy conviction" of God's supremacy), one sees one's actions and thoughts conformed to righteousness and morality.

> This is a way in which [God] constituted [Gr. *kataskeuazô*] a pure disposition of soul [Gr. *psychês kathara diathesis*], which is able to accept the noblest things, and which, turning to the highest one, the piety [Gr. *eusebeia*], directs everything according to a rule which does not err. (*Let Aris* 2)

The prologue continues by emphasizing the "love of learning" (Gr. *philomatheia*) and "the desire of the good" that bring Aristeas and Philocrates

---

16. The quoted iambic triameter is not identifiable in any known poetic work. Thackeray (*The Letter of Aristeas*) holds that it is the result of two Sophoclean hemistichs.

together in wanting to follow this itinerary, a theme that will be taken up again several times in the body of the *Letter* (cf. *Let Aris* 7, 171, 300, 322). Aristeas volunteers "with enthusiasm" (*Let Aris* 4) as the king's ambassador to the high priest for no other reason than "a set purpose devoted to the special study of the things of God" (*Let Aris* 3). As for Philocrates, being "favorably inclined toward the piety and disposition [Gr. *diathesis*] of those who live by the sacred law" (*Let Aris* 5), he will certainly accept willingly his brother's account as "matters pertaining to the edification [Gr. *episkeuê*] of the soul" (*Let Aris* 5; cf. 7).

The (saving) value of this "edification" is such as to encourage every effort in acquiring it and also to justify unreserved praise of the Greek *paideia* and its propaedeutic function—the praise that closes the prologue of the *Letter*:

> The joy [originated] from gold or any other formation [given] by those things highly prized by the empty-headed does not possess the same value, as compared with the moral course [given] by the education [Gr. *paideia*] and with the care for it. (*Let Aris* 8)

In virtue of this "moral course" Aristeas has arrived at the recognition that "the God who prospers your kingdom, [O king], is the same [God] who appointed [the Jews] their law, as my research has ascertained" (*Let Aris* 15).

The study of the Greek *paideia* substantially allows the overcoming (if only one wants to) of what appears to Pseudo-Aristeas as the primary, if not the sole obstacle: polytheism. A condemnation without appeal is reserved for polytheism for its impiety but most of all for its "senselessness," using the same arguments that Greek philosophy had used against it:

> It is profitless and useless to deify equals. And yet, even today, there are many of greater inventiveness and learning than the men of old, who nevertheless would be the first to worship them. Those who have invented these fabrications and myths are usually ranked to be the wisest of the Greeks. There is surely no need to mention the rest of the very foolish people, Egyptians and those like them, who have put their confidence in beasts and most of the serpents and monsters, worship them, and sacrifice to them both while alive and dead. (*Let Aris* 137–38)

If Aristeas is the prototype of the saved Gentile, the king is also seen to be moving in the right direction. For him too the *philomatheia* represents a rule of life.

> The king, out of his love of culture, considered it of supreme importance to bring to his court any man, wherever he might be found, of outstanding culture and prudence who excelled among his contemporaries. (*Let Aris* 124; cf. 321)

The section on the banquets closes with the praise of the king's *philomatheia*. He loves to read (*Let Aris* 283), to watch decorous games and edifying performances (*Let Aris* 284–85), and to surround himself with "lovers of learning" (*Let Aris* 286). In this way he shows through his actions that he is a "philosopher" (*Let Aris* 285) and that he possesses a temperament that unites "goodness of soul" and "cultural education" (*Let Aris* 290). To the king—as to all those who are lovers of learning (Gr. *philomatheis*) and therefore "are beloved of God, having trained their hearts [Gr. *dianoia*] for the noblest things" (*Let Aris* 286–87)—God has allowed a "pure heart free of all evil" (Gr. *hagnên kai amigé pantos kakou tên dianoian; Let Aris* 292) and "has constituted [him] pious" (Gr. *eusebei de soi kathestôti; Let Aris* 233).

The road that permits the Gentiles, or at least some of them, to become "men of God" and not simply "men of drink, food and clothing" is the Greek *paideia*. The "love of learning" *can* guide them, if they wish, on this road of "purification" and "awareness," where the merciful God awaits them with gifts of salvation.

10. THE MEETING OF GREEK *PAIDEIA* AND JEWISH *PAIDEIA*

On these bases the cultural, religious, and even physical meeting between the Jews and the Gentiles is made possible because the conditions of impurity have lessened and the same awareness has united them. This is what the *Letter of Aristeas* visualizes in the seven banquets offered by the king, in which we see the Jewish translators seated at the same table with the Greek philosophers, eating the same food (*Let Aris* 182–86). It is enough that the idolatrous rituals have been expressly eliminated.

> When they had taken their places, the king ordered [his steward] Dorotheus to carry everything out in accordance with the customs practiced by all his visitors from Judea. So Dorotheus passed over the sacred heralds, the sacrificial ministers and the rest, whose habitual role was to offer the prayers. Instead, he invited Eleazar, the oldest of the [Jewish] priests. (*Let Aris* 184)

The meeting is realized in the (possible) convergence of the Greek *paideia* and the Jewish *paideia*, in the awareness of God's uniqueness and supreme and provident power, as solemnly recognized on the part of the Greek king and the invited philosophers. Every day of the banquet, during which the king poses a question to each of the seventy-two Jewish guests, is drawn to a close with expressions of rejoicing and consensus from all parts, "and especially by the philosophers" (*Let Aris* 235, 296). Once again, as in all the truly important moments, the *Letter* sees the necessity of introducing the

testimony of an authoritative historical figure, in this case the philosopher
Menedemus of Eritrea:

> All the assembled company acclaimed and applauded loudly, and the king said
> to the philosophers, of whom there were many among them, "I think that
> these men excel in virtue and have a fuller understanding, because when asked
> questions of this sort unexpectedly they give appropriate answers, all making
> God the basis of their argument." The philosopher Menedemus of Eritrea
> said, "Yes, indeed, O king, for since the whole cosmos is governed by
> providence, and on the correct assumption that man is a creature of God, it
> follows that all power and beauty of argument has its origin in God." (*Let Aris*
> 200–201; cf. 235)

If the Greeks must recognize the superior *paideia* of their guests, the Jews
are asked to make a change of mentality of no less importance: to abandon
every feeling of distrust (if not hostility) for the Greek *paideia* and the Gentiles in general. We could reverse Aristeas's "confession" as it had to resonate
in the ears of the Alexandrian Jews—"the God who appointed us the law is
the same [God] who prospers King Ptolemy's kingdom" (cf. *Let Aris* 15)—
and imagine their shock upon hearing the high priest proclaim the *eusebeia*
of the gentile king. Such a sentiment of welcome would certainly not have
been shared by Ben Sira, so different is the *Letter*'s rereading of Judaism.
The example of Eleazar is posed as the opposite of the culturally and reli-
giously "self-sufficient" model of the scribe (the "reader" of the *Prologue to
Sirach*). Eleazar selects as translators men who are experts in both Jewish and
Greek culture, are ready for dialogue, and are free from every prejudice,
every idea of presumption or contempt for the others.

> Eleazar selected men of the highest merit and of excellent education [Gr.
> *paideia*] due to the distinction of their parentage; they had not only mastered
> the Jewish literature, but had made a serious study of that of the Greeks as
> well. They were therefore well qualified . . . for the negotiations and questions
> arising from the law, with the middle way as their commendable ideal; they
> had rid their heart [Gr. *dianoia*] of any uncouth and uncultured attitude of
> mind; in the same way they rose above conceit and contempt of other people,
> and instead engaged in discourse and listening to and answering each and
> every one, as is meet and right. (*Let Aris* 121-22)

The stated primacy of "hearing" over the "reading" of the law is also part
of this new attitude of mind: "The good life consists in observing the law,
and this aim is achieved by hearing much more than by reading" [Gr. *anag-
nôsis*] (*Let Aris* 127). In the *Prologue to Sirach* the primacy of "reading" is
the primacy of salvation through "literal" observation; in Pseudo-Aristeas the
primacy of "hearing" is the primacy of salvation through the "sense" of
the law—the effects that its practice induces and produces in people. As the

impossibility of substituting the original Hebrew text is derived from the exclusiveness of the Jewish *paideia*, the equal dignity claimed for the Greek translation is derived from the primacy of the sense.

The way the *Letter* treats the theme of the sacral character of the law is indicative of this. It is the motive, states Demetrius of Phalerum, for which "writers and poets and the whole army of historians have been reluctant to refer to [it]" (*Let Aris* 31; cf. 312–13). Again from Demetrius of Phalerum we learn that Theopompus the historian and Theodectus the tragic poet, the (inevitable) historical witnesses, ran up against divine punishment for having tried to insert biblical quotations into their works. Yet they were dealing with "some passages of a previous translation of the law" (*Let Aris* 314), a translation that could not have been very accurate, at least judging from the poor quality of the Hebrew manuscripts then extant in Alexandria and the librarian's solicitude to ask for a reliable text from Jerusalem (cf. *Let Aris* 30, 32). Obviously, the force of the law had remained untouched even in these fragments of translation.

What should be said then of the new translation, made "so well, with respect for the piety and with rigorous accuracy" (*Let Aris* 310), the fruit of the philological capabilities and religious zeal of the seventy-two translators (cf. *Let Aris* 301–7)? As pointed out by H. M. Orlinsky, the studied ceremonials with which the Alexandrian Jewish community accepts the Greek translation (cf. *Let Aris* 308–12) make it the exact equivalent of the Hebrew text.[17] Every gesture and every detail, repeating the events of the original, contribute to this identification: the public reading before the priests, the notables, and the assembly of the people (*Let Aris* 308); the presence of the translators as representatives of the "twelve tribes" ("six from each tribe"; *Let Aris* 46–50); the "curse" pronounced so that "the text [of the translation] be conserved forever without change over the course of time" (*Let Aris* 310–11); the reading before the king (*Let Aris* 312); and the renewal of the same admiration and prostration that the king showed before the original scrolls when they arrived from Jerusalem (*Let Aris* 317; cf. 176–77).

The text of the Septuagint is the divine law *tout court*; it has the same sacral character, the same force (pace Ben Sira's "grandson"), and the same capacity to produce the effects of salvation. The "hearing" that the translation guarantees makes the "reading" of the original inessential and frustrates the cogency of the teaching pretense of the "readers" and their zealous

---

17. H. M. Orlinsky, "The Septuagint as Holy Writ and the Philosophy of the Translators," *HUCA* 46 (1975): 89–114 (esp. 94–103).

disciples, freeing the Jews of the Diaspora from the necessity of a suffocating discipleship.

11. A DIALOGICAL JUDAISM

Faced with a model such as the one outlined by Ben Sira, in which there is no room for the Gentile or gentile culture if not in the opposition between true and false *paideia*, the *Letter of Aristeas* manifests a type of Judaism capable of entering into a dialogue with the Greek culture, both giving and receiving value. This type of Judaism does not even find any need to "Judaize" the Greek *paideia*, making it dependent on the greater antiquity of the Jewish *paideia* through a process already used by Aristobulos.[18] A completely autonomous value and foundation to salvation are recognized in the Greek *paideia*. Thus, any sentiment of proselytism is equally extraneous to Pseudo-Aristeas. The Gentile is not asked to be converted or to obey the law; rather, nothing is asked of the Gentile because the *Letter* is directed to the Jews. The example offered by the gentile "authors" and protagonists of the writing teaches the Jews to see the Greek world in a more favorable light, to see open-mindedly a world in which there are similar potentialities for salvation and similar interlocutors.

At the same time that the Jews are asked to abandon every prejudice (cf. *Let Aris* 122), the *Letter* wants also to teach them to keep alive the meaning and value of their own uniqueness, without letting it be dissolved in the meeting of cultures. Thanks to the "constituting" intervention of God, and to the law that upholds and prolongs its effects, as a people the Jews are already what only a few Gentiles can become individually. In their own being, therefore, there is both the salvation and the "mission" of Israel; in the faithful observance of their own traditions, the Jews live for themselves and teach others the "holy conviction" that all things have their beginning in the one God.

At the end of the second century B.C.E. such a model of Judaism must

---

18. On Aristobulos, see Riessler, *ASB* (1928), 179–85, 1275 (German trans.); N. Walter, *Der Thoraausleger Aristobulos: Untersuchungen zu seinen Fragmenten and zu pseudepigraphischen Resten der jüdisch-hellenistischen Literatur,* TU 86 (Berlin, 1964); M. Hengel, "Schöpfung und Weisheit bei Aristobul, dem ersten jüdischen 'Philosophen' in Alexandria," in *Judentum und Hellenismus,* WUNT 10 (Tübingen, 1969), 295–307 (*Judaism and Hellenism,* trans. J. Bowden, 2 vols. [Philadelphia, 1974], 1:163–69); A.-M. Denis, *Fragmenta Pseudepigraphorum quae supersunt Graeca* (Leiden, 1970 [Greek text]); C. Kraus Reggiani, "Aristobulo e l'esegesi allegorica dell'Antico Testamento nell'ambito del giudaismo ellenistico," *Rivista di Filologia e Istruzione Classica* 101 (1973): 162–85; N. Walter, *JSHRZ* 3.2 (1975): 261–79 (German trans.); and A. Y. Collins, *OTP* 2 (1985): 831–42 (English trans.).

have still seemed possible, even able to appeal to the authority of the high priest of Jerusalem. The necessity of the apology and the bitterness of the debate remind us, however, that the climate was rapidly changing. The emergence and affirmation in the Alexandrian Diaspora of the self-sufficient course of the *Book of Sirach* and its prologue would block the development of this dialogical line. The only alternative to confrontation and indifference, on the one hand, and assimilation, on the other, would be the "Judaization" of the Greek *paideia* and proselytism as the condition for an enduring cultural exchange. This was, in fact, the line of development in the Hellenistic Jewish tradition Wisdom *of Solomon* and Philo of Alexandria in particular— that would also leave a deep mark on early Christianity. When a comprehensive history of the many middle Judaisms—a history encompassing the winning and the losing movements, those that remained viable and those that did not—is written, an important place will be reserved for the *Letter of Aristeas* and its unique testimony.[19]

19. This chapter is the revision of a paper I delivered at the 1987 AISG Meeting in S. Miniato, Pisa. See G. Boccaccini, "La Sapienza dello Pseudo–Aristea," in *Biblische und judaistische Studien: Festschrift für Paolo Sacchi*, ed. A. Vivian (Frankfurt, 1990), 143–76.

PART III

SOME PREPARATORY
SKETCHES

6

PHILO
OF ALEXANDRIA

A Judaism in Philosophical
Categories

At the beginning of the Common Era, the Hellenistic Jewish tradition offers, in Philo of Alexandria, its most significant attempt at a synthesis of the Jewish and Hellenistic cultures.[1] In spite of the possession of one of the largest and most complete corpora to have come down to us from antiquity, the work of the Alexandrian philosopher and exegete is much less known and studied than would be expected. The greatest obstacle to understanding this protagonist of middle Judaism seems to lie in historically determined prejudices. These prejudices result, on the one hand, from the early appropriation of his work by the Christian apologists as a "precursor" of Christian philosophy and theology, and on the other hand, from his consequent devaluation by the rabbinic tradition, which, mercilessly judging him "non-Jewish," does not even mention him. Thus his figure is familiar at the most to historians of Greek philosophy (and even to patrologists) and practically alien to scholars of Judaism. It is as if his thought could be understood only in terms of contemporary Hellenistic philosophy or in the light of later

---

1. The fundamental critical edition of the works of Philo of Alexandria is L. Cohn, P. Wendland, and S. Reiter, eds., *Philonis Alexandrini opera quae supersunt*, 6 vols. (Berlin, 1896–1930; repr., 1962). L. Cohn is also the editor (with I. Heinemann, M. Adler, and W. Theiler) of the German translation, *Die Werke Philos von Alexandria in deutscher Übersetzung*, 7 vols. (Breslau, 1909–38; 2d ed., Berlin, 1962–64). There are three other modern complete translations: F. H. Colson, G. H. Whitaker, and R. Marcus, eds., *Philo*, 12 vols. (London and Cambridge, Mass., 1929–62 [English trans]); R. Arnaldez, C. Mondésert, and J. Pouilloux, *Les oeuvres de Philon d'Alexandrie*, 35 vols. (Paris, 1961–79 [French trans.]); and J. M. Triviño, *Obras completas de Filón de Alejandría*, 5 vols. (Buenos Aires, 1975–76 [Spanish trans.]). A great deal of Philo's corpus can also be found in Italian. See C. Kraus Reggiani, *Filone Alessandrino e un'ora tragica della storia ebraica* (Naples, 1967); idem, *De Opificio Mundi: De Abrahamo: De Josepho* (Rome, 1979); G. Reale, ed., *La creazione del mondo: Le allegorie delle Leggi* (Milan, 1978); idem, *L'erede delle cose divine* (Milan, 1981); idem, *Le origini del male* (Milan, 1984); idem, *L'uomo e Dio* (Milan, 1986); idem, *La filosofia mosaica* (Milan, 1987); and idem, *La migrazione verso l'eterno* (Milan, 1988).

Christian theology, and not in terms of his own environment: the culture and faith of his people in his time.

In order to disprove such a charge of "non-Jewishness," it should be enough to present the biographical information we have about Philo. He was one of the most influential and esteemed members of the Jewish community of Alexandria, so much so as to be designated, in 39–40 C.E., officially to represent that community before the Roman emperor Caligula (cf. Philo, *Leg Gai*; Josephus, *Ant* 18.259–60). As with the *Letter of Aristeas*,[2] the use of the Greek language and attention to intercultural dialogue does not signify a lesser degree of commitment to the intellectual, religious, and even political problems that were then emerging within Judaism. In respect to the *Letter of Aristeas*, Philo is even much less willing to grant autonomy to the Greek *paideia*. He does not hesitate to assume concepts and methods of philosophical investigation and systematically to apply the allegorical method to Scripture. Consequently, from the very letter of Scripture the foundations of the religion of Israel emerge, exposed "rationally." Yet he never forgets that his primary role is as the custodian of a divinely revealed wisdom, held to be infallible and comprehensive. It is only divine revelation that makes Moses the greatest philosopher or, better, the "perfect" philosopher,

> both because he had attained the very summit of philosophy, and because he had been divinely instructed in the greater and most essential part of Nature's lore. (*Op Mund* 8)

Greek philosophy is offered an important place and an organically recognized role, but on the condition that it accepts its dependence on Scripture, both chronologically and in terms of content (Moses, the perfect philosopher, lived before the Greek philosophers; cf. *Her* 214; *Aet Mund* 19) and that it subordinates itself to an ancillary function, respectful of the primacy of revelation.

> And indeed just as school subjects contribute to the acquisition of philosophy, so does philosophy to the getting of wisdom. For philosophy is the practice or study of wisdom, and wisdom is the knowledge of things divine and human and their causes. And therefore just as the culture of the schools is the bond-servant of philosophy, so must philosophy be the servant of wisdom. (*Congr* 79)

Biblical commentary is imposed as the philosophical work par excellence, in which it is possible to use the classical sources with unprejudiced freedom and even to bend biblical texts to the most bold allegories without lessening the integrity of the system. One of the most effective syntheses of Greek

---

2. On the frequent references to the *Letter of Aristeas* and its ideology, see chap. 5.

philosophy and "Mosaic philosophy" results, unfolding in one of the most unique and fascinating systems of thought in middle Judaism.

I do not intend to present here the comprehensive framework of Philo's thought, nor even a broad outline, but only two concrete examples of his methods. This will be done through a critical approach (one I hope will be no less exemplary) that does not proceed from outside or backwards, but *from within* the middle Jewish problematic, fully returning a voice that has been long and culpably forgotten to its proper context.

I. Memory as a Philosophical and Religious Concept

1. BETWEEN CLASSICAL CULTURE AND THE JEWISH TRADITION

In ancient and middle Jewish traditions (and, therefore, also in early Christianity) the theme of memory occupies an unquestionably significant role, although with different emphases, as contemporary scholars from J. Pedersen on have noted.[3] Philo's approach is unique: thanks to his adoption of the allegorical method, the theme of memory is conceptualized to reemerge in the meeting and confrontation between the Jewish and classical cultures as one of the constituent elements of "Mosaic philosophy."

Philo's immediate points of reference are Aristotle's naturalistic treatise *De Memoria et Reminiscentia* (On memory and recollection)[4] and an excursus in the *Letter of Aristeas* on the religious value of memory (*Let Aris* 150–61). The review often seems servile, even in the examples put forward, and comes close to being simply a paraphrase. The context that the two sources are forced into, however, makes them formal references and not substantial ones: they are reappropriated in an ideological sense as building-blocks, unrecognizably revitalized, for a completely coherent and original development of thought.

---

3. On the importance of the theme of memory in the ancient and middle Jewish traditions, see chap. 8. On memory in Philo see also G. Boccaccini, "Il concetto di memoria in Filone Alessandrino," *Annali dell'Istituto di Filosofia dell'Università di Firenze* 6 (1984): 1–19.

4. For the Greek text of the Aristotelian treatise, see the critical edition by W. D. Ross, *Aristotelis: Parva Naturalia* (Oxford, 1955). For an English translation, see W. S. Hett, *Aristotle: On the Soul, Parva Naturalia, On Breath*, Loeb Classical Library (London, 1935), 279–307.

2. THE RELATIONSHIP WITH THE
CLASSICAL SOURCES

Philo paraphrases the beginning of Aristotle's treatise in *Leg Alleg* 2.42–43 (cf. *Spec Leg* 1.334) in order to state that "memory" (Gr. *mnêmê*) is a natural human faculty through which the "mind" (Gr. *nous*) collects the past (cf. Aristotle, *Mem* 449b). Even the mechanisms through which the recollections of "what is not present" are produced are described in conformity to Aristotle (cf. *Mem* 450a):

> "Presentation" is an imprint made on the soul. For, like a ring or seal, it stamps on the soul the image corresponding to everything which each of the senses has introduced. And the mind like wax receives the impress and retains it vividly, until forgetfulness, the opponent of memory, levels out the imprint, and makes it indistinct, or entirely effaces it. (Philo, *Deus Imm* 43)

The central distinction in the Aristotelian text between "memory" (Gr. *mnêmê*) and "recollection" (Gr. *anamnêsis*) is thus arrived at:

> Recollection [Gr. *anamnêsis*] is neither the recovery nor the acquisition of memory [Gr. *mnêmê*]; for when one first learns or receives a sense impression, one does not recover any memory—for none has gone before—, nor does one acquire memory from the first impression. . . . But when one recovers knowledge or sensation which one had before, or recovers that the condition of which we have previously called memory, at that moment this may be called recollection. . . . Then the process of recollection implies memory, and is followed by memory. (Aristotle, *Mem* 451a–b)

Aristotle had only developed a theme already dealt with by Plato (*Phaedrus* 73ff.; *Menexenus* 81c–d; *Philebus* 34b), emptying it, however, of every metaphysical connotation that had made it the foundation of the preexistence of the soul; recollection (Gr. *anamnêsis*) is simply one of the functions of psychic life.

Philo undoubtedly follows the same line of thought; in only two passages is there any indirect and polemical trace of reference to the Platonic conception. Learning can be said to be recollection, but only in the sense that God in providence has already arranged everything.

> For from the beginning at the first creation of all things God provided beforehand, raised from the earth, what was necessary for all living animals and particularly for the human race to which He granted sovereignty over all earthborn creatures. For none of the works of God is of later birth, but all that seems to be accomplished by human skill and industry in later time was there by the foresight of nature lying ready half made; thus it is not wrong to say that learning is recollection [Gr. *hôs mê apo skopou tas mathêseis anamnêseis einai legesthai*]. (Philo, *Praem Poen* 9)

And in *De Vita Mosis* 1.21, in order to exalt Moses's ease in learning, it is said:

> In a short time he advanced beyond the capacities [of his teachers]; his gifted nature forestalled their instruction, so that his seemed a case rather of recollection than of learning [Gr. *hôs anamnêsin einai dokein, ou mathêsin*].

These turns of phrase ("it is not wrong to say"; "his seemed a case") indicate that it is not possible to go further. Philo assumes the Platonic conception in order to neutralize it; it is much too contrary to his religious and cultural positions. On one hand, he reduces its meaning to banality; on the other, he loads it with contents foreign to it. The relationship with Aristotle remains the only one that can possibly support the much more pressing suggestions that come from the Jewish tradition.[5]

In five parallel passages from as many works (*Leg Alleg* 3.90–94; *Sobr* 27–29; *Migr Abr* 205–6; *Congr* 39–43; *Mut* 97–102) Philo confirms the Aristotelian distinction between memory and recollection, which he sees symbolized in the biblical figures of Joseph's two sons, Ephraim and Manasseh.

Ephraim, in a figurative sense, is the name of memory. In fact, Philo states that this name translated into Greek means "production of fruits" (Gr. *karpophoria*),

---

5. There is another passage in which some scholars see an explicit adherence to the Platonic doctrine of recollection. Philo, when speaking of the Therepeutae and their way of interpreting the Scripture, states: "The exposition of the sacred scriptures treats the inner meaning conveyed in allegory. For to these people the whole law book seems to resemble a living creature with the literal ordinances for its body and for its soul the invisible mind laid up in its wording. It is in this mind especially that the rational soul begins to contemplate the things akin to itself and looking through the words as through a mirror beholds the marvelous beauties of the concepts, unfolds and removes the symbolic coverings and brings forth the thoughts and sets them bare to the light of day for those who *ek mikras hypomnêseôs* are able to discern the inward and hidden through the outward and visible" (*Vit Cont* 78). Colson translates, "for those who need but a little reminding to enable them to discern . . . ," and specifies in a note: "I think this should be taken as an allusion to the Platonic doctrine that learning is recollection. The knowledge is latent in the mind and the teacher only brings it into consciousness" (Colson, Whitaker, and Marcus, eds., *Philo*, 9:161, 523; see also Cohn et al., eds., *Die Werke Philos*, 8:68). As we have seen, however, Philo tends to keep his distance from the Platonic doctrine of recollection. His total adherence to it here in such an engaged context would be strange indeed. The key to reading this passage must be sought elsewhere. In the ancient rabbinic literature (*Mishnah, Tosefta, Mekilta, Sifra, Sifre*) we often find the Hebrew formula: *'yn r'yh ldbr zkr ldbr* ("there is no proof in the Scripture, but a reminder [clue, allusion]"). The expression indicates that the interpreter faces a law or a teaching that is not written explicitly in the text but can be drawn from it. The exegetical work consists in drawing from the smallest *zeker* ("clue") those norms and teachings hidden in the Scripture but not clearly expressed. The Greek *hypomnêsis* is the exact semantic correspondent of the Hebrew *zeker*. Hence, in my opinion, F. Daumas's intuition is completely justified in translating, "from a little clue" (Fr. *à partir d'un indice infime*)," excluding any reference to the Platonic doctrine of recollection (Arnaldez, Mondésert, and Pouilloux, eds., *Les oeuvres de Philon*, 29:139).

for the soul of the lover of learning [Gr. *philomathês*] has borne its proper fruit when it is able by means of memory to hold securely the principles of the art [that is being learned]. (*Leg Alleg* 3.93; cf. *Sobr* 28; *Migr Abr* 205; *Congr* 41; *Mut* 96)

Manasseh, on the other hand, is the symbol of recollection, because the translation of his name is "out of forgetfulness" (Gr. *ek lêthês*),

and he who escapes from forgetfulness necessarily recollects. (*Leg Alleg* 3.93; cf. *Sobr* 28; *Congr* 41; *Mut* 100)

Based on the idea already expressed in Aristotle's work that "the very young . . . have poor memory" because due to "their growth" they are "in a state of flux . . . just as if a stimulus or a seal were impressed on flowing water" (Aristotle, *Mem* 450 a–b; cf. 453b), Philo can justify the fact that Manasseh is the elder and Ephraim the younger.

Now memories [Gr. *mnêmai*] belong to those who have reached settled manhood and therefore, being late-born, are accounted younger. But forgetfulness and recollection follow in succession in each of us almost from our earliest years. And therefore theirs is the seniority in time. (*Sobr* 29; cf. *Leg Alleg* 3.92)

The analogies with the Aristotelian treatise and with all of the classical philosophical tradition end here, little more than a premise for successive development. However, it is a premise, as we shall see, wide open and susceptible to new ideas.

3. THE SUGGESTIONS OF THE JEWISH TRADITION

In *Genesis* 48 Philo reads that Jacob ("the overthrower of the passions and the trained seeker of virtue"; *Leg Alleg* 3.93) sanctioned the superiority of the younger Ephraim over the elder Manasseh.

When Joseph brought [to Jacob] his two sons, the elder Manasseh and the younger Ephraim, Jacob crossed his hands and placed his right hand on Ephraim the younger son and his left hand on Manasseh the elder; and when Joseph was distressed by it and imagined that his father had made an unintentional mistake in so placing his hands, [Jacob] said it was no error, but . . . "his younger brother shall be greater than he" (*Gen* 48:19). (*Leg Alleg* 3.90)

Likewise, Philo concludes, of

the two exceedingly necessary faculties created in the soul by God . . . memory is the better, recollection is inferior. For while the former keeps everything that it has apprehended fresh and distinct, so as to go wrong in nothing owing to ignorance, recollection is in all cases preceded by forgetfulness, a maimed and blind affair. (*Leg Alleg* 3.91)

The presupposition that allows such a radical change of perspective (in a moral sense) is the one pronounced in *De Opificio Mundi*:

The cosmos [Gr. *kosmos*] is in harmony with the law, and the law with the cosmos, and the man who observes the law is constituted thereby a loyal citizen of the cosmos, regulating his doings by the purpose and will of Nature, in accordance with which the entire cosmos itself also is administered. (*Op Mund* 3)

Therefore, there is a perfect correspondence between the structure of the cosmos and the Torah, between the physical order and the moral one; both are the fruit of the one Creator.

The distinction between memory and recollection, which is only physical for Aristotle, immediately becomes a moral distinction through its connection with the virtue represented by Jacob.

The birthrights of virtue[6] will be due to memories, and the God-loving [Jacob] will lay on them his right hand and adjudge them worthy of the better portion which is his to give. (*Sobr* 29)

In this context, "forgetfulness" (Gr. *lêthê*) also comes to assume a morally negative connotation.[7] From the physical point of view it is an involuntary *pathos*, but it is still a state of illness that needs healing.

The conditions of [the rememberer and the recollecter] resemble respectively continuous health and recovery from disease, for forgetting is a disease of memory. (*Congr* 39; cf. *Quaest Gen* 4.45)

The fact is that for Philo the Jew, memory is essentially memory of God, of God's absolute lordship. This *mnêmê theou* is "the greatest good" (*Spec Leg* 1.133; 2.171), the "beginning and end of the greatness and large number of the good" (*Migr* 56). With a unique midrashic reinterpretation of the Greek legend of Mnemosyne, the mother of the Muses, Philo makes it one of God's powers.

There is an old story on men's lips. . . . When, they say, the Creator had finished the whole cosmos, He inquired of one of His subordinates whether he missed anything that had failed to be created, aught of created things beneath

---

6. The Greek expression is *tôn de aretês hai mnêmai koinônêsousi presbeiôn*. The opposition is between he who has "the birthrights of time" (*ta chronou presbeia*; *Sobr* 29), that is, Manasseh, and he who obtains instead "those of virtue," that is, Ephraim.

7. It is common in the ancient and middle Jewish traditions to speak of human unfaithfulness in terms of a guilty "forgetfulness." See W. Schottroff, "*škḥ*," *THAT*.

the earth or beneath the water, aught found in air's high realm or heaven's, furthest of all realms that are. He, it is said, made answer that all were perfect and complete in all their parts, and that he was looking for one thing only, namely the word to sound their praises. . . . The story runs that the Author of the universe on hearing this commended what had been said, and that it was not long before there appeared the new birth, the family of the Muses and hymnody, sprung from the womb of one of His powers, even virgin Memory, whose name most people slightly change and call "Mnemosyne." (*Plant* 127–29)

Of the Therapeutae, proposed as a living model of virtue, it is said with great admiration: "they keep the memory of God alive and never forget it." (*Vit Cont* 26).

In these expressions we find an echo of the High Priest Eleazar in the *Letter of Aristeas*, tracing out the praise of memory as a fundamental religious virtue for the Jew. Commenting allegorically on the norms for the purity of animals contained in *Lev* 11:3-8 and *Deut* 14:6-8 ("Whatever parts the hoof and is cloven-footed and chews the cud, among the animals, you may eat"; *Lev* 11:3), the text opens a long excursus:

The cloven hoof, that is the separation of the claws of the hoof, is a sign of setting apart each of our actions for good, because the strength of the whole body with its action rests upon the shoulders and the legs. The symbolism conveyed by these things compels us to make a distinction in the performance of all our acts, with righteousness as our aim. This moreover explains why we are distinct from all other men. The majority of other men defile themselves in their relationships, thereby committing a serious offense, and lands and whole cities take pride in it: they not only procure the males, they also defile mothers and daughters. We are quite separated from these practices.

The man with whom the aforesaid manner of disposition is concerned is the man on whom the legislator has also stamped that of memory. For all cloven-footed creatures and ruminants quite clearly express to those who perceive it, the phenomenon of memory. Rumination is nothing but the reminder of [the creature's] life and constitution, life being usually constituted by nourishment.

So we are exhorted through scripture also by the one who says thus, "Thou shalt remember the Lord, who did great and wonderful things in thee." When they are [really] understood they are manifestly "great and glorious"; first, there is the construction of the body, the digestion of the food, and the specific function connected with each limb. Much more, the orderly arrangement of the senses, the operation and unseen activity of the mind, and the speed of its reaction to each stimulus and its invention of arts and crafts involves an infinite variety of methods.

So [Moses] exorts us to remember how the aforesaid blessings are maintained and preserved by divine power under his providence, for he has ordained every time and place for a continual reminder of the supreme God and upholder [of all]. Accordingly in the matter of meats and drinks he commands men to offer first fruits and to consume them there and then straightaway. Furthermore in our clothes he has given us a distinguishing mark as a reminder, and similarly on our gates and doors he has commanded us to set up the "Words," so as to be a reminder of God. He also strictly commands that the sign shall be worn on our hands, clearly indicating that it is our duty to fulfill every activity with justice, having in mind our own condition, and above all the fear of God. He also commands that "on going to bed and rising" men should meditate on the ordinances of God, observing not only in word but in understanding the movement and impression which they have when they go to sleep, and waking too, what a divine change there is between them—quite beyond understanding.

I have thus demonstrated to you the extraordinary nature of the sound reason behind our distinctive characteristic of memory by expounding the cloven hoof and chewing the cud. (*Let Aris* 150–61)

Memory (Gr. *mnêmê*, *mneia*), therefore, is essentially a virtue of the righteous, mindful of God and of themselves, of the infinite lordship of the *kyrios* and their position as creatures submitted to God. Feasts, signs, ritual gestures: everything in the *Letter of Aristeas* has this double memory at the end.

Philo is rooted in this tradition. Even in his rigid censuring of the theme of God's memory, he confirms the model of the *Letter of Aristeas*; in the eyes of an educated and intellectually demanding audience, this theme would have seemed an unpleasant anthropomorphism.[8] Philo even avoids quotations from Scripture in which it is said that "God remembers" (hardly an unimportant omission in a work presented as a great commentary on the Torah). The theme of divine providence is emphasized with a completely different terminology—for example, the definition of God as "Creator and Father" (Gr. *Poiêtês kai Patêr*). Only in one instance, when speaking of the flood, does Philo state:

God, remembering His perfect and universal goodness, . . . takes mankind under His protection and suffers not the race to be brought to utter destruction and annihilation. (*Deus Imm* 73)

This evidences a nonextraneous mode of expression when speaking of God's intervention. However, it is also proof that a certain language could only be maintained on the condition of being philosophically understood, meaning nothing other than the fact that God acts in conformity with God's nature. Therefore, in Philo's work we should not search for the many implications that such language had in most Jewish traditions.

---

8. The theme of God's memory does not appear in *Wisdom of Solomon* or *Sibylline Oracles* even though, through the Septuagint, it is part of the tradition of the western Diaspora.

Remembering is a human action; human beings are called to remember God and to remember themselves and their own condition as creatures. The two aspects are inseparably linked, as they already were in the *Letter of Aristeas*. Here Philo speaks the words of Eleazar:

> When will you not forget God? Only when you do not forget yourself. For if you remember your own nothingness in all things, you will also remember the transcendence of God in all things. (*Sac* 55)

The immediate link between the physical order and the moral order continues to distinguish Philo's thought. Being mindful designates the righteous person and is at the same time a characteristic of a "good nature" (Gr. *euphyia*; *Leg Alleg* 1.53–55; *Cherub* 101–2; *Somn* 2.37; *Mut* 97–102, 212). Feasts, the traditional memorial signs, remind humankind both of the moral law and of the principles of the cosmos. They always have "a twofold significance, partly to [our] nation in particular, partly to all mankind in general" (*Spec Leg* 2.188).[9]

Once again we find ourselves at the beginning of an itinerary of thought that, from these traditional though carefully chosen givens, will be developed and take shape along previously untraveled paths.

4. THE ACQUISITION OF MEMORY AS A MORAL ITINERARY

The good of memory, Philo states, belongs firmly only to the "ideal man," created "after God's image" (Gr. *kat'eikona*). Among the virtues that God gave him, planted in the mind (Gr. *nous*) to form the marvelous Garden of Eden, we find "memories [Gr. *mnêmai*] . . . [and] ability to take in and retain the learning of every virtue" (Gr. *tôn aretês hapasês theôrêmatôn alêstos analêpsis*; *Plant* 31).

The "concrete man"—the one "molded" from mud and earth (Gr. *ho plastos*), according to Philo's well-known theory of double creation—does not possess this good but must conquer it through hard work, because by nature he tends to forget. Out of this arise the different destinies that (according to the allegorical interpretation of Genesis 2–3) await

> the two men introduced into the garden. . . . The one that was made after the archetype has his sphere not only in the planting of virtues but is also their

---

9. The expression is used by Philo in reference to the "trumpet feast," but it is the key to his interpretation of all the Jewish festivals (see *Spec Leg* 2.145ff.).

tiller and guardian [Gr. *ergatês kai phylax*], and that means that he is mindful of all that he heard and practiced in his training; but the "molded" man neither tills the virtues nor guards them, but is only introduced to the truths by the rich bounty of God, presently to be an exile from virtue. . . . [God] receives the one, and the other He casts out. And He confers on him whom He receives three gifts, which constitute good-nature [Gr. *euphyia*]: perspicacity [Gr. *euthixia*], perseverance [Gr. *epimonê*], memory [Gr. *mnêmê*]. Perspicacity is the placing in the garden, perseverance is the practice of good deeds, memory is the guarding and retaining of the holy precepts [Gr. *hê mnêmê phylakê kai diatêrêsis tôn hagiôn dogmatôn*]. But the "molded" mind neither remembers nor carries out in action the good things, but is only perspicacious. Accordingly after being placed in the garden he soon runs away and is cast out. (*Leg Alleg* 1.53–55; cf. 1.89)

"Perfect" memory is therefore something more than an act of reverent recognition of God's lordship—it is "the guarding and retaining of the holy precepts." Because it does not firmly belong to the "concrete man," a tension arises between what is "perfect" and what is "imperfect." Philo resolves this tension through a moral path, whose stages he calls humankind to take.

The distinction between memory and recollection is brought back into this tension; from statically descriptive it becomes dynamically active. First, he derives an equivalence between recollection and "repentance" (Gr. *metanoia*):

In the scale of values the primary place is taken in bodies by health free from disease, in ships by traveling happily free from danger, and in soul by memory of things worth remembering without lapse into forgetfulness. But second to these stands rectification in its various forms, recovery from disease, deliverance so earnestly desired from the dangers of the voyage, and recollection supervening on forgetfulness. This last has for its brother and close kinsman repentance [Gr. *to metanoein*], which though it does not stand in the first and highest rank of values has its place in the class next to this and takes the second prize. (*Virt* 175–76)

Philo applies the same scheme to the interpretation of *Num* 9:1–14:

Moses awards special praise among the sacrificers of the Passover to those who sacrificed the first time, because when they had separated themselves from the passions of Egypt by crossing the Red Sea they kept to that crossing and no more hankered after them, but to those who sacrificed the second time he assigns the second place, for after turning they retraced the wrong steps they had taken and as though they had forgotten their duties they set out again to perform them, while the earlier sacrificers held on without turning. So Manasseh, who comes "out of forgetfulness," corresponds to those who offer the second Passover, the fruit-bearing Ephraim to those who offer the earlier one.[10] (*Leg Alleg* 3.94)

Second, recollection is linked to "learning" (Gr. *mathêsis*). Ephraim and Manasseh are compared respectively to Reuben and Simeon.

Again, when the sons of Joseph, Ephraim and Manasseh, were likened to the two elder sons of Jacob, Reuben and Simeon, have we not something perfectly true to nature? [Jacob] says [to Joseph], "Your two sons who were born in Egypt before I came to Egypt are mine. Ephraim and Manasseh shall be as Reuben and Simeon to me" (*Gen* 48:5). Let us observe how the two pairs tally with each other. Reuben, whose name is by interpretation "Seeing son," is the symbol of good-nature [Gr. *euphyia*], because the man who enjoys perspicacity and good-nature is endowed with sight. Ephraim, as we have often said elsewhere, is the symbol of memory . . . and no two things can be so close akin as memory and good-nature. Again, Simeon is another name for learning and teaching [Gr. *mathêsis kai didaskalia*], since Simeon is by interpretation "hearing," and it is the peculiar mark of the learner that he hears and attends to what is said, while Manasseh is the symbol of recollection, . . . and recollection is akin to learning. For what he has acquired often floats away from the learner's mind, because in his weakness he is unable to retain it, and then emerges and starts again. The *pathos* of flowing away is called forgetfulness, that of flowing back recollection.

Surely then memory closely corresponds to good-nature and recollection to learning. And the same relation which Simeon or learning bears to Reuben or [good-]nature is borne by Manasseh or recollection to Ephraim or memory. For just as good-nature which resembles sight is better than learning which resembles hearing, the inferior of sight, so memory is in every way the superior of recollection, since while that is mixed with forgetfulness memory remains from first to last free from mixture or contamination. (*Mut* 97–102)

And certainly,

study [Gr. *askêsis*] is a mean, a half-way stage, not a perfect final achievement. It is seen in souls that are not perfect, but bent on reaching the summit. Guarding [Gr. *phylakê*] is something complete, consisting in entrusting to memory those principles of holy things which were acquired by study. To do this is to commit a fair deposit of knowledge to a trustworthy guardian, to her who alone makes light of the nets of forgetfulness with all their cunning devices. "Guardian" [Gr. *phylax*] is therefore the sound and appropriate name which he gives to the man who remembers what he had learnt. (*Det* 65)

Before the "perfect" good of memory, recollection is the road, the "half-

---

10. The equation of *anamnêsis* ("recollection") and *metanoia* ("repentance") is also present in Josephus's *Antiquitates Iudaicae*, in which it is placed in the mouth of Moses: "When you undergo these trials, all unvailing will be repentance and recollection of those laws which you have failed to keep" (*hê metanoia kai hê tôn ou phylachthentôn nomôn anamnêsis*; *Ant* 4.191).

way stage," that leads to the goal, belonging to "souls that are not perfect, but bent on reaching the summit."

5. MEMORY AND PERSEVERANCE

Therefore, it is morally necessary for humankind to follow the road that leads to the acquisition of memory not subject to forgetfulness. The "mnemonic processes" (Gr. *to mnêmonikon*), through which humankind conserves the learned wisdom of God, must in the end meet with "perseverance" (Gr. *epimonê*).

For Philo, this is the meaning of the trip Abraham's servant makes to procure Rebecca as Isaac's wife (cf. *Genesis* 24):

> this is the high truth, which the servant of the lover of learning [the servant of Abraham] had mastered when he went as ambassador on that splendid errand, wooing for the man of self-taught wisdom [Isaac] the bride most suited to him, perseverance [Rebecca]. (*Congr* 111)

The servant takes ten camels with him; we already know from the *Letter of Aristeas* that the camel is the symbol of the mnemonic processes.

> For the camel is a ruminating animal softening its food by chewing the cud. Moreover, when it has knelt and had a heavy load laid on it, it nimbly raises itself with astonishing agility. In the same way the soul of the lover of learning also, when it has been laden with the mass of teachings, does not stoop indeed, but springs up rejoicing, and through repetition and (so to speak) rumination of the original deposit of [mental] food, gains power to remember the teachings. (*Post* 148–49; cf. *Quaest Gen* 4.92)

Therefore, the servant "caused the camels to rest outside the city beside a well of water at evening, when the [women-]drawers of water came out" (*Gen* 24:11; quoted in *Quaest Gen* 4.94). There he meets Rebecca, who gives him springwater to drink; that is, she instructs him in all the truths.

> The literal significance is clear, for it is the custom of wayfarers to spend the night by springs in order to rest themselves and their asses for the needs of the journey. But as for the deeper meaning, it is as follows. . . . When the memory happens to be awake, it wakens the mind by entering the city, that is, by dwelling within us. But when sleep overtakes it—and sleep is forgetfulness of memory—, it necessarily removes its dwelling from that place, namely from us, until it is once again aroused. . . . Forgetfulness however is not perpetual or daily, since the spring is near by, from which the memory-form is drawn and enters the soul, and sleep, which by another name is called "forgetfulness," is shaken off. And when wakefulness comes in, of which the true name is "memory," it remains by the spring to which the drawers of water come out at evening. . . . At [that] time . . . when the senses are far gone . . . [the mind]

receives impressions of a more lucid reason from the things seen, and, behold, it arrives at the divine spring, and this is wisdom, which takes the appearance of water by its power. (*Quaest Gen* 4.94)

Consistently, Rebecca offers water not only to the servant but also to the camels, so that the servant may, by means of memory, fix firmly the teachings. She then gives him water to drink again; the water he receives now is God's wisdom.

For perfect enjoyment on the pupil's part, it is not enough that he should simply take in all the instruction given by the teacher. He needs the further boon of memory. Accordingly Rebecca exhibits her generosity by promising, when she gives the servant all he can drink, to water the camels also. . . . [Then] she comes again to the well to draw, to the ever-flowing wisdom of God, that her pupil may, by means of memory, fix firmly what he has learned, and drink in draughts of knowledge of yet other fresh subjects; for the wealth of the wisdom of God is unbounded and puts forth new shoots after the old ones, so as never to leave off renewing its youth and reaching its prime. (*Post* 148, 151)

Rebecca and her handmaidens then mount the camels (cf. *Gen* 24:61); that is, they are carried by a memory become strong and enduring in the divinely received teachings, no longer subject to forgetfulness.

The mounting of the camels shows that character and religion are superior to the mnemonic form. . . . The maids are the servants of Perseverance . . . and [their] names are Inflexible, Unbending, Unvacillating, Unrepentant, Unchanging, Indifferent, Firm, Stable, Unconquerable, and Upright, and all their brothers who desire lasting perseverance. (*Quaest Gen* 4.136)

Isaac finally "lifted up his eyes and saw the camels coming" (*Gen* 24:63; quoted in *Quaest Gen* 4.141), not with the eyes of his body, Philo tells us, but with those of the mind. And so

from other memories, he perceives the presence of the woman, whom [the camels] easily bear as a burden, [namely] the perseverance of the finest virtues. (*Quaest Gen* 4.141)

6. MEMORY AND DISCERNMENT

On the path that leads humankind to a stable and enduring memory, however, there is an obstacle that poses both a physical and a moral problem: sensation. There are also "negative" memories that distract human beings from God and distance them from the "holy truths." These memories come from the senses.

For instance, if you have caught sight of beauty and been captivated by it, and if it is likely to be a cause of stumbling to you, fly secretly from the vision of it, and give no further report of it to your mind [Gr. *nous*], that is to say, do not give it another thought or ponder it: for to keep on recalling anything is the way to engrave on the mind distinct outlines of it, which injure the thought [Gr. *dianoia*] and often bring it to ruin against its will. The same principle holds in the case of every kind of attraction by the avenue of whatever sense [Gr. *aisthêsis*] it may reach us; for here safety lies in secret flight; but recalling the attractive object in memory, telling of it, turning it over, spells conquest and harsh slavery for our reasoning faculty. (*Leg Alleg* 3.16–17)

From this comes the passionate appeal that Philo makes to thought (Gr. *dianoia*), so as not to become a prisoner of such memories:

If, therefore, O my thought [Gr. *dianoia*], you are in imminent danger of falling a prey to some object of sense that has shown itself, never report it to yourself, never dwell on it, lest you be overcome and plunged into misery. Nay, rush forth at large, make yourself escape, choose the freedom of the wild rather than the slavery of the tame. (*Leg Alleg* 3.17; cf. 3.36)

Therefore, it is not enough to know how to remember; one must also know how to distinguish between good and bad memories. In other words, memory cannot be split from its object; only a memory that keeps "good" memories is "good."

In developing this theme Philo takes up the allegorical interpretation of *Lev* 11:3-8 and *Deut* 14:6-8 offered in the *Letter of Aristeas*. However, the same correspondences (chewing the cud = remembering; dividing the hoof = distinguishing) are applied to a more demanding and refined elaboration of thought and also to a completely different conceptual framework. Compared to the rather lame interpretation of the *Letter*, in which the two elements are juxtaposed as characteristics of the "righteous" person without indicating an internal bond of reciprocity, Philo, by labeling the distinction a quality of memory itself, is able to center his reflection precisely on the strange interdependence between "chewing the cud" and "dividing the hoof," which Scripture poses in characterizing the purity of animals. As for the many ideological developments to be found in the allegorical reading, these simply reveal the long path followed by Philo from the assumption of the *Letter*.

Do you not see that the law says that the camel is an unclean animal, because, though it chews the cud, it does not part the hoof (*Lev* 11:4)? . . . Not all memory, in fact, is a good thing, but that which is brought to bear upon good things only, for it would be a thing most noxious that evil should be unforgettable. That is why, if perfection is to be attained, it is necessary to divide the hoof, in order that, the faculty of memory [Gr. *to mnêmonikon*] being cut in twain, language as it flows through the mouth, for which nature wrought lips as twin boundaries, may separate the beneficial and the injurious forms of memory [Gr. *mnêmê*].

But neither does dividing the hoof by itself apart from chewing the cud appear to have anything advantageous on its own account. For what use is there in dissecting the natures of things, beginning from the beginning and going on to the minutest particles? . . . Day after day the swarm of sophists to be found everywhere wears out the ears of any audience they happen to have with disquisitions on minutiae, unraveling phrases that are ambiguous and can bear two meanings and distinguishing among circumstances such as it is well to bear in mind—and they are set on bearing in mind a vast number. . . .

And if the mind putting a still finer edge upon itself dissect the natures of things, as a surgeon does men's bodies, he will effect nothing that is of advantage for the acquiring of virtue. It is true that, by reason of this power to distinguish and discriminate in each case, he will "divide the hoof," but he will not "chew the cud" so as to have at his service beneficial nourishment with its wholesome reminders [Gr. *hypomnêseis*], smoothing out the roughness that had accrued to the soul as the result of errors, and producing an easy and truly smooth movement. . . .

Excellently, therefore, does the lawgiver compare the race of sophists . . . to swine. . . . For he says that the pig is unclean, because, though it divide the hoof, it does not chew the cud (*Lev* 11:7). He pronounces the camel unclean for the opposite reason, because though chewing the cud it does not divide the hoof. But such animals as do both are, as we might expect, set down as clean, since they have escaped the unnatural development in each of the directions named. For indeed distinguishing without memory and without conning and going over of the things that are best is an incomplete good, but the meeting and partnership of both in combination is a good most complete and perfect. (*Agric* 131–45; cf. *Spec Leg* 4.106–9)

7. THE FINAL STEP: MEMORY OF GOD AND FORGETFULNESS OF THE SELF

Recognizing God's lordship and one's own condition as a creature subject to God, acquiring a stable and persevering memory of the holy truths, and knowing how to defend it through discernment: once a human being has followed the steps of this moral and philosophical path, a new horizon, infinite and inaccessible, is opened beyond the achieved goal. The mystical encounter with God awaits the mind (Gr. *nous*).

The human mind occupies a position in men precisely answering to that which the great Ruler occupies in all the cosmos. It is invisible while itself seeing all things; . . . and while it opens by arts and sciences roads branching in many directions, all of them great highways, it comes through land and sea investigating what either element contains. Again, when on soaring wing it has contemplated the atmosphere and all its phases, it is borne yet higher to the ether and the circuit of heaven, and is whirled round with the dances of planets and fixed stars, in accordance with the laws of perfect music, following that love of wisdom which guides its steps. And so, carrying its gaze beyond the confines of all substance discernible by sense, it comes to a point at which it reaches out after the intelligible world, and on descrying in that world sights of surpassing loveliness, even the patterns and the originals of the things of sense which it saw here, it is seized by a sober intoxication, like those filled with Corybantic frenzy, and is inspired, possessed by a longing far other than theirs and a nobler desire. Wafted by this to the topmost arch of the things perceptible to mind, it seems to be on its way to the Great King Himself; and, amid its longing to see Him, pure and untempered rays of concentrated light stream forth like a torrent, so that by its gleams the eye of the understanding is dazzled. (*Op Mund* 69–71)

In that supreme instant the memory of God cancels all other memories into total oblivion; only the greatness of the one Lord stands out. Forgetfulness is the fulfillment of memory.

When the mind is mastered by the love of the divine, when it strains its powers to reach the inmost shrine, when it puts forth every effort and ardor on its forward march, under the divine impelling force it forgets all else, forgets itself, and fixes its thoughts and memories on Him alone Whose attendant and servant it is. (*Somn* 2.232)

II. Virginity as a Religious Ideal

1. SEXUAL SIN AS "THE MOST SERIOUS OF ALL EVILS"

A vital need for confrontation pushes the Jews of Alexandria to a continuous search for essentiality, which is often translated into a willingness to attenuate the rigor of some of the Jewish law's norms, emphasizing instead their allegorical value.

In one area, however, no compromise seems to have been possible—that of sexual morality. Even in the documents that are most open to dialogue with non-Jews, the polemic against gentile amorality is radical. On this topic even the *Letter of Aristeas* is imperious:

We are distinct from all other men. The majority of other men defile themselves in their relationships, thereby committing a serious offense, and lands and whole cities take pride in it: they not only procure the males, they also defile mothers and daughters. We are quite separated from these practices. (*Let Aris* 151–52; cf. *Sib Or* 5.386–96)

Even on the popular level edifying stories circulate; the protagonists, from Joseph to Susanna,[11] offer heroic examples of moral rigor.

The fact is that through a gradual process of identifying the "impure" with the "morally bad," a negative conception of sexuality was being formed in middle Judaism. This conception led to a view of sexual sin, in its various expressions, as "the most serious of all evils."[12] The complexity of this phenomenon has already been treated by other scholars.[13] I have mentioned it here because it constitutes the context and point of departure for Philo's reflection on virginity.

2. VIRGINITY AS A
FLIGHT FROM EVIL (AND FROM WOMAN)

Philo fully shares this negative vision of sexuality, whose value he strictly limits to the procreative ends of marriage. The idea of premarital chastity as a moral obligation for both men and women is derived from this conception. Following a recurrent motif of Jewish Hellenistic literature (cf. *Jos Asen* 4:9; 8:1; 21:1), Philo attributes the proclamation of such an ideal to Joseph, whose refusal to give in to Potifar's wife made him the model of chastity.

> We children of the Hebrews follow laws and customs which are especially our own. Other people are permitted after the fourteenth year to deal without interference with harlots and strumpets and all those who make a traffic of their bodies. . . . Before the lawful union we know no mating with other women, but come as virgin men to virgin maidens. The end we seek in wedlock is not pleasure but the begetting of lawful children. (*Jos* 42–43)

For Philo, the procreative end regulates sexuality even within marriage, to the point that he sharply condemns those who have sexual relations dur-

---

11. Joseph, Jacob's son, is also the protagonist of the pseudepigraphon called *Joseph and Aseneth* (see chap. 10). The story of Susanna is one of the so-called apocryphal additions to *Daniel* (see *Dan* 13 [LXX]). See above, p. 126 n. 1. See also E. C. Bissell, *Additions to Daniel* (New York, 1880 [English trans.]); C. J. Ball, *The Addition to Daniel*, ed. H. Wace (London, 1888 [English trans.]); J. W. Rothstein, *APAT* 1 (1900): 172–93 (German trans.); D. M. Kay, *APOT* 1 (1913): 638–51 (English trans.); D. Matthias, *Le livre de Daniel* (Paris, 1971 [French trans.]); O. Plöger, *JSHRZ* 1.1 (1973): 63–87 (German trans.); and C. A. Moore, *Daniel, Esther and Jeremiah: The Additions*, AB 44 (Garden City, 1977), 77–116 (English trans.).

12. In the Septuagint the prohibition of adultery is already placed at the top of the list of sins against one's neighbor, before murder and theft, even though this changes the biblical order of the Decalogue (cf. *Exod* 20:13-15 [LXX] and *Deut* 5:17-19 [LXX] with the original Hebrew texts). Philo takes up the same scheme, encompassing all the sexual sins within this commandment (*Dec* 121–32; *Spec Leg* 3.8–82). See G. Boccaccini, "Il valore della verginità in Filone Alessandrino," in *La verginità cristiana*, ed. E. Bianchi, Parola Spirito Vita 12 (Bologna, 1979), 217–27.

13. See L. Rosso Ubigli, "Alcuni aspetti della 'porneia' nel tardo-giudaismo," *Henoch* 1 (1979): 201–42.

ing the infertile periods of the woman's menstrual cycle (cf. *Spec Leg* 3.32–33) or who marry women known to be sterile (cf. *Spec Leg* 3.34–36).

Continence is thus affirmed as the supreme ideal of conjugal life; incontinence is made the equivalent of adultery or other illicit unions.

> And because, with a view to the persistence of the race, you were endowed with generative organs, do not run after rapes and adulteries and other unhallowed forms of intercourse, but only those which are lawful means of propagating the human race. . . . So let us make it our earnest endeavor to bind up [our faculties] with the adamantine chains of self-control. (*Det* 102–3)

The negative conception of women as objects of pleasure is not unrelated to this vision; most middle Jewish men saw women as an instrument of the devil or evil. Philo, in his allegorical reading of the Scriptures, also interprets Adam's sin as the process by which "pleasure" (Gr. *hêdonê*), or the serpent, through the "senses" (Gr. *aisthêsis*), or the woman, succeeds in fooling the "mind" (Gr. *nous*), or the man (cf. *Op Mund* 165–66). For Philo,

> pleasure . . . is the beginning of wrongs and violation of Law, the pleasure for the sake of which men bring on themselves the life of mortality and wretchedness in lieu of that of immortality and bliss. (*Op Mund* 152)

In this sense, "woman has been for man the beginning of blameworthy life" (*Op Mund* 151).

The Essenes' refusal of marriage, as presented by Philo in the *Apologia pro Iudaeis*, is the logical conclusion of this vision. The flight from evil, for those who intend to pursue it with extreme radicalness, necessarily involves a flight from woman.

> Furthermore they eschew marriage because they clearly discern it to be the sole or the principal danger to the maintenance of the communal life, as well as because they particularly practice continence. For no Essene takes a wife, because a wife is a selfish creature, excessively jealous and an adept at beguiling the morals of her husband and seducing him by her continued impostures. For by the fawning talk which she practices and the other ways in which she plays her part like an actress on the stage she first ensnares the sight and hearing, and when these subjects as it were have been duped she cajoles the sovereign mind [Gr. *nous*]. And if children come, filled with the spirit of arrogance and bold speaking she gives utterance with more audacious hardiness to things which before she hinted covertly and under disguise, and casting off all shame she compels him to commit actions which are hostile to the life of fellowship. For he who is either fast bound in the lures of his wife or under the stress of nature makes his children his first care ceases to be the same to others and unconsciously has become a different man and has passed from freedom into slavery. (*Apologia* 11.14–17)

Premarital chastity, continence among spouses, and even the refusal of marriage make sense, therefore, because they keep evil at bay; the exercise of sexuality as a source of pleasure (and impurity) is always morally bad.

3. VIRGINITY AS A ROAD TO PERFECTION

Up to this point we have seen nothing new. Philo has limited himself to ideas prevalent in middle Judaism, translating them into his own philosophical language. However, along with these negative formulations of the problem we find in Philo the idea that continence represents a positive road to perfection for men and women. Following this path, he even arrives at a vision of a perpetual virginity, freely accepted "to please God."

"Continence" [Gr. *sôphrosynê*] is part of the capacity for self-control, and control of the passions is the characteristic prerogative of every righteous person. In *De Josepho*, Philo also emphasizes the civil value of this virtue:

> While in all the affairs of life self-mastery [Gr. *egkrateia*] is a source of profit and safety, it is particularly so in affairs of state, as those who will may learn from plentiful and obvious examples. Who does not know the misfortunes which licentiousness brings to nations and countries and whole latitudes of the civilized world on land and sea? For the majority of wars, and those the greatest, have arisen through amours and adulteries and the deceit of women, which have consumed the greatest and choicest part of the Greek race and the barbarian also, and destroyed the youth of their cities. And, if the results of licentiousness are civil strife and war, and ill upon ill without number, clearly the results of continence [Gr. *sôphrosynê*] are stability and peace and the acquisition and enjoyment of perfect blessings. (*Jos* 55–57)

However, the authentic peace that Philo aspires to is that of the soul. In this peace even Adam's sin would be annulled and God would again allow humanity to taste the happiness of Eden. Philo's tone becomes hearty as he writes,

> If the unmeasured impulses of men's passions were calmed and allayed by continence [Gr. *sôphrosynê*], . . . the warfare in the soul, of all wars veritably the most dire and most grievous, would have been abolished, and peace would prevail, . . . and there would be hope that God . . . would provide for our race good things all coming forth spontaneously and all in readiness. (*Op Mund* 81)

4. THE VOYAGE OF THE SOUL TOWARD GOD

The ethical-religious aspiration is absolutely central to Philo's thought. The search for God, welcoming God's grace, and the ecstasy of meeting

God mark the steps of a voyage of the soul, prefiguring a theme that would later be embraced in the Christian mystical traditions.

Humankind's point of departure is the recognition of its own impotence and of God's absolute lordship, a recognition that only allows for the exercise of continence:

> It is impossible to lay hold of pleasure [Gr. *hêdonê*] . . . if the soul [Gr. *psychê*] first has not acknowledged that all its achievements and successes are due to God's impelling force and refer nothing to itself. (*Leg Alleg* 2.93)

Continence, therefore, plays a purifying role of liberation from every impediment and evil. Yet it is only a step, not an end in itself. It is the condition necessary for the soul to open itself to God's grace, to welcome God's gifts and give fruit.

> It is meet that God should converse with the truly virgin nature; but it is the opposite with us. For the union of human beings that is made for the procreation of children, turns virgins into women. But when God begins to consort with the soul, He makes what before was a woman into a virgin again, for He takes away the degenerate and emasculate desires which unmanned it and plants instead the native growth of unpolluted virtues. (*Cherub* 50)

5. A FERTILE AND FRUITFUL VIRGINITY

The soul that has joined God thus lives in a condition of virginity that is not an absence of passion, but a fruitful and "procreative" intercourse because it can welcome and nurture God's gifts. Philo can thus speak allegorically of the virginal conception of the wives of the patriarchs. The allegorical reading is complex, a mystery so great that Philo reserves it only for the "initiated."

> The persons to whose virtue the lawgiver has testified, such as Abraham, Isaac, Jacob and Moses, and others of the same spirit, are not represented by him as knowing women. For since we hold that woman signifies in a figure sense-perception [Gr. *aisthêsis*], and that knowledge comes into being through estrangement from sense and body, it will follow that the lovers of wisdom reject rather than choose sense. And surely this is natural. For the helpmeets of these men are called women, but are in reality virtues: Sarah . . . Rebecca . . . Leah . . . Zipporah. . . .
>
> The virtues have their conception and their birthpangs, but when I purpose to speak of them let them who corrupt religion into superstition close their ears or depart. For this is a divine mystery and its lesson is for the initiated who are worthy to receive the holiest secret, even those who in simplicity of heart practice the true piety [Gr. *eusebeia*]. . . .

Thus then must the sacred instruction begin. Man and woman, male and female of the human race, in the course of nature come together to hold intercourse for the procreation of children. But virtues whose offspring are so many and so perfect may not have to do with mortal man, yet if they receive not seed of generation from another they will never of themselves conceive. Who then is he that sows in them the good seed save the Father of all, that is God unbegotten and begetter of all things? He then sows, but the fruit of His sowing, the fruit which is His own, He bestows as a gift. For God begets nothing for Himself, for He is in want of nothing, but all for him who needs to receive.

I will give as a warrant for my words one that none can dispute, Moses the holiest of men. For he shows us Sarah at the time when God visited her in her solitude (*Gen* 21:1), but when she brings forth it is not to the Author of her visitation, but to him who seeks to win wisdom, whose name is Abraham.

And even clearer is Moses' teaching of Leah, that God opened her womb (*Gen* 29:31). Now to open the womb belongs to the husband. Yet when she conceived she brought forth not to God (for He is in Himself all-sufficing for Himself), but to him who endures toil to gain the good, even Jacob. Thus virtue receives the divine seed from the Creator, but brings forth to one of her lovers, who is preferred above all others who seek her favor. Again Isaac the all-wise besought God, and through the power of Him who was thus besought Perseverance or Rebecca became pregnant (*Gen* 25:21). And without supplication or entreaty did Moses, when he took Zipporah the winged and soaring virtue, find her pregnant through no mortal agency (*Exod* 2:22). (*Cherub* 40–47; cf. *Post* 132–35)

To different degrees and with different characteristics, the patriarchs (Abraham, Isaac, Jacob, Moses) are the symbol of the soul that aspires to God. Their wives (Sarah, Rebecca, Leah, Zipporah) are the preliminary "virtues" the soul needs to approach the perfection of meeting with God. For this to come about, it is necessary that God "impregnate" them, in order that they produce fruit "for him who needs to receive." Human beings, in fact, cannot arrive at supreme happiness through their efforts alone if God does not intervene with grace. In itself, continence is sterile, whereas virginity is fertile.

For happiness consists in the exercise and enjoyment of virtue, not in its mere possession. But I could not exercise it, should you not send down the seeds from heaven to cause her pregnancy, and were she not to give birth to happiness. (*Det* 60)

6. SPIRITUAL VIRGINITY AND PHYSICAL VIRGINITY

We now arrive at the end of our itinerary, at the serene, almost idyllic vision that Philo gives in *De Vita Contemplativa* of the community of the

Therapeutae, which for him represents the ideal of the highest stage of perfection: the contemplative life.

Describing this extraordinary community whose monastic life style aroused a continuous sense of admiration in him, Philo mentions some women who had become old without ever having known a man. He extols the freedom of their choice, made not by force but spontaneously, to open themselves to God's grace.

> [Among them, there are] women also, most of them aged virgins, who have kept their chastity not under compulsion, like some of the Greek priestesses, but of their own free will in their ardent yearning for wisdom. Eager to have her for their life mate they have spurned the pleasures [Gr. *hêdonai*] of the body and desire no mortal offspring but those immortal children which only the soul that is dear to God can bring to the birth unaided because the Father has sown in her spiritual rays enabling her to behold the verities of wisdom. (*Vit Cont* 68)

Philo's allegory is fleshed out in these living examples in a concrete praxis of life. Physical virginity acquires an entirely original meaning as a sign of the spiritual virginity, which for Philo is fundamental to the path of everyone who aspires to God.

The novelty of this conception is much more apparent when we compare it with the previously examined passage about the Essenes (*Apologia* 11.14–17). The motivations that justify the choice of virginity are, in fact, radically different and cannot be attributed simply to the fact that we face two different communities. If Philo has any interest in historical description, it is only as a function of his thought, for which every description acquires a strongly emblematic value. The two passages are actually the conclusions of two different itineraries of thought, one emphasizing the value of virginity as a flight from evil, the other (and this is certainly the most original conclusion) as a path toward the good.

It is not, then, coincidental that Philo entrusts his intuition to groups of women (allegorically the wives of the patriarchs; historically the pious women of the Therapeutae's community). First, this removes the misogynous and erotophobic traits of his justification of the Essenes' refusal of marriage, which in this context would have obscured the positive value of virginity seen primarily as a spiritual rather than physical reality. Second, the image of woman allows Philo to insist, by analogy, on the procreative value of virginity, by which the soul, "impregnated" by its Lord, can generate "immortal offspring," the fruits of virtue that spring from the experience of the encounter with God.

It is easy to understand the suggestions that these concepts were destined to evoke in Christianity, from the fertile virginity of Mary (cf. *Matt* 1:18–25; *Luke* 1:26–38) to the virginity of the "eunuchs for the kingdom" (*Matt* 19:12; cf. *1 Cor* 7:32–34; *Rev* 14:4). The surprise with which Philo's passages, in particular those about the Therapeutae, were read by Christians caused the ancient commentators, from Eusebius on, to see in them the description of the first Christian communities in Egypt.[14] However, Philo's works testify to another contemporary and autonomous Jewish movement, deprived of its place in history by the triumph of other movements, but whose messages would continue to live triumphantly in the conscience of its defeaters.

14. Eusebius, *Historia Ecclesiastica* 2.16–17. On Eusebius of Caesarea, see K. Lake and J.E.L. Oulton, *Eusebius, Ecclesiastical History*, 2 vols. (London, 1926–32 [Greek text and English trans.]).

7

JAMES, PAUL
(AND JESUS)

Early Christianity and
Early Christianities

1. THE "MOST JEWISH" DOCUMENT IN
THE NEW TESTAMENT

The *Letter of James* is commonly referred to as the "most Jewish" document in the New Testament.[1] Its address to the "twelve tribes in the Diaspora" (*James* 1:1), its claim of the primacy of works, and the apparent marginality of the specifically Christian traits contribute to such a judgment.[2] Some scholars have even gone so far as to suggest that the document is an adaptation of an "originally Jewish" writing later "Christianized" by a few slight modifications.[3]

---

1. On the *Letter of James*, see F. Spitta, *Der Brief des Jacobus* (Göttingen, 1896); J. H. Ropes, *A Critical and Exegetical Commentary on the Epistle of St. James*, ICC (Edinburgh, 1916); M. Dibelius, *Der Brief des Jacobus* (Göttingen, 1921); J. Chaine, *L'épître de Saint Jacques*, EBib (Paris, 1927); H. Windisch, *Die katholischen Briefe*, 2d ed., HNT 15 (Tübingen, 1930; 3d ed., 1951); J. Marty, *L'épître de Jacques*, EBib (Paris, 1935); P. de Ambroggi, *Le Epistole Cattoliche di Giacomo, Pietro, Giovanni e Giuda* (Turin and Rome, 1947; 2d ed., 1949; repr. 1954); A. Ross, *The Epistles of James and John*, NICNT (Grand Rapids, 1954); R.V.G. Tasker, *The General Epistle of James*, TNTC (Grand Rapids and London, 1957); L. Simon, *Une éthique de la sagesse: Commentaire de l'épître de Jacques* (Geneva, 1961); M. Dibelius, *Der Brief des Jakobus*, 11th ed., rev. H. Greeven (Göttingen, 1964) (*James*, trans. M. A. Williams [Philadelphia, 1976]); B. Reicke, *The Epistles of James, Peter, and Jude*, AB (Garden City, 1964; 2d ed., 1967; 3d ed., 1975); F. Mussner, *Der Jacobusbrief*, 3d ed., HTKNT 13.1 (Freiburg, 1964; 2d ed., 1967; 3d ed., 1975; 4th ed., 1981); J. Cantinat, *Les épîtres de Saint Jacques et de Saint Jude* (Paris, 1973); K. Aland, et al., eds., *The Greek New Testament*, (New York, 1975 [Greek text]); J. B. Adamson, *The Epistle of James*, NICNT (Grand Rapids, 1976); S. Laws, *A Commentary on the Epistle of James*, HNTC (London and San Francisco, 1980); P. H. Davids, *Commentary on James*, NIGNTC (Grand Rapids, 1982); F. Vouga, *L'épître de Saint Jacques* (Geneva, 1984); D. J. Moo, *The Letter of James: An Introduction and Commentary* (Leicester and Grand Rapids, 1985); and R. P. Martin, *James*, WBC 48 (Waco, Tex., 1988).
2. See A. Wikenhauser and J. Schmid, *Einleitung in das Neuen Testament* (Freiburg, 1973).
3. The origins of this interpretative tradition are L. Massebieau, "L'épître de Jacques, est-elle l'oeuvre d'un chrétien?" *RHR* 32 (1895): 249–83; and Spitta, *Der Brief des Jacobus*.

Even the mistrust that Christian theologians (especially Protestants) have often harbored against *James* might be attributed to its suspected "Jewish" nature. Luther did not hesitate to call it "a straw letter," thus wanting to underscore its extraneousness to the corpus of the New Testament and to Pauline theology in particular.[4]

But what does it mean to say that *James* is the "most Jewish" (or even "originally Jewish") compared to the other writings in the New Testament, which are considered "less Jewish" or even "not Jewish at all" (Paul, for example)? At the bottom of this way of thinking there is a serious misunderstanding, an anachronistic a posteriori presupposition. What is only the (contingent) point of arrival of a long historical process is projected into the past: it is assumed that Christianity and Judaism are parallel phenomena, existing distinctly and separately.

When we speak of Judaism we tend to think of the Judaism we know from the rabbinic writings (*Mishnah*, Talmudim, Midrashim, and so forth), that is, of the Judaism of the dual Torah, which prevailed as "the" Judaism only from the second century C.E. onward. Before that, it was, like Christianity, only one possible way of understanding Judaism among other equally possible ways.

The image of the Judaism of the dual Torah as the officially recognized "mother Judaism" from which Christianity was born as a "son" (whether legitimate or illegitimate does not matter) is historically just as misleading as the exclusively Christian pretense of being the coherent and natural heir to ancient Israel. In reality, neither rabbinic Judaism nor Christian Judaism is *sic et simpliciter* the continuation of the ancient religion of Israel; both are children of reforms that developed from within the religion of Israel during the first centuries of the Common Era.[5]

2. ANTI-JUDAISM AND ANTI-PHARISAISM

The opposition between orthodoxy and heresy was unknown to first-century Judaism. Ideologically this is an extremely complex and ill-defined period, in which even the most diverse of experiences coexist (Pharisees, Sadducees, Zealots, followers of Jesus, apocalyptics, Essenes, Judeo-Hellenists, and so forth) and from which both Christianity and Rabbinism emerge, through a homologous yet divergent process of elaboration and restructuring of the same religious inheritance.

---

4. Preface to the so-called *Septemberbibel* of 1522.
5. See chap. 1.

Compared to this pluralistic phase of Judaism, no New Testament writing is "more" or "less" Jewish for the simple reason that they are all Jewish. The authors are Jews (in nationality, culture, or religious convictions) just as the movement to which they witness is integrally Jewish.

Even Paul belongs to Judaism; the ideas he expresses (including those that appear most extraneous, such as the theories of original sin and justification by faith) are an integral part of the Jewish cultural and religious patrimony of the first century. In this sense there is no anti-Jewish (much less anti-Semitic) trace in the New Testament, although certain passages would be reinterpreted that way in more recent times.

Of course, there is an obvious *ad extra* polemic in the New Testament, but this itself is part of the internal debate within Judaism at a time when the religion of the Jews, forced by history into a difficult corner, found itself as if it were compelled to bet on possible futures. Imagine a confused crowd at a crossroads that opens onto many equally passable roads, all of them plausible in the light of the common tradition. With the (not just verbal) intolerance characteristic of moments of crisis, each group tended to propose and, if possible, impose its own solution as the only one. Due to the capricious yet intelligible randomness of history, more than to any necessary logic inherent in different systems of thought, by the end of the first century C.E. the crossroads had been reduced to a simple fork. After having tried long and hard to convince one another of their own conviction that they represented the true Israel, the Christian and the Pharisaic roads grew further apart, finally reaching a reciprocal estrangement. A pluralistic Judaism had generated two much less pluralistic and tolerant but more homogeneous Judaisms.

Having clarified what is meant by "Jewish" in the first century, we might conclude that the so-called "anti-Jewish" expressions in the New Testament are in reality "anti-Pharisaic," testimony to a debate between rival groups within middle Judaism. But even posed in these more historically correct terms, the point needs further clarification. The polemical attacks are not, in fact, spread with equal intensity through all the documents in the New Testament. Instead of speaking of "more" or "less" Jewish works, we might speak of New Testament writings that are closer to or farther from Pharisaism. There is even a current of criticism that tends to see Jesus as a Pharisaic rabbi and the early Judeo-Christian movement not only as a movement within middle Judaism (as is obvious from what we have seen so far) but an internal movement within Pharisaism itself—a school, however unique, among other schools. According to this critical trend, only with Paul do we seen a true change in quality that places Christianity outside the Pharisaic "orthodoxy." This created the basis for the Christian schism at the end of the second century, when Pharisaism identified itself *tout court* as "the" Judaism.[6]

Such a formulation would place James closer to the Pharisees than to Paul. Certainly, it is striking that the *Letter of James* lacks *ad extra* polemics against non-Christian Jews and contains instead *ad intra* polemics against other Christians (perhaps against certain ways of understanding or misunderstanding Paul, or even against Paul himself). But are we sure that the model of Judaism proposed by the Christian Jew James is compatible with the Pharisaic vision and that the "anti-Pauline" polemic he advances is made in the name of the principles of Pharisaism? Is it due to other factors? Just how far does James's image as defender of the law and its saving function correspond to reality? To answer such questions, we must first attempt to understand the somewhat mysterious ideology of this document and the elusive nature of its "anti-Pauline" polemic.[7]

3. IN THE FACE OF THE LAW

The asymmetry of the debate has already been noted. While Paul contests the saving value of "works of the law," James intends more generally to defend the saving value of human actions, of "works" *tout court*. What has not been sufficiently brought out by scholars is that on the only occasion that James speaks about the law, he curiously does so in the same terms as Paul:

> Whoever keeps the whole law but fails in one point has become guilty of all of it. For he who said, "Do not commit adultery," said also, "Do not kill." If you do not commit adultery but do kill, you have become a transgressor of the law. (*James* 2:10-11)

In substance, breaking one norm of the law is enough to be accused of being a transgressor and to be found guilty. It is precisely what Paul says in the *Letter to the Galatians*,[8] on the basis of *Deut* 27:26.

6. See H. Maccoby, *The Mythmaker: Paul and the Invention of Christianity* (New York, 1986); and idem, *Judaism in the First Century* (London, 1989), esp. 34–37. On Jesus as a Pharisee, see H. Falk, *Jesus the Pharisee: A New Look at the Jewishness of Jesus* (New York and Mahwah, N.J., 1985).

7. There is a vast bibliography on the debate between James and Paul. See esp. W. Schmithals, *Paulus und Jakobus* (Göttingen, 1963) (*Paul and James*, trans. D. M. Barton [London, 1965]). The problem has been reexamined and its essential terms focused in an interesting article by R. Penna, "La giustificazione in Paolo e in Giacomo," *RivB* 30 (1982): 337–62.

8. On the *Letter to the Galatians*, see esp. P. Bonnard, *L'épître de Saint Paul aux Galates* (Neuchâtel, 1953; 2d ed., 1972); H. Schlier, *Der Brief an die Galater*, 5th ed. (Göttingen, 1971); U. Borse, *Der Standort des Galaterbriefes* (Bonn, 1972); F. Mussner, *Der Galaterbrief* (Freiburg, Basel, and Vienna, 1974); Aland, et al., eds., *Greek New Testament*; and H. D. Betz, *Galatians* (Philadelphia, 1979).

All who rely on works of the law are under a curse; for it is written, "Cursed be every one who does not abide by all things written in the book of the law, and do them." . . . I testify again to every man who receives circumcision that he is bound to keep the whole law. (*Gal* 3:10; 5:3)

From *Qohelet*[9] on, it is a given in the Jewish tradition that "there is not a righteous man on earth who does good and never sins" (*Qoh* 7:20); the consistent conclusion reached by both James and Paul is that God's justice based on the law cannot lead to salvation. God's law, like every human law, is only used for punishing transgressions; for human beings, who are known not to be immune to guilt, facing God's judgment means being destined to an inevitable condemnation. Therefore, another path must be taken, placing one's hope not in God's justice but in God's mercy.

For Paul, "Christ redeemed us from the curse of the law" (*Gal* 3:3). For James, hope lies in the chance to be judged by a different law, "the law of liberty," and in the certainty that mercy will triumph. God's mercy over God's justice, and humankind's mercy over God's judgment.

So speak and so act as those who are to be judged under the law of liberty [Gr. *dia nomou eleutherias*]. For judgment [Gr. *krisis*] is without mercy [Gr. *aneleos*] to one who has shown no mercy [Gr. *eleos*]; mercy triumphs over the judgment [Gr. *katakauchatai eleos kriseôs*]. (*James* 2:12-13)

4. SALVATION: BETWEEN MERCY AND JUSTICE

The diversity of the solutions adopted by the two New Testament authors (whose meaning I will try to clarify in this chapter) should not make us lose sight of their substantial agreement; each bases his solution on the broken link between God's mercy and God's justice. In my opinion, this is the generative idea of Christianity; it makes Paul and James representatives of the same system of thought and at the same time makes their understanding of Judaism incompatible with (and unintelligible within) the Pharisaic system.

Within the Pharisaic-rabbinic system it is possible to discuss whether God's mercy or God's justice is greater. For example, demonstrating the validity of the principle, "With what measure a man metes it shall be measured to him again," *Mishnah Sotah* (1:7-9) affirms that "with the same measure" God gives justice when punishing bad deeds, and mercy when rewarding good deeds. On the other hand, the parallel text in *Tosefta Sotah* (3:1—4:19) claims that "the measure of mercy is five hundred times greater

9. On *Qohelet*, see chap. 3.

than the measure of justice." But the two divine attributes are never opposed; on the contrary, their necessarily complementary nature is emphasized.[10]

Because no one is without sin, justice without mercy would be cruel and implacable. No one could be saved if God did not forgive sins and give an expiatory value to good deeds. God's mercy makes God different from human judges; a judge's duty lies only in applying the law and punishing transgressions.

On the other hand, mercy without justice would become a shocking and arbitrary act. Such is the behavior of the householder in the Gospel parable who pays the same salary to those who worked all day and to those who only worked a few hours, opposing the (just) remonstrances of the former with his arbitrary freedom to be merciful (*Matt* 20:1-16).

The more effective synthesis of the Pharisaic-rabbinic view of salvation can be found in a saying that tradition attributes to Rabbi Aqiba, at the beginning of the second century C.E.:

> All is foreseen, but freedom of choice is given; and the world is judged by mercy, yet all is according to the quantity of [good or evil] works. (*m. Aboth* 3:16)

Rabbinism is far from being the legalistic and ritualistic system it has been portrayed by ancient and modern Christian apologists, who state the superiority of religions without law. The position of the Rabbis is logical and consistent. Human freedom coexists with God's freedom and omniscience. Salvation lies in God's mercy, without which every judgment would inevitably be a condemnation. On the other hand, God's mercy is dispensed following the criterion of justice, so that the two attributes of God remain complementary, God's behavior is not cruel or arbitrary, and obedience to the law is for humankind an effective means of salvation. The antiquity and necessity of such a position stem from the centrality of the problem of the relationship between God's mercy and justice in the entire history of middle Jewish thought. The question is already found in its essential terms in the *Book of Sirach*[11] at the beginning of the second century B.C.E. and is still open in the early second century C.E. in the apocalyptic *4 Ezra* and *2 Baruch*.

---

10. On the relationship between God's mercy and God's justice in rabbinic thought, see E. E. Urbach, *The Sages: Their Concepts and Beliefs* (Jerusalem, 1975), 448–61.

11. On the *Book of Sirach* and its ideology, see chap. 3. On *2 Baruch*, see above, p. 115 n. 40. On *4 Ezra*, see J. Schreiner, *JSHRZ* 5.4 (1981): 291–412 (German trans.); A.F.J. Klijn, "Textual Criticism of IV Ezra," in *SBL Seminar Papers 20, 1981*, ed. K. H. Richards (Chico, Calif., 1981), 217–25 (Latin text); B. M. Metzger, *OTP* 1 (1983): 517–59 (English trans.); R.J.H. Shutt, *AOT* (1984): 927–41 (English trans.); P. Geoltrain, *BÉI* (1987), 1393–1470 (French trans.); and P. Marrassini, *AAT* 2 (1989): 235–377 (Italian trans.).

How do Jesus of Nazareth and his Palestinian movement fit into this debate? According to the testimony of all the synoptic Gospels, Jesus does not deny the validity of the retributory principle or the existence of judgment; however, for him humankind acquires no merit through obedience to the law and is condemned for the smallest transgression. In line with the thought already expressed in the second century B.C.E. by Antigonus of Soko (cf. *m. Aboth* 1:3), the person who is faithful to the law is presented as a "useless servant who has only done what was his duty" (cf. *Luke* 17:7-10). Certainly, obeying the law is a good thing; Mark tells us that Jesus "loved" the man, observant of the law, who one day stopped him on the road wanting to know the way to eternal life. In many respects, Jesus interprets the law even more rigidly than the scribes and Pharisees: "You have heard that it was said to the men of old . . . but I say to you . . ." (cf. *Matt* 5:20-48). But this radicalization of the law, which asks total abandon of one's heart to God's will, precludes even more any hypothesis of salvation. "Then who can be saved?" ask Jesus' disciples, amazed and anguished when the man observant of the law goes away disappointed after Jesus' peremptory invitation to abandon all his goods. Jesus' reply to his disciples, witnessed by all three synoptic Gospels, is likewise peremptory: "With men it is impossible, but not with God; for all things are possible with God" (*Mark* 10:27; *Matt* 19:25; *Luke* 18:26).

Salvation, then, is not to be looked for in humankind's righteousness and God's justice, but exclusively in God's mercy. In Jesus' parables, the two attributes of God are radically separated, at times opposed to one another. "Am I not allowed to do what I choose with what belongs to me? Or do you begrudge my generosity?" responds the owner of the vineyard when accused of an open injustice for paying the same salary for different "measures" of work (*Matt* 20:15). Salvation is the unconditioned work of God, who justifies whom God wants. In Jesus' teachings and self-consciousness, the "Son of man," the eschatological judge of the apocalyptic tradition (cf. *Book of Similitudes* [*1 Enoch* 37–71]), turns above all into he who "has authority on earth to forgive sins" (*Mark* 2:10; *Matt* 9:6; *Luke* 5:24).

The Beatitudes furnish us with a list of the "justified" (the poor, the afflicted, the meek, the hungry, the merciful, the pure in heart, the peacemakers, the persecuted) according to categories that are not connected to observance of the law (cf. *Matt* 5:3-12; *Luke* 6:20-23). The debate with the Pharisees on this point must have been extremely intense, as shown by the famous parable in which the righteous man and the sinner are a Pharisee and a publican, respectively; at the end the parts are emblematically reversed—

the one who is righteous according to the law is wicked and the sinner is justified (*Luke* 18:9-14).

The road to salvation indicated by Jesus is radically different from the one conceived by the Pharisees. For the Pharisees, as we have seen, salvation is a consequence of obedience to the law on the part of humankind and of an interaction between mercy and justice in judgment on the part of God. For Jesus and his early followers, however, salvation is based on one's acknowledgment of being a sinner, on merciful and forgiving practices, and on the faithful hope of the merciful and forgiving intervention of God through the eschatological judge, the Son of man. In other words, salvation is the consequence of an interaction between human mercy and God's mercy, through which humankind is freed from judgment and from God's justice; for the sinner (that is, for everyone), in fact, being judged would only mean being irremediably condemned. The same "measure for measure" principle discussed in the Pharisaic-rabbinic tradition is used in the Gospels to synthesize a radically different concept. "Be merciful, even as your Father is merciful. Judge not, and you will not be judged; condemn not, and you will not be condemned; forgive, and you will be forgiven. . . . For the measure you give will be the measure you get back" (*Luke* 6:36-38; cf. *Matt* 7:1-2).

Jesus was not unfaithful to the law in his life; observance of the law remains a good thing. However, the separation he makes between obedience to the law and salvation (that is, between God's mercy and God's justice as a means of salvation) is the logical premise of every future development of early Christianity, just as the nascent rabbinic Judaism will be consolidated around the opposing Pharisaic principle of an inseparable bond between human righteousness and salvation (that is, between God's mercy and God's justice).

5. PAUL'S CHRISTIANITY

In stating the neutrality of the law as a means of salvation, James and Paul are consistently connected to the line of thought opened by Jesus. This does not mean that there are not profound differences between James and Paul but rather that their differences are internal differences within the same system of thought. This allows us better to focus on James's "anti-Pauline" polemic that lies not in a different conception of the law but, as we shall see, in a different conception of the origin of evil and of human freedom. The fact is that Paul and James, beginning with the same generative idea, place and therefore reread the Christian system in a line of continuity with two distinct strains of thought present in the Judaism of their day.

Paul links himself to the apocalyptic tradition in the conception of evil as an autonomous reality, predating human transgression, fruit of an "original sin" that corrupted human nature together with the whole of creation.[12] Such is the sense of "Adam's sin" (cf. *Rom* 5:12-21), which for Paul has made humankind unable to do good, even "enslaved to sin" (*Rom* 6:6).

> Sin came into the world through one man and death through sin, and so death spread to all men because all men sinned—sin indeed was in the world before the law was given. (*Rom* 5:12-13a)

Sin, in fact, is responsible for the unleashing of "all sorts of passion" in humankind (cf. *Rom* 7:8). A cause-and-effect chain is thus created: "sin" (Gr. *hamartia*) produces "desire" (Gr. *epithymia*) and desire in turn brings "death" (Gr. *thanatos*).

Humanity is left with the will to do good but neither the freedom nor the ability to do it:

> I know that good does not dwell within me, that is, in my flesh. I can will what is right, but I cannot do it. For I do not do the good I want, but the evil I do not want is what I do. . . . I delight in the law of God, in my inmost self, but I see in my members another law at war with the law of my mind and making me captive to the law of sin which dwells in my members. (*Rom* 7:18-19, 22-23)

Israel, indeed, has received from God ("Who will render to every man according to his works"; *Rom* 2:6) an effective instrument of salvation: the law. But the simple possession of the law does not suffice; to be effective it should be observed, "For it is not the hearers of the law who are righteous before God, but the doers of the law who will be justified" (*Rom* 2:13).

For Paul, the tragic paradox of the law is that it guarantees salvation to those who observe it, yet no person, as "slave to sin," will ever be able to do so. The law can only provide "a full awareness of the fall" (*Rom* 3:20) and uncover the common condition of sin that people, be they Jews or Gentiles, live in. Paradoxically, sin has taken further advantage of the "holy" law: knowing the transgressions could only be a stimulus for the sinner to com mit them (cf. *Rom* 7:7ff.). The conclusion is bitter: "the law which promised life proved to be death to me" (*Rom* 7:10).[13] The appeal to God's mercy is

---

12. On the apocalyptic tradition, see chap. 4.

13. The debate on the law's value for Paul is still wide open. See H. Hübner, *Das Gesetz bei Paulus: Ein Beitrag zum Werden der paulinischen Theologie* (Göttingen, 1978) (*Law in Paul's Thought*, ed. J. Riches, trans. J.C.G. Grieg [Edinburgh, 1984]); H. Räisänen, *Paul and the Law* (Philadelphia, 1983); E. P. Sanders, *Paul, the Law and the Jewish People* (Philadelphia, 1983); J.D.G. Dunn, *Jesus, Paul and the Law* (London, 1990); and A. F. Segal, *Paul the Convert* (New Haven and London, 1990). Such a complex problem certainly cannot be resolved in a note. I believe, however, that the relationship with the apocalyptic tradition and its peculiar conception

thus raised up with an anguished tone, almost a cry of desperation: "Wretched man that I am! Who will deliver me from this body [destined to] death" (*Rom* 7:24).

6. JAMES'S CHRISTIANITY

James returns to the writings of the wisdom tradition (*Sirach* and especially the *Testaments of the Twelve Patriarchs*)[14] that see in humankind the manifestation of a radical ambivalence, the emergence of evil from a self that appears dramatically double and unstable.

This ambivalence, whose ontological significance Ben Sira had strongly denied, in the *Testaments of the Twelve Patriarchs* (at least in the last of its pre-Christian redactions, mid–first century B.C.E.) becomes the effect of the internal conflict that opposes God to Beliar. The devil has a key for direct access to the human self, that is, the "seven spirits of deceit" posed by Beliar within and against humankind (cf. *T Reub* 2:1–2). These spirits are human desires; once a person "is subjected to the passion of desire [Gr. *epithymia*] and is enslaved by it" (*T Jos* 7:8), losing integrity, that person is led to the deadly sin (Gr. *hamartia eis thanaton*; *T Iss* 7:1). As in *Sir* 28:12-26, the image of the double tongue is used to describe human ambivalence, but the ideological framework is totally changed: Beliar is the protagonist.

> The good set of soul does not talk with a double tongue: praises and curses, abuse and honor, calm and strife, hypocrisy and truth, poverty and wealth, but it has one disposition, uncontaminated and pure, toward all men. There is no duplicity in its perception or its hearing. Whatever it does, or speaks, or

---

of the origin of evil is the right approach for explaining the complexity and paradox of Paul's vision of the law. On the *Letter to the Romans*, see esp. C. K. Barrett, *A Commentary on the Epistle to the Romans* (London, 1957); E. Käsemann, *An die Römer* (Tübingen, 1974) (*Commentary on Romans*, trans. G. W. Bromiley [Grand Rapids and London, 1980]); Aland, et al., eds., *Greek New Testament*; C.E.B. Cranfield, *A Critical and Exegetical Commentary on the Epistle to the Romans*, 2 vols. (Edinburgh, 1975–79); O. Michel, *Der Brief an die Römer*, 14th ed. (Göttingen, 1978); and H. Schlier, *Der Römerbrief* (Freiburg, Basel, and Vienna, 1978).

14. On the *Testaments of the Twelve Patriarchs*, see R. Sinker, *The Testaments of the Twelve Patriarchs* (Edinburgh, 1871 [English trans.]); F. Schnapp, *Die Testamente der zwölf Patriarchen* (Halle, 1884 [German trans.]); idem, *APAT* 2 (1900): 458–506 (German trans.); R. H. Charles, *The Greek Versions of the Testaments of the Twelve Patriarchs* (Oxford, 1908; repr., Darmstadt, 1966 [Greek text with the variants of other ancient versions]); idem, *APOT* 2 (1913): 282–367 (English trans.); P. Riessler, *ASB* (1928), 1149–1250, 1335–38 (German trans.); J. Becker, *JSHRZ* 3.1 (1974): 1–164 (German trans.); M. de Jonge, H. W. Hollander, H. J. de Jonge, and T. Korteweg, *The Testaments of the Twelve Patriarchs* (Leiden, 1978 [Greek text]); P. Sacchi, *AAT* 1 (1981): 725–948 (Italian trans.); H. C. Kee, *OTP* 1 (1983): 775–828 (English trans.); M. de Jonge, *AOT* (1984), 505–600 (English trans.); and M. Philonenko, *BÉI* (1987), 811–944 (French trans.).

perceives, it knows that the Lord is watching over its life, for he cleanses his soul in order that he will not be suspected of wrongdoing either by men or by God. The works of Beliar are twofold; he knows no simplicity. (*T Benj* 6:5-7)

Against this ambivalence, even the practice of the law is ineffective. "The commandments of the Lord are double" (*T Naph* 8:7), their goodness depending on humankind's good soul.

If the soul is disposed toward evil, all of man's deeds are wicked; driving out the good, he accepts the evil and is overmastered by Beliar. Even when man does good, it is turned into evil. (*T Ash* 1:8)

Salvation consists in the attainment of an integrity and simplicity (Gr. *haplotês*) of soul, based on the fear of God and love toward one's neighbor.

The Lord I loved with all my strength; and I loved every human being. You do these as well, my children, and every spirit of Beliar will flee from you . . . so long as you have the God of heaven with you, and walk with all mankind in simplicity [Gr. *haplotês*] of heart. (*T Iss* 7:6-7; cf. 3:6—5:3; *T Reub* 4:1)

James places the Christian system in this conceptual framework. Again, the "double tongue" symbolizes human ambivalence:

We all make many mistakes. If any one makes no mistakes in what he says, he is a perfect man, able to bridle the whole body also. If we put bits into the mouths of horses, we can guide their whole bodies. Look at the ships also; though they are so great and are driven by strong winds, they are guided by a very small rudder wherever the will of the pilot directs. So the tongue is a little member and boasts of great things. How great a forest is set ablaze by a small fire! And the tongue is a fire, the world of iniquity; the tongue lives among our members, defiles the whole body, sets on fire the course of life, and is set on fire by Gehenna. Every kind of beast and bird, of reptile and sea creature, can be tamed by humankind, but no human being can tame the tongue—a restless evil, full of deadly poison. With it we bless the Lord and Father, and with it we curse men, who are made in the likeness of God. From the same mouth come blessing and cursing. My brethren, this ought not to be so. Does a spring pour forth from the same opening fresh water and brackish? Can a fig tree, my brethren, yield olives, or a grapevine figs? Neither can a source of salt water yield fresh. (*James* 3:2-12)

James, therefore, agrees with the *Testaments of the Twelve Patriarchs* that the source of evil is "the world of iniquity," that is, the devil, whose power is manifested in the apparently uncontrollable emergence of "passions."

What causes wars, and what causes fightings within you? Is it not your passions [Gr. *hêdonai*] that are at war in your members? You desire [Gr. *epithymeô*]; and do not have, so you kill and covet; and cannot obtain, so you fight and wage war. You do not have, because you do not ask. You ask and do not receive, because you ask wrongly, to spend it on your passions [Gr. *hêdonai*]. (*James* 4:1-3)

As a result the Pauline series of causes and effects is significantly modified. At the base of everything there is "desire" [Gr. *epithymia*], fomented by
the devil, which leads to sin [Gr. *hamartia*], which, once committed, leads to
death [Gr. *thanatos*].

> Let no one say when he is tempted, "I am tempted by God"; for God cannot
> be tempted with evil and He Himself tempts no one; but each person is
> tempted when he is lured and enticed by his own desire [Gr. *epithymia*]. Then
> desire when it has conceived gives birth to sin [Gr. *hamartia*]; and sin when it
> is committed brings forth death [Gr. *thanatos*]. (*James* 1:13-15)

The double nature of the devil is faced by God's simplicity. If the *Testament of Benjamin* claims effectively that Beliar "knows no simplicity" (*T Benj*
6:7), James reminds us that "in God there is no variation or shadow of
turning" (*James* 1:17). The "jealous" God demands of humankind an equally
simple, undivided love.

> Adulterers! Do you not know that loving the world is hating God? Whoever
> wishes to be a friend of the world makes himself an enemy of God. Or do you
> suppose it is in vain that the scripture says, "[God] loves jealously the spirit
> which He has made to dwell in us"?[15] (*James* 4:4-5)

It is thus understandable why for James religious experience consists not
only of a positive sense of doing good, but primarily in a defensive stance in
order to conserve one's original simplicity.

> If any one thinks he is religious, and does not bridle his tongue but deceives
> his heart, this man's religion is vain. Religion that is pure and undefiled before
> God and the Father is this: to visit orphans and widows in their affliction, and
> to keep oneself unstained from the world. (*James* 1:26-27)

Human beings, therefore, find themselves torn between two opposing
principles, enemies to themselves in their own ambivalence, but not entirely
deprived of freedom and simplicity. Because of this condition they are ready

---

15. The quotation of the Scripture contained in this passage poses serious problems of
interpretation: first, because it does not correspond to any known Scripture (canonical or
apocryphal); second, and most importantly, because it lends itself to divergent readings. What
exactly is the "spirit" it speaks of? Is it the "vital breath" that God calls "jealously" to God, as
most scholars understand it—even the "holy spirit," according to a certain theological tradition
that today has rightly fallen into disuse? Or is it "the inclination toward evil [that] seduces us
even to the point of jealousy [and] that God has made live in us," as hypothesized by J. Marcus
("The Evil Inclination in the Epistle of James," *CBQ* 44 [1982]: 606–21)? Marcus's thesis is
based on the (in my opinion, incorrect and anachronistic) attribution of the rabbinic conception
of *yeṣer haraʿ* ("the evil inclination") to the *Letter of James* and, even earlier, to the *Book of Sirach*.
The theme of God's "jealousy" (also a theme of the Scripture) is easily adapted to the
"simplicity-doubleness" contrast that James uses to resolve the problem of evil and the opposition of God and Satan.

joyously to receive the "good news" of the decisive help the Creator offers, through the Messiah, in the struggle against the devil.

7. HUMAN FREEDOM AND THE VALUE
OF PRAXIS

We now can better understand why the common appeal to God's mercy assumed different traits in Paul and James. For Paul, human beings are innocent victims of the evil that dominates them, and yet are responsible before God for their sins. They must be redeemed from this paradoxical and hopeless condition in virtue of an event that is absolutely independent of their (useless) efforts to do good. Such an event is the redeeming work of Jesus the Christ; his blood is the "price" of redemption.

> Now the righteousness of God has been manifested apart from law, although the law and the prophets bear witness to it, the righteousness of God through faith in Jesus Christ for all who believe. For there is no distinction; since all have sinned and fall short of the glory of God, they are justified by His grace as a gift, through the redemption which is in Christ Jesus, whom God put forward as an expiation by his blood, to be received by faith. This was to show God's righteousness, because in His divine forbearance He had passed over former sins; it was to prove at the present time that He Himself is righteous and that He justifies him who has faith in Jesus. (*Rom* 3:21-26)

In this way grace has contrasted sin through a symmetrical process of restoring the order overturned by Adam's sin.

> As one man's trespass led to condemnation for all men, so one man's act of righteousness leads to acquittal and life for all men. For as by one man's disobedience all men were made sinners, so by one man's obedience all men will be made righteous. (*Rom* 5:18-19)

Salvation is the fruit of an individual acceptance of this event of justification. In virtue of a pure act of will human beings, redeemed from the slavery of sin, can accept this redemption, subjecting themselves to the liberating lordship of God and of Christ. The proof for this in the Scriptures is drawn from *Gen* 15:6; Abraham becomes the model of the man who is justified by faith.

> What does the scripture say? "Abraham believed God, and it was reckoned to him as righteousness." Now to one who works, his wages are not reckoned as a gift but as his due. And to one who does not work but trusts Him who justifies the ungodly, his faith is reckoned as righteousness. (*Rom* 4:3-5)

From such faith a consistent style of life will naturally spring forth, expressing itself in works that conform to the new condition of being justified, in a "faith working through love," to use Paul's pregnant expression (*Gal* 5:6). Useless and neutral as a means for salvation, human works become the evidence that the graciously offered goal of salvation has been reached through faith.

For James too, humankind is dramatically oppressed by its own ambivalent nature and is in need of a supplementary intervention from above. This is "the implanted word" or "the law of liberty" (cf. *James* 1:21, 25), that is, the message of "our Lord Jesus Christ, the Lord of glory." Such a message is the source of salvation for those who are willing to accept the "greatest gift" that the "jealous" God has given to the "humble."

> Do you suppose it is in vain that the scripture says, "[God] loves jealously the spirit which He has made to dwell in us"? But He gives a greatest gift; therefore it says, "God opposes the proud, but gives His gift to the humble." (*James* 4:5-6)

Acceptance of and faith in such an opportunity for salvation does not consist in a pure act of the will so much as in putting it into practice. It is human freedom that enables each individual to act as God's collaborator. Humankind must do its part, putting aside every desire, accepting "the implanted word with simplicity [Gr. *haplotēs*]," and becoming "doers of the word."

> You know this, beloved brethren. Let every man be quick to hear, slow to speak, slow to anger; for the anger of man does not work the righteousness of God. Therefore put away all filthiness and rank growth of wickedness and receive with simplicity the implanted word, which is able to save your souls. But be doers of the word, and not hearers only, deceiving yourselves. For if any one is a hearer of the word and not a doer, he is like a man who observes his face in a mirror; he observes himself and goes away and at once forgets what he was like. But he who looks into the perfect law, the law of liberty, and perseveres, being no hearer that forgets but a doer that acts, he shall be blessed in his doing. (*James* 1:19-25)

Between faith and works, grace and merit, an unbreakable bond is thus created. Again, the example of Abraham is recalled, but for James the experience of the biblical patriarch (together with that of Rahab the harlot) demonstrates how works should cooperate with faith if faith is to be completed. Human action should cooperate with God's grace for God's grace to have effect.

> What does it profit, my brethren, if a man says he has faith but has not works? Can his faith save him? . . . You believe that God is one; you do well. Even the demons believe—and shudder. Do you want to be shown, you foolish fellow, that faith apart from works is barren? Was not Abraham our father justified by works, when he offered his son Isaac upon the altar? You see that faith was

active along with his works, and faith was completed by works, and the scripture says, "Abraham believed God, and it was reckoned to him as righteousness"; and he was called the friend of God. You see that a man is justified by works and not by faith alone. And in the same way was not also Rahab the harlot justified by works when she received the messengers and sent them out another way? For as the body apart from the spirit is dead, so faith apart from works is dead. (*James* 2:14, 19-26)

In James's conclusion ("a man is justified by works and not by faith alone") we can see many things: the polemical reaction to "rampant" Paulinism; the diffidence of Christian Jews in the face of the increasingly cumbersome presence of Christian Gentiles; and, in the adverb "alone," the worried precision of one who wants to clarify, without breaking, a bridge (even a concession) laid in an otherwise frontal attack. Primarily, however, James's conclusion is the logical and consistent expression of a synergetic process in which he sees salvation.

Submit yourselves to God. Resist the devil and he will flee from you. Draw near to God and He will draw near to you. Cleanse your hands, you sinner, and purify your heart, you men of double soul. Be wretched and mourn and weep. Let your laughter be turned to mourning and your joy to dejection. Humble yourselves before God and He will exalt you. (*James* 4:7-10)

8. CHRISTIANITY AND CHRISTIANITIES

The preceding analysis restores a more historically plausible image of James: he is much closer to Paul than to the Pharisees. This has been done without playing down the differences between the two Christian authors. Both of them begin from the same generative idea, that is, the split between God's mercy and God's justice. Their conclusions are so different, however, that it is impossible even to speak of an authentic debate or dialogue between the two. The interpreter is left rather with a sense of a profound, unsolvable incommunicability and incomprehension. James and Paul confront the same themes, offer the same examples, and even say the same words. At times they assume accusatory tones, at other times defensive ones. Both seem almost surprised at the possibility of being misunderstood. Their discourses are interwoven without ever really meeting, without any real possibility of changing, or of changing each other.

Having begun with the analysis of the many "Judaisms" of the first century, we have now faced the no less complex problem of the dialectics within each system. The themes and tensions that characterize this phase of the history of Jewish thought reemerge, stronger than any pretentious solutions, as elements of an internal debate. In this respect, James and Paul offer an emblematic example in the diversity of their Christianities. Both of them are exponents of a Jewish movement convinced that it bears God's final and definitive answer. Without being aware of it, however, they also carried within themselves the unresolved questions of their times. Our culture, which owes so much to them, has inherited their doubts no less than their certainties.

8

"DO THIS IN REMEMBRANCE OF ME"

The Memorial Value of Worship
in Middle Judaism

1. A PROBLEM OF METHOD

The imperative, "Do this in remembrance of me" (Gr. *touto poieite eis tên emên anamnêsin*), which the tradition of Luke and Paul (*Luke* 22:19; *1 Cor* 11:24-25) adds as an explanation for the Lord's Supper, represents without doubt one of the most important expressions in Christian theology, one that would lead to many later developments. Determining its original meaning still constitutes an open historical problem.

Since the second and third centuries the Christian liturgical tradition has seen in this imperative the attitude and the motive that bring the faithful to repeat Jesus' ritual gesture, understood as an offering to God the Father, according to the formula already present in Hippolytus of Rome: "Mindful of [Jesus'] death and resurrection, we offer up the bread and the cup to [God]" [Lat. *memores igitur mortis et resurrectionis eius, offerimus tibi panem et calicem*]; Hippolytus of Rome, *Traditio Apostolica* 4).[1] This interpretation has never satisfied contemporary scholars, who in this century have been repeatedly engaged in the attempt to reconstruct the exact background of the expression.

Research initially was directed toward the Hellenistic environment; the formulas of commemoration of the dead, as well as some mystery rituals, present some possible points of contact with the passages of Luke and Paul. But the analogies are more apparent than real, as Justin had already noted, not without a certain embarrassment, in his *First Apology* (mid–second century):

---

1. See H. Leclercq, "Messe," *DACL* 6 (1933): 513–774.

The wicked devils have imitated [Jesus' gesture] in the mysteries of Mithras, commanding the same thing to be done. For, that bread and a cup of water are placed with certain incantations in the mystic rites of one who is being initiated, you either know or can learn. (Justin Martyr, *First Apology* 66)

The exegetic work of J. Jeremias definitively shifted scholars' attention to the Jewish background of the expression.[2] The proposed translation, "That God may remember me," had the merit of bringing to light that God's memory was no less important than human memory in the Jewish tradition—a fact that was being rediscovered and emphasized in Jeremias's time by a whole series of semantic and theological studies.[3]

The theological work of M. Thurian marks another fundamental shift.[4] A conceptual value came to be attributed to the term "memorial" (Heb. *zikkaron*; Gr. *anamnêsis*), so as to encompass all the various meanings expressed by the Hebrew root *zkr*, in relation to both human memory and God's memory. Thus, the "memorial concept" became the interpretative theological category par excellence of Jewish and Christian worship: Jesus' Supper is a "memorial," as is Passover.

This formulation, reproposed in important later works,[5] seems today to be universally accepted, even in church documents.[6] It has also been given its most organic synthesis in a recent book by F. Chenderlin.[7] The proposed translation, "Do this as my memorial," would, in its comprehensiveness, fully express the complexity of the "memorial concept" as a reminder that recalls both human memory and God's memory. "Jesus' memorial . . . would have involved his reminding God and the disciples present: reminding them of God's promises, of Jesus himself and his promises, of the disciples themselves, of his and the disciples' intentionalities. . . . It would also be 'his' because . . . he would be reminding God and God would be reminded of him."[8]

---

2. See J. Jeremias, *Die Abendmahlsworte Jesu*, 3d ed. (Göttingen, 1960) (*The Eucharistic Words of Jesus*, trans. N. Perrin [New York, 1966]).

3. See esp. J. Pedersen, *Israel: Its Life and Culture* (London and Copenhagen, 1926); and O. Michel, "*mimnêskomai*," *TWNT*. Pedersen even made memory an exclusive category of thought of Israel: "The peculiarity about the Israelite is that he cannot at all imagine memory, unless at the same time an effect on the totality and its direction of the will is taken for granted" (p. 106).

4. See M. Thurian, *L'eucharistie, mémorial du Seigneur* (Neuchâtel and Paris, 1959) (*The Eucharistic Memorial*, trans. J. G. Davies, 2 vols [Richmond, Va., 1960–61]).

5. See esp. the excursus dedicated to the theme by R. Le Déaut in *La nuit pascale* (Rome, 1964), 66–71.

6. The World Council of Churches, in the document *Baptism, Eucharist and Ministry* (Lima, 1982), assumes "the biblical concept of memorial" as a possible base of ecumenical consensus among Christians on the Eucharist.

7. See F. Chenderlin, *Do This as My Memorial* (Rome, 1982).

8. Ibid., 226.

Such conclusions cannot help but raise questions of method. How much of the "memorial concept" belongs to the history of Jewish thought, and how much is a projection of contemporary theological problems and interests? Is there not perhaps a risk of improperly transferring the data of linguistic analysis to the ideological plane, constructing an abstract "theology of the root"?[9]

These questions are more than legitimate because the meaning of an expression is given completely only within and by the ideological context that uses it. It is primarily to this context that we must refer in order to avoid dangerous misunderstandings and confusion of the historical and theological planes. To understand the passages of Luke and Paul fully they must be correctly placed within their ideological context. The memorial value attributed to acts of worship does in fact vary in the history of Jewish thought according to the various ideological strains present in it.

2. THE MEMORIAL VALUE OF WORSHIP IN ANCIENT JUDAISM

As the ancient documents in the Hebrew Bible witness,[10] the memorial value of worship was understood in ancient Judaism in various modalities, at times in relation to human memory, at times in relation to God's memory.[11]

First, we have a series of passages that place worship in relation to the saving events in the history of Israel—particularly in the exodus, in which God's power was fully shown and God's promise fulfilled. In the face of the graciousness and benevolence of divine intervention, the memory of the past holds a specific saving value for human beings as the means that places them and makes them participants in the divine plan. Through worship (and its memorial power) this saving past makes itself present in every person. The goal of the feast of the unleavened bread is to recall the event of the exodus.

You shall eat no leavened bread . . . ; seven days you shall eat . . . unleavened bread, the bread of affliction—for you came out of the land of Egypt in

---

9. This is the risk indicated by J. Barr's critical lesson, *The Semantics of Biblical Language* (London, 1961).

10. On the texts of the Hebrew Bible quoted here, see K. Elliger and W. Rudolph, eds., *Biblia Hebraica Stuttgartensia* (Stuttgart, 1967–77).

11. On the theme of memory in ancient Judaism, see P.A.H. de Boer, *Gedenken und Gedachtnis in der Welt des Alten Testaments* (Stuttgart, 1962); B. S. Childs, *Memory and Tradition in Israel* (London, 1962); W. Schottroff, *Gedenken im Alten Orient und im Alten Testament*, WMANT 15 (Neukirchen-Vluyn, 1964); and G. Boccaccini, "Il tema della memoria nell' ebraismo e nel giudaismo antico," *Henoch* 7 (1985): 165–92.

> hurried flight—that all the days of your life you may remember the day when
> you came out of the land of Egypt. (*Deut* 16:3; cf. 16:9-12, with reference to
> "the feast of weeks")

This is the same criterion enunciated in *Exod* 13:3-10:

> And Moses said to the people, "Remember this day, in which you came out
> from Egypt, out of the house of bondage, for by strength of hand the Lord
> brought you out from this place; no leavened bread shall be eaten. . . . And you
> shall tell your son on that day, 'It is because of what the Lord did for me when
> I came out of Egypt.' And it shall be to you as a sign on your hand and as a
> memorial between your eyes, that the law of the Lord may be in your mouth;
> for with a strong hand the Lord has brought you out of Egypt." (*Exod* 13:3, 8-9)

In *Josh* 4:1-9, the pile of stones erected in remembrance of the crossing of
the Jordan has the purpose of perpetuating through continual narration a
saving memory. Just as in *Exod* 13:9, the ritual action is a "reminder," "a
memorial sign" (Heb. *zikkaron*) for future generations.

> When your children ask in time to come, "What do those stones mean to
> you?" you shall tell them that the waters of the Jordan were cut off before the
> ark of the covenant of the Lord. . . . These stones shall be to the people of
> Israel a memorial for ever. (*Josh* 4:6-7)

The later placement of these ancient passages within the context of a
theology of the covenant did not modify the memorial value of worship for
future generations; historical memory was simply subordinated to the memory of the covenant as that which pushes human beings to recognize God's
benevolence and the necessity of obeying the law.

The Hebrew Bible also testifies to a different conception of worship, as
fully expressed in the priestly traditions. We are still within the sphere of a
theology of the covenant, but the stress falls rather on the eternal order fixed
by God through the covenant, so that the main concerns are to insure the
duration of that order and to refer Israel to it. The regularity of worship is
its principal guarantee. The objects and acts of worship are placed as a
"memorial [Heb. *zikkaron*] for the children of Israel before the Lord" (*Exod*
12:14; 28:12, 29; 30:16; *Lev* 23:24; *Num* 10:10; 17:5; 31:54), so that, as *Num*
10:9 explains about the ritual sounding of the trumpets, Israel will be
remembered before God and God will intervene in its favor. In essence, for
the priestly traditions worship regards not human memory but God's memory, so that God will continue to remember the chosen.

The act of worship is always related to God's memory, even when it may
bring with it a punitive intervention. The ordeal of the woman suspected of
adultery (*Num* 5:11-31) provides for the presentation of an offering, among
other things. It is an "offering of jealousy, an offering of remembrance, that

unveils transgression" (*Num* 5:15) and calls down divine judgment, which may be a condemnation.

3. WORSHIP AS
A MEMORIAL "BEFORE GOD"

In middle Judaism the situation becomes decidedly more complex, as does the evolution of Jewish thought. Judaism appears increasingly to be divided into often contradictory ideological systems.

The priestly conception is reproposed by the *Book of Sirach* (early second century B.C.E.)[12] in which three elements of worship are mentioned as a "memorial before the Most High for the children of His people" (Gr. *eis mnêmosynon enanti hypsistou huiois laou autou*; Heb. *lzkrwn* [or *lhzkyr*] *lpny 'lywn lbny 'mw*): the ringing of the golden bells of Aaron's robe (*Sir* 45:9), the precious stones with seal engravings in golden settings on the ephod (*Sir* 45:11), and the sounding of the trumpets (*Sir* 50:16).

A more ample list of "memorials before God" is offered by Pseudo-Philo's *Liber Antiquitatum Biblicarum* (first century C.E.):[13] the rainbow (*Lib Ant Bib* 3:12; 4:5), the tithes (*Lib Ant Bib* 14:4), the staff of Moses (*Lib Ant Bib* 19:11), the festival of the unleavened bread (*Lib Ant Bib* 13:4), and the stones put in the ark of the covenant (*Lib Ant Bib* 26:12). The (lost) original Semitic can easily be seen through the Latin formula: *in conspectu meo in memoriam* (or *in testimonium*).

The Palestinian Targum (*Neofiti*; cf. *Fragment-Targums* and *Pseudo-Jonathan*) interprets in the priestly sense ("before God"; Aram. *qdn yyy*) all of the passages of the Pentateuch in which the term *zikkaron* appears, even in the cases in which the original meaning was different (cf. *Exod* 13:9; 17:14).[14] To the Aramaic term *dokran* (corresponding to Heb. *zikkaron*) the specification *tob* ("good," "favorable," "acceptable"), characteristic of God's memory,

12. On the *Book of Sirach*, see chap. 3. For more detailed information on the theme of memory in middle Judaism, see G. Boccaccini, "Ricordare—dimenticare nella tradizione giudaica e cristiana antica" (diss., Università di Firenze, 1983).

13. On Pseudo-Philo, *Liber Antiquitarum Biblicarum*, see M. R. James, *The Biblical Antiquities of Philo* (London, 1917 [English trans.]); P. Riessler, *ASB* (1928), 735–861, 1315–18 (German trans.); G. Kisch, *Pseudo-Philo's Liber Antiquitatum Biblicarum* (Notre Dame, 1949 [Latin text]); C. Dietzfelbinger, *JSHRZ* 2.2 (1975) (German trans.); D. J. Harrington, ed., and J. Cazeaux, C. Perrot, and P. M. Bogaert, trans., *Pseudo-Philon: Les Antiquités Bibliques*, 2 vols., SC 229–230 (Paris, 1976 [Latin text and French trans.]); A. de la Fuente Adánez, *ApAT* 2 (1983): 195–316 (Spanish trans.); D. J. Harrington, *OTP* 2 (1985): 297–377 (English trans.); and J. Hadot, *BÉI* (1987), 1225–1392 (French trans.).

14. On the *Targum Neofiti*, see A. Díez Macho, ed., *Neophyti 1*, 5 vols. (Madrid and Barcelona, 1968–78 [Aramaic text and French, Spanish, and English trans.]); and R. Le Déaut

is added regularly, except in *Num* 5:15, 18. (See *tg.* [*Ne*] on *Exod* 12:14; 13:9; 17:14; 28:12; 39:7; on *Lev* 23:24; on *Num* 17:5; *tg.* [*Ne*; *Jo*] on *Exod* 28:29; 30:16; on *Num* 10:10; 31:54; cf. *Exod* 28:29 [LXX] [Gr. *eis to hagion mnêmosynon enanti tou theou*]; *T Naph* 8:5 [Gr. *mnêmê para theou agathê*]). The hermeneutic criterion is precisely that expressed in the Tosefta,[15] in a discussion that tradition places at the beginning of the second century C.E.:

> R. Tarfon says, "Every point at which *zikkaron* is mentioned in the Torah, [God's] intention is favorable [Heb. *ltwbh*], except for this one, since it is said, 'It is an offering of remembrance, unveiling transgression' (*Num* 5:15)." (*t. Sotah* 1:10)

Even the objection raised by R. Aqiba is part of the same logic that sees *zikkaron* as a memorial sign that *exclusively* regards God's memory:

> R. Aqiba says, "Also this one is favorable [Heb. *ltwbh*], since it is said, 'And if the woman has not been made unclean and she is clean, then she will be guiltless and will conceive a child' (*Num* 5:28)." (*t. Sotah* 1:10)

In particular, the Palestinian Targum emphasizes the memorial value "before God" of the Passover, explaining its role within the divine order of history:

> It is a night that is preserved and prepared for salvation before the Lord [Aram. *qdm yy*], when the Israelites went forth redeemed from the land of Egypt. For four nights are written in the Book of the Memorials [Aram. *bspr dwkrnyy'*]. . . . The first night: when the Word of the Lord was revealed upon the world to create it. . . . The second night: when the Word of the Lord was revealed unto Abraham between the pieces. . . . The third night: when the Word of the Lord was revealed upon the Egyptians in the middle of the night. . . . The fourth night: when the world will reach its fixed time to be redeemed. . . . This is the Passover night before the Lord [Aram. *qwdm yy*]; it is preserved and prepared for all the Israelites, through their generations. (*tg.* [V] on *Exod* 12:42; cf. *tg.* [*Ne*; *Jo*] on *Exod* 12:42; *tg.* [P] on *Exod* 15:18)[16]

---

and J. Robert, *Targum de Pentateuque*, 5 vols. (Paris, 1978–81 [French trans.]). On the *Fragment-Targums*, see M. L. Klein, ed., *The Fragments-Targums of the Pentateuch*, 2 vols. (Rome, 1980 [Aramaic text and English trans.]). On the *Targum Pseudo-Jonathan*, see J. W. Etheridge, *The Targums of Onkelos and of Jonathan ben Uzziel on the Pentateuch*, 2 vols. (London, 1862–65 [English trans.]); D. Rieder, *Pseudo Jonathan* (Jerusalem, 1974 [Aramaic text]); and Le Déaut and Robert, *Targum de Pentateuch* (French trans.).

15. On the *Tosefta*, see M. S. Zuckermandel, *Tosephta* (Halberstadt, 1881; repr., Jerusalem, 1963 [Hebrew text]); S. Lieberman, *The Tosefta*, 4 vols. (New York, 1955–73 [Hebrew text]); D. W. Windfuhr, et al., *Die Tosefta*, 5 vols. (Stuttgart, 1960–67 [German trans.]); and J. Neusner, *The Tosefta*, 6 vols. (New York, 1977–86 [English trans.]).

16. A detailed analysis of the passage is in Le Déaut, *La nuit pascale*.

4. WORSHIP AS
A MEMORIAL "FOR FUTURE GENERATIONS"

In spite of the fact that the continuity of the priestly conception is amply documented, its influence appears limited to the Temple rituals. Outside the Temple, the memorial value of worship "for future generations" is instead emphasized.

Festivals such as Purim and Hanukkah are born as commemorative festivals to celebrate the victories obtained by Israel over its enemies, thanks to God's help and to faithfulness to the law, and to conserve their memory for posterity. For example, it is said of the institution of the feast of Purim:

> These days shall be remembered and kept throughout every generation, in every family, province, and city; these days of Purim shall never fall into disuse among the Jews, nor shall the commemoration of these days cease among their descendants. (*Esther* 9:28)[17]

The memorial value of worship for future generations is the only one that the western Diaspora seems to share, whether for cultural reasons (that lead to keeping quiet about a theme that is too "Jewish," too anthropomorphic, like God's memory) or due to a greater distance (physical and religious) from the priestly circles of the Temple of Jerusalem. The *Letter of Aristeas* and both of the great expositions of the Jewish law, by Philo of Alexandria and by Josephus,[18] are in perfect agreement on this point.

For Pseudo-Aristeas, Moses "has ordained every time and place for a continual reminder of the supreme God and upholder [of all]" (*Let Aris* 157). Consistent with his cosmic perspective, Philo states that Passover is for Israel "a reminder [Gr. *hypomnêma*] and thank-offering [Gr. *charistêrion*] of the great migration from Egypt" (*Spec Leg* 2.146), as well as the occasion for God to "remind [Gr. *hypomimnêskô*] all mankind of the creation of the world by setting before our eyes the spring when everything blooms and flowers" (*Spec Leg* 2.152). As for the "trumpet feast,"

> it is a reminder [Gr. *hypomnêsis*] of a might and marvelous event which came to pass when the oracles of the law were given from above. . . . This is a significance peculiar to [our] nation. What follows is common to all mankind. . . . The law instituted this feast figured by that instrument of war the trumpet, which gives it its name, to be a thank-offering [Gr. *eucharistia*] to God the peace-maker and peace-keeper, Who destroys faction both in cities and in

---

17. On the *Book of Esther*, see Elliger and Rudolph, eds., *Biblia Hebraica Stuttgartensia* (Hebrew text).

18. On the *Letter of Aristeas*, Philo, and Josephus, see chaps. 5, 6, and 9, respectively.

various parts of the universe and creates plenty and fertility and abundance of other good things and leaves the havoc of fruits without a single spark to be rekindled. (*Spec Leg* 2.188–92)

For Josephus, too, the feast of the unleavened bread is celebrated "in memory of that time of scarcity" (Gr. *eis mnêmên tês tote endeias*; *Ant* 2.317). The three annual pilgrim festivals remind the dispersed Jews that "they are members of the same race and partners in the same institutions; and this end is attained by such intercourse, when through sight and speech they recall those ties in mind" (Gr. *tê te opsei kai tê homilia mnêmên autôn entithentas*; *Ant* 4.204). The septennial reading of the laws has the same memorial function:

> Every seven years at the season of the feast of tabernacles, the high priest, standing upon a raised platform from which he may be heard, recites the laws to the whole assembly; and neither woman nor child are excluded from this audience, nor yet the slaves. Thus the laws are so graven on their hearts and stored in the memory that they can never be effaced. (*Ant* 4.209–10)

The memorial value of certain cult objects is also emphasized by Josephus. For example, the tribe of Reuben, with that of Gad and all those of Manasseh who accompanied them, raise an altar on the bank of the Jordan "as a memorial to future generations [Gr. *mnêmeion tois epeita genêsomenois*], as a sign [Gr. *symbolon*] of their relationship to the inhabitants on the other side" (*Ant* 5.100). Similarly, after the revolt of Korah and his house (cf. *Num* 16), Moses,

> wishing their penalty to be commemorated and future generations to learn thereof, ordered Eleazar, the son of Aaron, to deposit their censers beside the brazen altar, as a reminder to posterity [Gr. *hôs an hypomnêsis eiê tois authis*] of the fate which had befallen them for imagining that it was possible for deceit to be practiced on the power of God. (*Ant* 4.57–58)

Even in the rabbinic texts and especially in the ritual of the *Haggadah of Pesah*, the formula "in memory of the exodus from Egypt" appears repeatedly as the founding recollection of the people of Israel's national and religious identity. After 70 C.E. the memory of the city and the Temple's destruction is added to the memory of the exodus:

> [R. Joshua] said to them, "My children, to mourn too much is not possible. But thus have the sages said: A man puts on plaster on his house but he leaves open a small area, as a memorial to Jerusalem. A man prepares what is needed for a meal but leaves out some small things, as a memorial to Jerusalem. A woman prepares her ornaments, but leaves out some small things, as a memorial of Jerusalem, since it is said, 'If I forget you, O Jerusalem, let my right hand wither! Let my tongue cleave to the roof of my mouth, if I do not remember you, if I do not set Jerusalem above my highest joy!' (*Ps* 137:5-6)." (*t. Sotah* 15:12-14; cf. *Baba Bathra* 2:17)

The same traditional festivals, such as the feast of Tabernacles, are further enriched by memorial elements.

> Before time the *lulab* [lit. "palm branch," but here denoting the bunch of palm, myrtle, and willow branches] was carried seven days in the Temple, but in the provinces one day only. After the Temple was destroyed, Rabban Johanan b. Zakkai ordained that in the provinces it should be carried seven days in memory of the Temple. (*m. Sukkah* 3:12; *Rosh ha-Shanah* 4:3)[19]

In the end, the mechanism is the same as the one already pointed out concerning the Hebrew Bible. The memory of past events shows that God acts in history in conformity to the covenant, in rewards as well as in punishments and tests. Before good or bad luck, every generation is brought back by the historical memory to the only memory that counts, that is, the memory of the law.

5. THE MEMORIAL VALUE OF WORSHIP IN ESSENISM

The Essene movement carries the dissolution of the traditional figure of the righteous person, understood as "he who fulfills the law," to its extreme consequences.[20] Humankind's incapacity to do justice is implicit in its very nature; human beings are impure and in a state of sin from the time they are in their mother's womb (cf. 1QH 4.29–31). Salvation can exist only as a gracious act of God that "remembers" human beings and "justifies" them.

---

19. On the Mishnah, see V. Castiglioni, *Mishnaiot*, 3 vols. (Rome, 1894–1928; 2d ed., 1962–64 [Italian trans.]); G. Beer and O. Holtzmann, eds., *Die Mischna* (Berlin, 1912– [Hebrew text and German trans.]); H. Danby, *The Mishnah* (Oxford, 1933; repr., 1964 [English trans.]); P. Blackman, *Mishnayoth*, 7 vols. (London, 1951–56 [vocalized Hebrew text and English trans.]); C. Albeck and H. Yalon, *The Six Orders of the Mishnah* (Jerusalem and Tel Aviv, 1952–59 [vocalized Hebrew text]); and C. Del Valle, *La Misna* (Madrid, 1981 [Spanish trans.]).

20. On the Dead Sea Scrolls, see M. Burrows, J. C. Trever, and W. H. Brownlee, *The Dead Sea Scrolls of St. Mark's Monastery*, 2 vols. (Oxford, 1950–51 [Hebrew texts]); A. Dupont-Sommer, *Les écrits esséniens découverts près de la Mer Morte*, 2d ed. (Paris, 1959; 3d ed., 1964 [French trans.]) (*The Essene Writings from Qumran*, trans. G. Vermes [Oxford, 1961; rist., Gloucester and Magnola, Mass., 1973]); J. Maier, *Die Texte vom Toten Meer*, 2 vols. (Munich and Basel, 1960 [German trans.]); J. Carmignac and P. Guilbert, eds., *Les textes de Qumrân*, 2 vols. (Paris, 1961–63 [French trans.]); G. Vermes, *The Dead Sea Scrolls in English* (Harmondsworth, 1962; 2d ed., 1975; 3d ed., 1987 [English trans.]); E. Lohse, *Die Texte von Qumrân hebräische und deutsch* (Munich, 1964; 2d ed., 1971 [vocalized Hebrew texts and German trans.]); F. Michelini Tocci, *I manoscritti del Mar Morto* (Bari, 1967 [Italian trans.]); L. Moraldi, *I Manoscritti di Qumrân* (Turin, 1971; 2d ed., 1987 [Italian trans.]); J. A. Fitzmayer and D. J. Harrington, *A Manual of Palestinian Aramaic Texts* (Rome, 1978 [Aramaic texts and English trans.]); E. Qimron, *The Hebrew of the Dead Sea Scrolls* (Atlanta, 1986 [Hebrew texts]); M. A. Knibb, *The Qumran Community* (Cambridge, 1987 [Hebrew texts]); and A. Dupont-Sommer and A. Caquot, *BÉI* (1987), 1–460 (French trans.).

The emphasis placed on God's initiative and on human insufficiency over-shadows human freedom and results in predestination. God has *ab aeterno* decided the lot of every one of God's creatures; God fixed the times of history, and created the righteous to love God and the wicked to hate God.

> When can I say that is not foreknown,
> and what can I utter that is not foretold?
> All things are graven before You
> on a written reminder
> for everlasting ages,
> and for the numbered cycles
> of the eternal years
> in all their seasons;
> they are not hidden or absent from You.
>   (1QH 1.23–25)

Everything, therefore, happens "in its appointed time" and depends on God's memory. Even worship is "a memorial before God in its appointed time" (Heb. *lzkrwn bmw' dyhm*, 1QS 10.5; Aram. *qwdm 'l dkr*[n], 11QJN ar). Hence, an almost obsessive concern is given to the determination of the calendar, of the exact moment when worship should take place in order to be valid. For example, we find in the *Book of Jubilees*[21] concerning the feast of Passover:

> And you [Moses], remember this day all of the days of your life and observe it from year to year all the days of your life, once per year on its day according to all of its laws and you will not delay [one] day from [its] day or from [one] month to [another] month. For it is an eternal decree and engraved upon heavenly tablets for all of the children of Israel that they might observe it in each and every year on its day once per year in all of their generations. And there is no limit of days because it is ordained forever. . . . And you command the children of Israel to observe the Passover on their days in every year, once per year, on its appointed day. And it will come as an acceptable memorial

---

21. On the *Book of Jubilees*, see A. Dillmann, "Das Buch der Jubiläen," *Jahrbuch der biblischen Wissenschaft* 3 (1851): 72–96 (German trans.); idem, *Mashafa Kufâlê sive liber Jubilaeorum aethiopice* (Leipzig, 1859 [Ethiopic version]); A. M. Ceriani, *Monumenta sacra et profana* vol. 1.1 (Milan, 1861): 9–54, 63–64 (Latin fragments); H. Rönsch, *Das Buch der Jubiläen oder die kleine Genesis* (Leipzig, 1874; repr., 1970 [Latin fragments and German trans.]); R. H. Charles, *The Ethiopic Version of the Hebrew Book of Jubilees* (Oxford, 1895); E. Littmann, *APAT* 2 (1900): 31–119 (German trans.); R. H. Charles, *The Book of Jubilees or the Little Genesis* (London, 1902; repr., 1972 [Greek, Latin, and Syriac fragments and English trans.]); idem, *APOT* 2 (1913): 1–82 (English trans.); P. Riessler, *ASB* (1928): 539–666, 1304–11 (German trans.); A.-M. Denis, *Fragmenta Pseudepigraphorum quae supersunt graeca* (Leiden, 1970 [Greek fragments]); L. Fusella and P. Sacchi, *AAT* 1 (1981): 179–411 (Italian trans.); K. Berger, *JSHRZ* 2.3 (1982): 275–575 (German trans.); F. Corriente and A. Piñero, *ApAT* 2 (1983): 65–193 (Spanish trans.); R. H. Charles (rev. C. Rabin), *AOT* (1984), 1–139 (English trans.); O. S. Wintermute, *OTP* 2 (1985): 35–142 (English trans.); and A. Caquot, *BÉI* (1987), 627–810 (French trans.).

from before the Lord [Lat. *et erit in testimonium in cospectu Dei acceptabile*]. And the plague will not come to kill or to smite during that year when they have observed the Passover in its [appointed] time in all [respects] according to his command. (*Jub* 49:7, 15)

The priestly origin and ideology of the Essene movement are also manifested in the *War Scroll*'s presentation of the eschatological battle as a great liturgy. The phases of the battle will unfold to the rhythm of the sounding of the "memorial trumpets" (Heb. *ḥwṣrwt ḥzkrwn*; 1QM 7.13; 16.4; 18.4) that the priests will sound "in favor of the combatants" (1QM 16.4). On the trumpets it is written, "memorial of vengeance in the time appointed by God" (Heb. *zkrwn nqm bmw'd 'l*; 1QM 3.7-8). At that time the promise of *Num* 10:9 will be fulfilled ("you will sound with your trumpets, and you will be remembered before your God, and you will be saved from your enemies"; 1QM 10.7-8), and those who have been "justified" by God will win the definitive victory over Beliar (the devil) and over those destined *ab aeterno* to perdition.

6. "DO THIS AS A SIGN THAT REMINDS YOU OF ME"

Like the Essenes, early Christians claim that salvation can only come from God's mercy because, sin being inevitable, humankind would always be guilty before the law and God's punitive justice. Early Christians also believe, however, that the awaited intervention of God's mercy has already been realized in Jesus, the Son of man, the Christ, who with his mission, death, and resurrection has opened the way to salvation to humankind. God has already remembered God's promises; from now on memory is a duty above all for humankind, whose salvation depends on a saving past event.

Paul's passage in *1 Corinthians* 11 must be read within this context.[22] As has been pointed out by some scholars, Paul's text appears to be a paraphrase of the *Haggadah of Pesah*. [23] In this, the former Pharisee Paul places himself directly in line with his teachers. In *1 Cor* 11:26 he explains that the disciples, repeating the ritual gestures of Jesus (putting in practice the impera-

22. On *1 Corinthians*, see esp. C. K. Barrett, *A Commentary on the First Epistle to the Corinthians* (London, 1968); H. Conzelmann, *Der erste Brief an die Korinther* (Göttingen, 1969) (*1 Corinthians*, trans. J. W. Leitch [Philadelphia, 1975]); H. Lietzmann, *An die Korinther 1.2.*, 5th ed., ed. W. G. Kümmel (Tübingen, 1969); and K. Aland, et al., eds., *The Greek New Testament*, 3d ed. (New York, 1975 [Greek text]).

23. See W. D. Davies, *Paul and Rabbinical Judaism* (London, 1948), 242. On the interpretation of *1 Cor* 11:25-26, see G. Boccaccini, "Il valore memoriale dell'atto eucaristico alla luce della tradizione giudaica," in *Gesù ebreo*, ed. I. Gargano (Camaldoli, 1984), 107–17.

tive, "Do this in remembrance of me"), proclaim (Gr. *kataggellô*) his death, just as the exodus from Egypt is told, and through the telling is announced (Heb. *nagad*), when celebrating Pesah.

The difference, however, lies in the value of the event remembered. The exodus from Egypt is only one event, albeit fundamental, of divine mercy whose memory spurs humankind to give God just recognition and to obey the law; Jesus' mission, death, and resurrection is *the* single and unrepeatable event of God's mercy, whose memory and inclusion makes the Christian one of the faithful and grateful "justified." Jesus' Supper (as a "memorial sign") reminds the disciples of this reality until the Christ returns—that is, until this reality is fully manifest (*1 Cor* 11:26).

The emphasis is exclusively on human memory; no sign is made in the text (or from the context) of God's memory, except at the cost of an undue conceptualization of the term *anamnêsis*. In the ancient and middle Jewish traditions, worship implies human memory *or* God's memory, never both of them contemporaneously. The term "memorial" (Heb. *zikkaron*; Aram. *dokran*; Gr. *anamnêsis* [or *mnêmosynon*]) can be found in each of these two prospects. The context and a different technical terminology specify who is reminded of. When the Lukan tradition wants to take up the priestly idea of worship "before God," it does properly by using the right terminology. In *Acts* 10 an angel of God appears to the centurion Cornelius, announcing the fulfillment of his hopes of salvation: "Your prayers and your alms have ascended as a memorial before God" (Gr. *eis mnêmosynon emprosthen tou theou*; *Acts* 10:4; cf. *1 Enoch* 13:4; 99:3; *Tobias* 12:12 [Gr. *mnêmosynon enôpion tês doxês kyriou*]; *t. Rosh ha-Shanah* 1:12 [Heb. *zkrwn lpny yy ltwby*]; *tg.* [*On*] on *Gen* 30:22 [Aram. *dwkrn qdn yy*]). The expression means, as Cornelius then relates to Peter, "Your prayer has been heard and your alms have been remembered before God" (10:31). This technical terminology, used regularly when worship reminds God, is significantly lacking in *Luke* 22:19 and *1 Cor* 11:24-25; the repetition of Jesus' gesture does not imply God's memory.

As for the later Christian liturgical tradition, it has simply misunderstood and overturned the terms of Paul's formulation. The memory of those faithful to the Christ, from being the end of the act of worship, became its premise. Hence the problem of the completed act's meanings and ends was placed on an entirely new basis, opening the way for the most diverse reflections along the whole history of Christian theology. The "memorial concept" is a part of that history and finds its value and dignity therein. However, what is a significant concept of contemporary theology should not be transferred backwards to the historical plane, in which it turns into a misleading hermeneutic category.

9

FLAVIUS JOSEPHUS

The Betrayed Memory

1. APOLOGETIC MOTIFS IN
JOSEPHUS'S WORK

Flavius Josephus's work is marked by the accusation of betrayal for his having gone during the Jewish War from being the head of resistance in Galilee to being a personal friend of the Flavian emperors, whose name he took with Roman citizenship.[1]

In reality, Josephus did nothing more than adhere to the philo-imperial positions of a large part of the western Diaspora. Engaged in finding an advantageous modus vivendi with the Romans,[2] many Jews living in the Roman Empire essentially had remained outside of the nationalistic currents then arising in Palestine. This did not necessarily mean renouncing their identity, as seen from many examples, including Pseudo-Aristeas and Philo of Alexandria; their effort was rather to make Judaism a fundamental component of the cosmopolitan culture of the Roman Empire. It can be understood how Josephus can at the same time exalt the Romans and the Jews, two great nations that God has called to work together and that only the folly of a few fanatics has brought into conflict.[3]

---

1. See P. Vidal-Naquet, "Du bon usage de la trahison," in *Flavius Josèphe, La guerre des Juifs*, ed. P. Savinel (Paris, 1977).

2. In King Agrippa's speech to the people of Jerusalem (*Bellum* 2.345–401), in which he tries to convince them willingly to accept Roman domination, there is a preoccupation with the Diaspora: "There is not a people in the world which does not contain a portion of our race. All these, if you go to war, will be butchered by your adversaries" (2.398).

3. This is the basic thesis put forward by Josephus in *Bellum Judaicum*, clearly pronounced in the introduction to the work: "[my country] owed its ruin to civil strife" (1.10).

Just how much this corresponds to reality—the Roman Empire was a great power with better things to do than worry about a weak and even disdained minority (one needs only to think of Tacitus's description of the Jews in Book 5 of his *Historiae*)[4]—may be of little importance. Josephus's work is not that of a base quisling but that of an apologist who proclaims his faithfulness to the fathers and tries to give his culture and his people a consideration denied by many.[5]

Acting as his own apologist before his compatriots and apologist of his people before the Romans, Josephus holds these two awkward and diffident audiences present throughout his work. To the former he must demonstrate his enduring attachment to his national and religious identity; to the latter the value of this proudly and "incomprehensibly" maintained identity.

2. FAITHFULNESS TO THE RELIGIOUS IDENTITY AND TRADITION

The God professed by Josephus is a just and merciful God who looks upon the people of Israel with benevolence for their forefathers' merits. This idea is placed in the mouth of Nehemiah as a proclamation of faith:

> Fellow Jews, you know that God cherishes the memory of our fathers Abraham, Isaac and Jacob, and because of their righteousness [Gr. *dikaiosynê*] does not give up His providential care for us. (*Ant* 11.169)

Jews' mindful obedience to the law is explained above all as an act of recognition toward a provident and mindful God. The blessings poured out by God on God's people are in fact so great that "they would be deemed impious [Gr. *asebeis*] not to hold in remembrance" (*Ant* 2.214).

Josephus also knows, however, that in God's justice God has tied recompense and punishment, salvation and ruin, to humankind's practice of piety

---

4. Tacitus, *Historiae* 5.2–13. On this section, see A.M.A. Hospers-Jansen, *Tacitus over de Joden: Hist. 5, 2–13* (Kampen, 1949 [in Dutch, with an extensive English summary]).

5. The fundamental critical editions of Josephus's works are B. Niese, *Flavii Josephi opera*, 7 vols. (Berlin, 1887–95; repr., 1955); and S. A. Naber, *Flavii Josephi opera omnia*, 6 vols. (Leipzig, 1888–96). Among the modern translations, those of note are T. Reinach, ed., *Oeuvres complétes de Flavius Josèphe*, 7 vols. (Paris, 1900–1932 [French trans.]); H. St. J. Thackeray, R. Marcus, and L. H. Feldman, *Josephus*, 9 vols. (London and Cambridge, Mass., 1926–65) [English trans.]; G. Ricciotti, *Flavio Giuseppe tradotto e commentato*, 4 vols. (Turin, 1937–63 [Italian trans.]); J.A.G. Larraya, *Las guerras de los Judios* (Barcelona, 1952 [Spanish trans.]); and A. Shalit, *Yosef ben Mattityahu (Flavius Josephus), Qadmoniyot ha-Yehudim (Antiquitates Iudaicae)*, 3 vols. (Jerusalem, 1955–63, 2d ed., 1967 [Hebrew trans.]). Recently published in Italian are G. Vitucci, ed., *La Guerra Giudaica*, 2 vols. (Milan, 1974 [critical text and Italian trans.]); and L. Troiani, *Commento storico al "Contro Apione" di Giuseppe Flavio* (Pisa, 1977 [introduction, historical commentary, translation, and index]).

[Gr. *eusebeia*]. In a haggadic expansion of the biblical text of *Exod* 2:1, Amram, the future father of Moses, is presented in the act of raising his supplication to God with trust; he knows that the faithfulness of the people is a guarantee and a safe defense against the pharaoh's intentions to kill all the newborn Jewish children. Amram

> accordingly recoursed to prayer to God, beseeching Him to take some pity at length on men who had in no wise transgressed in their worship of Him, and to grant them deliverance from the tribulations of the present time and from the prospect of the extermination of their race. And God had compassion on him and, moved by his supplication, appeared to him in his sleep, exhorted him not to despair of the future, and told him that He had their piety [Gr. *eusebeia*] in remembrance and would ever give them its due recompense. (*Ant* 2.210–12)

As a Jew, Josephus knows no distinction between religious law and civil law; they are both part of the same divine tradition and their transmission engages the people of Israel from generation to generation. He can therefore state that

> above all we [Jews] pride ourselves on the education of our children and regard as the most essential task in life the observance of our laws and of the piety [Gr. *eusebeia*] based thereupon, which we have inherited. (*Ap* 1.60)

Hence memory is affirmed as the very foundation of the national and religious identity of the Jewish people.[6] With admiration Josephus tells us of some priests conducted in captivity to Rome. Even in their difficult situation "they had not forgotten the piety [Gr. *eusebeia*] owed to God, and supported themselves on figs and nuts" (*Vita* 14) in order to avoid breaking the dietary laws. In praise of the young King Solomon, the memory of his father's teaching is closely linked to his justice and fidelity to the law. Solomon "was not hindered by his youth from dealing justice and observing the laws and remembering the injunctions of his dying father" (*Ant* 8.21).

We must bear in mind this complexity in order to understand fully passages such as *Ant* 5.107–8, in which memory of the forefathers' laws contrasts with both forgetting God and introducing foreign customs (cf. *Ant* 8.127, 194). Josephus reformulates the warning that the Israelites direct to the eastern tribes accused of having abandoned the common tradition (*Josh* 22:13-20):

---

6. On the importance of the theme of memory in the ancient and middle Jewish traditions, see above, chap. 8. On Josephus in particular, see G. Boccaccini, "Il tema della memoria in Giuseppe Flavio," *Henoch* 6 (1984): 147–63.

We could not conceive that you, with your experience of instruction in the will of God, you who had been hearers of those laws which He Himself has given us, once parted from us and entering on your own heritage, which by the grace of God and His providential care for us has fallen to your lot, could have straightway forgotten Him and, abandoning the tabernacle and the ark and the altar of our fathers, introduced some strange gods and gone over to the vices of the Canaanites. Howbeit you shall be in no wise held guilty, if you repent and carry this madness no farther, but show that you revere and are mindful of the laws of your fathers. (*Ant* 5.107–8)

Forgetfulness therefore has a great moral weight; it is idolatry and betrayal[7] and as such is justly the object of God's wrath (cf. *Ant* 1.194; 2.327; 8.270). Even when it may be involuntary, it is always guilty and requires an expiatory sacrifice.[8] This is the sense Josephus gives to the sacrifice prescribed in *Num* 28:15.

On the new moon, besides the daily sacrifices, [the priests] offer . . . also a kid in expiation for any sins which may have been committed through forgetfulness [Gr. *kata lêthên*]. (*Ant* 3.238)

For this reason the great heads of Israel, such as Moses, Joshua, and Samuel, continually call the people to remember: they remind them of the signs of God's blessing (*Ant* 5.115), and reproach their forgetfulness (*Ant* 6.60) so that memory and perseverance should never be lacking, even in the most difficult moments, and so that the prospect of divine punishment is kept at bay. In Josephus's description of the people's revolt at Elis (Elim, cf. *Exod* 15:27) during the exodus from Egypt, the interdependence of these elements is quite evident.

With mind obsessed with their present woes, precluding all memory [Gr. *mnêmê*] of past blessings which they owed to God on the one hand, to the virtue and sagacity of Moses on the other, they viewed their general with indignation and were eager to stone him. . . . But he advanced into their midst . . . and exhorted them not, with present discomforts engrossing all their thoughts, to forget [Gr. *lêthên echô*] the benefits of the past. . . . It was probably to test their manhood, to see what fortitude they possessed, what memory [Gr. *mnêmê*] of past services, and whether their thoughts would not revert to those services because of the troubles now in their path, that God was exercising them with these trials of the moment. But now they were convicted of failure, both in perseverance [Gr. *hypomonê*] and in memory [Gr. *mnêmê*] of benefits

----

7. In the ancient and middle Jewish traditions it is common to speak of unfaithfulness to God in terms of a guilty "forgetfulness." See W. Schottroff, "*škh*," *THAT*.

8. The link between "forgetfulness" and expiatory sacrifice is common in the rabbinic halakhic tradition that, aware of human weakness, makes any effort to define the remedies to the inevitable "forgetfulnesses" (see, e.g., *m. Shabbath* 19:4).

received, by showing at once such contempt of God and of His purpose. . . .
Thus [Moses] calmed them, restraining that impulse to stone him and moving
them to repent of their intended action. (*Ant* 3.12–16, 22)

Because the history of Israel unfolds according to the rules of the covenant, beside the memory of blessings received lies the memory of evils
endured for having been unfaithful, as a perennial warning for future generations. What is experienced by Moses in the desert is no less than the
disdain and shame that Ezra presents before a people openly accused by him
of "having put out of their minds [Gr. *tês mnêmês ekballô*] all the things that
had befallen our fathers because of their impiety [Gr. *asebeia*]" (*Ant* 11.143;
cf. Samuel's exhortation to the people in *Ant* 6.97).

To keep alive the memory of the people through generations, the law
itself prescribes particular moments and gestures. In Josephus's interpretation, worship is basically "a memorial for future generations" (*Ant* 4.57;
5.100; cf. 2.317; 4.210).[9]

3. ISRAEL'S PRIMACY IN FIDELITY TO
THE FOREFATHERS' LAWS

In exalting the value of fidelity to tradition, Josephus intended primarily
to reconfirm his own enduring fidelity before his compatriots. He was equally
cautious to use language perfectly comprehensible to his gentile audience,
for whom gratefulness toward a benevolent divinity and attachment to the
national laws represented virtues that were difficult not to share and esteem.

The goal Josephus worked toward, however, was much more ambitious:
silently he was laying the foundations for a pedestal to put his small and
defeated people upon. In a culture that placed an almost absolute value on
antiquity, Josephus gave at least one primacy (and what a primacy!) to the
people of Israel: their faithfulness to the laws inherited from their forefathers. This virtue is such that even the much-proclaimed Spartan model is
humiliated in comparison.

The praises of Sparta are sung by all the world, because she remained for
so long faithful to [Lycurgus's] laws. . . . But let the admirers of the
Lacedaemonians set the duration of that state over against the period of
upwards of two thousand years of our constitution. Let them further reflect
that the Lacedaemonians thought good strictly to observe their laws only so
long as they retained their liberty and independence, but when they met with
reverses of fortune forgot wellnigh all of them. We, on the contrary, notwith-

9. On the "memorial" value of worship in middle Judaism, see chap. 8.

standing the countless calamities in which changes of rulers in Asia have involved us, never even in the direst extremity proved traitors to our laws. (*Ap* 2.227)

4. THE BETRAYED MEMORY

If memory is seen from inside as fundamental to the national and religious identity of the people of Israel, and from outside as the reason of their superiority among peoples, Josephus's choice to surrender and collaborate with the Roman enemy exposes him to an intolerable accusation: his soldiers threaten to kill him as a "traitor."

> Is life so dear to you, Josephus, that you can endure to see the light in slavery? How soon have you forgotten yourself! . . . Nay, if the fortune of the Romans has cast over you some strange forgetfulness of yourself, the care of our country's honor devolves on us. We will lend you a right hand and a sword. If you meet death willingly, you will have died as general of the Jews; if unwillingly, as a traitor. (*Bellum* 3.357–59)

Josephus is not a hero; he would not kill himself or let himself be killed by his fellows. He surrenders and sides with the Romans. But even below the walls of Jerusalem, facing the contempt of (and the stones thrown by) his compatriots and former companions in revolt, he would continue to defend his choice with vehemence and passion, crying out his innocence.

> I am a Jew. . . . Never may I live to become so abject a captive as to abjure my race or to forget the traditions of my forefathers! (*Bellum* 6.107)

The reason for his choice must lie, then, in the tradition to which he continues to declare himself faithful. The same memory of Israel that incites the rebels to redeem the nation[10] must for Josephus become his justification for "betrayal" and surrender.

Josephus turns the accusal around and becomes the accuser. It is not he who has betrayed the country; rather, those who, rebelling against Rome, have brought the nation to ruin by opposing the very will of God are the true traitors. His discourse to the besieged people of Jerusalem to convince them to surrender (*Bellum* 5.362–419) is indeed typical. The rebels have forgotten that the true power of the people of Israel consists in the intervention of God.

> Ah, miserable wretches, unmindful of your own true allies, would you make war on the Romans with arms and might of hand? What other foe have we

---

10. The Maccabean revolt offered a significant example, a model that was still alive in the consciousness of the people of Israel (see *1 Macc* 2:50–61; 4:8–11).

conquered thus, and when did God who created, fail to avenge, the Jews, if they were wronged? . . . Will you not recall your fathers' superhuman exploits and what mighty wars this holy place has quelled for us in days of old? . . . Nechaos, also called Pharaoh, the reigning king of Egypt, came down with a prodigious host and carried off Sarah, a princess and the mother of our race. What action, then, did her husband Abraham, our forefather, take? Did he avenge himself on the ravisher with the sword? He had, to be sure, three hundred and eighteen officers under him, each in command of a boundless army. Or did he not rather count these as nothing, if unaided by God, and uplifting pure hands toward this spot which you have now polluted enlist the invincible Ally on his side? . . . Need I speak of the migration of our fathers to Egypt? Oppressed and in subjection to foreign monarchs for four hundred years, yet, though they might have defended themselves by resort to arms and violence, did they not commit themselves to God? . . . You know, moreover, of the bondage in Babylon, where our people passed seventy years in exile and never reared their heads for liberty, until Cyrus granted it in gratitude to God. . . . In short, there is no instance of our forefathers having triumphed by arms or failed of success without them when they committed their cause to God. . . . Again, when our ancestors went forth in arms against Antiochus, surnamed Epiphanes, who was blockading this city and had grossly outraged the Deity, they were cut to pieces in the battle, the town was plundered by the enemy and the sanctuary for three years and six months lay desolate. Why need I mention more? (*Bellum* 5.376–95)

Josephus does not hesitate to appeal to the same memory of Israel upon which the rebels base their hopes of victory. In his mouth, the invitation to remember is the equivalent of an appeal to surrender. In fact, he uses the same past examples to show the impiety of the revolt; God intervened in worse situations and against even stronger enemies, but now God remains silent and leaves the city prey to destruction. The unfavorable outcome of the military operations can only be a sign of the revocation of divine favor, of the blasphemy of the very prosecution of the war.

You are warring not against the Romans only, but also against God. . . . The Deity has fled from the holy places and taken His stand on the side of those with whom you are now at war. (*Bellum* 5.378, 412)

The complete failure of the nationalistic experience is placed, through able rhetorical artifice, in the mouth of Eleazar, chief of the garrison of Masada, who has vowed to commit suicide. For Josephus the episode is emblematic of the whole Jewish War: the fall of Masada, which follows that of Jerusalem, far from being a glorious chapter in the history of the resistance,[11] is rather the demonstration that the rebels' logic can only result in

---

11. See P. Vidal-Naquet, "Flavius Josèphe et Masada," *Revue Historique* 260 (1978): 3–21.

the death and annihilation of the Jewish nation—suicide in fact, the very loss of its memory.

> Where now is that great city [Jerusalem], the mother-city of the whole Jewish race, intrenched behind all those lines of ramparts, screened by all those forts and massive towers, that could scarce contain her munitions of war, and held all those myriads of defenders? What has become of her that we believed to have God for her inhabitant? Uprooted from her base she has been swept away, and the sole memory of her remaining is that of the slain still quartered in her ruins! (*Bellum* 7.375–76)

5. MEMORY VINDICATED

Personal defense thus becomes national defense. In a much different way the memory, history, and traditions of the people should be defended. This is Josephus's great challenge: to place side by side, if not opposite one another, the memory of the Greek and Roman peoples and the memory of the Jewish people—Jewish antiquities against Greek and Roman antiquities.

Josephus lives in a world where all people seem desirous of, even obsessed with, establishing an eternal memory for themselves. This condition of immortality is the fruit of great undertakings and is reserved mainly for the heroes and valorous dead on the battlefield, an idea widespread in classical antiquity. Thus Titus incites his soldiers:

> What brave man knows not that souls released from the flesh by the sword on the battlefield are hospitably welcomed by that purest of elements, the ether, and placed among the stars, and that as good genii and benignant heroes they manifest their presence to their posterity; while souls which pine away in bodies wasted by disease, however pure they may be from stain or pollution, are obliterated in subterranean night and pass into profound oblivion, their life, their bodies, aye and their memory, brought simultaneously to a close? (*Bellum* 6.47–48)

If dying in battle is the action that most deserves memory, there are other accomplishments that can ensure immutable fame through the centuries. Herod, who erects splendid monuments in his memory (*Bellum* 1.419; *Ant* 15.380), who builds a city "in memory of his father" (*Bellum* 1.417) and a tower in "memory of the dead [brother]" (*Ant* 16.144), represents the typical mentality of the Hellenistic sovereign, who likes to be named "Hevergetes" (that is, benefactor) and is

> ambitious to leave behind to posterity more and more great monuments of his reign. . . . For Herod loved honors and, being powerfully dominated by his passion, he was led to display generosity whenever there was reason to hope for future remembrance or present reputation. (*Ant* 15.330; 16.153; cf. 17.163)

Motivated by the same "passion," Titus, after destroying Jerusalem, saves some towers "as a memorial of his attendant fortune, to whose cooperation he owed his conquest of defenses which defied assault" (*Bellum* 6.413).

The Greek–educated Josephus is the son of this culture and mentality. With these words, worthy of a Roman commander, he sends his own soldiers on the assault: "Fine is to sacrifice life for renown and by some glorious exploit to ensure in falling the memory of posterity!" (*Bellum* 3.204). He too feels the words he puts in the mouth of the dying Mattathias: "Though our bodies are mortal and subject to death, we can, through the memory of our deeds, attain the heights of immortality" (*Ant* 12.282). And Moses, in his last will and testament, claims to have always labored in his long life "to secure for [his fellows] the everlasting enjoyment of good things and for [himself] an abiding memory" (*Ant* 4.178).

However, true to his religious tradition, Josephus also knows that memory is justly destined for the righteous as God's recompense.[12] This is the Lord's promise to Abraham and Isaac:

> that their race would swell into a multitude of nations, with increasing wealth, nations whose founders would be had in everlasting remembrance. (*Ant* 1.235)

This is also the promise to Moses' father at the announcement of the birth of his son:

> He shall deliver the Hebrew race from their bondage in Egypt, and be remembered, so long the universe shall endure, not by Hebrews alone but even by alien nations. (*Ant* 2.216)

A link unknown to classical antiquity is thus established between memory and piety [Gr. *eusebeia*]. The two terms can be opposed, and their opposition is a sort of bad omen, unveiling the transience of human glory, as in the speech that the Essene Menaemus (Menahem) addresses to King Herod:

> You will be singled out for such good fortune as no other man has had, and you will enjoy eternal glory, but you will forget piety [Gr. *eusebeia*] and justice [Gr. *dikaion*]. This, however, cannot escape the notice of God, and at the close of your life His wrath will show that He is mindful of these things. (*Ant* 15.376)

In the eyes of Josephus the condition of the biblical heroes is quite different. They accomplished extraordinary undertakings and were righteous people who feared God—for this they are more worthy of eternal memory than

---

12. In the ancient and middle Jewish traditions this idea is expressed in terms of a conservation of the "name," assured to the "righteous." See H. Schult, "*šm*," *THAT*; and H. Bietenhard, "*onoma*," *TWNT*.

any other. Josephus explicitly states that Moses (*Ant* 4.178), Saul (*Ant* 6.345), Elijah (*Ant* 9.182), Jeconiah (*Bellum* 6.105), Daniel (*Ant* 10.266), Nehemiah (*Ant* 11.183), Judas Maccabeus (*Ant* 12.434), and also the Hasmonean Queen Helena, so dear to the Pharisees (*Ant* 20.52), have left an eternal memory of themselves and glorious monuments of their worth.

For him, therefore, the weak echo accorded to the people of Israel in Greek historiography is inconceivable. The entire first volume of *Contra Apionem* is dedicated to this problem. Josephus points out that not only do the people of Israel have a greater sense of *memoria patria* than the Greeks themselves (cf. *Ap* 1.8–10) but they also have left works worth remembering. That the Greeks do not recall them can only be the fruit of a conspiracy of silence.

> I can prove that some writers have omitted to mention our nation, not because they knew nothing of us, but because they envied us, or for some other unjustifiable reasons. (*Ap* 1.213)

By means of his writings Josephus intends to respond to this unpardonable omission. From the mouth of the "traitor" come words of pride and revenge:

> I, a foreigner, present to Greeks and Romans this memorial of great achievements. . . . Let us hold historical truth in honor, since by the Greeks it is disregarded. (*Bellum* 1.16)

10

BOUNDLESS SALVATION

Jews and Gentiles in
Middle Judaism

1. UNIVERSALISM:
A CHRISTIAN EXCLUSIVE?

One of the worst stereotypes of the Christian theological tradition is that of a "universalistic" Christianity emerging from a "particularistic" Judaism. History instead reveals a great variety of attitudes of middle Judaisms toward Gentiles as well as divisions among and within these Judaisms on the question of the possible salvation of Gentiles. The debate was made all the more complex by the fact that even the most divergent and opposing groups could share the same attitude toward this question.

I have stated several times that the soteriological thought in middle Judaism oscillates between the supremacy of God's justice and that of God's mercy. Even so, the emphasis placed by the different Judaisms of the time on one or the other perspective does not in itself imply an attitude of openness or exclusion toward the Gentiles, or a particularistic vision of the problem of salvation rather than a universalistic one. Obedience to the norms of the covenant can be understood as the only means of salvation, in which case the question is whether or not salvation is accessible to those Gentiles who convert; or the covenant can be interpreted as the sign of a morality that even Gentiles can live by, more or less consciously adhering with their own will to the will of the only God. Likewise, pessimism regarding humankind's capacity to do good can lead to the belief that only the people of Israel—and even only a select few of them—are destined to be saved; or it can bind Jews and Gentiles together in a common condition of sin and a common need for salvation.

Within the limits of this chapter, it is impossible to account for all of the positions on this issue manifested in middle Judaism. I will, therefore, draw attention to some aspects of Hellenistic Judaism as well as the Essene and apocalyptic movements. The choice is strictly illustrative; it has the function of fixing—as in a series of snapshots—the processes within the Judaism of this period through which equally universalistic results were reached from contradictory points of departure.[1]

2. PROSELYTISM AND THE ANTI-GENTILE DEBATE

The relationship between Jews and Gentiles, in Palestine as well as in the Diaspora, was not always an easy one. In fact, it was often marked by incomprehension and intolerance.[2] The refusal of the Jews to be assimilated to the pagan rites—a refusal intrinsic to a jealous monotheism such as that of Judaism—created in the Gentiles contrasting feelings of appreciation and contempt because the Jews opposed the dominant climate of religious syncretism. The argument against pagan idolatry, a leitmotif of Hellenistic Jewish literature, occasionally materialized in radical opposition between Jews and Gentiles, seemingly negating any reciprocal relationship. This opposition was immediately perceived on a day-to-day level in the refusal to dine together and the prohibition of mixed marriages.

This did not, however, prevent the emergence of an active and militant proselytism. If we trust the testimony of *Matthew*—and we have no reason not to—the Pharisees in particular were animated by such a missionary zeal as to "traverse sea and land to make a single proselyte" (*Matt* 23:15). Without denying the principles of polemical opposition, or rather basing itself on these principles, this proselytism had the aim of drawing Gentiles into the Jewish community. Thus, the salvation of Gentiles was believed possible and even desirable on the condition that they converted to the covenant and were purified through obedience to the law.[3] The strength with which

---

1. This chapter is a revision and amplification of G. Boccaccini, "Prospettive universalistiche nel tardo-giudaismo," in *Testimoni fino all'estremità della terra*, ed. A. Filippi, Parola Spirito Vita 16 (Bologna, 1987), 81–98. Some interesting indications on the same topic can be found also in M. Pérez Fernández, "La apertura a los gentiles en el judaísmo intertestamentario," *EB* 41 (1983): 83–106.

2. On the complex relationship between Jews and Gentiles in middle Judaism, see E. Schürer, *The History of the Jewish People in the Age of Jesus Christ*, a new English version rev. and ed. G. Vermes, F. Millar, and M. Goodman, Vol. 3.1 (Edinburgh, 1986), 150–76.

3. On proselytism in the Judeo-Hellenistic world, see esp. W. G. Braude, *Jewish Proselytising in the First Five Centuries of the Common Era* (Providence, 1940); and P. Dalbert, *Die Theologie der hellenistisch-jüdischen Missions-Literatur unter Ausschluss von Philo und Joseph* (Hamburg and Volksdorf, 1954).

authors such as Philo and Josephus defend this viewpoint indicates that it was not universally accepted. The argument is also taken up in one of the classics of Jewish proselytism, *Joseph and Aseneth*,[4] which, like Philo and Josephus,[5] sustains the possibility of reconciling the bitter anti-Gentile debates with an affirmation of the proselyte's dignity.

In *De Specialibus Legibus* Philo is equally clear in defining the characteristics of the convert's "new life" and defending the convert's complete equality with those born into the Jewish faith:

> All of like sort of [Moses], all who spurn idle fables and embrace truth in its purity, whether they have been such from the first or through conversion to the better side have reached that higher state, obtain [God's] approval, the former because they were not false to the nobility of their birth, the latter because their judgment led them to make the passage to piety. These last [Moses] calls "proselytes," or newly-joined, because they have joined the new and godly commonwealth. Thus, while giving equal rank to all in-comers with all the privileges which he gives to the native-born, he exhorts the old nobility to honor them not only with marks of respect but with special friendship and with more than ordinary goodwill. And surely there is good reason for this; they have left, he says, their country, their kinsfolk and their friends for the sake of virtue and religion. Let them not be denied another citizenship or other ties of family and friendship, and let them find place of shelter standing ready for refugees to the camp of piety. For the most effectual love-charm, the chain which binds indissolubly the goodwill which makes us one is to honor the one God. (*Spec Leg* 1.51–52; cf. 1.309)

Thus the convert abandons the condition of being a Gentile, deserts previous nationality, and becomes a Jew in all respects, equally sharing rights and responsibilities.

Josephus is of the same opinion, although in his apologetic work he is much more careful to soften the biting tones of the anti-Gentile debate:

> The consideration given by our legislator to the equitable treatment of aliens also merits attention. It will be seen that he took the best of all possible measures at once to secure our own customs from corruption, and to throw them open ungrudgingly to any who elect to share them. To all who desire to

---

4. On *Joseph and Aseneth*, see E. W. Brooks, *Joseph and Aseneth* (New York, 1918 [English trans.]); P. Batiffol, "Le livre de la Prière d'Aseneth," in *Studia Patristica*, Vol. 1 (Paris, 1889), 1–115 (Greek text); P. Riessler, *ASB* (1928), 497–538 (German trans.); M. Philonenko, *Joseph et Aséneth*, SPB 13 (Leiden, 1968 [Greek text and French trans.]); R. Martínez Fernández and A. Piñero, *ApAT* 3 (1982): 189–238 (Spanish trans.); M. Cavalli, *Storia del bellissimo Giuseppe e della sua sposa Aseneth* (Palermo, 1983 [Italian trans.]); D. Cook, *AOT* (1984), 465–503 (English trans.); C. Burchard, *OTP* 2 (1985), 177–247 (English trans.); and M. Philonenko, *BÉI* (1987), 1559–1601 (French trans.).

5. On Philo of Alexandria and Flavius Josephus, see chaps. 6 and 9, respectively.

come and live under the same laws with us, he gives a gracious welcome, holding that it is not family ties which constitute relationship, but agreement in the principles of conduct. (*Ap* 2.209–10; cf. 2.261)

The experience of conversion—seen with particular effectiveness through the eyes of the proselyte—is the theme of *Joseph and Aseneth*, another work dating from the Roman period. This poetic midrash reveals a behind-the-scenes view of the "scandalous" marriage of Joseph (by then viceroy of Egypt) to "Aseneth, the daughter of Potiphera priest of On" (*Gen* 41:45, 50; 46:20).

The irreconcilability of Jews and Gentiles is confirmed in the traditional terms of rigid separation: "Joseph never ate with the Egyptians, for this was an abomination to him" (*Jos Asen* 7:1). Consistently, Joseph at first refused any relation with Aseneth (herself an idolatress and daughter of idolaters), even refusing her polite kiss, which Pentephres (Potiphera) had ordered as an homage to their illustrious houseguest:

> It is not fitting for a man who worships God, who will bless with his mouth the living God and eat blessed bread of life and drink a blessed cup of immortality and anoint himself with blessed ointment of incorruptibility to kiss a strange woman who will bless with her mouth dead and dumb idols and eat from their table bread of strangulation and drink from their libation a cup of insidiousness and anoint herself with ointment of destruction. But a man who worships God will kiss his mother and the sister [who is born] of his clan and family and the wife who shares his bed, [all of] who[m] bless with their mouths the living God. (*Jos Asen* 8:5-6)

There is only one road open to a possible relationship between the two— her conversion. This is the road that Aseneth takes, following its radicalness to the end. In the midrash we find the same elements as in Philo, although emphasized with great psychological subtlety. Conversion is a personally traumatic experience, characterized by a complete break with the past, the repudiation of family and social ties, sincere and suffering penitence, and the expiation of the impurity and sin lived until that moment.

> And Aseneth hurried and put off her linen and gold woven royal robe and dressed in the black tunic of mourning. . . . And she took her chosen robe and the golden girdle and the headgear and the diadem, and threw everything through the window looking north to the poor. And Aseneth hurried and took all her gods that were in her chamber, the ones of gold and silver who were without number, and ground them to pieces, and threw all the idols of the Egyptians through the window looking north from her upper floor to beggars and needy [persons]. And Aseneth took her royal dinner and the fatlings and the fish and the flesh of the heifer and all the sacrifices of her gods and the vessels of their wine of libation and threw everything through the window

looking north, and gave everything to the strange dogs. . . . And after that Aseneth took the skin [full] of ashes and poured it on the floor . . . and fell upon the ashes and wept with great and bitter weeping all night with sighing and screaming until daybreak. (*Jos Asen* 10:10-15)

Aseneth is now alone and trusts only in God's help:

My father and my mother disowned me and said, "Aseneth is not our daughter," because I have destroyed and ground [to pieces] their gods. . . . And I am now an orphan and desolate, and I have no other hope save in you, Lord. (*Jos Asen* 12:12-13)

At this point, with the same decisiveness used in sanctioning the impossibility of communication between Jews and Gentiles, the text proclaims God's pleasure with the conversion. An angel appears to Aseneth to announce:

Courage, Aseneth, chaste virgin. Behold, I have heard all the words of your confession and your prayer. . . . Your name was written in the book of the living in heaven . . . and it will not be erased forever. (*Jos Asen* 15:3-4)

Aseneth is a new creature "renewed and formed anew and made alive again" (*Jos Asen* 15:5), from now on her name will be "City of Refuge" and future proselytes can look to her example with trust:

In you many nations will take refuge with the Lord God, the Most High, and under your wings many peoples trusting in the Lord God will be sheltered, and behind your walls will be guarded those who attach themselves to the Most High God in the name of Repentance. (*Jos Asen* 15:7)

The second part of the midrash is a hymn to the protection of God, "Father of Repentance" (*Jos Asen* 15:7), who ensures the convert against diffident or even hostile members of the Jewish people. As the story tells us, the pharaoh's son tries to seduce Aseneth and draw her away from Joseph— notably, with the complicity of two of Joseph's brothers, Dan and Gad. But God is watching over Aseneth and "fights against [them] for Aseneth" (28:1). Thanks also to the help offered her by the other sons of Jacob, Aseneth overcomes the danger, mending the strife within the house of Israel; she is finally recognized as a legitimate member of the chosen people.

The experience of Aseneth is certainly an exceptional one. Even in the text it is not difficult to detect a certain skepticism, especially when it states the premise that

she had nothing similar to the virgins of the Egyptians, but she was in every respect similar to the daughters of the Hebrews; she was tall as Sarah and handsome as Rebecca and beautiful as Rachel. (*Jos Asen* 1:5)

It is significant, however, that in the story Aseneth is an idolatrous Egyptian, like in *Genesis*, while the rabbinic midrashic tradition would solve the aporia by making her a Jew by birth, the daughter of Dina and therefore the niece of Joseph.[6] Aseneth is and remains a proselyte and is celebrated as such. She proudly displays this identity not as a disgrace, but as a praise to the power of God.

3. COMMITTED IN A COMMON WILL
TO DO GOOD

Beside the tendency that resolves the opposition between Jews and Gentiles by means of conversion—that is, by the elimination of the other (in religious terms)—another tendency springs up that poses the question of proselytism in a completely different way.

We have clear evidence of this tendency in Josephus. While narrating the story of the conversion of Izates, king of Adiabene (perhaps the most striking success of Jewish proselytism), the historian tells us of a conflict between two characters obviously presented for their paradigmatic value: "a certain Jewish merchant named Ananias" (*Ant* 20.34) and "another Jew, named Eleazar, who came from Galilee and who had a reputation for being extremely strict when it came to the ancestral laws" (*Ant* 20.43). The conflict is about the manner of the king's conversion. For Ananias it is enough to fulfill the moral principles of the Jewish religion, "because this was more important than circumcision" (*Ant* 20.41). For Eleazar, on the other hand, the morality is worthless if not accompanied by the integral and literal observance of the law:

> In your ignorance, O king, you are guilty of the greatest offense against the law and thereby against God. For you ought not merely to read the law but also, and even more, do what is commanded in it. How long will you continue to be uncircumcised? If you have not yet read the law concerning this matter, read it now, so that you may know what an impiety it is that you commit. (*Ant* 20.44–45)

The episode reveals that there was a clear tendency in Hellenistic Judaism to identify the fulfillment of the norms of the covenant as a sign of morality and to attribute the power of salvation to this morality. Even Josephus admits that at least in some circumstances God owes some compensation to Gentiles who have shown themselves to be righteous. When Caligula ordered that his own image be fixed to the Temple of Jerusalem, the Roman legate,

---

6. See *tg.* [Jo] on *Gen* 41:45; 46:20; 48:9; and *Pirke of Rabbi Eliezer* 38:1.

Petronius, opposed the imperial order, risking his own life. With sincere gratitude Josephus comments on the fortunate outcome of the episode:

> Indeed, God could never have been unmindful of the risk that Petronius had taken in showing favor to the Jews and honoring God. No, the removal of Gaius in displeasure at his rashness in promoting his own claim to worship was God's payment of the debt to Petronius. (*Ant* 18.306)

Some texts go even further in this direction, especially the *Letter of Aristeas*,[7] according to which the motive for the separation of Jews and Gentiles springs from the dominant idolatry and injustice. For this reason Moses

> surrounded us with unbroken palisades and iron walls to prevent our mixing with any of the other peoples in any matter, since we have been constituted pure in body and soul, preserved from false beliefs, and worshiping the only God, omnipotent over all creation. (*Let Aris* 139)

The terminology used here in reference to the law reminds us of the famous expression that opens *Mishnah Aboth*:[8]

> Moses received the law from Sinai and committed it to Joshua, and Joshua to the elders, and the elders to the prophets; and the prophets committed it to the men of the great synagogue. They said three things: "Be deliberate in judgment, raise up many disciples, and make a palisade around the law." (*m. Aboth* 1:1)

The ideological difference between the two texts, however, is immense. In *Mishnah Aboth* it is the law that is to be defended with a palisade. In the *Letter of Aristeas* we find the opposite: the palisade is the law itself, defending what really counts—the morality of the people.

> So, to prevent our being perverted by contact with others or by mixing with bad influences, [Moses] hedged us in on all sides with strict observances connected with meat and drink and touch and hearing and sight, after the manner of the law. (*Let Aris* 142)

After using the allegory to clarify the moral value of these norms, the *Letter* concludes:

---

7. On the *Letter of Aristeas* and its ideology, see chap. 5.

8. On *Aboth*, see the works on *Mishnah* cited above, p. 237 n. 19; see also R. T. Herford, *APOT* 2 (1913): 686–714 (English trans.); Y. Colombo, *Pirkê Aboth* (Rome, 1977 [Italian trans.]); and F. Manns, *Pour lire la Mishnah* (Jerusalem, 1984) [French trans.]). The Italian edition of Manns's work contains an Italian trans. of *Aboth* by G. Busi (*Leggere la Mishnah* [Brescia, 1987], 180–206).

In the matter of meats, the unclean reptiles, the beasts, the whole underlying rationale is directed toward righteousness and righteous human relationship. (*Let Aris* 169)

The law, then, has no value in and of itself, but only as a function of its moral message. Thus, observing the law and even belonging to the community of Israel are not determining factors in salvation; neither, for Pseudo-Aristeas, is the explicit profession of faith in the God of Israel. In this literary invention, Aristeas is portrayed as a gentile functionary full of respect and admiration for Judaism. Before his king he affirms:

The [same] God who appointed them their law lets your kingdom prosper, as my research has ascertained. These people worship God the overseer and creator of all, whom all men worship including ourselves, O king, except that we use a different name. (*Let Aris* 15–16)

The universalistic ideal put forth by the *Letter* finds its exact visualization in the seven banquets offered by King Ptolemy Philadelphus to his Jewish guests. The banquets are held according to Jewish custom (see *Let Aris* 184), yet Jews and Gentiles are brought together at the same table. Jewish sages and Greek sages speak the same language, express the same wisdom, find themselves animated by the same desire for the good, and agree that they worship the same God, even though they invoke the one deity with different names.

Two centuries later in another Hellenistic Jewish work, the *Testament of Abraham* (late first century C.E.),[9] we find the same universalistic spirit and the same emphasis on salvation through morality—a morality constituting the very contents of the law, but going beyond the confines of the covenant.

Abraham, curiously awkward and reluctant when faced with his own death (a death God had preannounced to him with great delicacy), asks first to visit "all the inhabited world" (*T Abr* 9:6). Seeing the wrong brought about by some people, Abraham would have all the evildoers executed immediately. His request provokes the decided and sarcastic response of God:

---

9. On the *Testament of Abraham*, see W. A. Craige, "The Testament of Abraham," in *The Ante-Nicene Fathers*, ed. A. Roberts and J. Donaldson, Vol. 10 (Edinburgh, 1872; repr., Grand Rapids, 1952), 183–201 (English trans.); M. R. James, *The Testament of Abraham*, TS 2.2 (Cambridge, 1892 [Greek text]); G. H. Box, *The Testament of Abraham* (London, 1927 [English trans.]); Riessler, *ASB* (1928), 1332–33 (German trans.); M. E. Stone, *The Testament of Abraham*, TT 2 Pseudepigrapha Series 2 (Missoula, Mont., 1972 [James's Greek text and English trans.]); M. Delcor, *Le Testament d'Abraham*, SVTP 2 (Leiden, 1973 [French trans.]); E. Janssen, *JSHRZ* 3.2 (1975): 193–256 (German trans.); E. P. Sanders, *OTP* 1 (1983): 871–902 (English trans.); N. Turner, *AOT* (1984), 393–421 (English trans.); and F. Schmidt, *BÉI* (1987), 1647–90 (French trans.).

Abraham has not sinned and he has no mercy on sinners. But I made the world, and I do not want to destroy any one of my creatures; but I delay the death of the sinner so that he should convert and live. (*T Abr* 10:14)

The trip is abruptly interrupted and Abraham is led "toward the east, to the first gate of heaven" (*T Abr* 11:1), so that he can understand how God judges human beings. A first selection is made immediately: those few who have never known sin are directly granted salvation and Adam, father of all, joyously greets them at heaven's gate, yet feels sorrow for the multitude awaiting judgment (see *Testament of Abraham* 11). Judgment is applied in the same way to all the descendants of Adam, with no differentiation between Jews and Gentiles: with a scale Abel measures the good against the evil done by each person, thus deciding his sort. The unit of measure is not the law, but rather a universally applied morality for which not even idolatry is a sin (see *Testament of Abraham* 12–13). Convinced of the benevolence of God toward all creatures, Abraham intercedes so that, in case the good and evil works should balance, precedence will be given to the good (see *Testament of Abraham* 14). Thus, even the "merits of the fathers" acquire universal validity.

If, then, the Gentile can gain salvation by practicing the same morality that the Jew learns through the law, what sense is there in speaking about proselytism, about the repudiation of national and religious identity, about "desertion," and about entrance into a new people? While the rabbinic midrashic tradition exalts the proselytic work of the patriarch,[10] the *Testament of Abraham* exalts his hospitality instead. Along with the banquets described in the *Letter of Aristeas*, the opening image of the *Testament of Abraham* is perhaps the most emblematic image of this tendency in Hellenistic Judaism. Israel is the hospitable Abraham who "pitched his tent at the crossroads of the oak of Mamre and welcomed everyone—rich and poor, kings and rulers, the crippled and the helpless, friends and strangers, neighbors and passersby" (*T Abr* 1:2), doing good and asking only the acceptance of his example.

4. FROM A CHOSEN PEOPLE TO A COMMUNITY APART

With the apocalyptic movement and the related tradition of Essenism, we are faced with a line of thought completely different from that examined thus far. All optimism and enthusiasm about humankind's ability to gain

---

10. See *tg.* [*Ne; P; V; Jo*] on *Gen.* 12:5.

salvation through its own efforts to do good have disappeared. These traditions are dominated by an acute perception of evil as an autonomous and
preexisting reality, both conditioning and limiting human liberty; evil, as the
fruit of an "original sin," has irremediably marred God's creation.[11]

In this context, in which all hope for salvation is placed in a gracious
intervention by God, nothing is simpler than to perceive and translate the
idea of a chosen people in terms of rigid separation, as an exclusive and
excluding condition for salvation; the more Israel is separated from the
Gentiles, the more its salvation is assured. If we add to this the idea that
identifies the contaminating force of evil with impurity, the rigid expressions
of the *Book of Jubilees*[12] immediately become intelligible. Ideologically close
to Essenism, *Jubilees* excludes all contacts between Jews and Gentiles:

> Separate yourself from the Gentiles, and do not eat with them, and do not
> perform deeds like theirs. And do not become associates of theirs. Because
> their deeds are defiled, and all of their ways are contaminated, and despicable,
> and abominable. . . . And for all of those who worship idols and for the hated
> ones, there is no hope in the land of the living; because they will go down into
> šeol. And in the place of judgment they will walk, and they will have no
> memory upon the earth. (*Jub* 22:16, 22)

For *Jubilees* this is a universal rule, valid since the creation; the election of
Israel consists precisely in its decreed separation *ab aeterno*. God

> completed all his work on the sixth day. . . . And He gave us a great sign, the
> sabbath day. . . . And He said to us, "Behold I shall separate for Myself a
> people among all the nations. And they will also keep the sabbath. And I will
> sanctify them for Myself and I will bless them. . . . And they will be My people
> and I will be their God. And I have chosen the seed of Jacob from among all
> that I have seen. And I have recorded him as My firstborn son, and have
> sanctified him for Myself forever and ever." (*Jub* 2:16-20)

Even on the individual level, relations with Gentiles are a mortal danger
for the entire chosen people. Bringing with it a contamination of evil and
impurity, a relationship with a Gentile signifies the weakening and eventually the end of the requirements for salvation. It is, therefore, a possibility
that must be fought with every means available, with the conscious and
unpitying energy of a doctor trying to avoid the spread of a contagious
mortal disease. The ruthless revenge of Jacob's sons against the Shechemites
(cf. *Genesis* 34) is raised to the level of a paradigm:

---

11. On this conception of evil as the characterizing element of the apocalyptic tradition, see
chap. 4.
12. On the *Book of Jubilees*, see above, p. 238 n. 21.

And if there be any man in Israel who wishes to give his daughter or his sister to any man who is from the seed of the gentiles, let him surely die, and let him be stoned because he has caused shame in Israel. And also the woman will be burned with fire because she has defiled the name of her father's house and so she will be uprooted from Israel. . . . And there is no limit of days for this law. And there is no remission or forgiveness. . . . And it is a reproach to Israel, to those who give and those who take any of the daughters of the gentile nations because it is a defilement and it is contemptible to Israel. And Israel will not be cleansed from this defilement. . . . For there will be plague upon plague and curse upon curse, and every judgment, and plague, and curse will come. And if he does this thing, or if he blinds his eyes from those who cause defilement and from those who defile the sanctuary of the Lord and from those who profane His holy name, [then] all of the people will be judged together on account of all the defilement and the profaning of this one. . . . Therefore I command you saying, "Proclaim this testimony to Israel: See how it was for the Shechemites and their sons, how they were given into the hand of the two children of Jacob and they killed them painfully. And it was a righteousness for them and it was written down for them for righteousness." (*Jub* 30:7-17)

These are the same positions we find expressed at Qumran:[13]

The seed of man did not understand all that You caused them to inherit; they did not discern You in all Your words and wickedly turned aside from every one. They heeded not Your great power and therefore You did reject them. For wickedness pleases You not, and the ungodly shall not be established before You. But in the time of Your goodwill You did choose for Yourself a people. You did remember Your covenant and [granted] that they should be set apart for Yourself from among all the peoples as a holy thing. (1Q34bis 2.3–5)

The theology of separation reaches its peak at Qumran, where it is not only applied to Gentiles, but also to Jews not belonging to the community. Whoever joins the community

shall undertake by the Covenant to separate from all the men of falsehood who walk in the way of wickedness. For they are not reckoned in His Covenant. They have neither inquired nor sought after Him concerning His laws that they might know the hidden things in which they have sinfully erred, and matters revealed they have treated with insolence. Therefore wrath shall rise up to condemn, and vengeance shall be executed by the curses of the Covenant, and great chastisements of eternal destruction shall be visited on them, leaving no remnant. . . . No man shall consort with him with regard to his work or property lest he be burdened with the guilt of [his] sin. He shall indeed keep away from him in all things. . . . No member of the community shall follow them in matters of doctrine and justice, or eat or drink anything of theirs. . . .

---

13. On the Dead Sea Scrolls, see above, p. 237 n. 20.

For all those not reckoned in His Covenant are to be set apart, together with all that is theirs. (1QS 5.10–18)

For the Essene tradition, belonging to a community apart is the definitive proof of being included among the elect. According to their ability to persevere in this condition, individuals can verify their own preordained destiny— whether they belong to the chosen loved by God or to the wicked hated by God and condemned to perdition.

5. JOINED IN SIN

Drawing on this same pessimism, however, some of the voices of the apocalyptic tradition pronounce a very different attitude toward the Gentiles.

For the *Book of Dream Visions* (second century B.C.E.), part of the Enochic pentateuch (*1 Enoch*),[14] the spread of evil in the world has deprived Israel of any superiority whatsoever over other peoples; the chosen people are victims of evil as much as any other. The degeneration of God's creation, brought about *ab origine* by the sin of the angels, continues relentlessly on through history at an accelerating rate. In the characteristic animal symbolism of the book, the Jews from "oxen" have become "sheep" and are subject to rebel angel "shepherds." Only God's cathartic intervention—the end of history— can eliminate evil from the world and return God's creation to its original goodness. Thus a messianic era of salvation will be opened for all humanity, just as evil has condemned all; the "new Temple" will gather within its walls the elect from among both Jews and Gentiles.

> All those [sheep] which have been destroyed and dispersed [i.e., the Jews], and all the beasts of the field and the birds of the sky [i.e., the Gentiles] were gathered together in that house [i.e., the new Temple, the new Jerusalem]; and the Lord of the sheep rejoiced with great joy because they had all become gentle and returned to His house. (*1 Enoch* 90:33)

We find a similar prospect in the *Testaments of the Twelve Patriarchs* (first century B.C.E.).[15] Evil is an ingrained characteristic of humankind. Beliar (Satan) placed "the seven spirits of deceit" in every human being "against mankind" (*T Reub* 2:12). The seven spirits of deceit interact with the seven "neutral" spirits that make up the human being, but most of all they interact with the last of these "neutral" spirits, "the spirit of procreation and intercourse, with which come sins through fondness for pleasure" (*T Reub* 2:8).

---

14. On the *Book of Dream Visions* and its ideology, see chap. 4.
15. On the *Testaments of the Twelve Patriarchs*, see above, p. 222 n. 14.

This is the motive behind every transgression:

> And thus every young man is destroyed, darkening his mind from the truth, neither gaining understanding in the law of God nor heeding the advice of his fathers. (*T Reub* 3:8)

Every human being, therefore, longs for a redemption that liberates from the slavery of sin. And this redemption will be brought about in full during the messianic era, when "God will appear . . . to save the race of Israel, and to assemble the righteous from among the nations" (*T Naph* 8:3; cf. *T Levi* 2:11; *T Ash* 7:3; *T Benj* 9:2). Eschatological universalism is a traditional concept in Judaism; here, however, as in the *Book of Dream Visions*, it receives peculiar connotations from the context, affirming the common solidarity of humankind in sin. Israel undoubtedly has a unique vocation that, if put into action, places it in a privileged position:

> If you achieve the good, my children, men and angels will bless you; and God will be glorified through you among the Gentiles. The devil will flee from you; wild animals will be afraid of you, and the angels will stand by you. (*T Naph* 8:4)

But God's benediction hides an equivalent malediction that weighs on the people:

> The one who does not do the good, men and angels will curse, and God will be dishonored among the Gentiles because of him. The devil will inhabit him as his own instrument; every wild animal will dominate him, and the Lord will hate him. (*T Naph* 8:6)

If the forces of evil are so relentless in every human being, is Israel perhaps left only with an inability to bring about good, its only potential privilege transformed into an even harder condemnation? In the *Testament of Benjamin*, Israel, called to such an exalted mission, must undergo the insult of being convinced of its guilt by the elect among the Gentiles:

> Then shall we also be raised, each of us over our tribe, and we shall prostrate ourselves before the heavenly king. Then all shall be changed, some destined for glory, others for dishonor, for the Lord first judges Israel for the wrong it has committed and then He shall do the same for all the nations. Then He shall judge Israel by the chosen Gentiles as He tested Esau by the Midianites who loved their brothers. (*T Benj* 10:7-10)

God indiscriminately loves those who fear God and those who love their neighbor, regardless of the apparent human boundaries between groups of people:

> If you continue to do good, even the unclean spirits will flee from you and wild animals will fear you. For where someone has within himself respect for good

works and has light in the understanding, darkness will slink away from that person. (*T Benj* 5:2-3; cf. 3:4; 6:1)

With the disappearance of any consciousness or pretense of superiority, the idea of proselytism clearly remains a foreign one. The Jews, as human beings among other human beings, discover themselves to be as much sinners as the Gentiles and, like the Gentiles, in need of salvation. Salvation is a gift from God to the elect, to those who desire it and entrust themselves to God's mercy.

Paul's universalism also draws on the apocalyptic line of thought.

All men, both Jews and Greeks, are under the power of sin, as it is written: "None is righteous, no, not one; no one understands, no one seeks for God. All have turned aside, together they have gone wrong; no one does good, not even one." (*Ps* 14:1-3; *Rom* 3:9b-12)

The ignorance of good (of the law) does not reduce the Gentile's responsibility:

For what can be known about God is plain to them, because God has shown it to them. . . . So they are without excuse; for although they knew God they did not honor Him as God or give thanks to Him. . . . They exchanged the truth about God for a lie and worshiped and served the creature rather than the Creator. . . . All who have sinned without the law will also perish without the law. (*Rom* 1:19, 21, 25; 2:12a).

The knowledge of good (of the law) does not prevent the Jew from sinning:

You call yourself a Jew and rely upon the law and boast of your relation to God and know His will and approve what is excellent, because you are instructed in the law. . . . You then who teach others, why do you not teach yourself? . . . You who boast in the law, why do you dishonor God by breaking the law? (*Rom* 2:17-18, 21, 23)

The necessity of the expiatory death of the Christ—a gracious and totally unilateral death (*Rom* 5:6-11)—comes precisely from this common admission of guilt and common need of salvation.

There is no distinction; since all have sinned and fall short of the glory of God, they are justified by His grace as a gift, through the redemption which is in Christ Jesus, whom God put forward as an expiation by his blood, to be received by faith. (*Rom* 3:22b-25a)

If the fulfillment of God's promises through God's son Jesus "has broken down the dividing wall of hostility" (*Eph* 2:14) between the Jew and the Gentile, it has set a new boundary within humankind, between the believer and the nonbeliever, between those who receive salvation by faith and become Christians and those who refuse the good news and fellowship in the community of the saints. A universal announcement of salvation embodies itself in an active proselytism, borrowing schemes and modalities of Pharisaic proselytism. Although it tends to embrace all humankind, the definitiveness and exclusiveness of the new fellowship breeds the same seeds of intolerance that the Qumran community did, first of all against those among the Jewish people who have remained nonbelievers.

6. AT THE ROOTS OF UNIVERSALISM

In conclusion, if universalism means the capacity of attaching value to being different, then its opposite is not particularism or nationalism, but dogmatism and intolerance, namely, the pretense of possessing the whole truth or of having the only key to salvation. By this definition, some middle Judaisms were undoubtedly sectarian and intolerant; others were able to develop mature positions that were much more universalistic than those of early Christianity. Early Christians, in fact, were quite willing to accept pagan proselytes, but much less willing to recognize the possibility of salvation for nonbelievers, be they Jews or Gentiles.

We have seen identical universalistic conclusions emerging from diametrically opposed starting points, with Jews and Gentiles placed on the same level for quite opposite reasons. In the Hellenistic Jewish tradition, Jews and Gentiles are equally committed in a will to the good; in the apocalyptic tradition, Jews and Gentiles are equal as victims of evil and are equally in need of salvation. This is not a paradox or a surprise; whether the universalism arises from mutual respect or from a confession of impotence, it is none other than a recognition of solidarity, of a common commitment or a common suffering.

It is true that those middle Judaisms did not succeed in surviving as distinct groups, while Christianity was even able to adapt the positions of these fellow Judaisms to its own proselytic ends and forced Rabbinism to renounce any missionary activity. But thanks to these forgotten voices the hope for a boundless salvation has been taken up by both of the main modern Judaisms—Rabbinism and Christianity—and it resounds today with its original force *from within these traditions*, the echo of an ancient and unforgotten dream.

INDEXES

[Pages on which passages are quoted in full are *italicized*.]

ANCIENT JEWISH LITERATURE

MIDDLE JEWISH LITERATURE

GREEK–ROMAN LITERATURE

ANCIENT RABBINIC LITERATURE

ANCIENT CHRISTIAN LITERATURE

MEDIEVAL AND MODERN AUTHORS

CONTEMPORARY AUTHORS